Thick Concepts

EDITED BY
Simon Kirchin

UNIVERSITY PRESS

OXFORD
UNIVERSITY PRESS

Great Clarendon Street, Oxford, OX2 6DP,
United Kingdom

Oxford University Press is a department of the University of Oxford.
It furthers the University's objective of excellence in research, scholarship,
and education by publishing worldwide. Oxford is a registered trade mark of
Oxford University Press in the UK and in certain other countries

© the several contributors 2013

The moral rights of the author have been asserted

First Edition published in 2013

Impression: 1

British Library Cataloguing in Publication Data
Data available

ISBN 978–0–19–967234–9

Printed by the MPG Printgroup, UK

Acknowledgements

Many of the papers in this volume started life as presentations at a conference—called 'Thick Concepts'—that was held in July 2009 at the University of Kent. The Mind Association was the main sponsor, with other financial assistance provided by The Aristotelian Society, The Analysis Trust, and the University of Kent. For the record, the main speakers were: Jonathan Dancy, Daniel Elstein, Edward Harcourt and Alan Thomas, Allan Gibbard, Chris Hookway, Michael Smith, Pekka Väyrynen, Nick Zangwill, and myself. Not all of those who spoke were able to write papers for this volume, but all of these good folk were important in providing initial impetus for it. And, of course, I am very grateful to all of the authors whose papers are contained in this volume; grateful for their time, energy, and patience with my editorial nagging.

I am also grateful to all at OUP, especially Peter Momtchiloff and Eleanor Collins, for their support in bringing this collection to completion. Two readers for OUP gave a series of comments that helped to make a set of very good drafts even better. The Mind Association's support for this volume goes beyond financial matters, and I am proud that it has found a home in their series.

Lastly, as ever I owe a large debt to Penny and our children who have allowed me the time and space to finish this book.

Simon Kirchin

June 2012

Contents

Contributors

SIMON BLACKBURN was educated at Cambridge, and was Fellow and Tutor in philosophy at Pembroke College, Oxford from 1969 to 1990. He became Edna J. Koury Distinguished Professor of Philosophy at the University of North Carolina at Chapel Hill in 1990, returning to Cambridge in 2001. Retired from the University of Cambridge he remains Fellow of Trinity College, distinguished research professor at Chapel Hill, and Professor at the New College of the Humanities. He is the author of many articles—many of which are collected in *Essays in Quasi-Realism* and *Practical Tortoise Raising*—and a number of books, including *Spreading the Word*, *Ruling Passions* and *Truth*.

TIMOTHY CHAPPELL is Professor of Philosophy at The Open University, and Visiting Fellow in the Philosophy Departments, University of St. Andrews. He has published widely on ethics, Plato, and Aristotle.

JONATHAN DANCY is Professor of Philosophy at the University of Texas at Austin, and Professor Emeritus at the University of Reading. He has worked mainly in epistemology, moral philosophy, and the philosophy of action. Among his books are *Moral Reasons*, *Practical Reality* and *Ethics Without Principles*. His current focus is on the nature of practical reasoning.

MATTI EKLUND is Associate Professor of Philosophy at Cornell University. He has published articles in many areas of philosophy, primarily metaphysics, philosophy of language, and philosophy of logic.

EDWARD HARCOURT is Fellow and Tutor in Philosophy at Keble College, Oxford. His research interests include ethics (in particular moral psychology, neo-Aristotelianism and child development, ethical dimensions of psychoanalysis, metaethics, and Nietzsche's ethics); literature and philosophy; and Wittgenstein.

SIMON KIRCHIN is Senior Lecturer in Philosophy at the University of Kent. He is the author of *Metaethics*, and the editor of *Arguing about Metaethics* (with Andrew Fisher), and *A World without Values: Essays on John Mackie's Moral Error Theory* (with Richard Joyce). He is currently writing a book about thick and thin concepts.

DEBBIE ROBERTS is Lecturer in Philosophy at the University of York. She writes mainly on ethics and metaethics, and has interests in philosophy of law.

MICHAEL SMITH is McCosh Professor of Philosophy at Princeton University. He is the author of *The Moral Problem*, *Ethics and the A Priori: Selected Essays on Moral Psychology and Metaethics*, and the co-author with Frank Jackson and Philip Pettit of *Mind, Morality, and Explanation: Selected Collaborations*.

ALAN THOMAS is Professor of Ethics at Tilburg University in the Netherlands. Educated at Cambridge, Harvard, and Oxford, his research interests are in moral and political philosophy, and the philosophy of mind. He is currently writing a book about egalitarianism.

VALERIE TIBERIUS is Professor of Philosophy at the University of Minnesota. Her work explores the ways in which philosophy and psychology can both contribute to the study of well-being and virtue. She is the author of *The Reflective Life: Living Wisely With Our Limits*.

PEKKA VÄYRYNEN is Senior Lecturer in Philosophy at the University of Leeds. He has published articles on a wide variety of topics in metaethics and is the author of *The Lewd, the Rude and the Nasty: A Study of Thick Concepts* (Oxford University Press).

ERIC WILAND is Associate Professor of Philosophy at the University of Missouri-St. Louis. He is the author of *Reasons* and various articles concerning moral advice, indirection, and the objectivity of normative concepts.

NICK ZANGWILL is Professor at Durham University. He is the author of *The Metaphysics of Beauty, Aesthetic Creation*, and papers on metaethics, aesthetics, philosophy of mind, and metaphysics.

1

Introduction: Thick and Thin Concepts

Simon Kirchin

Thick and thin concepts have been the focus of significant debate over the past few decades, particularly in moral philosophy. However, there has not been a collection of papers on the topic. This volume, which grew out of a conference, is designed both to encapsulate some of the current thoughts about these concepts, and to encourage discussion about new ideas in relation to them.[1] In this introduction I lay out a number of the key points of interest about thick and thin concepts, and then summarize each of the papers in this volume.

I

Thick and thin concepts are best introduced by way of examples. Imagine we are discussing the merits of a mutual friend, Peter. I describe Peter as being good. Perhaps because of something I say explicitly, or the context in which we are talking, you correctly infer that I mean 'morally good', rather than good at cooking or good on the guitar. Even so, describing Peter in this way does not tell us much about his character. There are plenty of ways in which people can be morally good, and plenty of types of action that they typically perform. In contrast, imagine that our discussion continues and I describe Peter as being honest. There are plenty of ways in which people can be honest or show their honesty. However, this more specific description gives us more of a sense of what Peter is like, and perhaps why we think of him as good. We would have created a different impression of him if we had described him as being brave or generous or sympathetic. There is a further, interesting point. If I say of Peter that he is honest then, given typical linguistic conventions, you should be able to pick up that I approve of Peter, or think you should approve of Peter, or similar. These more specific sorts of concept—HONEST, BRAVE, and the like—are said to have both evaluative conceptual content, for they seem to be essentially keyed in to approval (and disapproval), and descriptive

---

[1] For details on the conference, see 'Acknowledgements' at the start of this volume.

conceptual content, for they help to give us a specific idea of the character of the person, object, or action so characterized.[2] More briefly we may say that thick concepts are both evaluative and descriptive. In contrast, thin concepts although clearly evaluative, are thought not to have much or any descriptive conceptual content: we get little if any sense of what the object is like beyond the fact that the user of the concept likes (or dislikes) it, thinks others should do the same, and so on.

Although ethical examples are often used when discussing thin and thick concepts, the division and various ideas that I will sketch below apply to all sorts of thick concept: aesthetic concepts (such as GLAMOROUS, GROTESQUE, SUBLIME), epistemic concepts (such as OBSERVANT, RELIABLE, DULL-WITTED), and many other concepts that might be used to pick out characteristics, of people and other things (such as CORNY, FOLKSY, TERRIBLE, TRIUMPHANT, JEJUNE, FASCINATING, IDIOTIC, MESMERIZING, DISAPPOINTING). Similarly, there may be a range of thin concepts. For a start, we may have GOOD as applying to no specific domain (or, alternatively, as applying to all domains), and we then further distinguish different senses of it: MORALLY GOOD, AESTHETICALLY GOOD, and so on. Other examples of thin concepts might be RIGHT and OUGHT. Note that in displaying things in this fashion, we need not assume that concepts operate only in one discrete domain of thought and use. Some concepts can be used—literally or metaphorically—across different domains. Indeed, some concepts seem to have associations and functions from a number of different areas. Nice examples abound in the border between ethics and aesthetics here: perhaps OBSCENE and HEROIC can be categorized in this way.

There is far more to say after this short introduction and lots to unpick just about the seemingly innocuous way in which things have been described. Here are five points of interest, which although important do not exhaust the discussion of thick and thin concepts.

(i) First, I deliberately slipped in the idea just now that thin concepts are thought not to have 'much or any' descriptive conceptual content. Alternatively, we may find thin concepts being characterized as predominantly or wholly evaluative. This seemingly innocent slip is crucial. If we define thick concepts as being both evaluative and descriptive in some way, then we have an important choice. Do we define thin concepts as being wholly evaluative, thus entailing a difference in kind between the two sorts of concept? Or, do we define thin concepts as being mainly (or predominantly, or primarily, or...) evaluative, thus giving us only a difference of degree? That difference of degree may still be significant, but any difference will not be as clear as a difference in kind.

Some commentators like the idea of there being a difference of degree.[3] We can imagine there being a continuum or spectrum of evaluative concepts, ranging from the very specific to the very general, and with no dividing lines to break it. A simple illustration:

---

[2] I follow a few of the writers in this volume and write concepts thus—GOOD or GOODNESS—when I am referring to them as concepts. In this convention, when we wish to speak of the associated term we write things thus: 'good' or 'goodness'.

[3] See Scheffler (1987) and Tappolet (2004).

GOOD or even PRO might stand at one end, with COMPASSIONATE, SYMPATHETIC and EMPA-THETIC towards the other, with KIND and THOUGHTFUL somewhere in the middle. Simi-larly, JUST, BEAUTIFUL, and KNOWLEDGABLE seem thicker than our typical thin concept examples, but not as thick or specific as KITSCH and CLEVER.

Not only does this picture have initial attraction, there is some reason to support it. We should be drawn to answer the question 'What is descriptive content?' We should note straightaway that we are not talking about any function some thin term may have in our language: we can certainly use 'good' to describe many things.[4] And that itself is telling. We can and do use GOOD and its corresponding term to represent. We do exactly the same with HONEST and 'honest'. The only difference is that, intuitively, we use HON-EST of fewer things than GOOD.[5] But that difference is one of degree, not of kind. As yet we do not have a basis for establishing any difference in kind.

However, now consider two ways in which we can try to draw a distinction of kind. First, Bernard Williams did much to arouse interest in the distinction between thin and thick concepts, particularly with his *Ethics and the Limits of Philosophy* (*ELP*). (Indeed, it is Williams who first coins the term 'thick concept' in print.) Williams says that whilst thin concepts are action-guiding alone, thick concepts are both action-guiding and world-guided. What does it mean to say that HONEST is world-guided and GOOD is not? After all, to repeat, there are things in the world that are good, and we are (seemingly) applying a concept or related term to them. For Williams, the idea is that one begins with thick concepts that seem to get purchase on people, actions, and things that we encounter, and which become understandable and categorizable to us because of how we describe them. (Indeed, one may go further and say that what it is for stuff to be *a* thing just is for it to be categorized.) We can extrapolate from what Williams says. We then notice that many different sorts of object get categorized in the same way. We can then abstract and work out what, say, HONEST is. Another process of abstraction can then happen. We abstract across many, many different objects, which are categorized using many different sorts of thick concept, all of which point in a positive direction. (Or, to anticipate a debate below: are used of certain objects in certain contexts in a positive way.) For example, not just HONEST, but also KIND, JUST, MERCIFUL, and the like. From this process of abstraction we arrive at the concept GOOD or, for slightly different associations, RIGHT. It is notable that Williams does not use the label 'thin concept' in *ELP*, but prefers to use phrases such as 'the most abstract concepts'. So, thin concepts can be applied to things and in this (minimal) sense are world-guided. But, they are not world-guided in

---

[4] Different theories of ethical language will then come in: some will think ethical terms and phrases do, ultimately, function to describe. Other options, such as prescriptivism, abound. I am here thinking of a debate before we get to this dispute: can we get a definite handle on how evaluative language *appears* to function, at first glance?

[5] We can imagine possible worlds where, for example, there are far fewer good things than there are wicked things, for example, so the numbers alone need not necessarily be the be-all and end-all. (And, if there are few good things, then it is likely that there will be few honest things.) But, in our world, there seem to be more good things than wicked things, anyway.

the sense that Williams means when formulating his distinction between the thin and the thick because these thin concepts do not have any real purchase on objects. They are derived and formed at a higher stage (or at higher stages) of abstraction.

This gives us one sense in which a thin concept may fail to be world-guided, or fail to be descriptive. An evaluative concept may fail to be world-guided or fail to have descriptive content simply because we are able to derive it and understand it away from the details of the objects on which it gets purchase. However, although this has some merit, Williams's treatment of the thick, particularly the priority it has over the thin, is controversial. It seems clear from his writings that Williams thinks of thick concepts as being more important than thin ones. He believes this because thick concepts are more or more directly connected with the objects of our social world. This is so precisely because of what they are: they are ways of directly classifying what we encounter, and are not abstractions from such classifications. Williams links this to his thoughts about relativism and evaluative knowledge. Once we encounter other societies with their different evaluative concepts we may call into question the usefulness and truth of our own. But, if anything can give us confidence in our moral dealings it is our thick concepts, as they (supposedly) get more purchase on the world.

Some people disagree with Williams's thoughts here. Thin concepts seem important to help create a social world, and there seems no reason to expect that thick concepts may survive better than thin ones when we encounter others. No matter what the outcome of this debate, we can worry that there is still no justified definite line between the thin and the thick, our main line of concern at present. How many stages of conceptual abstraction do there have to be before a concept has no descriptive content or before it is not world-guided? Indeed, we may not really have scratched the itch that we had before: do we really think that more abstract concepts get no purchase on the world, that they cannot be used to pick out things we notice about it? If one is an evaluative realist, for example, one will think that there are real moral properties of honesty and goodness, and that we need both concepts to pick these properties out. Just because one concept is less specific than the other, that fact should not alter the idea that we really have two aspects of the world that require categorization.

Here is a second way of trying to distinguish the thin from the thick. This respects the idea that both thin and thick concepts come in different 'thicknesses', but saying that is consistent with saying that we can draw dividing lines that indicate differences of kind. Think of the most minimal of thin concepts: PRO and CON. These simply stand for the barest sort of favouring and disfavouring one can imagine, they are just the most minimal sort of positive and negative stances. Beyond this, think of the traditional exemplar thin concepts: GOOD and RIGHT. The following may not be perfect, but here are definitions for both. We can think of GOOD as indicating some positive evaluation of something (of some strength) where we allow that other similarly placed things can be evaluated in the same way (and to the same or different strength). We can think of RIGHT, in contrast, as indicating some positive evaluation of something where we do not allow that any other similarly placed thing can be viewed positively. (There can be many good options, but, strictly, only one right one. All the other relevant options are wrong.) These concepts differ from each other: much of modern normative ethics makes little sense otherwise. They also both differ from PRO: they are more specific than it. But, how are they more specific? All we are told is that we have some positive evaluation of the object, and how the positive evaluation of it compares with evaluations of objects. That is, we have some sort of comparative or relational 'thickening'. Yet, we are not told anything about the character of the object itself when we hear that it is good or right, only that it is viewed positively.[6] On the other hand, traditional thick concepts do tell us something about the object itself beyond the fact that it is viewed positively (or negatively). A similar point can be made concerning a run of (possible) thin concepts such as EXCELLENT, GOOD, FAIR, FINE, OKAY. Here the strength of positive evaluation diminishes, but this strength is also comparative: assuming typical linguistic conventions we are not told anything directly about the character of the objects so classified beyond the fact that they are viewed positively.[7] So, this might be the start of some difference in kind between the thin and the thick. Thin concepts indicate some pro or con evaluation, and may indicate how that evaluation compares with the evaluation of other objects. Thick concepts can do this, obviously, but in addition they tell us something about the character of the object directly. This sort of division allows for thin and thick concepts to be more or less specific, yet it also indicates a nice intuitive dividing line.

Despite that, this second way of distinguishing thin from thick may be imperfect. The slightly 'thicker' thin concepts such as OUGHT might prove tricky to place. If we ought to do an action then we are told that the action is viewed positively, and more positively than other potential actions. In addition, if some popular conceptions of OUGHT are to be believed, we are told that we can do it. Does this extra requirement take it beyond the thin? Is the fact that the action is 'do-able' for certain people a feature of the action itself, or something relational? It is this sort of issue that advocates of this way of dividing things will have to sort out. It may not prove to be a fatal flaw, but it will need some thought.[8]

---

[6] An anonymous referee raised the possibility that we do learn something about an object (in the broadest sense) if it is right, namely that it is an action or act-type. I think this is wrong. For example, an answer can be right, even though that is not an action-type; an answer*ing* is an action. Still one might think that the answer and the action of answering are close such that associations involved in calling the latter right 'rub off' on the former. Less close is this example pair. The *placing* of a painting in a certain point in one's house can be right and is an action, but the right *position* of a painting is not an action. When one thinks of an answer, one cannot—I think—help but think of someone giving the answer. Yet, although the painting has to have got where it is in some manner, when we call the position right I think that we are far more concerned simply with the painting's position, not its placing. In my view, things are so loose and vague here when we call something right, that finding out that an object is right gives us little or no information about it beyond the fact that we think it right and are viewing it positively, in the way set out in the main text.

[7] These concepts may be used of other ideas, not just 'positive evaluation of some strength'. Certainly the corresponding words might be. I am just trying to indicate that sometimes we do have a run of positive evaluation in mind and the concepts used, however we label them, can be thin.

[8] Additional thought should be given, perhaps, to the fact that 'ought' is a modal auxiliary verb, whereas 'right' and 'good' are adjectives, and further that the former of these probably has more limited application than the latter. These linguistic facts may affect how we classify OUGHT.

So, despite the attraction of thinking of thin and thick concepts coming in a continuum, there is also some attraction for thinking of there being a division. Work on this issue is still in its early stages.

(ii) Here is a second issue. Although people often talk of thick and thin concepts as being evaluative, a number of words are used to pick them out. Some prefer to talk of these concepts as being normative, with the contrast being between normative and nonnormative conceptual content. At other times, one might hear mention of the factual as well as the descriptive. As we have already seen, Williams's formulation talks of action-guidingness rather than evaluation. In brief, Williams thinks that thick concepts are fundamentally practical concepts: even though they may not always lead to direct action, they usually provide such reasons even if they work only indirectly. (Arguably he is led to this thought because his chief examples are ethical concepts, which do seem practical.)

Should we favour one word over others here? Is it better to choose to say that thick concepts—*all* sorts of thick concept—are fundamentally evaluative rather than action-guiding? Even if ethical concepts can guide action, are we so keen that aesthetic concepts should be thought to have this as their chief and significant characteristic? Perhaps calling thin and thick concepts normative is better. But, that will make sense only once we have a clear idea of what it is for a concept to be normative, and that is far from settled in current philosophical work. It has something to do with providing reasons and influencing us, and it is tied to action. But, there are various sorts of action: physical actions, the formation of beliefs, moral actions, prudential actions, and so on. It may not be helpful here to subsume all such things under some general classification of the normative since this might obscure differences between thin and thick concepts from different domains. Again, is it obvious that a chief function of aesthetic concepts is to provide reasons, even if we agree that the use of such concepts can influence action and the belief-formation of others?

This may be an issue where progress can be made only by working through the details of how a large number of different types of supposed thin and thick concepts work. We may suspect that because of the variety of thick concepts with which we are dealing, then perhaps we should be liberal and say that whatever it is that is nondescriptive or non-world-guided, it is something very broad and multi-various. It may be evaluative-cum-normative-cum-action-guiding. Thick concepts have appeal as a topic because they force us to think hard about how terms such as 'evaluative' and 'normative' relate, as too often they can be run together and used unthinkingly as synonyms.

(iii) More progress can be made on a related issue concerning evaluation or, at least, we can see better what the options are. (I will stick with 'evaluative' now, as well as 'descriptive'.) This issue concerns the idea that thick concepts can be disentangled or separated into distinct, isolable and independently intelligible parts: typically some evaluative conceptual content and some descriptive conceptual content. Arguably it is this issue that people associate most with the idea of thick concepts. In effect, we are asking whether thick concepts are whole concepts, or whether they can be broken into more basic elements such that we use thick terms only as a convenient shorthand. On this issue hangs a lot of the point of modern metaethics. This issue gets to the heart of our thoughts about how the evaluative relates to the descriptive, and what the evaluative is.

To introduce the idea and explain why thick concepts are so important for modern metaethics, we should consider some history. In the middle part of the twentieth century, it is commonly said, noncognitivist positions were very popular in moral philosophy. Although they came in varieties, noncognitivists were united by the thought that we lived in a natural, nonmoral world, where actions, people, and other things should properly be characterized in nonmoral ways only. So, for example, one could praise the helping of someone or object to the stealing of something. This could be analyzed thus: we have an action or person characterized nonmorally, with some bare evaluative attitude or stance attached to it. Similarly, evaluative concepts such as HONESTY could be separated and assumed to be composed of some bare attitude with some descriptive conceptual content. It was this latter sort of content that distinguished the honest from the brave and all the rest. Some positions—such as emotivism—characterized the attitude in terms of emotions that were evinced. Other positions, such as R. M. Hare's prescriptivism, characterized this attitude in terms of some prescription or demand.[9] Hare explicitly talked about thick concepts, albeit briefly and not under that label.[10] He assumed of TIDY and INDUSTRIOUS that the descriptive meaning or content could be separated from the evaluative and, further, that the evaluative meaning was of less importance than the descriptive. 'Tidy' and 'industrious' are value-words for Hare, but it is clear to him that we can separate them into more basic parts. The same held for all moral concepts.

Standing behind noncognitivism, and other ideas, lay a distinction that many people held dear, namely that between facts and values. Supposedly these were very distinct, different types of thing. It is a fact that the table exists and a fact that Mabel likes it, but for Mabel to say that the table is good or elegant would be for her to express values. Values, it was assumed, could not be studied or measured by the empirical sciences. This, amongst other things, cast doubt on whether they 'really' existed. Again, we can use value terms and concepts for convenience, but that is all: they are not really picking out things we should think exist in any meaningful and important sense. Many value terms could be broken down into terms that refer to things that do exist and could be understood better.

This sort of general intellectual stance began to be challenged. In a seminar run during the 1950s in Oxford, Philippa Foot and Iris Murdoch questioned the fact-value distinction and primarily had Hare in their sights. Indeed, although it is Williams who

---

[9] There are interesting details I am skating over here, such as the relationship between speech acts and mental states. For more on this, see Schroeder (2010).

[10] Hare (1952), 121ff.

first coined 'thick concept', he himself notes that he was developing ideas he first aired in the Foot-Murdoch seminar.[11] They used the idea of thick concepts to call into question the fact-value distinction directly, and specifically prescriptivist views of it. As I put their question, when we say of someone that she was honest, or rude, are we stating a fact about her or are we expressing a value of her? Even if we wholeheartedly say the latter, it is not so clear that we cannot endorse the former option also. This should make us pause to think hard about whether there is such a hard and fast distinction between facts and values in the first place. Perhaps we can think of some occasions, and some concepts, where the two are intertwined in a way that this distinction rules out.

Let us now tackle the specific idea of disentangling or separating. Note that it is probably fine when introducing thick concepts to indicate the supposed aspects they have. But, to leave things there, and assume that we have separable elements, is hugely controversial. Note also that for much of the time, this debate raged between cognitivists and noncognitivists.[12] But, it is important to realize that one can adopt (what I call) 'separationism'—which says that supposed thick concepts can be split into separable and independently intelligible elements—and be a cognitivist about both or all elements that thick concepts are thought to be composed of. Or, in other words, the evaluative conceptual content is best not seen as the expression of some attitude, but is itself some representing concept such as GOOD or PRO. For that reason, some of the writers in this volume like to characterize the central dispute as that between separationists and nonseparationists, or between reductivists and nonreductivists.

The thought raised by nonseparationists was that one cannot disentangle thick concepts into their supposed parts. Why not? We have to assume that there is some rationale, however basic and vague, to the application of concepts. We cannot decide only on a whim to call each of a group of things 'honest'. There has to be something about these things such that our concept application is justified, in some minimal sense. Now, nonseparationists believe that this 'something' is best thought of as the quality of honesty, which cannot be reduced into further parts. (Talk of 'quality' suggests a realistic take on their conclusion. This is justified in part by some nonseparationist writings, but the conclusion need be only that thick concepts refer and are as conceptually irreducible as, say, concepts such as CARPET and COMPUTER.) To keep things simple, imagine we have just two elements: some thin evaluation and some descriptive conceptual content.[13] We need to make sure that one or other element is sufficient to justify our conceptual divisions; it

---

[11] Williams (1985), 217–18, n. 7. Williams also notes that Wittgenstein is an influence on the idea. As I note in my contribution to this volume, the first to use 'thick' to indicate ideas in this *general* ballpark was Gilbert Ryle. I regret to say that I have not been able to confirm how much, if at all, Ryle or Hare knew about the Foot-Murdoch seminar. Some writings that connect with that seminar are Foot (1958) and (1958–9), and Murdoch (1956), (1957), and (1962).

[12] For example, see the exchange between Blackburn (1981) and McDowell (1981).

[13] Separationists differ exactly on how these two elements combine for most or all thick concepts, or whether we have just two. For reasons of space I do not detail that debate here, but for an introduction to this idea, see the exchange between Blackburn (1992) and Gibbard (1992), and also Elstein and Hurka (2009).

has to justify us saying why all of *these* things are kind whilst all of *those* things are just (and such that it can accommodate overlap between the two camps, of course). Can the evaluation do the work necessary to divide conceptually the just from the kind from the sublime? No, because it is far too coarse-grained. Perhaps it is not thin evaluation, but there is a whole range of particular evaluative elements that attach to the relevant descriptive contents and are such as to distinguish the concepts in the way we want. Whether there is such a range is an empirical question. However, some worry if there could be such a fine-grained range of responses and, secondly, that evaluations divide as clearly as they may have to when it comes to mapping and explaining our conceptual divisions. Furthermore, we would have to be certain that we could (logically) pick out the evaluations without recourse to the concepts, for we are trying to show that these things are derived and constructed. It is unclear whether that is possible: perhaps we see the differences between certain sorts of evaluative feeling only because of the concepts we are used to.

Most work has focused on the descriptive conceptual content. This brings in the so-called shapelessness hypothesis. The hypothesis is that evaluative concepts are shapeless with respect to the descriptive. In other words, there is no way of descriptively recharacterizing the evaluative concepts (or parts thereof) that is such that our new descriptive concept maps onto all and only all of the instances that the evaluative concept is used of. It may be extremely hard to get at a high-level, reasonably short descriptive characterization of our various evaluative concepts. Utilitarian failures to convince people that we can recharacterize our moral notions in terms of the maximization of happiness come to mind here. Similarly, dictionary definitions of all of the evaluative notions we are considering standardly use other evaluative notions and synonyms, and that will not do for our present purposes. Attention has focused on longer, lower-level sorts of recharacterization, where we create disjunctive definitions of evaluative concepts, with each descriptively characterized disjunct representing an example that we have encountered and agreed to be an example of the concept under consideration. For example, we might say that x is kind if and only if x has features $<a, b, c>$ or $<d, e, f>$ or $<a, b, d$, but if e is present, then g and not $d>$ or . . . and so on. The key problem here is whether we can be certain that we will ever capture all of the instances of, say, KIND. The ' . . . and so on' is crucial. It cannot be left there because if it does it signifies the thought that, after a time, one can pick up what is common to all of these examples and extend it to an indefinite number of new cases. But, the whole point of this debate is whether this understanding can be captured—fully—in a descriptive way, or whether such understanding is, ultimately, evaluative. The charge is that separationists are supporting the former option, so they cannot leave us with an ' . . . and so on' clause. To put this another way, what we are doing with our disjuncts is reporting cases we have encountered. But, what of the future? How can we be sure that new cases will be just the same as the old ones? Even if they are *like* them, we need to codify the understanding that categorizes new cases to be like the old ones, and not unlike them. And that understanding cannot be evaluative understanding, if one is a separationist. We have to be able to represent it descriptively.

Is there any reason to think that a full descriptive disjunctive definition could not be given for our common-or-garden evaluative concepts? Consider this sort of example. Imagine we are told that lying is wrong. (So, we have part of some full recharacterization of WRONG: '*x* is wrong if *x* is...or is...or is the deliberate act of saying something to someone that one thinks he or she will believe and which one knows is not correct, or is...and so on.[14]) But, there are plenty of cases where lying is permitted, even right. Imagine when someone asks you whether she looks good in a certain dress. She doesn't, but you don't want to hurt her feelings and, so, it would be wrong to tell the truth. So we get a suitably worded clause added. However, imagine further that she is wearing the dress to her birthday party, and you know that she doesn't want to be made fun of. So, even though it will hurt her feelings, you need to tell her the truth, and so we get another clause. The philosophical supposition is that we could continue like this all day, inventing new situations that justify new clauses. In which case, we will never get to rule out the '...and so on', simply because we will never reach the end of the wrong (and right) actions.

This sort of example, and the idea behind it, has quite a pull. It does seem as if we could go on like this all day. But, other people will say that we could not. At some point, we will be able to capture evaluative concepts descriptively, for at least some level of description. All we have at present is a nice example illustrating the view, or prejudice, that separationism is a non-starter. We do not have an argument here.

There may be no way out of this impasse. The debate could continue differently, however, with disputants arguing about whether we could ever *know* that we had successfully captured an evaluative concept descriptively irrespective of whether we in fact had. Surely there would always be the worry that the future might throw up something new, even if it would not. In that case, it might be best to adopt a nonseparationist view of evaluative concepts if only as a safety-first option.

There is a lot more to say about shapelessness and disentangling.[15] For now, we should note that the debate about disentangling does not usually lend itself to discussion of thin concepts, for we typically do not have some descriptive aspect to disentangle from something evaluative. (However, that remark may be countered by the reflection on a discussion above. If GOOD and RIGHT differ, perhaps that difference can be classed as a difference of descriptive content of some sort.) Whatever is said about thin concepts, the debate concerning shapelessness does seem relevant to thin concepts. Just as we can speculate about the many types of thing that can be deemed honest, so we can speculate about the many types of thing that can be deemed good. Indeed, just now I used WRONG as an example. We might speculate further and ask about the extent to which the phenomenon of shapelessness is confined to evaluative concepts, or whether it concerns many other sorts of concept where there is the prospect of some reduction or separation. Perhaps CARPET and COMPUTER are not so different after all in this regard.

---

[14] This is just for illustrative purposes. I am not too fussed about getting a relevant definition of lying perfect here.

[15] For more on this, see Kirchin (2010).

More generally, we are now in a better place to ask what the point of discussion about shapelessness and disentangling is. Although a debate about whether or not a descriptive disjunctive description could capture all of an evaluative concept is interesting and relevant, if nonseparationists rest their hopes on the success of this argument then they may be missing out on other options. Recall that Foot and Murdoch were opposed to the prescriptivist analyses given by Hare because it seemed to them that there was less difference between values and facts than was assumed. One way to run with this idea is to show, through thoughts about entanglement, that an assumed separation of fact and (thin) value cannot account for what happens with thick evaluative concepts. A different way of showing this is to claim that value—or evaluation—does not always have to be thin. That is, it does not always have to be pro or con, or even pro-in-a-way or con-in-a-way. It is certainly the case that, for example, if some action is honest or some painting grotesque, this can imply or entail thin-in-a-way judgements. But some writers wish to argue that HONEST and GROTESQUE themselves can be evaluations where one does not automatically have to peg them to thin evaluations, that is peg them to pro and con summaries. When I call a figurine grotesque I am judging it, and I may be offering some evaluation of it that is not just conveying nonevaluative meaning. But, I may also not be indicating that it is pro-in-a-way or con-in-a-way. Despite the link back to Foot and Murdoch, this sort of idea, categorized as an option in the modern debate between separationists and nonseparationists, is still in its infancy. Although this option is intriguing, advocates have to walk a fine line between thinking of evaluation as different from PRO and CON and thinking of these (supposed) evaluative concepts as being nothing more than specific nonevaluative, descriptive concepts.

(iv) A fourth topic follows directly on from that of disentangling. When Williams cites the Foot-Murdoch seminar in *ELP*, what he specifically says is that it is in these seminars that he heard the idea that it 'might be impossible to pick up on an evaluative concept unless one shares its evaluative interest'. The understanding and appreciation of others' thick and thin evaluative concepts is something that does not get as much attention as, for example, shapelessness, but is arguably just as important.[16] Disentangling was introduced as a problem for separationists, and whilst understanding can cause a problem for them, it can also cause a headache for nonseparationists.

The thought goes like this. Imagine an anthropologist going into a society and trying to pick out what a certain evaluative concept stands for. As part of this, or perhaps first of all, she will have to work out what the concepts are that are in use, which ones are evaluative, and so on. Outsiders such as anthropologists are often used to convey some of the thoughts about shapelessness. Perhaps the outsider encounters a friendly insider who

---

[16] For more on this topic, see Sreenivasan (2001). The anthropologist Clifford Geertz picked up on Ryle's thoughts and moulded them into his work. For a classic introduction, see Geertz (1973).

points out which collection of descriptively characterized things are kind and which are not. But, after the insider leaves the outsider, will she be able to continue and apply her knowledge to descriptively new cases? (Think, again, about the lie and the party dress.) The problem for separationists is supposedly that the outsider will not be able to. Why not? Because people can see what various descriptively characterized collections have in common only if they can latch onto the evaluative point of putting these items into a collection in the first place. For example, we can classify various things—beatings, tongue-lashings, silences—as harms only because we do not like harm and are interested in the ways in which one person or group can cause negative feelings in another (in a particular way). Applications of more involved and specific concepts such as BRASH and PICARESQUE will be more complicated than that, although the philosophical moral stays the same.

Indeed, and further, Foot herself was fond of pointing out the flaws of separationism (or, rather, emotivism and the like) by pointing out that there were certain limits on what types of thing one could be proud of and what types of thing one could think of as rude.[17] Without further (and quite contrived) explanation, it would be silly to be proud of the number of planets in one's galaxy, and silly to think that someone is rude simply by breathing. Indeed, it seems that one cannot simply apply (bare) pro or con attitudes to these things, let along moral versions of these attitudes, in a way that makes sense. Separationism—or at least emotivism and prescriptivism—seems to imply heavily that any pro or con attitude can be conjoined with any sort of descriptively characterized action or thing, and some of these conjunctions are the basis of analyses of familiar thick concepts. But, says Foot, not everything can be found to be rude or kitsch or terrifying or disappointing, and not everything can be found to be good. Certain attitudes are fitted to certain objects, and vice versa. When we are thinking about our outsider we are showing that she has to be able to latch onto the ideas and evaluations that are common in a society with which she is not quite familiar. Again, what makes it the case that all of *these* things are categorized together using a certain concept and what makes it the case that *those* other things are categorized differently is determined partly by human interests, views, and evaluations. The outsider has to be able to pick up on those in order to understand the concept and not simply list all of the descriptive features that she encounters.

All well and good. But in offering this story I have used a few telling words: the outsider has to *latch onto* evaluations and uses, and has to *appreciate* what is going on. With this we now raise a key question for nonseparationists. To what extent does the outsider have to hold the exact same evaluation as those she is investigating in order to understand their concepts, its applications, and its withholdings? Indeed, does she have to hold such evaluations sincerely? If we imagine a Martian anthropologist coming to Earth, do we have to claim that for them to be successful they have to have exactly the same responses we have to the grotesque as we do? Although there are no doubt cases of investigators going native, it seems too much to claim that such a stance is necessary for understanding other

---

[17] See Foot (1958) and (1958–9).

people's evaluative concepts. The possibility of anthropology does not depend on something so extreme, surely. So, something lesser is required, and indeed that is suggested by the vague phrase 'latch onto'. But what exactly is the mental state that an anthropologist has to employ? Pretence? Imagination? Appreciation? These ideas themselves invite a host of different interpretations and, despite the simplicity of the terms, they hide a lot of complexity. To complicate matters further, different groups and different concepts and different investigators will require different stances. Sometimes an anthropologist will have to spend years understanding what is going on, whereas in other contexts translation and understanding will be a straightforward and quick affair. Indeed, although I have run this idea with talk of anthropology, the sort of phenomenon goes on most days in most of our lives where we have to understand other people whose use of words is not quite our own.

As with previous discussions, raising the question 'What sort of stance does one have to take in order to understand another's evaluative concepts?' is not fatal to the nonseparationist enterprise. But, it is a question that does deserve a detailed answer. A considered view, introduced via the separationist-nonseparationist debate, is, as yet, lacking.

(v) Consider the phenomenon that I call 'evaluative flexibility'. This occurs when a thick concept is used to imply a pro idea in one context, but a con idea in another. For example, we may praise some poems as elegant, but often we may think of others as bad precisely because they are elegant. Given the material and the feelings they are trying to convey, what we want is something wild and messy, not something elegant. Similarly, people can go wrong in being honest, when really they should be discrete. Being knowledgeable can often stand in the way of action. Cherubic children can sometimes be a bore; cheekiness occasionally has its merits. And so on. Some separationists—notably Hare and Blackburn—think that separationism (or, at least, the type of separationism they propose) has the virtue of being able to accommodate evaluative flexibility very easily. For them, (supposed) thick concepts are constructed from some thin evaluation and some descriptive conceptual content that can stand on its own as a concept.[18] So, we can easily add some pro or con element to whatever descriptive content has been chosen for the (supposed) thick concept in order to get some analysis of what is going on in a particular context.

This view stands opposed to other views. Some separationists do not think that (supposed) thick concepts should be characterized as Hare and Blackburn do. They prefer more detailed accounts that assert, in various ways, that a certain sort of evaluation is tied to the descriptive content and that it is more specific than anything pro or con (but such that it can be analyzed noncognitively and hence is not itself some thick concept), or that a certain specific evaluation is tied more intimately to some descriptive content

---

[18] Blackburn's position is, in fact, more complicated than this. I detail this complication in chapter 2 of Kirchin (ms).

which is not itself enough to become a concept on its own, or some other option.[19] Nonseparationists will clearly disagree with what Hare and Blackburn say. Often they are cast as thinking that a concept has to be either pro or con, but not both. Common to all of these positions that oppose Hare and Blackburn's stance, then, is that they invite this challenge: How can your position accommodate the phenomenon of flexibility?

One could challenge whether the phenomenon of flexibility exists. Perhaps for any thick concept we have two or more concepts in operation, concepts such as HONEST-pro, HONEST-con, and perhaps HONEST-neutral. They have much in common, perhaps, but in the circumstances envisaged above, we have to be aware that only one is applicable in any circumstance. Perhaps. But, this option is simply to repeat the separationism of Hare and Blackburn in another guise, for HONEST in this analysis is functioning, it seems, as a fully determinate concept with descriptive conceptual content. And, given the set-up, it might be difficult to arrive at a different explanation of the phenomenon that relied on their being different versions of the same concept (or just different concepts that were linked in some way).

Let us take the phenomenon of flexibility at face value. Here I focus on nonseparationism.[20] It would be a mistake to think that nonseparationists are committed to there being just one, specific thin evaluation that is tied into any thick concept. They can perfectly well say that honesty can sometimes be good and sometimes be bad. All that nonseparationists were ever committed to was the idea that evaluation—not *an* evaluation—was irreducibly linked to descriptive content. In certain circumstances a pro-evaluation may be appropriate, in other cases one needs to use con-evaluation. Mastery with a thick concept involves knowing which evaluation applies when and where. Indeed, further, we can underline a point from section (iii). Why think that evaluation is limited solely to thin pro and con? Perhaps the evaluative content of HONEST is just something that we should label as, well, HONEST. On occasion—on many occasions—it can offer or convey a clear pro-evaluation. On other occasions it can offer or convey a con-evaluation. It may even occasionally carry no evaluation, although we may wish to introduce a different but related concept for that.

---

[19] See the papers referenced in n. 13 for discussion amongst separationists. One worry with the Hare position (that Blackburn may also once have indicated some support for) is that it may not be able to account for disagreement satisfactorily. Perhaps you want to say of something that it is just whilst I do not think it is. You are for it and I am not. It seems, ordinarily, that both of us can agree generally on what it is for something to be just, but differ on the details. On the Hare-Blackburn view, supposedly our disagreement looks mysterious, even impossible. You apply JUST to a thing, with a pro-evaluation, I apply a con-evaluation. Crucially, what sort of descriptive content do we each apply? We cannot both apply the very same overall, namely a constructed concept JUST, given our different evaluations. Similarly, in order for us to disagree rather than merely talk past each other, we cannot be using radically different concepts. Finally, it could be that we both apply the very same wholly descriptive content, but have different evaluations. But our disagreement does not seem to be analyzable as 'we both agree that this is JUST (descriptive only), it is just that you are pro it and I am not'. Elstein and Hurka (2009) use this worry to introduce their separationist alternatives.

[20] For more on this line of thought, see Dancy (1995).

This sounds all well and good. But, this final point again invites a worry from earlier: can we really make out the idea of there being evaluative conceptual content that is neither pro nor con? For those that find it hard to do so, is it simply that they are in awe of the separationist (or other) illusion that we must be forced to choose between positive or negative? After all, simple as it may be, that picture is rather inviting, and it may be inviting because it is true. If it is true, then nonseparationists may be thrown back onto disentangling and shapelessness as their main form of attack, and if that is so then their arguments may not convince neutrals, let alone separationists.

These five points do not exhaust everything that is of interest about thin and thick concepts, nor indeed do they cover everything that will be raised and debated in the pages of this book. I have barely touched on the workings of thick language, for example, nor of how thick concepts may be more important than thin concepts in classifying objects and of how they may be more important when justifying what we do. Further, many of the points I have made can be put in terms of the question, 'Which type of concept, if either—thin or thick—is conceptually prior?' and this raises a whole series of questions revolving around the idea of conceptual priority. But I hope that these points highlight why so many people find thin and thick concepts worth thinking about. I now turn to sketch the contributions to this collection.

II

The first four pieces form a group of papers that are explicitly in favour of a nonseparationist outlook. In the first piece Edward Harcourt and Alan Thomas begin by offering a few helpful correctives on various assumptions in the debate. Thereafter, in the main meat of their paper, they argue for a nonreductive account of thick concepts. In their view, one cannot analyze thick concepts, but that is no embarrassment, nor does it threaten the importance of thick concepts and how we use and understand them. Along the way they criticize various sorts of reductive views developed by Christine Tappolet, and by Daniel Elstein and Thomas Hurka. They also criticize a counter-criticism developed by Pekka Väyrynen.

In his contribution Jonathan Dancy ranges across a variety of issues—evaluative flexibility, the distinction between thick and thin, the evaluative and the non-evaluative—in order to articulate a nonseparationist view of thick concepts. In doing so he focuses on and uses Williams's characterization of the thick as being both action-guiding and world-guided. He ends by suggesting that thick concepts are evaluative because 'competence with them requires a general understanding of their evaluative point, including the range of their practical relevance, the sorts of difference it can make that the concept is here instantiated'.

In my contribution I seek to compare Williams on thin and thick concepts with Gilbert Ryle on thick descriptions. As we have seen, Williams's official characterization of thin concepts has them as being wholly action-guiding, whilst thick concepts are both action-guiding and world-guided. I argue that the official characterization of

Williams's view—in terms of action-guidance and world-guidedness—is a misleading summary of what Williams himself says, and is wrong as a summary of thin and thick concepts. I analyze these failures by looking to Ryle. One of the upshots is that I suggest a view of the thick mooted in this introduction: that we understand the thick better if we do not always understand it as being either pro or con. Thick evaluation is understandable on its own away from these thin notions.

Debbie Roberts takes this suggestion—which she calls the 'Inclusive' view—and shapes her whole paper around it. She argues that this idea can be obscured if we think that evaluation is simply to be identified with thin evaluation. She concentrates on the shapelessness hypothesis, as found in John McDowell's work, in order to tease out how a different sense of evaluation emerges that is friendly to the Inclusive view. She argues in the end that the best way to understand thick concepts is by viewing them in relation to the (supposed) thick properties that they (supposedly) pick out.

The next two papers offer opposition to the first four as both are separationist in spirit. Michael Smith takes as his cue Hare's work on the thick. He sets himself two questions to answer. First, in what way do thick concepts differ from thin ones? More specifically, is Williams correct in thinking that the difference lies in the world-guidedness of the former? Secondly, what should we say about the issue of conceptual priority? Is one of these types of concept prior to the other when we analyze what is going on? Smith argues that Williams is wrong since thin concepts are as world-guided as thick ones. From the way in which he argues for this, he then argues that the thin is conceptually prior to the thick, in a way that Hare's work showed us all along.

Simon Blackburn focuses on the work of Hilary Putnam. Putnam uses the idea of the thick to unseat the supposed distinction between facts and values. Blackburn criticizes Putnam's view, and those who share it, focusing on language with a variety of well-chosen examples. For Blackburn the thick is pressed to do work for which is it unfit and there is good reason to retain faith in the fact-value distinction.

We then have a change of tack, although we do not leave behind the debate between separationists and nonseparationists. There is a standard view, endorsed by nonseparationists, that all thin and thick concepts are in some way inherently evaluative. (Some separationists assume that this is what they should be arguing against at the start.) Pekka Väyrynen claims that as part of this there is a presumption that non-evaluative aspects of thick concepts are not enough to determine such concepts' extensions. Väyrynen argues that one can explain this underdetermination without assuming that thick concepts are, as a general class, inherently evaluative. Some thick concepts may work in this way, but many do not. If he is right, it should make us rethink a lot of the debate between separationists and nonseparationists, and other aspects of thick concepts.

In his contribution, Matti Eklund also highlights and discusses an aspect of the debate about thick concepts that often resides in the background: What is it for something to be evaluative? In asking this question, Eklund explicitly considers the differences between concepts (and predicates), and properties. He discusses and dismisses a number of views. He does not advance any positive view of his own, but he does draw a number of consequences. One of the most important is that evaluation (or 'evaluativeness') is a feature of predicates and not properties.

Throughout much of this book and in other places, there is an assumption that it is clear what thin and thick concepts are. Some writers go further and argue that thin concepts are stand-alone concepts. Some go further still and argue for the conceptual priority of the thin to the thick, or of the thick to the thin. In this last view people sometimes think that thin concepts are (mere) abstractions from their thick cousins. In his contribution Timothy Chappell picks up on some of these thoughts. He argues that 'thin concepts' are dubious entities. He uses a careful analysis of some of the usual examples of thick and thin to raise serious doubts about both their conceptuality and their thinness. Confusions aside, he sees little obvious use for them in ethics or metaethics. The very idea that there could be a naturally occurring, purely evaluative moral concept, with no descriptive content, no cultural setting, and no capacity for distanced or ironic use, is—he argues—as chimerical as any other ahistorical illusion. He also suggests that our concentration on thick and thin has distracted us from thinking about other interesting and important ethical distinctions—evidential/verdictive, evaluative/prescriptive, determinable/determinate, Zangwill's because-relation, Anscombe's brute-relative-to relation—which he thinks have something genuine and non-illusory on *both* sides of them.

Although when discussing thin and thick concepts, writers aim to say something general about all of them, too often they fall back on moral examples. The conclusions they draw therefore may not be as general as they think, nor correct. In a frank piece, Nick Zangwill traces his own prejudices against moral thick talk and how this used to be different from his attraction to thick aesthetic talk. In doing so he compares thick talk about ethics and aesthetics and highlights the use of moral metaphor. In his view the phenomenon of metaphor is unjustly neglected in much that is written about thick moral concepts and moral language generally. In showing the importance of metaphor for moral language and thought, Zangwill in effect shows why Wittgenstein was correct when he drew attention to the literal indescribability of the moral. (Readers should be warned that Zangwill boldly discusses many swearwords, particularly in §3.)

Eric Wiland focuses on a topic that appears small but which reveals something significant. As should be apparent, one cannot discuss the topic of thick concepts without at least mentioning, if not engaging with, the work of Williams. But, it is important to see how the topic of thick concepts connects with other parts of Williams's thought. Wiland focuses on how Williams's views about thick concepts links with his conclusion that there are no true external reasons statements. Wiland argues that there is a tension: Williams thinks that thick concepts are guided by the world and (it seems) they are applicable to people no matter who they are, yet Williams also thinks that reasons for action for any individual depend only on their pre-existing motives. (The concept REASONABLE shows this tension.) If Wiland is right, not only does he make us think hard about Williams's overall views, but he also gets us to think hard about reasons and what is involved in an evaluative concept being world-guided.

In the final contribution, Valerie Tiberius extends thoughts about thick concepts in an interesting fashion. Focusing on the concepts WELL-BEING and WISDOM, she argues that a certain view of the relation between (academic) psychology and philosophy is wrong. What is wrong is to think that philosophers define and characterize various positions, ideas and phenomena, and then psychologists investigate the phenomena to see if what philosophers say is true. (Or, at least, Tiberius thinks this picture is wrong with regards to WELL-being and WISDOM.) In arguing in this way, Tiberius shows why it is that thick concepts hold 'special' promise for moral progress, an idea that can be found in Williams's writings.

We can extend that last thought and end this piece. Thick concepts hold our interest in part because they seem to unite evaluation and description, in some way and, further, make us question what evaluation *is*. But, if that was all that they did, our interest in them would not be as high as it is. They are practical concepts and everyday concepts. They are concepts that pull us—and others—in certain directions and justify some actions and not others. We can use them to shape our world and colour it in special ways. Thick concepts are important to us and our world because they seem to be a necessary way of understanding what the world and its people are. If we understand what these concepts are and how they work, we might better understand ourselves and the world we find ourselves in.[21]

References

Blackburn, Simon (1981) 'Rule-Following and Moral Realism', in Stephen Holtzman and Christopher Leich (eds.) *Wittgenstein: To Follow a Rule* (London: Routledge and Kegan Paul), 163–87.

—— (1992) 'Morality and Thick Concepts: Through Thick and Thin', *Proceedings of the Aristotelian Society, Supplementary Volume* 66: 285–99.

Dancy, Jonathan (1995) 'In Defense of Thick Concepts', in Peter A. French, Theodore E. Uehling, and Howard K. Wettstein (eds.) *Midwest Studies in Philosophy* XX, 263–79.

Foot, Philippa (1958) 'Moral Arguments', *Mind* 67: 502–13.

—— (1958–9) 'Moral Beliefs', *Proceedings of the Aristotelian Society* 59: 83–104.

Elstein, Daniel and Hurka, Thomas (2009) 'From Thin to Thick: Two Moral Reductionist Plans', *Canadian Journal of Philosophy* 39: 515–35.

Geertz, Clifford (1973) 'Thick Description: Toward an Interpretive Theory of Culture', in his *The Interpretation of Cultures* (New York: Basic Books), 3–30.

Gibbard, Allan (1992) 'Morality and Thick Concepts: Thick Concepts and Warrant for Feelings', *Proceedings of the Aristotelian Society, Supplementary Volume* 66: 267–83.

Hare, R. M. (1952) *The Language of Morals* (Oxford: Clarendon Press).

Kirchin, Simon (2010) 'The Shapelessness Hypothesis', *Philosophers' Imprint* 10: 1–28.

—— (ms) *Thick Evaluation*.

---

[21] Thanks to Tim Chappell for his comments on an earlier draft.

McDowell, John (1981) 'Non-Cognitivism and Rule-Following', in Stephen Holtzman and Christopher Leich (eds.) *Wittgenstein: To Follow a Rule* (London: Routledge and Kegan Paul), 141–62.

Murdoch, Iris (1956) 'Vision and Choice in Morality', *Proceedings of the Aristotelian Society, Supplementary Volume* 30: 32–58. Reprinted in her *Existentialists and Mystics*, Peter Conradi (ed.) (London: Chatto and Windus, 1997), 76–98.

—— (1957) 'Metaphysics and Ethics' in *The Nature of Metaphysics,* D. F. Pears (ed.) (London: Macmillan). Reprinted in her *Existentialists and Mystics*, Peter Conradi (ed.) (London: Chatto and Windus, 1997), 59–75.

—— (1962) 'The Idea of Perfection', based on the Ballard Matthews Lecture delivered at the University College, North Wales. Reprinted in her *Existentialists and Mystics*, Peter Conradi (ed.) (London: Chatto and Windus, 1997), 299–336.

Scheffler, Samuel (1987) 'Morality through Thick and Thin: A Critical Notice of *Ethics and the Limits of Philosophy*', *Philosophical Review* 96: 411–34.

Schroeder, Mark (2010) *Noncognitivism in Ethics* (London: Routledge).

Sreenivasan, Gopal (2001) 'Understanding Alien Morals', *Philosophy and Phenomenological Research* 62: 1–32.

Tappolet, Christine (2004) 'Through Thick and Thin: *Good* and its Determinates', *dialectica* 58: 207–21.

Williams, Bernard (1985) *Ethics and the Limits of Philosophy* (London: Fontana).

2

Thick Concepts, Analysis, and Reductionism

Edward Harcourt and Alan Thomas

'Thick concepts' has emerged as a topic of interest because it sits on a fault-line in metaethics. Some utterances which deploy 'thick' ethical vocabulary—terms such as 'obsequious', 'small-minded', 'priggish', 'resilient', 'tolerant', each with different and comparatively specific satisfaction-conditions—have been claimed to express ethical *concepts* thanks to which the thoughts and judgments expressed by these utterances on the one hand are candidates for truth and falsity ('world-guided') and, on the other, supply defeasible reasons for action ('action-guiding').[1] But it is a widely-held doctrine in meta-ethics that no single thing can play both roles. So there is considerable pressure to find an alternative account of the same phenomenon.

The alternatives take two basic forms. One is an account of the thoughts and judg-ments expressed by 'thick' ethical vocabulary according to which their truth-evaluability and their relation to action are carried by two independently specifiable components, typically—though only typically—something with a truth-value plus an expressive or otherwise non-cognitive extra. The other affirms the simplicity of these thoughts and judgments while denying the link to action. This is externalism in the theory of motiva-tion. As we will assume for present purposes that externalism is unattractive, it looks as if either the former alternative must be made to work, or else utterances deploying 'thick' ethical vocabulary really do—contrary to the doctrine—express ethical concepts of the kind we have outlined.

Our aim in this paper is to defend the latter view. However, some preliminary com-mentary is required on the way the dispute about 'thick concepts' is often set up.

2.1 How *not* to identify the issue

Let us assume for the time being that the ethical concepts whose existence we wish to defend are usefully labelled 'thick ethical concepts', or 'thick concepts' for short. (We will return to this assumption later.) Thick concepts are commonly defined as concepts that

[1] Williams (1985), 141.

'have both a descriptive and an evaluative component', perhaps with the qualification that these components are a 'compound…rather than a mixture'[2] or an indissoluble 'amalgam'.[3] We object to this kind of definition, with or without the qualification, because the word 'descriptive' has acquired a technical usage in philosophy according to which it has come simply to *mean* 'non-evaluative'. Defining thick concepts as concepts that have both an (in this sense) descriptive and an evaluative component thus implies that, even if utterances deploying thick vocabulary *do* express judgments deploying thick concepts, the fact that judgments deploying these concepts express evaluations can be no thanks to whatever it is that makes them truth-evaluable. So our position, namely, that what it *is* for judgments to deploy ethical concepts is for them to be apt to express evaluations precisely thanks to what makes them truth-evaluable,[4] goes out of the window with the mere definition of the topic.

A related and equally objectionable idea is that the most visible version of the view we are opposing here—the claim that what is expressed by utterances deploying 'thick' vocabulary resolves into a truth-evaluable component plus a non-cognitive extra—is properly characterized as the claim that thick *concepts* are capable of a two-component reductive analysis. When 'bachelor' is analysed into 'unmarried person' and 'man', both components of the analysis are themselves concepts. But when it comes to what is expressed by thick ethical vocabulary, on the view now in focus this is not so. For, assuming a connection between conceptually structured judgments and truth, the second component of the analysis is precisely *non*-conceptual, since by the non-cognitivist's lights whatever connects the judgment to action cannot be truth-relevant. But now if the two supposed analysantia of what thick vocabulary expresses are a conceptual and a non-conceptual item, what it expresses is not, properly speaking, a thick *concept* after all. Those who deny that utterances involving thick ethical vocabulary express thoughts and judgments with the two features we claim for them ought to deny that there are any thick ethical concepts, not concede their existence and then offer a reductive analysis of them.[5]

This complaint connects with Elstein and Hurka's helpful point that two-component approaches (or indeed multiple-component ones, but we suppress this qualification henceforth for the sake of brevity) to the thick are not the exclusive preserve of non-cognitivists.[6] They observe that though non-cognitivism *requires* a two-component approach, it is also open to 'Moorean' cognitivists, who hold that the word 'good' expresses a concept apt to figure in truth-evaluable judgments but that is also simple and

[2] Blackburn (1992), 298.   [3] Payne (2006).

[4] Cf. David Wiggins (2006), 378: 'the commendatory or approbatory force of (ethical) terms (where that force is present and in operation) (is) not an extra input into their full meaning but…*results(s) from what they already mean*'.

[5] The point is formulated with admirable clarity by Simon Blackburn in his (1992). For further recognition of the difference between these two strategies, one eliminative, and one reductive, see Väyrynen (2009).

[6] Elstein and Hurka (2009).

unanalysable, to argue that the concepts expressed by thick ethical vocabulary have a reductive analysis (into 'good' plus some non-evaluative component). That seems exactly right about 'Mooreans', but Elstein and Hurka do not quite go far enough. If non-cognitivists ought properly speaking to deny that there are any thick concepts, reductive analyses of thick ethical concepts are in fact on offer *only* from 'Mooreans', because only they combine a two-component approach to what the thick vocabulary expresses (and so have an analysis to offer) with the claim that *both* its evaluative and its non-evaluative functions are carried by semantic features of the utterance (and so can properly claim that there are some thick concepts, rather than merely some uses of 'thick' vocabulary, to analyse). We reject two-component approaches whether in their 'Moorean' (properly speaking reductionist) or in their more visible, non-cognitivist (properly speaking eliminativist) version, though for ease of comprehension we use 'reductive' and 'two-component' interchangeably as there is no contradictory of 'two-component' ready to hand.

A distinct reason to protest at the way the topic is usually presented relates not to the thick but to the thin, and this point applies as much to Bernard Williams's definition as it does to, say, Simon Blackburn's.[7] 'Action-guiding and world-guided' as a characterization exclusive to the thick strongly suggests that thin ethical concepts are *not* world-guided since, on pain of abolishing the thick/thin distinction, there must be something that thick concepts have as a class which thin ones do not. So, for example, an utterance deploying only the paradigmatically thin term 'good' will (just as non-cognitivists say) not express anything that is a candidate for truth. That is far too substantial a conclusion to get out of a mere definition. In order that the discussion not be skewed in favour of the non-cognitivist from the very start, therefore, this familiar definition of the thick/thin contrast must be rejected.

But why persist in the assumption we have been making so far, that the thick/thin distinction is needed at all? One bad reason for distinguishing the thin from the thick would be to appeal to the idea that thin evaluative concepts distinctively express *verdictive* ethical considerations.[8] If that were so, it would imply that judgments deploying thin concepts are, distinctively, not *both* truth-evaluable *and* expressive of reasons for action, on the grounds that they are not expressive of reasons for action. A compressed argument to this conclusion is that verdictive judgments expressed by the word 'right', for example, express a verdict on one's reasons and cannot in themselves *add* a further reason on pain of launching a regress of reasons.[9] However, while the evidential/verdictive distinction is a good one, we see it as marking off two distinct functional roles for a reason involving *any* kind of term (thick or thin), and thus as orthogonal to the thick/thin distinction. It cannot, therefore, be used to differentiate thin and thick judgments as a class.

---

[7] Blackburn (1992).

[8] This is a recurring theme in many of the essays in Foot (2002), especially 'Moral Arguments' and 'Moral Beliefs'.

[9] Stratton-Lake (2000), 14–15; Dancy (2004), 16–17.

In fact we agree with Samuel Scheffler that the distinction between thick and thin ethical concepts is best seen as a continuum.[10] If this is right, for a concept to be (relatively) thick is just for it to be more specific and to have narrower satisfaction conditions than one that is (relatively) thin, so there is no need to make differentiating claims about the marks of thick and thin concepts as classes. Moreover our non-reductive cognitivism about judgments deploying thick vocabulary applies just as much to judgments expressed by paradigmatically thin vocabulary such as 'good'. (This simply mirrors something the non-cognitivist can also say, namely that even 'good' places *some* restrictions on the range of things that can satisfy it—as it might be, persons or states of affairs—but in so far as it does, even here there is room to unbundle what the word does into 'description'—which earns the utterance its truth-conditions—and evaluation.)

But it does not follow from any of this that there is nothing interesting going on towards one end of the continuum that is not also going on towards the other. For instance, the thicker the concept, the more likely it is to be merely local, and the less likely it is to be portable outside a larger web of sensibilities, understandings, and ways of life whose characterization will require further use of thick concepts.[11] So we feel no sense of awkwardness in continuing to claim that the ethical concepts expressed by (relatively) thick vocabulary are indeed (relatively) thick ethical concepts, rather than just ethical concepts without qualification. It is also consistent with this to maintain that the concepts expressed by *thin* ethical vocabulary are sometimes (relatively) thick—but that is another story.

What of the converse worry, that there's nothing to distinguish ethical concepts (thick or thin) from concepts generally? Some very general reflections on concept use, derived from the later Wittgenstein, can make it seem as if the claims that non-reductive cognitivists make about thick ethical concepts stem from a generalized operationalism that ties all concept use to practicality, and so rope in non-ethical concepts as well as ethical ones. Operationalism is at home in the philosophy of science as a distinctive kind of explanation of concept use: grasp of a concept is identical to grasp of 'a certain set of operations'.[12] But this view is open to decisive objections even in its proper domain.[13] So we need to show that the practicality of ethical concepts rests on something different, and proper to those concepts in particular.

The answer is that both thick and thin evaluative concepts presuppose that which David Wiggins and John McDowell have called a prior 'evaluative interest' in a way that other concepts do not. Adrian Moore explains clearly why there have to be two arguments here, not one:

Practical reasoning, on this reconstruction, includes a pure element: keeping faith with concepts. Theoretical reasoning also involves keeping faith with concepts. What makes it possible for keeping faith with concepts to have a practical dimension as well as its more familiar theoretical

---

[10] Scheffler (1987).   [11] Thomas (2006), 156–60.   [12] Bridgman (1927).
[13] Chihara and Fodor (1965).

dimension is, ultimately, the fact that some concepts—. . . ethical concepts—equip those who possess them with certain reasons for doing things.[14]

Because of the role of an evaluative interest in explaining ethical concepts, the interpretation of both thin and thick concepts places special demands on the interpretation of social groups, demands that do not extend to the explanation of all concepts. Given the nature of the ethical, we can expect both classes of ethical concepts to be highly perspectival: they are tied to our human perspective and its distinctive peculiarities. Once again, however, it is a matter of degree that thick concepts place more demands on social explanations than do the thin. That is because they give you more specific information about the particular way in which, to use Williams's phrase, users of thick concepts 'find their way around' a particular social world.[15] This fact is simply a consequence of their comparative specificity compared to thin concepts. They capture that which is to be explained in a more fine-grained way than descriptions that deploy thin concepts.

In this paper we cannot hope to say all that needs to be said in defence of non-reductive cognitivism about what thick ethical vocabulary expresses. In particular we do not address what, to some, fundamentally underpins opposition to it, namely the doctrine that nothing can be both truth-evaluable and bear the relation to action which we claim for ethical concepts. (If correct, this would of course rule out reductive ('Moorean') cognitivism about the thick as much as it would our own view.) We focus instead on considerations as it were upstream of that doctrine designed to make two-component accounts seem inevitable, arguing that our non-reductive view is at least as well-motivated as its rivals.

2.2 Evaluative properties and the determinate/ determinable relation

One of the main arguments in favour of a two-component approach to judgments deploying thick vocabulary is that a two-component approach *follows from* the idea that the thick/ thin contrast is a contrast between more and less 'descriptive content'. As long as 'more descriptive content' means 'greater specificity' or 'narrower satisfaction-conditions', this interpretation of the contrast in unimpeachably neutral, so we now want to show why it is no argument for a two-component approach.

Consider a thick ethical concept such as BRUTAL and an occasion of its use, such as 'the prisoners were treated brutally'.[16] We can form a corresponding judgment using one of its thin counterparts such as BAD, and substitute the judgment 'the prisoners were treated badly' as a less specific description of the same situation. In the former case you know much more specifically the particular way in which the prisoners were treated badly. Furthermore, one can establish a defeasible tie to a reason for action (perhaps preventing

---

[14] Moore (2006), 143.   [15] Williams (1985), 155.
[16] We follow the convention of referring to concepts in small capitals.

the brutal treatment if it is in your power to do so) in virtue of the correct application of a more fine-grained description. Now it is tempting to imagine that what one is doing here is subtracting the extra descriptive content contributed by 'brutal' to isolate the element—whether it is regarded as purely evaluative or not is another matter, though it usually is—expressed by 'bad'. But this explanation is far from mandatory.

Consider an analogy with colours. 'Red' has more 'descriptive content' than 'coloured', in that whatever is red is coloured but we don't learn *which* colour something is—as it might be, red—just by being told that it is coloured. But there is no property distinct from redness itself such that something is red iff it has that property and is coloured. There is nothing one can conjoin with colouredness to yield redness; or to put the point the other way about, colouredness is not a *component* of redness.[17] But since it is not, it is a mistake to infer from the mere fact that 'brutal' has more descriptive content than 'bad' that brutality can be analysed into two components, badness plus some further independently specifiable condition. You could say, trivially, that *x* is brutal iff it is bad and brutal, but that is no comfort to a two-component approach.

Does this show that thick concepts are unanalysable? No: at this stage all we have shown is that a two-component analysis of what thick ethical vocabulary expresses is not inevitable, because the data is compatible both with that proposal and with an alternative, namely that 'bad' stands to 'brutal' as 'coloured' stands to 'red', at least in so far as the former is an *abstraction from* the latter (or the latter a *specification of* the former). However, we mention the alternative not just because its mere possibility shows no two-component approach can be inferred straight from the agreed facts about more and less 'descriptive content', but because we think this view is correct. To elaborate: following Christine Tappolet, we argue that a *pro tanto* judgment using the word 'good' stands to a counterpart judgment using a thick ethical concept in a way analogous to that in which the concept RED stands to the concept COLOURED, namely, the relation of a determinate to its covering determinable at the level of the corresponding properties.[18]

Why only 'analogous to'? Because evaluative properties lack the kind of necessary inter-property relations within the entire field of properties that allowed Wittgenstein to speak of a 'geometry of colour' in the case of colour concepts.[19] (There is no analogy, in the case of evaluative properties, to a colour wheel exhibiting these necessary relations within a holistic structure.) Nevertheless, the relations between properties such as the property of badness and the property of being brutal preserve the truisms that Funkhouser lists as minimally required for the presence of this kind of determination relation between properties.[20]

First, it is a relation that holds relative to pairs of properties. So, on this account, the property of brutality is determinable relative to thuggish, but determinate relative to bad. Secondly, any determinate property is an instantiation of a determinable in some

[17] Williamson (2000), x; Jackson (2002), 518ff.
[18] Johnson (1921); Prior (1949); Funkhouser (2006).
[19] Wittgenstein (1977).   [20] Funkhouser (2006), 548–9.

specific way, where specificity is distinct from, inter alia, the genus-species relation, so brutality is a determinate way of being bad. Thirdly, we agree with Judith Jarvis Thomson when she claims that

it seems very plausible to think that a thing's being good must consist in its being good in some way... if that is the case then there is no metaphysically mysterious property goodness.[21]

Compare: no object is just coloured without being some particular colour. This preserves the truism that an object which instantiates a determinate instantiates all determinables that it falls under, so a thuggish action is also brutal and bad. The way in which the relation between properties picked out by thick and thin predications matches this profile seems to us a strong indication that our account is correct.

We would like to add a further, epistemic gloss to Thomson's ontological claim that to be good is always to be good in a particular way. It is an advantage of our account that it promises to explain, in a way that is favourable to cognitivism, a line of thought which has been made to bear too much weight in metaethics. Consider a uniformly red surface filling one's field of vision. In a certain obvious sense there is no further feature of the surface one needs to see beyond its redness in order to judge that it is coloured. If one were sufficiently impressed by this fact, therefore, it might be tempting to say that the colouredness of the surface is a property of it that cannot be seen. One would then need a theory of what sort of property colour is, and how it relates to the visible. But there's a simpler explanation of the facts stated. The reason there is no further feature of the surface one needs to see beyond its redness in order to judge that it is coloured is just the relationship between the two concepts: in someone who possesses both concepts, to see that it is red is to see that it is coloured. So there's no warrant for saying of colouredness, any more than there is of redness, that it is not a property that can be discerned by looking.

This allows one to see G. E. Moore as having taken a wrong turning precisely where the determinate/determinable analogy shows it to be avoidable. Moore's 'intuition' that good is simple, indefinable, but non-natural (that is, not discernible by the senses or by introspection) seems almost exactly to parallel the misguided construction of a theory of colouredness on the assumption that colour is not a visible feature. Goodness is a real property of things and, like yellow, it is (let us grant) simple; but unlike yellow—so Moore reasoned—it is unobservable. So we must come to know it by 'intuition'. We do not want to argue that the property of goodness can literally be seen, but Moore overlooked the possibility that, like the exercise of 'coloured', judgments of goodness might be the bringing to bear on the observable of a complex conceptual capacity, concluding instead that they must involve the exercise of a conceptually unstructured quasi-perceptual faculty which delivers knowledge of what cannot be perceived. That is one path towards an intuitionist moral epistemology that seems to us very unappealing. The positive model

---

[21] Thomson (1996), 128–9.

we have put forward explains how it can be avoided. If, as on our view, to be good is always to be good in some particular way, in coming to know (by whatever epistemic route) that something is that particular way one also comes to know (by that route) that it is good.

We now propose to strengthen our view by defending it against two recent rivals.

2.3 Tappolet's reductive account of thick concepts

Our non-reductive cognitivist treatment of what's expressed by thick ethical vocabulary claims that thick concepts are unanalysable. The first challenge to this view comes from Christine Tappolet.[22] Despite holding that the thin/thick relation is analogous to that of the determinable/determinate relation at the level of properties and the specific/abstract relation at the level of descriptions, Tappolet conjoins this with a further claim. She also maintains that as we have an independent theoretical grasp on a theory of warranted attitude expression, we must be able to develop a two-component analysis of thick concepts that is still at the service of cognitivism.

Throughout her paper she distinguishes between a determinate/determinable model of the relation between the thick and the thin and a species/genus model. The hallmark of the species/genus model is that species must always have an independently specifiable differentia, as in 'man is a rational animal' (contrast: 'man is a human animal'), while on the determinable/determinate model this is not the case. Tappolet then argues that thick ethical concepts cannot stand to 'good *pro tanto*' as species to genus because there is no such differentia. We agree. But she goes on to argue that the proper way to view thick ethical concepts is as conjunctions of what she calls an 'affective concept'—defined in terms of reasons for certain feelings, such as ADMIRABLE and DESIRABLE—and some further condition, the non-evaluative grounds in virtue of which one judges whatever it is to be admirable, desirable, and so on. So her putative analyses run as follows:

> BRAVERY = ADMIRABILITY + withstanding danger (or whatever other non-evaluative candidate would be adequate),
>
> KINDNESS = ADMIRABILITY + giving to others, etc.

Thus there's *some* relation between thick concepts and the determinates of *pro tanto* goodness, as Tappolet conceives of them, but not a straightforward one.

Tappolet's account seems internally inconsistent. If there is a reason to reject the species/genus model of the thick concept/*pro tanto* goodness relation, then that very same reason will force rejection of Tappolet's account itself. For what non-evaluative conditions are we to conjoin with admirability to give necessary and sufficient conditions for bravery, generosity and so on?

---

[22] Tappolet (2004).

At this point Tappolet faces a dilemma: if such conditions are statable, they could presumably also be pressed into service as differentiae on the species/genus model, which would leave Tappolet's account unmotivated vis-à-vis its closest competitor. Or she could argue that though there are such conditions, they are not statable by those competent with the concept. That is, following the example of a content-externalist treatment of natural kind terms, it might be argued that descriptive necessary and sufficient conditions for bravery are not part of the meaning of the term or of what it is to grasp the concept. So the fact that one could be competent in the use of the concept BRAVE and not be able to state any such conditions is compatible with the truth of the account. But if Tappolet can draw upon such an argument, so can the defender of the species/genus model. Furthermore, this is no longer an analysis: analyses have to be made up of other concepts. They cannot simply list what falls under the original concept.

At this point we appeal to a more general interpretationism about the mental: our aim is to characterize a thinker's grasp of concepts such as CRUEL, or BRUTAL, or BRAVE. Our methodological principle is that while there is no general interpretationist scruple about recognizing externally individuated contents, there must be some evidence, from within our ordinary grasp of the concepts that make up these contents, that we implicitly defer to a set of conditions beyond the concept user's grasp. (The alternative view simply rewards theft over honest toil.) It must be part of the concept user's self-understanding not simply that the concept *would* tolerate such an expansion, but also that it could be represented as an enrichment of what we took ourselves to be doing all along. Tappolet offers no grounds to substantiate this claim and is, in fact, commendably hesitant to endorse the externalist line:

> One might wonder whether it is plausible to claim that thick concepts and natural kind concepts are similarly out of the ordinary speaker's reach. The suggestion that the necessary descriptive underpinnings of a thick concept might be unknown to ordinary speakers is bound to appear implausible.[23]

She goes on to canvas the suggestion that determining the underlying nature of (say) cruelty is a (contestable) task for the community of concept users, but that suggestion is unconvincing. If the external determination of the set of descriptive necessary and sufficient conditions fails because there are no moral experts, then an appeal to community is not going to be an adequate substitute for that role. Deferring to community is simply a part of non-expert, quotidian, conceptual competence and does no work in substantiating Putnam-style externalism. We are, after all, perfectly good at applying a thick ethical concept without any theory of its underlying 'nature' that seeks to determine its extension. How can it be reasonable to set us the task of extension determination in this way, even if this task is distributed across the linguistic community?

We conclude that the unstatability by competent speakers of descriptive necessary and sufficient conditions for thick terms works—unless we have missed something

---

[23] Tappolet (2004), 215.

important—as much against Tappolet's own view as it does against the species/genus model. We suggest, then, that for the reasons we have given she stick with the separate proposal to understand the thin/thick relation in terms of the relation of determinable to determinate at the level of properties and abstract/specific at the level of concepts and descriptions.

2.4 Elstein and Hurka's sophisticated two-component account

Daniel Elstein and Thomas Hurka have jointly proposed a different kind of two-component approach to thick ethical judgments which differs both from Tappolet's and from the simple two-component views we have referred to so far.[24] They point out that the latter views all take a 'descriptively determinate two-part form', where the non-evaluative ('descriptive') component on its own fully determines the extension of the thick concept.[25] As such, all are indeed vulnerable to a well-known argument of McDowell's. But, they argue, it is a mistake to think that reductive analyses must be committed to 'descriptive determinacy'. As long as the non-evaluative component determines the concept's extension only partially, the analysis can escape the force of McDowell's argument while nonetheless meeting the standards for a reduction.[26]

The argument of McDowell's they have in mind is his 'disentangling' argument.[27] McDowell invites us to consider the things to which it is agreed that some thick ethical term applies, and then asks what all these things have non-evaluatively in common. The answer, he says, is 'nothing': that is what is meant by the claim that the extension of a putative thick ethical concept is non-evaluatively 'shapeless'. But because it is thus shapeless, there is no non-evaluative term mastery of which would have enabled its user to gather all and only the things to which it is agreed the thick term applies, or would enable the user to go on to new cases in the same way as one who has mastered the thick term itself. So, McDowell reasons, competence with a thick term cannot be broken down into competence with a non-evaluative predicate which determines the thick term's extension, plus a non-cognitive extra. (McDowell does not consider 'Moorean' reductionism, but for present purposes that is unimportant.)

In reply, Elstein and Hurka simply agree, but without abandoning reductionism about the thick, on the grounds that reductionists need not assume that the extension of a thick concept must be determined by a non-evaluative component all on its own. Thus on the

---

[24] Elstein and Hurka (2009).   [25] Elstein and Hurka (2009), 517.

[26] In order fairly to represent the Elstein and Hurka view we will engage with it in this form. But we do not think that it is, in fact, true that anyone in the existing debate thought that the two components of a putative analysis were merely conjoined. Blackburn and Allan Gibbard, for example, take the attitudinal component to be attitudes directed to the extension falling under the associated description. That is not a mere *conjunction*. It is true that Blackburn and Elstein and Hurka disagree about whether this extension can be captured in non-evaluative terms. But the difference between them is one of degree, not of kind.

[27] McDowell (1981).

simpler of their two types of analysis—they also advocate a more complex pattern of analysis for some virtue terms, of which more shortly—they propose:

> There can be concepts whose descriptive component defines an area in conceptual space within which admissible good- or right-making properties must be found, so any use of the concept associating it with properties outside that area is a misuse, but does not identity any specific point within the area as uniquely correct... The concept therefore has descriptive content, but this content is not completely determinate.... This pattern is reductive... But it accommodates the key premise of the disentangling argument because determining which properties... are the good-making ones, which we must do to determine the concept's extension, requires evaluative judgment.[28]

Thus 'x is selfish' is to be analysed as:

> Something like 'x is wrong, and there are properties X, Y, and Z (not specified) that acts have in virtue of somehow bringing about the agent's happiness rather than other people's, such that x has X, Y, and Z, and X, Y, and Z make any acts that have them wrong.[29]

'Brings about the agent's happiness rather than other people's' *partly* determines the extension of 'selfish', explaining for example why it would be a mistake to apply the term to distributions of goods between people. Thus a 'strict impartialist' (who thinks self-preference per se is never good) and a believer in 'agent-centred prerogatives' (who thinks it sometimes is) agree that satisfying 'brings about... (etc.)' is a necessary condition for satisfying 'selfish'. But it doesn't determine the extension of 'selfish' all on its own, because the moralists in dispute are plausibly to be pictured not as employing different concepts but as disagreeing over what falls under a given concept.[30] But because the non-evaluative component doesn't on its own determine any extension for 'selfish' itself, and so a fortiori not a 'shapeless' one, the proposed analysis is immune to the 'disentangling' objection. For all that, however, the analysis is reductive because it uses only thin evaluative terms (here, 'wrong') plus non-evaluative ones (here 'brings about the agent's happiness rather than other people's'): any other concepts are represented in the analysis only by means of quantifiers.

Before we raise a problem for Elstein and Hurka's two-part analysis, something needs to be said about the more complex three-part analysis they offer of 'some virtue-concepts'. Here their idea is that thin evaluative concepts figure in the analysis of the relevant virtue-concepts twice over: once as on the two-part analysis (the thin evaluation of some unspecified further properties) and once more, independently, in the specification of those further properties themselves. Thus their analysis of 'x is courageous' is (roughly):

> x is good, and x involves an agent's accepting harm or the risk of harm for himself for the sake of goods greater than the evil of that harm, where this property makes any act that has it good.[31]

[28] Elstein and Hurka (2009), 521.   [29] Elstein and Hurka (2009), 522.
[30] Elstein and Hurka (2009), 521–2.   [31] Elstein and Hurka (2009), 527.

As they say, the second 'good' here is the extra, 'embedded' evaluation. The three-part style of analysis is motivated by the quite proper observation that an act can only count as (say) courageous if it is done in pursuit of a good (or a good enough) end: drinking a pint of vodka in one go in order to show off is dangerous, but not courageous.

Two points about the three-part style of analysis deserve comment. The first is that whereas Elstein and Hurka's two-part analyses studiously avoid specifying *any* property that fully determines the extension of the analysandum (so the analysis of 'selfish' tells us merely that there are *some* (unspecified) wrong-making properties that an act has in virtue of satisfying the non-evaluative necessary but not sufficient condition for selfishness), the three-part analyses *do* specify an extension-determining property for the thick term—that of 'involving an agent's accepting harm or the risk of harm for himself for the sake of goods greater than the evil of that harm'. To be sure, the specification of that property embeds a thin evaluation, so the analysis does not violate the requirement that no extension-determining *non-evaluative* property should feature in it. But granted that, this property *does* determine the extension of 'courageous', whereas the counterpart specification in the two-part analyses merely 'narrows the extension of the target concept'.

One might therefore have expected the evaluation-embedding property in the three-part analysis (that is, 'involving an agent's accepting harm or the risk of harm' etc.) also to do no more than that, leaving the final determination of the target concept's extension to some further set of properties of an act, unspecified in the analysis. But if there is a problem here, we suspect it can be fixed by a more complex formula, so we will not dwell on it.

The second point is that we do not see the three-part style of analysis as supplying any further reasons, beyond those putatively supplied by the two-part style, for the priority of the thin over the thick in ethical judgments. Let us suppose for argument's sake that the embedded thin judgment (about the goodness of the end) is verdictive or all-in. It is thus determined by *all* the evaluative features bearing on judgment, both thick and thin, and thus is no argument for the priority of the thin. Now suppose that the judgment is not verdictive: in fact there's just one thing that makes it the case that the agent is acting courageously, namely that their end (in the relevant circumstances, in the presence of the appropriate emotional dispositions etc.) is honesty. Of course it would be proper to report this by saying that their end is good. But again, there is no evidence here for the priority of the thin: the data are compatible with the claim that 'good' here is an abstraction from the prior (evidential or *pro tanto*) thick judgment of honesty.

Either way, what we have in judgments of courage here is not evidence for the priority of the thin, but one point of entry into an inescapable holism of the thick. It is not clear in any case what marks off the cases that call for a three-part analysis from those where a two-part analysis is appropriate. ('Just', like 'courageous', is a virtue-term and 'lewdness'—another of Elstein and Hurka's examples—is a vice.) So perhaps the three-part treatment applies only to virtues like courage and integrity where there's no particular end or type of end for the sake of which one needs to act in order to display the virtue (all the more reason, we would have thought, for some quantifiers in the three-part analyses). Consequently we focus henceforth on Elstein and Hurka's proposed two-part style of analysis, to which our main objection to their view pertains.

To develop this objection let us return to the trivial kind of 'analysis' that we hinted at earlier, BRUTAL = BAD + BRUTAL or, as it might be, RED = COLOURED + RED. Here is a more complex (but no less trivial) version of it: RED = (is true of surfaces) + COLOURED + (there is some further property of surfaces such that any surface satisfies COLOURED in virtue of having this property). This cumbersome formulation mimics Elstein and Hurka's two-part analyses, because its first clause simply 'narrows the possible extension of the target concept'. However, it differs from our earlier 'analysis' of RED in that it does not specify *which* property needs to be added to COLOURED to yield RED: it just says there is one. But it will be obvious that the only property that can be a value of the property-variable in our new quantified 'analysis' is, in fact, RED itself. The example thus drama-tizes the fact that a would-be analysis is not improved just by quantifying in to the good- (or bad-) making property contexts if the only possible values of the good-mak-ing property variables are values that yield a merely trivial 'analysis'.

Now according to us, thin concepts are abstractions from (stand as determinables to) thick evaluations. So, according to us, the only value of the good-making property variable in Elstein and Hurka's bipartite analysis that will make the analysans true is the thick evaluative property which is in fact the analysandum—as it might be, 'distribu-tively just'. So cannot we just accept Elstein and Hurka's two-part style of analysis, on the grounds that its availability does not vindicate their reductionism over our anti-reductionism, as it is compatible with the only analysis available being the trivial one we have given?

That would in fact be hasty, for of course the unspecified good-making properties Elstein and Hurka have in mind are not just any old properties, but non-evaluative ones, while the good-making property which we acknowledge as satisfying the analysis is a thick evaluation itself. So the question is why we should accept that (once the range of application has been narrowed down) there is a further set of *non-evaluative* properties such that (whatever the example) *x* is wrong in virtue of having them, and anything that has them is thereby made wrong?

It might look as if our disagreement with Elstein and Hurka here concerns universal-izability, and of course it is controversial whether if some properties make an item dis-tributively just on one occasion, they make anything else that has them distributively just (for example, the property 'having an equal number of sweets'). However, Elstein and Hurka don't argue for universalizability: they merely say, reasonably enough, that since the disentangling argument has been claimed to rule out reductionism even on the assumption of universalizability, if they can show, on the same assumption, that the argument fails to do this, that is a worthwhile result, nothwithstanding the fact that some anti-reductionists reject the assumption.[32] So if our objection to their two-part

---

[32] Elstein and Hurka (2009), 520–1.

style of analysis depended only on rejecting universalizability, that would limit its scope and thereby its interest.

Now as it happens we do not think that if something makes an item (let us say) distributively just, it must make everything that possesses it distributively just. But that is not where the dispute between ourselves and Elstein and Hurka lies. Universalizability says that if something (as it might be within a given range) is made good by its being F, then anything else within that range that is F is also thereby made good. But it doesn't say that anything within that range that is good is made good *by being F*. That is, universalizability is a constraint on what counts as a good-making property on an occasion: if that property would not make everything else that has it good, then it is not good-making here and now. But it does not commit one to the claim that the extension of a thick evaluative term has non-evaluative 'shape'.

The focal point of our dispute with Elstein and Hurka is, rather, their claim that full 'descriptive determinacy' of a thick term is 'provided by evaluation', given that what they mean by 'evaluation' seems to be the mapping of some small set of non-evaluative properties onto goodness. The novel feature of their analysis is that it eliminates extension-determining non-evaluative terms in favour of quantifiers, so nothing non-evaluative that is specified in the analysis is itself extension-determining for the thick term in question.

But now consider what Elstein and Hurka's quarrelling egalitarian and desert-theorist each thinks. What each thinks is that x is distributively just (on any occasion) *if and only if* it falls within some non-evaluatively specified range and it is F, G, and H (for some non-evaluative F, G, and H). Now one can characterize the difference between them this way: they disagree over *which* property at least one of F, G, and H actually is. The striking thing here is not the commitment to universalizability (expressed by the 'on any occasion'), but rather the idea (expressed by 'if and only if') that any particular user of a thick evaluative term must take it that there *is* a fully determinate non-evaluative specification of the extension of the term, even though different users of the term may differ over what the non-evaluative specification is. Quantification into the relevant non-evaluative property contexts lifts the mention of any particular such properties out of the analysis, so mastery of the non-evaluative concepts that (according to each disagreeing theorist) unify the term's extension are not criterial for mastery of the thick term itself, thus allowing the egalitarian and the desert-theorist to agree in the concept they use.

But now: it seems only a slight improvement on the 'descriptive determinacy' view criticized by McDowell to say that someone who possesses the concept 'distributively just', or 'selfish', or whatever it might be, must be able to state in non-evaluative terms what (in his opinion) unifies its extension—even if doing that does not amount to saying what the word means. If the disentangling argument is right, there will not be anything non-evaluative that unifies it (the extension will be, as Elstein and Hurka seem to agree, 'shapeless'). So any opinions that users of a thick term may have about what non-evaluatively unifies its extension will be false. So—and to say this is simply to play a variation on the point we made by means of our complex but trivial 'analysis' of RED—

there will be no substitutions for X, Y, and Z in the two-part analysis which make the analysans come out true.

What if we drop the requirement that users of the term can state (or rather think they can state) what unifies the extension, and understand only that x is good, x falls within some non-evaluatively specified range, and there *are* some further non-evaluative properties that make x distributively just (etc.), though they cannot say what they are? There are two ways to understand this weakened requirement, neither of which helps this proposal.

First, if the extension of the thick term is non-evaluatively shapeless, there will not be any tidy set of non-evaluative properties (known or unknown) that unify its extension, at least if the disentangling argument is valid. If on the other hand all that is meant is that the members of the extension of 'distributively just' *have* some non-evaluative properties, then we can hardly disagree: there must after all be something in virtue of which an item picks up a thick evaluation. But could that understanding explain competence with the thick concept to be analysed? Of course not. (Compare our objection to the 'externalist' amendment to Tappolet's theory.) Indeed accepting this weakened formulation is consistent with maintaining that it is the evaluative interest that guides application of 'distributively just' from case to case, and that the concept itself is unanalysable. The fact that no extension-determining non-evaluative properties are actually mentioned in Elstein and Hurka's sophisticated two-part proposal does not, in the end, advance the cause of reductionism very far. Their putative refutation of the 'shapelessness' argument rests, fundamentally, on an assumption that grasp of a thick concept involves the belief that the extension of a thick term is, in fact, shaped by a determinate set of non-evaluative properties. Why would a non-reductionist accept *that*?

Some independent argument is needed to the effect that the unanalysability of thick concepts is problematic in its own terms. It would, indeed, be unfortunate if the thesis of unanalysability was constrained to a mute conservatism of the local folkways, but we do not think that it is. Is our thesis of unanalysability all that can be said about thick concepts? Can we say nothing about how such concepts are learned, how they can be essentially contested, or must we simply say 'this is how we go on' with such terms? This raises a whole host of issues that, for reasons of space, we cannot go into here. However, we do believe that given the connection between meaning and explanations of meaning, there is a great deal to be said about the use of thick concepts that does not constitute an analysis of them. Any competent use of a concept grasps various truisms about that concept, derived from rules of thumb used to teach the concepts, or specifications of its Aristotelian 'field of application'.[33] Allan Gibbard points out that a great deal of language-learning involves a lot of catching on in the absence of explicit 'definitions'.[34] But none of this folk wisdom constitutes an *analysis* of a thick concept and our practices with such concepts proceed without such analyses.

---

[33] For the latter, see Dancy (1995).   [34] Gibbard (1992), 271.

We also deny that Elstein and Hurka's analysis is needed in order to make sense of moral disagreement. We would naturally explain it using the distinction between concept and conception, introduced by H. L. A. Hart and made famous by John Rawls in the course of his own discussion of exactly the same example, differing conceptions of the concept of justice.[35] In drawing the concept versus conception distinction one must be careful, as Maite Ezcurdia notes, to distinguish 'having a conception *of a concept* from having a conception *associated with* the concept which one takes to be *analytic to* or *constitutive of* that concept'.[36] Conceptions are further beliefs about the proper domain of application of a concept that serve to vindicate the public character of meaning and the normativity of concept use. The fact that two people can disagree about justice while sharing the same concept is easily explained by appeal to the concept/conception distinction and we can appeal to that distinction even in the case of unanalysable concepts.

Elstein and Hurka's paper appeals to a further putative advantage that their view possesses over other views, namely, that it allows one to diagnose a kind of protracted disagreement that they take ethical disagreements to exemplify. Our response is that W. B. Gallie has identified certain kinds of concept as essentially contested in the sense that disagreements over evaluative concepts can be peculiarly intractable because they are evaluative 'all the way down'.[37] Once again, our view that the thin stands in no privileged relationship to the verdictive plays a role here. The grounds of concept application can, on our view, be characterized using either thick or thin ethical concepts. There is nothing in our use of ethical concepts to sustain the rationalist hope that greater abstraction correlates with greater suasive power, and with a special role for thin vocabulary. (Yet it is those assumptions that shape Elstein and Hurka's discussion.) We do not believe that it is always possible to identify a locus of disagreement in non-evaluative terms. But the main point is that you can believe that thick concepts are unanalysable but still explain reasonable disagreement between competent users of the concept by appealing to the concept versus conception distinction.

Our disagreement with Elstein and Hurka is a radical one: we claim that a set of concepts is in principle unanalysable while they claim actually to have provided the correct analysis. Are we embarrassed by the fact that an analysis of thick concepts *seems* available to such competent users of ethical concepts as Elstein and Hurka? Does any plausibility accrue to their view simply because their own linguistic intuitions suggest to them the correctness of their analysis? No, because the situation is directly analogous to other areas of philosophy, notably epistemology. Those who deny that knowledge can be analysed are very well aware of the large number of putative analyses of knowledge that epistemologists have been putting forward over a considerable period of time.

Nor do we believe that we have to enter into the game of putative-analysis-meets-counter-example. We have explained why the data cited by Elstein and Hurka is fully explained by our own view. Once again, we would draw a direct analogy with the putative

---

[35] Hart (1961/1994), 155–9; Rawls (1971), 5; Ezcurdia (1998).
[36] Ezcurdia (1998), 187.   [37] Gallie (1955–6).

definition of knowledge as justified true belief plus contested further factor x (where each reductively minded epistemologist solves this equation for x in his or her own proprietary way). Proponents of unanalysability are under no obligation to enter the over-familiar dialectic where putative analysis meets putative counter-example, resulting in an ad hoc clause added to the analysis, which meets with a further counter-example—and so on. Our aim throughout this paper has been well-captured by P. F. Strawson when he contrasted conceptual analysis with conceptual elucidation. The latter seeks the identification of 'general, pervasive, and ultimately irreducible' components in 'a structure which constitutes the framework of our ordinary thought and talk and which is presupposed by (our theories)'.[38] Ethical judgments that use thick ethical concepts seem to us to be an irreducible component of ordinary thought and talk of precisely this kind.

2.5 Thick concepts and presupposition

One further objection to our non-reductionist cognitivism about thick concepts, due to Pekka Väyrynen, deserves consideration.[39] Suppose two speakers take different evaluative attitudes to items to which they agree in applying a given thick term. If the difference in attitude induces a difference in what the speakers express, there is a mere illusion of communication. Väyrynen argues that anyone who agrees, as Blackburn has persuasively argued, that in reality there is communication and indeed disagreement here, must also concede that 'thick terms (do not) have evaluative content as part of their conventional meaning', that is, that thick terms do not express thick concepts in our sense.[40]

Let us call the agreed fact that 'the evaluative contents associated with them [thick expressions] enjoy a certain autonomy with respect to the attitudes and intentions of particular thinkers' the *slack* between attitudes and evaluative contents.[41] The most oft-cited example of slack in this sense is Oscar Wilde: if the evaluative content of 'blasphemous' had depended solely on Wilde's own attitudes, he need not have worried that by using that word he would have expressed condemnation of the thing, so he would not have needed to say that 'blasphemous' was 'not a word' of his. There's also another kind of case, which is very common, where—unlike Wilde—we use an expression in line with the usage of someone fully signed up to the evaluations associated with it, but while our own attitudes are still work in progress.

---

[38] Strawson (1998), 24.   [39] Väyrynen (2009).

[40] Väyrynen (2009), 442; Blackburn (1992). There is of course a larger issue not far off here: if we are to argue that difference in attitude does not induce difference in concept expressed, we also need to show—on pain of conceding externalism in the theory of motivation—how a deployment of the concept in question can on its own bear the right sort of connection with action, given that—by hypothesis—sometimes it does not. This is the large issue that we said in the introduction that we would put off till another occasion. Väyrynen's attack on non-reductionist cognitivism about the thick is independent, however, of any issues in the theory of motivation: independent, that is, of any further debts we stand to incur in defending that view.

[41] Väyrynen (2009), 441.

Väyrynen seems to be interested in cases of a third kind, where speakers have an expertise in the use of an expression comparable to that of someone fully signed up to the associated evaluations, but reject those valuations wholesale. Väyrynen describes these as cases where the speaker finds the concept 'objectionable'. We say that Väyrynen's 'objectors' must have an expertise comparable to that of someone fully signed up to the associated evaluations because he stresses that 'non-evaluative constraints' on the application of a thick expression are accepted both by the objectors and by those who are fully signed up to the associated evaluations (the 'non-objectors').[42]

In Väyrynen's example the concept under dispute is CHASTE. Now in some sense or other, Väyrynen has to be right about non-evaluative constraints: no one could count as understanding the term 'chaste' unless they understood that chastity has got something to do with sex, for example. But in Väyrynen's view, the constraints are much more specific than this. Although he does not claim that the relevant non-evaluative predicate 'is anything like extensionally equivalent to "chaste" or sufficient for it to apply, or even that it captures the full non-evaluative meaning of "chaste"',[43] he does claim that all will agree that 'if . . . conduct is to count as satisfying "chaste", it must have some properties which signal some kind of dedication to not being sexually provocative'.[44] So it seems as if these properties will be possessed—and agreed to be so by objectors and non-objectors alike—by everything in the extension of 'chaste'. To see how this is relevant to the level of linguistic expertise Väyrynen expects of his objectors, consider the fact that devotees of the concept CHASTE usually—as we understand it—acknowledge the possibility of chaste behaviour in marriage (and we do not mean *mariages blancs*). Now we are not quite sure what 'dedication to not being sexually provocative' actually means (nor whether 'provocative' is really non-evaluative). But let us say it means making an effort not to arouse another sexually. Assuming married persons may attempt to arouse one another sexually without offending against chastity, the case of chastity in marriage seems like a counterexample to Väyrynen's non-evaluative constraint. But to figure out whether it is a counterexample or not, one has to be rather expert—more expert than we are—at applying the term 'chaste'. And if the non-evaluative condition must be agreed to apply by non-objectors and objectors to 'chaste' alike, the objectors must have the same considerable level of expertise with the term as the non-objectors.

This combination—wholesale rejection of the concept plus unimpeachable expertise in how to apply it—must surely be something of a rarity. Wilde, after all, rejected any evaluations the word 'blasphemous' might be used to express, but refused even to use the word. If one really thinks there is nothing worthwhile to be said by means of a given thick expression, why retain the same interest in the niceties of its usage as would be shown by someone fully signed up to the associated evaluations? Indeed many speakers who are far from any such wholesale rejection—for instance, because they think the concept is an attractive one but they want to find out more—cannot match the expertise in use of those speakers who are fully signed up to it. This is not to say that we think the combination is impossible: it might be found in someone, for example, who was fully identified with the evaluations associated with a concept and had for some reason become suddenly and totally disillusioned. And even if it were impossible, that fact wouldn't magic away all the difficulties of occupying our position, since some of those stem from the phenomenon of slack generally, not from Väyrynen's very specific variant of it. However, the difficulties Väyrynen himself raises do arise from the specific variant, and not from the general phenomenon. We confine ourselves to noting this point for now; it will be important later on.

We turn next, however, to Väyrynen's main argument for the claim that the evaluative contents associated with a given thick expression are not part of the concept it expresses. His argument depends on the behaviour of 'objectionable' thick concepts—that is, thick expressions where the speaker retains full competence with the expression but objects wholesale to the attitude it expresses—in denials. The focus of Väyrynen's discussion is the sentence:

(5)   Abstinence from extramarital sex is chaste.

He claims that a wholesale objector to the concept CHASTE will disagree with (5), but will not 'typically . . . be willing to express their disagreement with (5)' by uttering

(6)   Abstinence from extramarital sex is not chaste.[45]

On the contrary, someone who asserts (6) will typically be a non-objector, who in addition thinks that abstinence from extramarital sex is not (for example) enough for chastity.[46] Again, argues Väyrynen, 'if we regard "chaste" as an objectionable concept, our objection to (5) isn't (merely) that it's false', for 'if (5) were false, then (6)', which Väyrynen says is the truth-conditional negation of (5), 'should be non-problematically true', though perhaps pragmatically odd without further explanation.[47] But only someone who *doesn't* think 'chaste' is objectionable could regard a sentence containing it as expressing something non-problematically true.

Now there's a danger of misunderstanding Väyrynen at this point. If objectors to the concept CHASTE really are unwilling to register their objection by uttering (6), then there should be no account to give of what they mean when they utter it. But that is exactly the thing Väyrynen seeks to give an account of. In fact, however, it is not that objectors do not utter (6): it's rather that they don't utter (6) on its own, but accompanied by an appropriate follow-up. The difference between objectors and non-objectors to 'chaste' is that the former must 'hesitate to express disagreement with (5) by uttering an expansion of (6) that uses negation truth-conditionally'.[48] Why? Because truth-conditional negation 'takes scope over the assertion that sentence S would have made if uttered, but not over other types of information its utterance would have conveyed [sc. non-semantically]'.[49] So 'assertions of "*a* is chaste" and of "*a* is unchaste" both convey the evaluative content

[45] Väyrynen (2009), 444.   [46] Väyrynen (2009), 448.   [47] Väyrynen (2009), 448.
[48] Väyrynen (2009), 448.   [49] Väyrynen (2009), 448.

which is associated with "chaste"'[50] and which is exactly what objectors want not to convey. Hence, on the lips of an objector, the negation in (6) and expansions of it need to be interpreted not as 'ordinary truth-conditional' negation but metalinguistically. As an analogy, compare negation directed towards someone's pronunciation: 'He didn't call the *po*lice, he called the po*lice*'.[51]

In reply, let us first of all explore the idea that objectors to CHASTE should after all be willing to express their objection by uttering (6), with negation understood truth-conditionally—that is, the idea that objectors regard (5) as straightforwardly false. Many virtue and vice terms have naturally associated contrasting terms that are not their contradictories, like 'just' and 'unjust' or 'brave' and 'cowardly'; the same goes for 'chaste' and 'unchaste'. As a result, (5) has two ways of being false: either because abstinence from extramarital sex is unchaste, or because—presumably like having books overdue at the library—it is neither chaste nor unchaste. Now if the non-objector—at least, the non-objector with the sort of fanatical first-order views Väyrynen has in mind—utters (6), it seems plausible that he would also be prepared to utter:

(5*)   Abstinence from extramarital sex is unchaste.

Certainly the objector would have no truck with that. But mightn't the objector nonetheless be willing to assert (6), because he thinks that sexual abstinence is neither chaste nor unchaste? Suppose he thinks that sexual conduct is a free-for-all, or at least, a free-for-all as long as other requirements are met (for example, absence of harm, or consent—in any case, no requirement it takes a distinctive concept of chastity to articulate). With an attitude like that, the objector would certainly satisfy the requirement, which Väyrynen rightly insists on, that there be genuine disagreement between the objector and the non-objector. What is more, the attitude would explain the objector's holding that no sexual conduct falls into the class either of the chaste or the unchaste: as far as chastity goes, all sexual conduct is like having books overdue at the library. This possibility opens the question whether objectionable thick concepts are to be thought of as empty, which we will consider in a moment.

But barring worries from that quarter, if the objector does assert (6) with that sort of attitude in mind, then there seems to be no difference in meaning between the kind of negation involved in his utterance of it, and the kind of negation involved in the non-objector's utterance of the same sentence. If the test for the detachability of attitude from what's semantically carried by thick expressions is that, in denials involving objectionable thick concepts, negation has to be interpreted as metalinguistic—because denial 'is directed specifically at the associated evaluative content'—on the present proposal denials involving objectionable thick concepts fail the test.[52]

We now need to confront the question that we have deferred up to now, namely whether objectionable thick concepts are empty, and this brings us also to the question whether the simple solution we have proposed so far to Väyrynen's challenge—namely,

---

[50] Väyrynen (2009), 448.   [51] Väyrynen (2009), 449.   [52] Väyrynen (2009), 446.

that the objector (of the niche variety Väyrynen has in mind) is disposed to utter the truth-conditional negation of (5) because he thinks precisely that nothing is either chaste or unchaste—is really a solution we can endorse ourselves, or just a dialectical move against Väyrynen.

First, we need to clarify some issues of terminology. Väyrynen says, 'what is wrong with wielding such concepts as CHASTE or LUSTFUL isn't merely the sort of fault that is involved in wielding such empty concepts as *phlogiston* or *Bigfoot*'.[53] He does not say what that sort of fault is, but he is right that these are not helpful analogies. At least the second of the latter two expressions is a putative singular term, whereas 'chaste' is ostensibly a first-level predicate, and emptiness for predicates cannot mean the non-existence of the object to which they purportedly refer, because they do not purport to refer to an object. So what does it mean? 'Empty' can—with some artificiality—be used in two ways. An empty term can be one that has nothing in its extension and, thereby, everything in its anti-extension, for example 'unicorn'. Terms that are empty in this sense nonetheless succeed in dividing (as it were) the universal domain in two, just as 'tiger' does. But a term can be empty in a second sense, that of failing to determine an extension (or therefore an anti-extension). Race terms may be of this kind—'Caucasian', 'black', or whatever the list is supposed to include: despite seeming to speakers for a good long time as if each such term determines a principle for dividing the universal domain, it may turn out that none does (because the terms' use is in some way incoherent).

Now in what sense, if any, should non-reductionist cognitivists say objectionable thick concepts are empty? The view we have been canvassing so far is that 'chaste'—if indeed it is objectionable—is empty in the first sense: since nothing is either chaste or unchaste, a fortiori nothing is chaste. So the concept CHASTE has nothing in its extension and everything in its anti-extension (since the not chaste includes the unchaste). This line certainly offers some straightforward solutions—(5) is supplied with a truth-value, for example (the value false). But there is something inappropriate about a wholesale objector to the concept CHASTE saying *in propria voce* that nothing is either chaste or unchaste. For we take it that what concerns wholesale objectors to the concept is the very idea that these terms serve to classify, not that they classify all right but place things on the wrong side of a boundary. People who deny that there are unicorns do not reject the *concept* UNICORN: on the contrary, they need it to articulate the thing they hold true (that there are not any things of that kind). Similarly, it is compatible with the free-for-all first-order sexual attitude we envisaged to think that CHASTE is a perfectly good concept—we can see exactly where it divides the chaste, the unchaste, and the neither-chaste-nor-unchaste. But whereas most people who deploy it are (according to the free-for-all view) prudes or 'repressed' or the like, the free-for-all user of it makes all sexual behaviour come out in the category of the neither-chaste-nor-unchaste. Our original objector seems not after all to be an objector to the *concept* CHASTE, but a non-objector with (compared to other non-objectors) non-standard sexual attitudes.

---

[53] Väyrynen (2009), 452.

If that really is the kind of objector Väyrynen had in mind, of course, then there is nothing wrong with the foregoing as a reply to him. However, it must be at least possible for there to be an objector of a more radical kind, who needs to be characterized as someone who holds that CHASTE is empty in the second sense. Väyrynen sees problems here for our view. If the concept is empty, he says, we must say (5) is neither true nor false. But 'lack of truth-value is most typically attributed to expressions with false presuppositions', and that diagnosis sits ill with our contention that the evaluative content associated with a thick expression is a *semantic* aspect of what is expressed by utterances of it.[54]

However, the link between lack of truth-value and presupposition-failure is weaker than Väyrynen thinks. Certainly in the cases of the singular terms he mentions ('Bigfoot' etc.), it is arguable that utterances involving the expression, far from being apt to express a thought but failing to do so because of a presupposition failure (as on some non-Russellian treatments of 'the King of France is bald'), aren't even apt to express a thought—which one would it be? When speakers attempt to formulate thoughts involving these terms, there is at best an illusion of a thought entertained. The race example suggests a parallel account might be made out for predicate expressions—and also reasons why we might be chronically unable to ascertain whether or not we are succeeding in expressing senses by means of these terms. That gives us an account of lack of truth-value without appealing to presupposition.

Moreover this explanation seems accurately to locate not only what the wholesale objector thinks—that 'chaste' does not express a concept—but also what less than wholesale objectors think, namely: here is a term, I can use it as well as anyone else, but am I really classifying anything? It also commits us to an account of what objectors—if their objection is indeed well founded—are doing with the objectionable terms. It is not that they are classifying in a way that is at variance with mainstream evaluations. All they are doing is applying the term as it is conventionally applied, but not in so doing grasping a sense and withholding an evaluation, because there isn't a sense to grasp. (That, by the way, is a very good reason why we might expect most wholesale objectors to be like Wilde rather than like Väyrynen's character: they refuse to use the word, because they believe there are no thoughts it is apt to express.)

This, ironically enough, chimes with an important aspect of Väyrynen's account. For if no sense is expressed by 'chaste' (or 'Caucasian'), and we believe this, then the correct account of what we say in order to register our objection to the concept, that is (6), cannot be that we are straightforwardly asserting the negation of the thought that a non-objector took himself to be asserting by uttering (5). That is because if there is no such thought, there is no such thing as its negation. It looks as if the correct account of (6) must after all be metalinguistic (compare 'that thing in the sky is not Vulcan'). Our difference from Väyrynen is just that we see no tension between the claim that negation is

<hr />

[54] Väyrynen (2009), 452.

metalinguistic and the claim that evaluative content, when there is such, is conveyed semantically, not pragmatically. Whether the objector is to be thought of as holding that everything is neither chaste nor unchaste (so that (5) is straightforwardly false and (6) true), or as holding that sentences featuring the term 'chaste' fail to express a sense (so (5) lacks a truth-value and (6)—if, unWildeanly, they utter it at all—is to be construed as metalinguistic negation), we do not see that Väyrynen has presented compelling reasons against the claim that the evaluative content of utterances involving a thick expression is due to a semantic feature of the expression; that is, that thick terms express thick concepts as we understand them.

2.6 Conclusion

In this paper we have argued that two- (or multi-) component reductive analyses of thick concepts are not required by the surface data, because there is another explanation of the data that suffices to explain it, namely, our own explanation. Reductionists need some independent motivation for their position and all the candidate reductionist proposals currently available are internally incoherent in one way or another. We have tried to go a little deeper into the motivations for reductionisms in this area. They are motivated, at least in part, by the thought that some such view has to be correct simply because of the difficulties facing the non-reductionist alternative. That is why we have related our own non-reductionist account to some of the standard objections to show that it can meet them.

References

Blackburn, Simon (1992) 'Morality and Thick Concepts: Through Thick and Thin', *Proceedings of the Aristotelian Society, Supplementary Volume* 66: 285–99.

Bridgman, Percy W. (1927) *The Logic of Modern Physics* (London: Macmillan).

Chihara, Charles and Jerry Fodor (1965) 'Operationalism and Ordinary Language', *American Philosophical Quarterly* 2: 281–95.

Dancy, Jonathan (1995) 'In Defense of Thick Concepts', in Peter A. French, Theodore E. Uehling, and Howard K. Wettstein (eds.) *Midwest Studies in Philosophy* XX: 263–79.

—— (2004) *Ethics Without Principles* (Oxford: Oxford University Press).

Elstein, Daniel and Thomas Hurka (2009) 'From Thin to Thick: Two Moral Reductionist Plans', *Canadian Journal of Philosophy* 39: 515–35.

Ezcurdia, Maite (1998) 'The Concept-Conception Distinction', *Philosophical Issues* 9: 187–92.

Foot, Philippa (2002) *Virtues and Vices*, 2nd edn. (Oxford: Oxford University Press).

Funkhouser, Eric (2006) 'The Determinable-Determinate Relation', *Noûs* 40: 548–69.

Gallie, W. B. (1955–6) 'Essentially Contested Concepts', *Proceedings of the Aristotelian Society* 56: 167–98.

Gibbard, Allan (1992) 'Morality and Thick Concepts: Thick Concepts and Warrant for Feelings', *Proceedings of the Aristotelian Society, Supplementary Volume* 66: 267–83.

Hart, H. L. A. (1961/1994) *The Concept of Law* (Oxford: Clarendon Press).

Jackson, Frank (2002), 'Critical Notice of *Knowledge and its Limits* by Timothy Wiliamson', *Australasian Journal of Philosophy* 80: 516–21.

Johnson, W. E. (1921) *Logic*, i (Cambridge: Cambridge University Press).

McDowell, John (1981) 'Non-Cognitivism and Rule-Following', in Stephen Holtzman and Christopher Leich (eds.) *Wittgenstein: To Follow a Rule* (London: Routledge and Kegan Paul), 141–62.

Moore, A. W. (2006) 'Maxims and Thick Ethical Concepts', *Ratio* 19: 129–47.

Payne, Andrew (2006) 'A New Account of Thick Concepts', *The Journal of Value Inquiry* 39: 89–103.

Prior, Arthur (1949) 'I. Determinables, Determinates and Determinants', *Mind* 57: 1–20.

Rawls, John (1971) *A Theory of Justice* (Cambridge, MA: Harvard University Press).

Scheffler, Samuel (1987) 'Morality Through Thick and Thin: A Critical Notice of *Ethics and the Limits of Philosophy*', *The Philosophical Review* 96: 411–34.

Stratton-Lake, Philip (2000) *Kant, Duty and Moral Worth* (London: Routledge).

Strawson P. F. (1998) *Analysis and Metaphysics* (Oxford: Oxford University Press).

Tappolet, Christine (2004) 'Through Thick and Thin: *Good* and its Determinates', *dialectica* 58: 207–21.

Thomas, Alan (2006) *Value and Context: the Nature of Moral and Political Knowledge* (Oxford: Clarendon Press).

Thomson, Judith Jarvis (1996) 'Moral Objectivity' in Gilbert Harman and Judith Jarvis Thomson, *Moral Relativism and Moral Objectivity* (Oxford: Blackwell), 65–154.

Väyrynen, Pekka (2009) 'Objectionable Thick Concepts in Denials', *Philosophical Perspectives* 23: 439–69.

Wiggins, David (2006) *Ethics: Twelve Lectures on the Philosophy of Morality* (London: Penguin Books).

Williams, Bernard (1985) *Ethics and the Limits of Philosophy* (London: Fontana).

Williamson, Timothy (2000) *Knowledge and Its Limits* (Oxford: Oxford University Press).

Wittgenstein, Ludwig (1977) *Remarks on Colour*, ed. G. E. M. Anscombe (Oxford: Blackwell).

3

Practical Concepts

Jonathan Dancy

Introduction

In this paper I revisit themes that I first treated in my 'In Defence of Thick Concepts' (1995). That paper grew out of the comments I had prepared to give as Chairman at the 1992 Joint Session Symposium on thick concepts, where the speakers were Allan Gibbard and Simon Blackburn. Those comments were suppressed on the occasion, for lack of time. But I had been impressed by some of the things Blackburn said about the thick, and thought that they required, not total abandonment of, but still significant adjustment to the standard conception of thick concepts.

The standard conception held that thick concepts somehow combine description and evaluation. The evaluative element would be either pro or con; some thick concepts are pro-concepts and the others are con-concepts. This picture seemed to me to be undermined by the example introduced by Gibbard, that of the lewd. The concept of lewdness looks like a perfectly standard thick concept, if there are any such, but it fails to fit the standard conception in two ways. First, some actions are the better for being lewd, though many lewd actions are the worse for it. So lewdness has a variable rather than a constant practical relevance. Further, when one calls something lewd one may be expressing a complex of attitudes rather than just one of the two super-attitudes of approval and disapproval. Another way of putting this point is that our response to the lewd is mixed, at least on occasions. There is a certain amount of lewdness on display at Mardi Gras, and my response to this is certainly neither simple approval, nor simple disapproval. In fact the choice between approval and disapproval, pro and con, doesn't seem to be exactly the point. I'll return to this later.

To sum up: the standard conception understood thick concepts as used to express just one attitude, and to express the same attitude on each occasion. They are all single attitude concepts, and they are invariable in the attitude they express. (Sometimes, as here, I speak of the concept as expressing an attitude, but of course no concept is capable of such a thing; it is the speaker, or the use, that really does the expressing.) My suggestion was that we abandon both of these elements of our conception of the thick. In their place, we should allow that thick concepts are, or at least can be, both multi-attitude concepts (expressing a mix of attitudes at once, most of which will be neither pro nor con—think of the embarrassment associated with even acceptable instances of lewdness) and variable in their practical relevance. Sometimes, as I said, an act can be the better for being lewd, for lewdness is occasionally exactly what is called for; isn't that exactly what carnivals are about (among other things, of course)? A display doesn't cease to be lewd for being acceptable and appropriate in its context.[1]

It is an interesting question, which I will address briefly here, whether all those thick concepts that are variable in this sort of way do enjoy nonetheless a sort of default valence. Lewdness, we might say, is generally not desirable, and when it is desirable, this is always because the circumstances are unusual in one way or another. Very many thick concepts are like this. Think of the courageous, the honest, the amusing, the light-hearted—and so on. I might be able to find a sort of case in which something, or some-one, is the worse for being amusing, but this will only be because something in the situation interferes to prevent things from being the way one would expect.[2] I don't have any trouble with this suggestion. Technically it allows the variability I want, and that is enough for me. But it would be good to find at least some examples of thick con-cepts that don't have a default valence in this sort of way. David Sosa suggested to me the provocative; another such would perhaps be the seductive.

There was a second theme in that early paper of mine. The interesting thing about thick concepts is not really whether they are single-attitude or multi-attitude concepts, variable or invariable in their practical relevance. It is the fact that they somehow hold together elements, or aspects, or evaluation and description. When I say that an action was lewd I am telling you quite a lot about what sort of action it was, even if by doing so I also express a certain mix of attitudes. (Note the way that attitude and evaluation are being run together here.) Now some people, known as the disentanglers, think that these two aspects can be disentangled from each other; though co-present here, one at least of them could be instantiated separately. I say 'one at least' because it is, or ought to be, common ground between entanglers and disentanglers that the evaluation is not capable of separate instantiation, since the evaluation at issue is linked to the description. A regrettably lewd action is not of such and such a sort, and bad; it is bad *for being of that sort*. All should accept that the evaluation is linked to the description in this way; we are not dealing here with a mere conjunction. The interesting question is whether the 'descriptive' element is capable of separate instantiation. To this question, the disentan-glers answer yes, the entanglers no. The disentanglers offer a reductive picture: use of a thick concept informs us that the relevant act (or whatever) has certain specifiable, and specified, features, and is the better or the worse for being so. This is a mere conjunction.

---

[1] I am told that North Americans are more likely to think of the bawdy than of the lewd as functioning in this variable way.

[2] I am intending these remarks to be reminiscent of the discussion of default reasons, especially the work of Lance and Little (2004) and (2007).

If we take things in this way, it is evident that the first bit of information can stand alone even though the second cannot; the action had those features, and this can be said, or thought, without any associated evaluation, any expression of attitude, at all.

So now the question arises for the entanglers: how can it be that the supposed descriptive 'element' is incapable of standing alone? Is it that there is not enough description here to make the content of a separable assertion? Hardly: any amount of description, no matter how slight, seems to be enough to make a content. But if not that, then what? The answer to this question is that just as the evaluation is linked to, penetrated by, the description, so the description is linked to, penetrated by, the evaluation. There is 'interpenetration'. But this is just a name for the thing we are trying to capture. Use of a thick concept characterizes the object in some way, describes it, ascribes some property or properties to it, and then evaluates it, expresses some attitude or response towards it. The interpenetration of description and evaluation is an interpenetration of property ascribed and attitude expressed. And that sort of interpenetration can be characterized in a way that is owed to David Wiggins: the property is to be understood as that of being such as to merit the response, and the response is to the object as meriting that response. Taken in this way, the response can only be understood in terms of the property to which it is a response, and the property is to be understood as the property of meriting that response. This overall picture was later called[3] the 'no-priority' view, because it maintained that neither property nor attitude enjoyed any sort of priority over the other. We cannot construct the property out of the attitude, nor construct the attitude out of the property, because as soon as we have one of the pair we already have the other.

Another way of making what is effectively the same point is to say that use of a thick concept does not express an evaluation of the relevant object for having certain specific features. The object is evaluated not just for having those features but for having them in the right sort of way. What is that way? It has those features in such a way as to make the evaluation appropriate.

The no-priority view, as I have expressed it so far, is merely formal. We have been shown a possible arrangement where the interpenetration is there for all to see, but we have not been shown how it works in any particular instance. No matter: our task at the moment was merely to make some sense of the entanglers' claim that neither description or evaluation was capable of standing alone, and I was persuaded that the no-priority view did achieve that end. One difficulty that immediately arises for it will be how to distinguish between different thick concepts. These are going to differ on the descriptive side, and it may be hard to see how to characterize descriptive differences without returning to a list of features that will, once more, be capable of standing alone. The answer that I gave to this difficulty was to appeal to an Aristotelian conception of a domain. A courageous act is one that is to be commended in the domain of response to

---

[3] McDowell (1987).

fear and danger. This specification of a domain seemed to me distinct from a list of features for which the action is to be commended. The act is not commendable for being in that domain, but for other features not specified.

There is a further attractive aspect to the no-priority view. Although property and response cannot be understood independently of each other, still there is an asymmetry of explanation involved. As Wiggins points out, the property both explains and justifies the response; he might have added that the response does neither of these things to the property. John McDowell later gives the example of fearfulness.[4] We can explain fear by showing that the feared object was indeed fearful, to be feared; that is, the fear is explained by being merited, appropriate, justified.

3.1

In this section I bring out some assumptions that have pervaded, or underpinned, recent discussion of the distinction between thick and thin concepts. I am not suggesting (yet) that these assumptions are sound.

First, the distinction between thick and thin is not just a matter of degree. Indeed, it is not a matter of degree at all. There may be more or less thick concepts; some are thicker than others, that is, some offer richer description than others. But thinness is not a matter of degree; all thin concepts are equally thin.

Second, there is therefore something that thick concepts have got and thin concepts don't have, and that something is the thing that those that are more thick have more of than do those that are less thick. We can (warily) call this something 'descriptive meaning'.

Third, the thick therefore combines something which it shares with the thin (call this 'evaluative meaning') with the descriptive meaning that it does not. Some thick concepts have more descriptive meaning than others, but there is no such thing as more evaluative meaning; each thin concept has as much evaluative meaning as any other, and the thick concepts have that much too.

Having got so far, we arrive at a position in which we can ask how the thick 'combines' these two sorts of meaning, and we have two possible answers, the disentanglers' answer and the entanglers' answer.

Finally, we notice the way in which the thick concepts are understood as, as one might put it, tending towards the thin. The paradigm thin concepts are good, bad, right, and wrong. Thick concepts have that sort of meaning in them added to some descriptive meaning. One wields a thick concept en route to a final, overall evaluation of the for/against sort. This sense in which the thin dominates was called 'centralism' by Susan Hurley, and the name has stuck. She wrote:

What makes an account centralist is …the conceptual independence and priority it allows to the general evaluative component in relation to specific reason-giving concepts.[5]

---

[4] McDowell (1985), §4.   [5] Hurley (1992), 13.

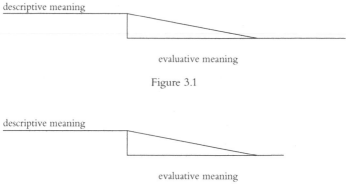

Figure 3.1

Figure 3.2

And this is just what we see in the standard picture of the relation between the thick and the thin. The thin is conceptually independent of the thick and the thick is not so independent of the thin. We can picture the situation as I have characterized it so far in Figure 3.1.

The triangle in the middle is the area of the (decreasingly) thick. The amount of descriptive meaning diminishes to zero, and at that point we encounter the thin. It has to be confessed, however, that it is not obvious why the line representing the thin has any significant length at all. For all thin concepts are, according to the assumptions, equally thin. Perhaps the diagram would look better like Figure 3.2.

In Figure 3.2 the length of the line representing the thin has been reduced almost to nothing; I wanted it to be almost invisible, but it still needs to be there. One could have similar worries about the long line representing those concepts that are neither thick nor thin. It is not easy to find an appropriate (that is, non-contentious) term for these concepts. We seem to have to choose between 'natural' and 'descriptive'. Both have their difficulties. First, it is not obvious that all these concepts can usefully be called 'natural' concepts. Clearly this depends on how one characterizes the natural, but if one took the standard approach and said that the natural is the domain of the natural sciences, there will be plenty of concepts that are neither thin nor thick nor natural. This does not mean that 'descriptive' is much better. The term 'descriptive' must get whatever sense it has from what it is to describe—which is something that people do, rather than concepts or terms. And it is not at all obvious that we misuse the notion of describing when we say that he described his star pupil as outstanding, excellent in every way, though even stronger in criticism than in invention. My solution to this terminological nightmare is to contrast the evaluative simply with the non-evaluative. This choice leaves it open to me to divide the left-hand line into two parts, the natural on the left and non-natural on the right, should that turn out to be worthwhile; to do this would of course be to adopt a conception of the natural that is narrower than is usual. So my diagram ends up looking like Figure 3.3.

When I presented Figure 3.3 at the 'Thick Concepts' conference, it was suggested that some thin concepts have some non-evaluative meaning. The example offered (by Pekka

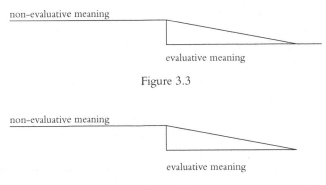

non-evaluative meaning

evaluative meaning

Figure 3.3

non-evaluative meaning

evaluative meaning

Figure 3.4

Väyrynen) was that 'ought' implies 'can', but not all thin concepts imply 'can'; perhaps 'is fitting to' does not, and maybe 'is a reason for' does not either. Now plainly, if some thin concepts have non-evaluative meaning, the diagram needs to be rethought entirely. And the general idea need not depend upon this contentious example. Michael Smith, in his paper, argued that the distinction between thick and thin is indeed a matter of degree, a sliding scale of evaluative concepts taking us from the least specific at the far right to the most specific where we hit the vertical line as we move towards the left.[6] So on his view there is no such thing as the sort of purely evaluative meaning standardly ascribed to thin concept, and the diagram should look like Figure 3.4.

In the remainder of this section, I respond to these suggestions. First, the argument that some thin concepts have non-evaluative meaning relies on the view that something non-evaluative can be inferred from the applicability of a thin concept. But this would not be enough to show that the thing inferred is itself part of the concept. It is in fact certain that many things that can be inferred in this way are not themselves part of the concept they are inferred from. For if they were (and this gives some sense to the dubious notion of 'part of a concept'), competence with that concept would require competence with the supposed part. But the concept 'is a cow' entails an enormous number of other concepts, such as 'is not a horse', 'is not a mountain', 'is not the Aga Khan', and so on; and these things entailed cannot sensibly be supposed to be part of the concept 'is a cow', on pain of rendering that concept unlearnable.

The question then is whether this implication is part of the concept of 'ought' and not part of the concept of 'reason'. I would say that the contentiousness of the implication is evidence that accepting the inference is no part of competence with the concept, since neither side in the debate accuses the other of conceptual incompetence. For what it is worth, then, I am not convinced by the examples that are supposed to show that some thin concepts have non-evaluative content. What is more, even if some thin concepts are a little thick, there will be some that are not (such as the concept of the fitting, which is

---

[6] See Smith (this volume).

allowed not to entail 'can'); so the idea of a concept that is purely thin will survive. But Smith's points are quite general, and do not depend on particular examples, and if correct would undermine the very idea of the 'purely' thin. For him, there is only the distinction between more or less specific.

There are two parts to Smith's paper, and I am going to take them in reverse order. The second part concerns Hurley's anti-centralism. As Hurley characterizes this position, it amounts to the denial that 'the general concepts right and ought are logically prior to and independent of specific reason-giving concepts such as just and unkind'.[7] Of course this does not reveal what logical priority is intended to mean. But it is clear that this denial is compatible with two positions. The first asserts the reverse priority, and the second simply denies any priority. I take Hurley to have intended the second of these. She contrasts a centralist account, not with the sort of view we associate with Bernard Williams, who definitely ascribed priority to the thick, but with what she called a 'coherence account'. The passage from her *Natural Reasons* which I quoted earlier continues:

A coherence account, by contrast, would hold the general and the specific concepts to be conceptually interdependent.[8]

But Smith supposes her to be committed to the reverse priority, because of the following remark:

According to [non-centralism], to say that a certain act ought to be done is to say that it is favoured by the best account of the relationships among the specific values that apply to the alternatives in question.[9]

Smith understands this sentence as saying that the concept of what ought to be done is a theoretical construct out of the values that we take to be relevant to whether something ought or ought not to be done. It must be a theoretical construct because on the non-centralist picture there is no prior concept of what ought to be done. But if so, he says, two people who operate with different sets of specific values could not even be said to disagree about what ought to be done, since they do not have the same concept. One's concept of ought is built out of the values that one takes to be relevant to determining ought-ness; so people with different values must have different concepts.

This is, however, a mistake. The sentence of Hurley's quoted above can be understood as offering an account of the concept of 'ought' that is entirely formal, as we see if we insert a caveat in it thus:

According to [non-centralism], to say that a certain act ought to be done is to say that it is favoured by the best account of the relationships among the specific values that apply to the alternatives in question (whatever they may be).

With this reading we can still respect the distinction between conception and concept. People who disagree in the values that they take to determine what ought to be done

---

[7] Hurley (1985), 56.   [8] Hurley (1992), 13.   [9] Hurley (1985), 56.

can still be said to have the same concept, and hence to be disagreeing about something, even though they have different conceptions. The difference in conception is not in danger of making a difference in concept, as it would be if one's concept was a theoretical construct out of one's conception.

Turning now to the body of Smith's paper, I am going to apply the distinction between concept and conception to the way in which Smith lays out a certain debate between R. M. Hare and his opponents. Hare starts by saying that calling an action right commits one to accepting a self-directed imperative instructing one to do any action that shares with the first action the features that led one to call it right. It was complained against him that not all such self-directed imperatives could be thought of as moral imperatives; morality has a certain restricted subject matter, and moral imperatives must relate to that. Philippa Foot, for instance, urged that moral requirements must have something to do with benefit and harm. Suppose we accept this amendment to Hare's picture. We now have a more specific picture of what moral judgement amounts to. And we could continue in the same vein, saying that considerations of justice and fairness are also relevant, or that considerations of simple identity are not relevant, ruling things out or in as we go along; but all we are doing is rendering more specific the thing we started with. But also, as we go along, we will be introducing the sorts of considerations that are standardly located within the thick: justice, fairness, impartiality, tolerance, and so on. So the difference between thin and thick is really nothing but a simple distinction between the more and the less specific. There is no difference that is not a matter of degree.

My response to all this is that we start with a concept of the right, namely of those responses that we have most moral reason to perform. This concept is thin, as is the concept of a reason that figures in it, and the broader concept of relevance that is lurking somewhere there too. What we then do is to develop a conception of the things that are morally relevant, which I take to be an elaboration of the moral domain as we conceive it. We thereby develop a conception of what counts morally in favour of what, and of the sorts of actions that are right or wrong. The increasing thickness of our conception of the morally relevant does nothing to undermine the pure thinness of our concept of the right, of reasons and of relevance.

My conclusion at the moment is that the distinction between thin and thick is not a matter of degree, but of type.

3.2

I 'solved' the interpenetration problem, on behalf of the entanglers, by appeal to the no-priority view, which I still think gives a good sense to the idea that property and attitude cannot be disentangled. But I confess to serious doubts about whether that view can be used to give a general account of thick concepts. Once we have a suitable attitude in place, and a suitable property, we get a nice picture. But it may not be right to think of all thick concepts as explicable in these terms. As I said above, the no-priority view as I expressed it was only formal. And it seems to be an open question whether all the concepts we want to think of as thick are capable of being explicated in its terms. So the question is: does the no-priority view generalize?

The only way to answer this question is to throw examples at it. The best case for the no-priority view, I think, is unsurprisingly the one that Wiggins and McDowell most often appeal to. This is the concept of the amusing, or funny. An amusing joke is one that merits a certain response, that of amusement or perhaps laughter; this is the property of being amusing. And when one is amused, one is amused by the object as meriting that amused response. The amusing joke calls for amusement; it says, as it were, 'laugh at me'. Of course one can be amused by a joke that is not funny. But this is a defective instance of the response.

This central example will only work if we can sustain the idea that our amusement is a response to the object as meriting just that response. And I have to confess that it is not absolutely clear to me that this account is true to the phenomenology of amusedness.[10] But I leave that aside, because my main focus here is on the question of whether an account of this style can be given across the board.

Wiggins, in his presentation of these themes, restricts his attention to two classes of concept.[11] The first class is what one might call the '-ings': the amusing, exciting, enticing, frightening, engaging, interesting, disturbing, alarming, challenging, and so on. We might include in this class the attractive, suggestive, provocative, impressive, festive, and other such; also the respectable, admirable, acceptable, understandable, desirable, and lovable. In all these cases it seems that things fit the pattern required. This is because in each case the distinction between property and response is already given; there is a distinct response-type served up by the concept. We are enticed by the enticing, disturbed by the disturbing, amused by the amusing, attracted by the attractive, provoked by the provocative, and alarmed by the alarming. We desire the desirable and fear the terrifying. Here, then, things work well.

Wiggins also considers thin concepts: the good and the right, just for a start. And here again things work well, because with the thin we are dealing with overall approval and disapproval. These are responses, and they may come in different forms; but at the level of the thin those different forms will need to be amalgamated into general-pro and general-con.

But there seem to be many thick concepts that do not work in this kind of way, since no clear response is there to be appealed to. In saying this, I am of course vulnerable to the charge that some of the examples I am about to give are not really examples of the thick at all. My response can only be that there are just too many of them for this style of rebuttal to be convincing overall. Consider then the list of thick concepts that Samuel Scheffler gave in his review of Williams's *Ethics and the Limits of Philosophy*:[12]

1. justice, fairness, impartiality
2. privacy, self-respect, envy

---

[10] For a recent expression of these doubts, see Dancy (2012).   [11] Wiggins (1998).
[12] Scheffler (1987).

3. needs, well-being, interests
4. autonomy, consent.

And here is another list:

1. relevant, rational
2. turn, share, help, promise
3. subtle, distinguished, sensible, responsive, fine, gross, coarse, balanced, lop-sided, harmonious, flabby
4. imaginative, resourceful, inventive, dull.

In very few of these cases is it easy to fix on a response that is served up by the concept in the sort of way that we have seen. Take the concept of a turn, as in 'it is not your turn'. There is the institution of waiting one's turn, which comes with respect for the fact that it is not one's turn but someone else's, not my turn but yours. It also comes with the practice of not pushing oneself forward, not going to the front of the queue, and so on; these are practical responses, but they are still responses. Similar things could be said of privacy, for instance. But the trouble is that the only way of making sure that there is a suitable response in each case is to read the response off the property. Take subtlety. What is the appropriate response to that? The only one I can think of is recognition of the subtlety, but neither that nor the sort of admiration that appropriate subtlety attracts seem to play the sort of role that the no-priority view adduces. It seems that in these cases, and in many others on the lists above, the property is prior to the response. Our response to subtlety is not a response to the subtle object as meriting our response, though if it is subtle it does merit that response. Its subtlety is not its meriting the appropriate response, but a feature in virtue of which it merits that response.

These are the reasons for thinking that the no-priority view does not generalize in the way required if it is to stand as the basis for a general account of the thick.

Have I somehow cheated here by imposing invariability or the single-attitude view on the discussion? Would things look any different if we adopt the positions I suggested above, understanding thick concepts as multi-attitude concepts and as variable in their practical relevance. I don't see that they would. One's response to subtlety can be as mixed as you like: it is still a response to a property in the object that is prior to that response. Maybe, again, some things are ruined by being subtle (which is not the same as being too subtle—sometimes subtlety is exactly what is not wanted); but this does not seem to change the situation either.

I conclude that the no-priority view cannot do everything that it is being asked to do.

3.3

Another aspect of the interpenetration problem for entanglers was the need to say something about the different non-evaluative meanings of different thick terms. 'Elegant' and 'clumsy' are both thick, and if we were invariabilists we would say that one is a pro-concept and the other a con-concept. But they clearly carry different 'non-evaluative meaning', no matter how wary one is of that notion. I tried to deal with this difficulty by appeal to Aristotelian domains: the courageous is the commendable (roughly) in the domain of responses to fear and danger. And that manoeuvre works well in general for the virtues, so long as we accept the Aristotelian way of distinguishing them, which I am not concerned here to dispute. But again it is not obvious how to make similar remarks across the board. One needs to be able to offer an independent specification of the relevant domain; otherwise nothing is gained. I would say that we can do this for one of Scheffler's list, impartiality, and for some of mine, such as resourcefulness, which is something like skill at finding solutions to problems; but then these two look very much like virtues. (It helps that they are predicated of people.) But what about the harmonious? This looks very much like that which is to be commended so far as harmony is concerned. And what is the domain for turns? Perhaps it is the domain of deciding who is to go next when there is competition for precedence. But this doesn't look sufficiently independent.

3.4

The interpenetration problem is proving very recalcitrant for entanglers. Their attempts to give a general characterization of the glue that holds what we are calling non-evaluative and evaluative meaning together in a thick concept are not meeting with much success. And I know of no further resource beyond those we have already tried and found wanting. A new start is needed. And what one tends to do in such cases is to examine as carefully as possible the contrasts in terms of which the debate has been posed, to see if one can unearth some challengeable presupposition in them. What are those contrasts? Here are some: descriptive vs. evaluative, property vs. attitude, attitude vs. response, concept vs. property.

Now my general feeling is that the debate about entangling and disentangling has been conducted in ways that reflect the main preoccupation of early writers in the field, namely the battle between cognitivism and non-cognitivism in value theory and ethics. It was that preoccupation that led to matters being presented in terms of property and attitude or response. The no-priority view was itself first presented as a weapon against non-cognitivism. Non-cognitivists, primarily Blackburn, supposedly maintained that the attitude of amusement, say, had the priority, and the so-called property of funniness was a construct out of that. Considered solely as a response to non-cognitivism, the no-priority view had no need to generalize. All it needed was a few good cases where the non-cognitivist account could not be got to work. If it could be run for the virtues and for the various concepts that I listed in section 3.2, it had no further pretensions and could be deemed successful in its own terms. It was not primarily intended as a contribution to an independent debate about thick concepts in general.

It now seems to me that we would do better to go even further back, to Williams' presentation of the thick/thin distinction in his *Ethics and the Limits of Philosophy*. The terms that Williams appealed to are quite different from the ones that we have come to use in our thinking about the thick. For Williams, thick concepts are world-guided and action-guiding. Non-evaluative concepts are only world-guided, and thin concepts are not world-guided at all.

I propose to try to make sense of this distinction. Note, first, that if it can be done it avoids entirely any worries about the glue that holds non-evaluative and evaluative meaning together in one concept. In place of such worries, we get instead a worry about the relation between being world-guided and being action-guiding in those concepts that are both. And it remains to be seen whether this new (or rather old) worry is any more tractable than the one that it is intended to replace (or that replaced it). The general idea, then, is to abandon the attempt to knit property and attitude together, and to try to make sense of the view that some concepts are intrinsically action-guiding, and that some of those are world-guided too.

Nobody could maintain that the contrast between world-guided and action-guiding is terribly happy as it stands. The obvious questions are whether the sort of guiding concerned is the same both times, and what is meant by 'the world' here. It looks as if some prejudicial conception of the world may be at issue. But in fact, as Williams uses it, this is not so. He writes, quite simply:

At the same time, their application is guided by the world. A concept of this sort may be rightly or wrongly applied, and people who have acquired it can agree that it applies or fails to apply to some new situation.[13]

This sort of 'guided by' is not very different from 'answerable to'. But when we ask what is meant by 'the world' we get a richer picture. It sounds initially as if 'the world' is supposed to mean 'what there is anyway'—a sort of nod towards the absolute conception which figures so largely in Williams' thought. But in fact he has two conceptions of 'the world'. The first is that of the world absolutely conceived, the world of primary qualities (roughly). The second is the human world, the world of desires, attitudes, and needs. Williams writes elsewhere:

Nevertheless, the nature of the shared practice shows that it is world guided, and explanation will hope to show how that can be. What the explanation exactly may be, is to be seen: but we know now that a vital part of it will lie in the desires, attitudes, and needs that we and they have differently acquired from our different ways of being brought into a social world. The explanation will show how, in relation to those differences, the world can indeed guide our and their reactions. 'The world' in that explanation will assuredly not be characterized merely in terms of primary qualities; the account of it will need to mention, no doubt, both secondary qualities and straightforwardly psychological items.[14]

So the idea that our use of thick concepts is world-guided is not based on some appeal to supervenience or anything like that. Perhaps we should not be spending time on the

---

[13] Williams (1985), 141.   [14] Williams (1995), 186.

notion of world-guidedness anyway, because Williams' real use of that notion lies in his denial that application of thin concepts is world-guided, and I do not want to go down that path at all. The idea that where non-evaluative meaning lapses we lose our sense that concepts of this sort can be rightly or wrongly applied and our sense that those competent with it can agree on its application to new cases, is not one that recommends itself to me. In my view, both thick and thin concepts are world-guided and action-guiding. The difference between thick and thin lies elsewhere.

So for me the real issue is how to characterize the action-guiding nature of thick concepts. Somehow we have to make sense of the idea that these concepts have an intrinsic practical relevance. Other, non-evaluative concepts may be such that their applicability makes a practical difference on occasion, but that relevance is extrinsic to them. It may make a difference that this car goes faster or uses less petrol than that one, but that difference is not intrinsic to those features.

It would be a mistake to read these initial remarks about having intrinsic practical relevance as remarks about being necessarily relevant. Only the thin concepts are necessarily practically relevant. The practical relevance of the thick must be consistent with the variability that I am persuaded is a feature of many thick concepts, and variability includes not only the idea that the applicability of the concept can make things now better and now worse, but also the idea that it may on occasion make no difference at all. The point has to be that in such a case there is something to explain, which there is not in the case of the non-evaluative concepts. By contrast, when the instantiation of a thick concept does make a practical difference, there is as yet nothing to be explained.

We explain the relevance of a non-evaluative concept by appeal to the co-instantiation of some other concept. (In less clumsy terms, the relevance of a non-evaluative property will be explained by the co-presence of some other property.) This sort of explanation is not necessary when a thick concept has practical relevance, for such a thing is to be expected. This is what makes it possible to think of these concepts as practical concepts. And competence with such concepts will be practical competence, since it consists in knowledge of the sort of difference it can make that the concept is here instantiated. This sort of knowledge brings with it the ability to tell one case from another in this respect; the competence is not just an ability to determine whether the concept is instantiated or not, but also the ability to determine what difference this makes on the present occasion. By contrast, competence with a non-evaluative concept requires only the former ability.

I said, however, that I intend this picture to be compatible with the variabilist picture that I adumbrated at the start of this paper. And here there is a difficulty for me. For suppose that a thick concept is here instantiated, and that it makes a difference. Still, as variabilism has it, the instantiation of that concept might have made a different difference, since it is capable of making any of a range of differences. Which difference it makes here will surely be to be explained by appeal to other features of the case. But haven't I said that if that is so, we are dealing with a non-evaluative concept?

Matters would be manageable if every thick concept had a default relevance. For in that case, those instances where the actual relevance is the default relevance are ones where no further explanation is needed, and that is all that is required to distinguish the thick concepts from non-evaluative ones. But I doubt that it is true that all thick concepts have a default relevance in the way required.

Luckily there is another way to distinguish the thick from the purely non-evaluative. For the instantiation of a thick concept may be practically relevant in a way that does not depend upon the co-instantiation of other concepts, even if the actual relevance that it has is so dependent. That is to say, that it is relevant at all needs no further explanation of that sort, even though the actual relevance it has may do so. And this is enough for the purpose of distinguishing the intrinsic practical relevance of a thick concept from the extrinsic practical relevance of the purely non-evaluative.

If we think in these terms, we make room for those thick concepts, such as a turn and a share, where the identification of a suitable attitude is rather a challenge, and undermines the general programme of characterizing the thick in terms of some combination of property and attitude, held together by some suitable sort of glue. But we can also allow a special place for the sort of thick concept that has dominated recent discussion, the sort that does indeed hold together property and attitude, or property and response. The no-priority view still seems to get it right about these concepts, but they are special in a way that cannot be extended to the thin (for example, the fitting), and that does little to sustain the sort of sentimentalism that Wiggins wanted to sustain for the evaluative quite generally.

I suggest, then, that thick concepts are those with an intrinsic practical relevance. But perhaps not all relevance is practical relevance. Simon Kirchin asked me about aesthetic concepts; these are often used in the appreciation of art rather than in the making of it. Do they have an intrinsic practical relevance? Yes, they do, because they are relevant to the choices of the artist. So there is a way out here, but still one might think that placing all the weight on the practical is a distortion, and will lead to a lop-sided conception of the thick. A different suggestion is that we should return again to Williams, and resuscitate his idea that thick concepts are more generally those that have an evaluative point. Miranda Fricker suggested this change of emphasis to me. Is there any reason to resist it? The notion of an evaluative point is perhaps less clear, less well focused than that of practical relevance. But this may be an advantage. We could say that competence with a thick concept requires an understanding of its evaluative point, and that this includes, but is not restricted to, a grasp of the sorts of practical difference it can make that the concept is here instantiated.[15]

3.5

In this final section I return to the topic of variability. Why have theorists been so tempted to suppose that thick concepts have an invariant relevance? I can think of three explanations for this. The first is simple. It is that, as commonly happens in philosophy, we work

[15] Both Kirchin's and Fricker's comments were made at the 'Thick Concepts' conference.

with a very limited range of examples. I am sure that this is part of the story, but it is not the only part, nor the most respectable. Another factor is a tendency to concentrate on the totalizing distinction between pro and con. I think of this tendency as a sign of a sort of centralism. Evaluative concepts are in the business of making cases for or against responses. That being so, they must carry elements of pro or con with them, to contribute to the mix. But I think this is a mistaken picture. Evaluative concepts are concepts with an evaluative point, and this is perfectly compatible with their not having elements of pro or of con in them. There is the appropriately lewd and there is the inappropriately lewd, the deliciously lewd and the unattractively lewd, and the fact that lewdness comes in all these forms does nothing to show that it is not a concept with an evaluative point.

Still one might think that there is some a priori consideration operating here in favour of invariabilism, and I end by considering one pressed on me by Michael Smith in conversation. He asked how it is possible for variabilists to explain the evaluative nature of thick concepts. There are two standard ways of doing that. The first says that thick concepts are evaluative because they entail a pro tanto evaluation. But this is what we have seen already, and it is not available to variabilists. The second says that thick concepts are evaluative because an ability to determine, or notice, instances of them requires what one might call an evaluative eye, an understanding of human practical purposes. The problem with this suggestion is that it seems possible for a non-evaluative concept to require the evaluative eye. I say that this might be so; I don't have a fully persuasive example. But one that has always appealed to me is Maggie Little's example of the child alone in a crowd. Loneliness is, I would say, a thick concept, but aloneness might not be, and one can imagine saying that it is a non-evaluative matter whether the child is accompanied or not, but that the ability to notice such a thing requires an understanding of human practical purposes. I'm not sure of this; one might say instead that what one notices is that the child is not appropriately accompanied, or accompanied by an appropriate person. Uncertainty here leads me to think that the second option is not reliable either, and variabilists need to look elsewhere.

My positive suggestion really appeals to points made earlier in this paper. It is that thick concepts are evaluative because competence with them requires a general understanding of their evaluative point, including the range of their practical relevance, the sorts of difference it can make that the concept is here instantiated. Thick concepts differ from non-evaluative concepts and from thin concepts in this respect.

References

Dancy, Jonathan (1995) 'In Defense of Thick Concepts', in Peter A. French, Theodore E. Uehling, and Howard K. Wettstein (eds.) *Midwest Studies in Philosophy* XX: 263–79.
—— (2012) 'McDowell, Williams, and Intuitionism', in Ulrike Heuer and Gerald Lang (eds.) *Luck, Value, and Commitment: Themes from the Ethics of Bernard Williams* (Oxford: Oxford University Press), 269–92.

Hurley, S. L. (1985) 'Objectivity and Disagreement', in Ted Honderich (ed.) *Morality and Objectivity* (London: Routledge and Kegan Paul), 54–97.

——(1992) *Natural Reasons* (Oxford: Oxford University Press).

Lance, Mark and Margaret Little (2004) 'Defeasibility and the Normative Grasp of Context', *Erkenntnis* 61: 435–55.

——(2007) 'From Particularism to Defeasibility in Ethics', in Mark Lance, Matjaž Potrč and Vojko Strahnovik (eds.) *Challenging Moral Particularism* (London: Routledge).

McDowell, John (1985) 'Values and Secondary Qualities' in Ted Honderich (ed.) *Morality and Objectivity* (London: Routledge and Kegan Paul), 110–29.

——(1987) 'Projection and Truth in Ethics', Lindley Lecture, University of Kansas. Reprinted in his *Mind, Value, and Reality* (Cambridge, MA: Harvard University Press, 1988), 151–66.

Scheffler, Samuel (1987) 'Morality through Thick and Thin: A Critical Notice of *Ethics and the Limits of Philosophy*', *Philosophical Review* 96: 411–34.

Smith, Michael (this volume) 'On the Nature and Significance of the Distinction between Thick and Thin Ethical Concepts'.

Wiggins, David (1998) 'A Sensible Subjectivism', in his *Needs, Values, Truth*, 3rd edn. (Oxford: Blackwell), 185–214.

Williams, Bernard (1985) *Ethics and the Limits of Philosophy* (London: Fontana).

——(1995) 'What Does Intuitionism Imply?' in his *Making Sense of Humanity* (Cambridge: Cambridge University Press), 182–91.

4

Thick Concepts and Thick Descriptions

Simon Kirchin

The first coinage in print of 'thick concept' was due to Bernard Williams, in *Ethics and the Limits of Philosophy* (hereafter *ELP*).[1] As many readers will know, we owe much of the current interest in thick concepts to Williams's work. However, Gilbert Ryle was the first to use the phrase 'thick description' to describe ideas in this general ballpark. A thick description is a more specific sort of description that one needs in order to categorize an action, personality trait, or other such thing. Ryle used this phrase in two papers from the late 1960s, although the idea runs through much of his work.[2] His idea of a thick description is, at first sight, broader than how Williams conceives of thick concepts. Williams characterizes thick concepts as being both action-guiding and world-guided, whilst thin concepts are action-guiding only. Many of Ryle's thick descriptions are not at all, on the face of it, involved in praise, blame, the guidance of action, and the like. They may be evaluations, of course, but only in the wide sense that is synonymous with 'judgement'; many of Ryle's examples are not straightforwardly or more narrowly evaluative in the way that Williams envisages thick concepts. However—and here is a key idea—there is no reason to think that amongst Ryle's thick descriptions there could not be terms that are action-guiding and evaluative in just the way thick concepts are thought about today. Indeed, we should note that thick descriptions and thick concepts have much in common. As well as them being notions that are more specific than other notions with which they are contrasted, both Ryle and Williams have opponents who can be classed as 'separationist' in outlook.[3]

---

[1] As far as I can see, the label 'thin concept' does not appear in *ELP*. Williams prefers phrases such as 'more abstract concepts'. He mentions 'thin concept' by name in his (1996), 25, but without fanfare. As I point out in my introduction to this volume, Williams acknowledges that he is developing ideas gained from Philippa Foot and Iris Murdoch.

[2] Ryle (1966–7) and (1968). Elsewhere he is fond of saying that there is a bottom (that is, thin) level of description that is contrasted with higher (that is, thicker) levels (or 'higher sophistication-levels'). For discussion of Ryle, see Tanney (2009) and (2010). Mention of Ryle is interesting here. Miranda Fricker mentions to me that Williams once said to her in passing that he regarded Ryle as his teacher and mentor.

[3] See my introduction to this volume, §I(iii), for discussion of this term.

What interests me in this paper is the connection between the notions of thick description and thick concept, and what ideas may come in the wake of thinking about them.

Like Williams and others I am a 'nonseparationist'. I will not argue for that view here. Instead I assume that this view has some attraction. I also assume that a certain theory of concepts, which we find in Ryle's work and which I sketch below, also has its attractions.[4] On the basis of that, I have two aims. First, I criticize the characterization, which is more often a slogan, that Williams gives of thin and thick concepts in terms of action-guidance. I do not think it fairly reflects some things that Williams says, and it is also an imperfect characterization of thin and thick concepts. One idea that has occurred to me more than once is that despite Williams's influence it is odd that few people *work explicitly* with his characterization of thin and thick concepts, preferring instead to talk of evaluative and descriptive content, or similar contrasts involving the normative and the factual.[5] My second aim is to try to understand the thin and thick better. In doing so, I argue that the work of Ryle is helpful here (well, helpful *if* one is sympathetic to nonseparationism). Along the way I consider the idea that thick concepts are just one type of thick description, the sort involved in evaluation and the guidance of action.[6] Whilst this idea has appeal, I suggest that the issue is more complex than it suggests: it implies a clear distinction between those thick descriptions that are thick concepts and those that are not, but I argue that this is not quite correct. In doing so, I hope to make attractive for nonseparationists one way of thinking about thick concepts.

In section 4.1 I begin with my first aim. I summarize Williams's view of thick concepts and criticize his official characterization of them. In section 4.2 I summarize Ryle's account of thick descriptions. I go into some detail here. Although not everything I say is of high relevance for my argument, I discuss Ryle at length to show that his thinking is similar to Williams's and, hence, that his position bears good comparison. In section 4.3 I make good on my second aim and analyse what goes wrong with Williams's characterization and what we should say instead, although the reader should know that for reasons of space what I offer is really only a promise of further exploration.

---

[4] The second assumption is a big one. The view I outline may be a minority view amongst modern analytic philosophers.

[5] In his contribution to this volume, Jonathan Dancy is a notable exception who runs with Williams's view. Tappolet (2004), 207 repeats this characterization but works with a different contrast.

[6] Descriptions are mainly linguistic devices that, for Ryle, are to be studied and thought about *in situ*, and from which we can abstract so as to get propositions, what we might term 'thick propositions'. So, technically we could voice the claim as 'thick concepts are a type of thick proposition', although this is also imperfect as we should not mix concepts and propositions in this way. It might be better to use 'thick term' to label the linguistic items that represent thick concepts, and wonder if they are a type of thick description. But, for simplicity's sake, I will talk of thick concepts being a type of thick description.

4.1 Williams on thick concepts

Williams's main discussion of thin and thick concepts occurs in *ELP* and this will be my focus.[7] In more detail, my main claim about Williams's view is as follows. His characterization of thick concepts as both action-guiding and world-guided, with thin concepts being action-guiding alone, is far too narrowly focused. What I concentrate on in this paper is the supposed action-guidance involved.[8] It may characterize some of what goes on with ethical concepts, but it falls short there and it is a misleading way of thinking about other evaluative concepts; I have aesthetic concepts particularly in mind. Oddly, Williams says things that cut against his main characterization which, if he had worked with them more, would have produced a more satisfactory generalizing slogan.

I begin by considering whether Williams's characterization summarizes everything important he says about the thick. In his first main description of thick concepts where he discusses theorists, such as prescriptivists, who distinguish sharply between fact and value, he says:

What has happened is that the theorists have brought the fact-value distinction to language rather than finding it revealed there. What they have found are a lot of those 'thicker' or more specific ethical notions I have already referred to, such as *treachery* and *promise* and *brutality* and *courage*, which seem to express a union of fact and value. The way these notions are applied is determined by what the world is like (for instance, by how someone has behaved), and yet, at the same time, their application usually involves a certain valuation of the situation, of persons or actions. Moreover, they usually (though not necessarily directly) provide reasons for action.[9]

Later on he says:

Many exotic examples of these [thick concepts] can be drawn from other cultures, but there are enough left in our own: *coward, lie, brutality, gratitude,* and so forth. They are characteristically related to reasons for action. If a concept of this kind applies, this often provides someone with a reason for action, though that reason need not be a decisive one and may be outweighed by other reasons... Of course, exactly what reason for action is provided, and to whom, depends on the situation, in ways that may well be governed by this and by other ethical concepts, but some general connection with action is clear enough. We may say, summarily, that such concepts are 'action-guiding'.

At the same time, their application is guided by the world.[10]

In a third key passage, when considering the possibility of ethical knowledge in the modern, post-Enlightenment West, he comments on thin concepts.

This brings us back to the question whether the reflective level might generate its own ethical knowledge.... [I see] no hope of extending to this level the kind of world-guidedness we have

---

[7] See also the aforementioned Williams (1996). Some of the issues relevant to thick concepts also crop up in Williams (1993) and (2002).

[8] I discuss world-guidedness in my introduction, §1(i).

[9] *ELP*, 129–30.   [10] *ELP*, 140–1.

been considering in the case of the thick ethical concepts. Discussions at the reflective level, if they have the ambition of considering all ethical experience and arriving at the truth about the ethical, will necessarily use the most general and abstract ethical concepts, such as 'right', and those concepts do not display world-guidedness (which is why they were selected by prescriptivism in its attempt to find a pure evaluative element from which it could detach world-guidedness).[11]

The official characterization of thin and thick concepts in terms of action-guidingness and world-guidedness is not wholly bad. It captures much of Williams's ideas. He clearly thinks there is some conceptual division between thin and thick concepts, and he clearly thinks that thin concepts are not world-guided. It is clear, lastly, that he thinks that both types of concept can be used to guide action. Even in the first passage quoted above, and certainly by the time he is summarizing his view later, I suspect that Williams thinks that action-guidingness is the prime function, or perhaps the 'foundational point', of thin and thick ethical concepts. (This is reinforced by much of *ELP*.)[12] By this I do not mean that this aspect is more important than any nonevaluative connotations that thick concepts might carry. Additionally, it seems that ethical concepts, both thin and thick, are practical in a way that many other concepts, such as CHAIR and GALAXY, are not. In the second passage quoted he says that thick concepts are 'characteristically related to reasons for action'. We apply these concepts to people, actions, and institutions, and we use such descriptions to shape our view of how we should act in relation to them. Thin and thick concepts are, to put it loosely, active. Despite the criticism I give below, no one should think that when characterizing thin and thick concepts the guidance of action is irrelevant or of only limited importance.

Yet, the official characterization has its flaws, even as a summary of what Williams says. In the first passage quoted he says that there will be some evaluation ('some valuation') when one applies some thick concept. He then says that some reason for action will usually, though not always, be provided and that the reason need not be direct. Let us take these points in turn. First, when it comes to the guidance of action, things are trickier when we are not talking of possible courses of action simply because we are not thinking about how to act. When evaluating a person, we might try to guide how others should treat her or refrain from following her lead. But, that need not always happen. Often our aim is simply to express some evaluation. Perhaps we take a negative view of someone, and our use of WICKED rather than BARBARIC is our way of indicating that, in the world-guided way associated with thick concepts. Similarly, when we praise an institution as just we might be wishing to do only that, namely express praise. We need not be trying to influence how others treat it. For us to assume that influence on action is (strongly and) typically to be present seems to shoehorn in something that may not be there.

So, the official characterization misses out on this important first point about thin and thick concepts. Secondly, we can show that talk of action-guidance alone disguises

[11] *ELP*, 151–2.   [12] See also Williams (1996), 32, for a casual repetition of this commitment.

something important about what Williams says: we miss out on the frequency and direct nature of the guidance provided. Williams says that through some evaluation there is usually some reason for action provided, even if it is only indirect. What might he mean here? We can imagine that if enough people describe some person as wicked the judgement will stick and that eventually, when some action involving our relation with her is possible, there will be some reason for us to act. Similarly, judging an institution to be just enough times will help to guide people to protect it, say, when it is under threat. But, even then, not only does the situation have to present us with some opportunity to act, Williams qualifies his comments in the first passage with the aforementioned 'usually'; there are cases when no reason is provided, even an indirect one. The link between some evaluative judgements and some actions are so loose and convoluted that it is strained to posit a link. Doing so might reflect only a philosophical prejudice, not the truth of the matter. Talking simply of action-guidingness, as the summary does, disguises this and implies that the use of thin and thick concepts always results in some direct guidance of action. Even the few brief examples I have given show this view to be wrong. It is wrong as a claim about Williams's view of thick concepts and—now a new claim—wrong about thick ethical concepts. Indeed, we can say that this summary makes Williams's thoughts about thick ethical concepts too concrete and narrowly discrete, something that goes against the spirit of his writings. After all, he is not developing a *theory* of the thick.

So: *contra* the official characterization of Williams's distinction, he thinks that thick ethical concepts have three aspects.[13] (i) They are world-guided because their correct application is determined by what the world is like and so, relatedly, they help to provide fair detail of what the items they categorize are like; (ii) they can be action-guiding, either directly or indirectly, since they can provide reasons for action; and (iii) they can be used to evaluate things where we simply wish to indicate, in more or less specific ways, whether we view something positively or negatively. The worry with the quick summary is that it could mislead one into forgetting about the important qualifications in (ii), and it misses out (iii) altogether. Even if the guidance of action is the foundational point of thin and thick concepts, putting everything about the thick that is 'non-world-guided' in terms of (ii) seems to misconstrue the phenomena.

It is odd that Williams did not embrace these points more. I think he forms his slogan in *ELP* because of his concentration on ethical concepts, and the fact that he generalizes from this case to all thick concepts. Here is another quotation that I have deliberately held back until now. At one point, earlier in *ELP* than the other passages quoted, he berates R. M. Hare for forcing all evaluative concepts into the prescriptivist mould.

In saying that anything is good or bad, admirable or low, outstanding or inferior of its kind, we are in effect telling others or ourselves to do something—as the explanation typically goes, to choose something. All evaluation has to be linked to action.

---

[13] I am not implying here that these aspects are separable in the way Williams argues against.

This result is not easy to believe. It seems false to the spirit of many aesthetic evaluations, for instance: it seems to require our basic perspective on the worth of pictures to be roughly that of potential collectors. Even within the realm of the ethical, it is surely taking too narrow a view of human merits to suppose that people recognized as good are people that we are being told to imitate.[14]

Williams himself gives a devastating criticism of his characterization. Imagine we had read the following in *ELP*: thin aesthetic concepts (such as [aesthetic] GOODNESS and BEAUTY) are wholly action-guiding whilst thick aesthetic concepts (such as ELEGANT and GAUDY) are both world-guided and action-guiding.[15] I think we would have been startled. Even if what Williams says goes for thick ethical concepts, he is making a claim in *ELP* about all thick concepts, and that general claim simply will not wash. Picking up on the second quotation from Williams above, aesthetic concepts are not characteristically related to action. We often use them simply to report how we view something in an aesthetic fashion and, in the way associated with thick concepts, express our evaluation of it. Do we like it? Does it transport us and our imaginings? Does it disquiet us or bore us? And so on.

This is not to say that aesthetic concepts cannot be used to guide action. Indeed, it happens a lot. Just think of an everyday action such as people choosing clothes. We do not pick *that* tie because it is gaudy, whereas we spend lots of money on *that* dress because it is so elegant. More general concepts, such as NAFF, TRASHY, COOL, and their many synonyms, will also be used aesthetically and influence action. Aesthetics matters a lot to us in our activities, and is not confined to some knowledgeable critic disinterestedly contemplating some work in the art gallery or concert hall. Furthermore, some people feel aesthetic matters very deeply, and sometimes more deeply than ethical matters. Some people will happily break promises so that they can attend concerts that they anticipate being majestic. Some people are happy to steal some article of clothing because it is simply divine. We could talk all day about the relationship between ethics and aesthetics in this regard.[16] However, it is enough for our purposes to note that when it comes to thin and thick aesthetic concepts, Williams's official characterization falls flat, and also does not represent at least one interesting passage in *ELP*.

The point applies to more than aesthetic concepts. Epistemic concepts such as WISE, RELEVANT, and KNOWLEDGABLE can guide action and be used to express evaluation, in the way that Williams qualifies in *ELP*. But, they can also influence the formation of beliefs. If you think that a scientific method is reliable, or if you think that a teacher is wise, then this alone gives you reason to change or maintain your other

---

[14] *ELP*, 124.

[15] I take no view here about whether BEAUTY is thin or thick; it is just an example.

[16] I think that individuals' psychology plays a huge role here, but we also seem more ready to generalize in the case of ethics than in aesthetics. We are more ready to say that an action should be done (no matter what your inclination) because it would be kind than we are to say that it should be done (no matter what your inclination) because it would be graceful. I refrain from talking more about this interesting topic here.

beliefs accordingly: although it is prudent to check the views of your teacher, her wisdom is itself a (defeasible) reason to believe what she tells you. As the reader might imagine, I think that the same sort of example will be forthcoming in ethical and aesthetic contexts. (If we favour a method because it is elegant, this might give us a reason to favour its results, as these too may be elegant.) The overall point is that although belief-formation may be a type of action, it would be a shame if we subsumed this function and characteristic point of epistemic concepts under the general catch-all of Williams's familiar description. What we see here, and previously, is that there are a number of functions and points that thick concepts have and that many of them are excised by Williams's summarizing slogan.[17] Our categorizations and lives are richer than Williams's contrast allows for.

To summarize, I think this general picture extends to thin concepts also. GOODNESS, say, can be used to influence action directly. Yet, often we call something good and simply wish to convey our positive view of it. Such a use may influence action indirectly, but the trail might be so indirect that it is not worth speaking of. A deontic concept such as RIGHTNESS differs. It seems more linked to the guidance of action simply because it is more often linked to choices, which in turn are more often linked to reasons. We can categorize an answer to an arithmetic sum as right, because it is the only one that fits. That is a type of evaluation and categorization, but there is surely some implication, even if indirect, that people should reason so as to arrive at that answer and no other. (Although, again, this might strictly be 'belief-formation' rather than action-guidance.) When it comes to moral RIGHTNESS I find it hard to imagine cases where no reason for action is implied, although some suggest themselves, such as 'This institution is right for us', which may not simply boil down to 'Enacting this institution is right for us'.[18] However, OUGHT I find impossible to think of without thinking of action-guidance. There is more to say about these and other thin concepts. The key thought here is that once we dig a little, we see that there may be some difference amongst thin ethical concepts which is not properly captured by Williams's official characterization of them. This is all grist to my mill.

I am ready to acknowledge that some of the things I have said are to be found in Williams, and that my target is (only) his official slogan. But, I think it fair to claim that even in some of his comments he has failed to recognize or has not sufficiently emphasized how thick and thin concepts should properly be conceived. Having completed my first aim, then, in showing the flaws in Williams's official summary, I now turn to Ryle to help diagnose what is happening.

---

[17] A further point. I do not think that we can clearly divide evaluative domains from one another, and so the functions that one associates with one sort of evaluative concept will bleed into the other domains. For example, OBSCENE has its ethical and aesthetic dimensions: the way in which an obscene object looks is partly what makes it (typically) ethically bad, and its ethical badness contributes to its aesthetic character. Similarly, WISDOM gets much of its point and content from how people treat and respect fellow humans, objects and institutions. It may be hard to separate ethical from epistemic content in some cases.

[18] Thanks to Tim Chappell for this example.

4.2 Ryle on thick descriptions

The best way to introduce the idea of a thick description is to think about some of Ryle's examples in his (1968). He thinks about how we distinguish different sorts of wink and imagines a succession of boys who wink in different ways and for different reasons.[19] The first boy has an involuntary twitch. The second winks conspiratorially to an accomplice. Yet, we learn that he does so in a slow, contorted, and conspicuous manner. The third boy parodies the second in order to give malicious amusement to his cronies. He acts in a clumsy way, just as the second did, but he is not himself clumsy. This third boy is later imagined in a different setting (and so becomes a fourth example): he practises his parody and so rehearses for a (hoped-for) public performance. And, this boy is later imagined in another setting, thereby creating a fifth example. When winking he had not been trying to parody the second boy, but had been 'trying to gull the grown-ups into the false belief that he was trying to do so'.[20]

Throughout his discussion of these and other examples, Ryle asks what is common to them. The obvious answer is the thinnest description, such as 'the boy contracted his eyelids'. Ryle thinks this applies to every case, and we can say of each that there is a physical movement. However, Ryle emphasizes two things. First, in order to distinguish the various boys and their actions—note, not just their physical movements—one needs to employ thick descriptions. This need (which is my word) is not just a matter of ease of language, that thick descriptions act merely as summations of various (separable) elements that could be expressed without them if only we had the time and patience. We can see this through a second point. Ryle argues that the boy who winks conspiratorially does not do, say, five separate things: (i) winks deliberately, (ii) to someone in particular, (ii) in order to impart a certain message, (iv) according to an understood code, (v) without the cognizance of the rest of the company. For him, the boy is not doing five separate things, but is rather doing one complex thing, where the implication is that aspects of the action stand and fall together. (In this case, you can be successful in one only if you are successful in the others.) Ryle refers to clauses such as those just expressed as embodying success-and-failure conditions. This is a key point for Ryle. Actions such as winks and conspiratorial winks are to be distinguished from physical movements, such as involuntary twitches, because the former have success-and-failure conditions, which in turn guide us in our descriptions or, better, are embodied in our descriptions.

We can elaborate this. Imagine an example just one step on from Ryle's list, where a boy is both parodying a fellow pupil (with the complexity familiar from Ryle's discussion) *and* is trying to win a girl's heart. On some understandings of this description, we can have a case where not all aspects of the action stand or fall together: the success-and-failure conditions are separate. One can parody the other boy without trying to impress the girl, and one can impress the girl in all manner of ways. In the sort of understanding of this

---

[19] The boys are not introduced immediately one after another. One has to look around (1968) to find them, between 494–6. In my descriptions I echo Ryle.   [20] Ryle (1968), 496.

type of case that I have in mind it seems right to say that our winker is trying to do two things; that clearly goes hand-in-hand with our thought that aspects can be dropped, but then what one is doing is dropping a separable second action, not an aspect of an action. To see this, note that a slightly different description—one that readers may also have in mind—will be such that the aspects of the action do stand or fall together: the boy is trying to win the girls' heart *by* parodying his fellow pupil. Perhaps someone corrects the previous description: 'No, Duncan isn't parodying *and* trying to win Daphne's heart. He's trying to impress her *by* impersonating Tommy'. Here I think it plausible to say that the winker is doing only one thing, albeit a complex thing that may be more complex than some of the other examples Ryle lists and which, uncomplicatedly, requires more words if we are to capture it.[21] This shows how and why, for Ryle, the description is paramount. As we might term it, there is the physical movement, which in this case is the contraction of the eyelids, and there are the various actions. Each individual physical movement can be picked out with the same thin description: 'the boy's eyelid contracted'. But for Ryle there seems to be no one core thing that is the action which then gets added to separable aspects, or to which separable aspects are added, in order to create more complex actions. Or, in other words, if one has a range of similar actions, described using related but different thick descriptions, then there is no core that all have in exactly the same way. This is even the case with 'the boy winked'. For a start, it will not cover our first case, of the involuntary twitcher. But, the ways in which people wink are different, for Ryle, and embody different success-and-failure conditions. There is no reason to think that we have one thing—winking—which is exactly the same thing at the core of each action. This is why I class Ryle as a type of nonseparationist on this point: there is no way of separating the individual aspects of the actions in such a way that they are independently intelligible and can be seen as different, 'sliceable' parts of the action.

This point can be hard to see when it comes to the winking example, simply because 'wink' can be colloquially used of the physical act of contracting the eyelid. It is easier to see the thought with the type of activity that is Ryle's prime focus in his (1968), namely thinking, for thinking is not colloquially thought of as a physical activity. We might say that there are many types of action that are called examples of thinking: pondering, meditating, coming to understand, and so on. And, these examples might be exemplified in many ways: mental arithmetic, writing on a piece of paper, chatting with others, arguing with others, manipulating some wood, playing notes on a piano, picking food from a shelf, and so on.[22] Now, are we confident that there is one separable core activity

---

[21] The final remark of Ryle (1968) shows this perfectly. 'A statesman signing his surname to a peace-treaty is doing much more than inscribe the seven letters of his surname, but he is not doing many or any more things. He is bringing the war to a close by inscribing the seven letters of his surname.' Here the word 'things' is key to understanding Ryle's point.

[22] Some of these examples are from Tanney (2009), xviii. I categorically do not wish to suggest that every instance of, say, playing notes on a piano is a type of thinking, just that some are. To elaborate these examples: the physical activity is not something separate from the thinking. It is how the thinking is exemplified and how an idea, some inspiration or frustration (etc.) is worked through.

called 'thinking' common to all these examples that we could isolate and that stands revealed as the same thing? Can we also, therefore, imagine that we would then be left with one or more separable aspects or elements for each action that would be our remainder? The answer is surely not an obvious yes, and, I think, we would and should be inclined to say no. (I temper my comments here, since some may disagree with Ryle, and my sympathy with his view is not my main focus. All that is needed is to understand what Ryle says and to see that it has some plausibility.) For Ryle, when we describe an action with a thick description, we are labelling something that is a unitary thing.

Here ends my summary of Ryle's view. Now for three points of elaboration. First, note that we can use one word to indicate a thick description, such as 'meditation' or 'parody'. But, we can and do also use appropriate multi-word phrases. Perhaps the boy is executing a skillful parody, and perhaps a thinker is weighing up the pros and cons. I point out here that it is no barrier to seeing a link between thick concepts and descriptions that the thick concepts traditionally used as examples are expressed with just one word. There is no reason why thick concepts cannot be encapsulated by phrases of more than one word, phrases such as 'something of the night'.[23]

Secondly, one key part of Ryle's thinking, through much of his writing career, was the thought that one could understand a concept only through its applications and use.[24] A concept is the abstraction from words and phrases used in all manner of ways in various contexts. Ryle thought that there was no fixed specific meaning for any concept.[25] The various inflections of meaning and the (sometimes) subtle differences in meaning across context are such as to affect our appreciation of what a concept is and what it means. Think again about THINKING. For Ryle, we appreciate what it is to think only if we understand the various exemplifications of the concept, which things count as thinking and which do not. Someone playing on a piano, fiddling around, might well be thinking, and this differs from the thinking that one typically gets in a philosophy seminar between two disputants trying out an idea on each other. It will also differ from idle fiddling around on a piano where someone is not thinking about anything but is just, well, fiddling. Appreciating the similarities and differences of these and other examples is simply to appreciate the contours of the concept THINKING and how it can be applied and withheld correctly and incorrectly, creatively and foolishly. Of course, once we do that,

---

[23] For more on this, see Zangwill (this volume). The example in the main text will be familiar to observers of UK politics. In the 1997 Conservative Party leadership election Ann Widdecombe described candidate Michael Howard, as having 'something of the night' about him. When it comes to this example, I dig my heels in: I think our phrase indicates a 'unitary' concept and it differs from, say, SHEEP IN THE GARDEN: the latter seems obviously constructed from smaller concepts, at least when it comes to English expression. How one decides the individuation of concepts is a big issue; I merely note it here as it does not hamper the discussion in this paper.

[24] The resemblances with the later Wittgenstein on this point are striking, but I will not comment on that here.

[25] This applies also to technical concepts for Ryle. We might find that hard to swallow when it comes to a concept such as H_2O, for example. However, we do not need to agree with Ryle here, nor investigate his idea further, to see how the idea can be worked out for more familiar, everyday concepts such as THINKING and WINKING.

we will appreciate what THINKING stands for. So, just on this basis, it would not be justified to say that there is no fixed meaning for THINKING, specific or otherwise. THINKING
means whatever our investigation of its uses reveals. However, once one accepts that
there can be all manner of different things that can be categorized as THINKING, with no
core element that THINKING stands for, one should appreciate that new uses will appear,
present uses will disappear and, therefore, that the concept itself—and not just applications of the concept—can, in theory, change.

Despite the claim that we can understand concepts only if we understand the many
and various contexts in which the concept is used, this is not to say that we have wild
and frequent changes in concepts' meanings across such uses, at least for every concept.
(In the case of a supposed single concept, that might well point to us having different
concepts to cope with.) Instead, we can talk of there being a common root, and rock-
solid commonality, and other such things. Philosophers are important because they can
point out this fact and map the ways in which different concepts work and their implications, as well as pointing out mistakes that fellow philosophers have made.

Again, this is not to argue for Ryle's view; it is merely to understand it. To aid our
understanding, here is a third idea that I, for one, like to join to what Ryle says. Consider
the distinction popular in political and legal philosophy between concepts and conceptions.[26] Consider the following explanatory example. Two people, John and Robert,
both know and agree in general what the concepts JUSTICE, JUST, and DISTRIBUTIVE JUS-
TICE refer to. That is, they agree about these related concepts and agree to what they can
plausibly be applied to. They apply to distributions of resources or effort or similar things.
In standard cases they simply do not apply to the distribution of planets in a galaxy nor
to chairs *simpliciter*. Indeed, because we have such a measure of agreement, then we can
say that John and Robert meaningfully disagree when it comes to particular examples
of possible just things, such as when they are evaluating various taxation proposals. They
have different conceptions of JUST, even though they operate with the same concept. In
other words, their application and extension of the concept JUST differs. Indeed, in this
sort of case we should note that there is little or no overlap between their applications of
the concept. What ties them in agreement about the concept is based on the (many)
sorts of case they would regard as things that simply cannot be described as just by
mature users of the concept.

I find it appealing to extend Ryle's thoughts by including this distinction. John appre-
ciates what JUST is only through his applications and withholdings of JUST in various
cases, and further can gain insight by thinking about how opponents such as Robert
apply the concept and for what reasons. However, despite the different conceptions, this
does not mean to say that we cannot formulate some general idea of what JUST is and

---

[26] The distinction is given voice by H. L. A. Hart in his (1961/1994), 155–9. See also Dworkin (1972) and
(2011), chapter 8, Lukes (1974), and Rawls (1971), 5, the last of whom arguably made the idea famous.
Other writers in this volume reference this idea.

the sorts of thing it applies to. We will even be able to form a first-stab dictionary definition of what 'just' means.

Now think about thin and thick descriptions. (And, for simplicity's sake, put out of your mind any disagreement scenarios.) We can get some sense of what THINKING is and to what is applies. But, that is achieved only through particular instances that are classed as ones of thinking, such as meditations and public arguments. It might well be that with some thin descriptions (although perhaps not all) one can develop different conceptions, even if one has a general sense of what the concept stands for. It is then a further question, the thing that Ryle wishes to push, that in most or even all cases there is no way of separating the thin description—THINKING—from (supposed) other aspects of related thicker descriptions, descriptions such as MEDITATION. Or, to return to our first example, even though we can describe many of our boys as winking, that does not mean we are committed to the idea that there has to be a specific, isolatable activity that is the very same thing and which stands at the core of their actions. Even though four of Ryle's boys are winkers, they wink in different ways. And we understand what winking is by understanding the different ways of winking.

Having summarized Ryle, we can think about the idea that may tempt: that thick concepts are a type of thick description.

4.3 Thick concepts and thick descriptions

So: both thick descriptions and thick concepts (or, the terms that indicate them) are thought of as being specific, or at least more specific than other descriptions/concepts with which they are contrasted. And, there seems no reason to think that Ryle would not have allowed some of the examples regularly touted as being thick concepts to be characterized as thick descriptions. (He does not say anywhere that such things cannot be used by speakers to guide action or express evaluations.) What would be involved in the claim that thick concepts are a type of thick description? First, it strongly implies that there are thick descriptions that are not thick concepts. Secondly, the difference between the two types of thick description comes down to this: one type is involved in praise, blame, the guidance of action, and the expression of evaluations (where 'evaluations' is here used narrowly and not as a general synonym for 'judgements'), whilst the other is not. As typically understood, concepts such as GOODNESS, RIGHTNESS, HONESTY, and EVIL (typically) imply or encapsulate a preference for or attachment to something (or aversion to something) and where, in the case of thick concepts, they also describe in some specific way the thing under consideration. In contrast when thinkers are described as meditating, of weighing up the pros and cons, the ideas of praise, blame, and other sort of pro and con evaluations do not spring readily to mind. Given all of that, it should be easy to see why thick concepts might be thought to be a type of thick description. Indeed, I do not think the idea of thick concepts being a type of thick description is silly and false. But, I do think there is more to the matter than this, as we saw with Williams's slogan. In short:

I think that *many* sorts of specific words can be used to evaluate and guide action, not just the well-worn examples familiar from the literature on thick concepts that are overtly pro and con evaluations. There will be differences, some pronounced, between various concepts in terms of how they are evaluative. And, some concepts may not be, as I will term it, 'essentially evaluative': when they are used for evaluative purposes and guide action this is only because of the tone of voice in which the relevant terms are expressed, the context in which they appear, and other such things. But, nevertheless, 'evaluative content' might cover more cases than one might at first think. Although it may be true to think that there are thick descriptions that are thick concepts and thick descriptions that are not, the former camp may extend fairly widely.

Let me first diagnose what is going on in *ELP*. Recall that Ryle thinks that there are success-and-failure conditions for concepts, and that the applications and withholdings of concepts, via some process of abstraction, presumably, will tell us what the concepts are and what their contours are. I added to this with the distinction between concepts and conceptions. My diagnosis of the failure of Williams's slogan, in light of what we learn from Ryle, is that it pays too much attention to how an ethical concept may be used on some occasions, and not enough attention to how the same concept can be used on other occasions, and how other similar concepts can also be used. In short, I think that Williams's appreciation of the success-and-failure conditions for thick concepts is far too narrow, at least in his official characterization. So, certainly a concept such as HONEST can be used to guide action directly. But, it can also be used to guide actions indirectly, and it can be used to evaluate, praise, express relief, voice hope, and many more things with no thought of future action. It can be used of people, of actions, of institutions. It can indicate a narrow judgement about a particular piece of language. It can be used of a document and what is said between the lines. It can also be used of the intentions of speakers and writers, and of their wider spirit of personality. Despite all of these various uses, we typically are able to get a handle on the concept through some process of abstraction, even if people will have different conceptions of that concept.

So: we can conclude here that a characterization of thin and thick concepts should use terms such as 'evaluative' or 'normative conceptual content' quite broadly. 'Action-guidingness' seems too narrow.

Now let me broaden things out. I think there is a tempting view before us, and one that should tempt those that follow Williams in spirit. How should we treat other examples? Consider these (likely) thick descriptions: MEDITATION, MANAGEABLE, TURN, PITHY, CONTORTED, INDUSTRIOUS, and TIDY.[27] Can they be used to guide action? Can they be used to indicate some preference or aversion? Surely all can. A religious teacher can praise a pupil who has finally succeeded in meditating: she has been trying for ages to get him to think correctly. Different sorts of teaching load can be advocated

---

[27] TURN appears as an example in Dancy (this volume). INDUSTRIOUSNESS and TIDY are discussed by a number of writers, but they enter our batch of examples with Hare (1952), 121.

as manageable. You may be prevented from doing something because it is not your turn. Comments can be held up as exemplary because they are pithy. Poems and dancers can be damned for being contorted, but they can also be admired for the same reason. And, as will be familiar to those knowledgeable of the literature on the thick, we can praise and condemn people at various times for being industrious and tidy.

Right away let me add an important qualification: I am not arguing that MEDITATION, say, as it is typically understood, is evaluative in the same way as, say, HONESTY is thought to be. The latter supposedly wears its pro evaluation on its sleeve. Even when people are blamed for being 'too honest' the qualifier, and possible tone of voice, are essential in converting pro to a con or overriding it. (Or some similar explanation.) Furthermore, the examples in the previous paragraph are not on their own supposed to show that there has to be something essentially evaluative about these concepts. For all I know, such matters could be signalled by the use of some of these concepts by context and tone of voice alone. But, I also think it would be wrong to think of MEDITATION as being completely different from more familiar thick concepts. Although I am wary of going straight to dictionaries, some of the OED's definitions are instructive: first of all we have 'to consider thoughtfully', and 'to consider deeply', and later on 'serious continuous contemplation'. It is not obvious to me that these ideas are nonevaluative. All three are suggestive of some positive idea. Of course, we can often use MEDITATION and not imply any sort of positive view: when asked, 'What are those monks doing over there?', we can simply report, 'They're meditating'. We can say similar things about CONTORTION: the idea here is of something that is uncomfortable, strenuous, and unusual. These words are not neutral: they have strong negative associations. But, they have positive ones also: sometimes it is good to make oneself uncomfortable, both physically and mentally, and I am all for strenuous activity at times. Lastly, one can note that an object such as a statue is contorted and be offering some nonevaluative description alone.[28]

So what? The evaluative nature of MEDITATION is more complex than we are used to when thinking about our (limited) diet of thick concepts: it is not always used evaluatively, and it need not always be used positively perhaps. Sometimes when it is used

---

[28] I realize that one sort of opponent will wish to keep firmly apart two words when it comes to concepts: content and function. What the concept's content (or meaning) is, is quite different from how it is used. Some people will hold this for all thick and other concepts. I have no problem with this idea when it comes to certain concepts. I may exclaim 'Tea!' in a positive fashion when at last someone brings me the cuppa I have been asking for following a succession of unwanted cups of coffee. I am not arguing for the crazy view that an essential (if infrequently activated) part of the concept TEA is some positive evaluation and that this is partly an action-guiding notion. What goes on here has all to do with the tone of voice and context and, as I treat them, these are matters that lie outside of the concept itself. (Further, it seems my exclamation is functioning as a quick way of saying, 'I am glad you have brought me tea at last'.) We would not wish to conclude from this case alone that positive evaluations have to be built into TEA. Indeed, my invocation of the concept-conception distinction is supposed to pacify slightly those that do wish to keep content and function completely separate. The various uses and functions of a concept help us to see what things the concept can be legitimately applied to, and when and where. From those occasions we can form a general idea of what the concept is, even if disputants might then disagree amongst themselves about how precisely it should be applied and withheld. Odd cases involving tone of voice and so on can be treated as odd cases for these reasons.

evaluatively, this is transmitted because of tone of voice or context. At other times, I think that the concept itself, because of what it is, conveys evaluation. My claim is that many concepts work like this. Without this insight they would be mistakenly classed as (mere) thick descriptions because our notion of a thick concept is limited.

This idea connects nicely with two points that have previously been raised in relation to thick concepts. First, Simon Blackburn, for example, argues that a strength of his account is that it can explain how thick concepts can be used with different (thin) evaluations attached, whereas the nonseparationist is committed to only one evaluation.[29] Jonathan Dancy has argued that a nonseparationist need not be so committed: whoever said that the evaluative aspect that mixes with the descriptive has to be only one thing or, far better, whoever said that the resulting content as characterized by a nonseparationist has to have only either pro or con mixed in?[30] We could have a concept that in some contexts is pro, and in other contexts is con, and this variation be something that is essential to its nature, revealed because of the context it is in. Allowing for this variation is consistent with some evaluative concepts being primarily or wholly pro or con.

Secondly, it may help give sense to the idea that I have sometimes heard, namely that we have 'thickness all the way down'. We may be familiar with the idea that thick concepts—those that have strikingly clear sorts of pro and con evaluations—can be interdefined with their various thick concept synonyms. But, we may also have thick concepts that cannot but be captured without resort to thick descriptions, some of which may not be totally evaluative-free. HONESTY may be defined (or partly defined) as 'providing information to others in a way that allows them to know or achieve what one thinks they wish to know or achieve'. The concept of ALLOW is not obviously pro or con. But, if TURN is treated as a thick description which has the possibility of action-guidance as part of its essential meaning, and hence is a thick concept of a sort, then we should treat ALLOW in a similar fashion. There may be no way of articulating many of our thick concepts without relying on other concepts that are evaluative in some way, even if they do not show their pro and con evaluations clearly and even if there may be times when they are not obviously either pro or con.

These two points open up another idea I hold to. I express it here only and leave arguing for it to another time. As well arguing for the variation of pro and con, Dancy argues that there may be some evaluation that is not obviously one thing or another. He is right, in my view. We should see that evaluative content itself can come in more varieties than pro and con, or even 'pro-in-a-way' and 'con-in-a-way'. Pro and con are clearly important evaluations, but they need not be the only thing that matters. We are so used to thinking in this way, I reckon, because of the concentration on ethical concepts and their relation to action and choice. In the case of ethics it is readily important that through dint of circumstance we have to go one way or another, and

---

[29] See Blackburn (1992).   [30] See Dancy (1995).

express a simple preference (even if it is a preference in a sort of a way). But, as we saw when thinking about Williams, aesthetic concepts may not be like that at all. When we use MACABRE of a story, say, we can indicate pro and con ideas, such as praise or worry. And, we can imply other ideas that themselves may be either wholly pro or wholly con, or also fluctuate in this respect: intrigue and fright come to mind. But, beyond that, perhaps we just wish to say that the story is macabre and this itself be an evaluation that is neither obviously pro nor obviously con, and that is, additionally, not just a recording of some nonevaluative descriptive aspect of the story. I see no reason to think that lots of thick concepts, including ethical ones, cannot or do not work in the same way.

If proved, this thought challenges separationism head-on. Separationists come in different varieties. Hare and Blackburn both believe, roughly, that there is some specific descriptive content to which a thin evaluation is added, whereas other separationists offer more complex accounts where the descriptive content does not come fully specified.[31] But, separationists typically assume that the evaluative content that is added to the descriptive is still pro or con, obviously so since separationists wish to argue that thick concepts can always be separated.[32] This, I believe, is a blind spot in the debate: commentators of all persuasions are so used to framing the debate in terms of 'evaluative and descriptive content' (or similar) that they fail to realize that the key aim of nonseparationism is to get us to see that evaluation can come in varieties. (That is surely the point of all the literature on 'disentangling' and 'shapelessness': even if these ideas are true, they are not ultimate ends in themselves to argue for.) If all that nonseparationists do is play around with the same materials—descriptive content of some specificity and some thin evaluation—in order to argue that the two are 'irreducibly entwined', then they may never win over neutrals, let alone turn separationists.

As mentioned, these end comments are really a promissory note: I realize that far more needs to be said about our range of thick concepts, about the idea of what evaluation is that is different from a mere (bland) judgement but which is also not pro or con in any way, and about what it is for something to be a concept.[33] All I do here is point out: (i) the plausibility of challenging the idea that there must be a narrowly construed one-size-fits-all characterization, such as Williams's slogan, that applies equally to all thick concepts, and (ii) that evaluative content could extend beyond pro and con. I think we should allow for more shades of grey than are typically included in debates about the thick.

---

[31] See Elstein and Hurka (2009).

[32] Gibbard (1992) probably stands out here, since at least part of his analysis of (his chief example) LEWD is 'L-censoriousness', which is a feeling that accompanies every case but which is separable. I have much to say about this but here I merely point out that (i) this specific attitude will not satisfy if one thinks a range of attitude will be forthcoming when it comes to many thick concepts (this is Blackburn's main worry), and (ii) it is not obvious that we have attitudes such that they can uniquely pick out all the concepts we want them to pick out and that such attitudes are prior to the things they supposedly attach to.

[33] I take up this challenge in chapter 6 of Kirchin (ms).

4.4 Conclusion

My first main target was Williams's official slogan. Williams's himself says many sensible things, although I think that he summarizes what he says misleadingly, and he fails to see and emphasize sufficiently other points. Thinking about Ryle and thick descriptions helps us to diagnose the failings of Williams's official characterization. It also helps open up the debate: we can see that there are many sorts of thick concept. I have ended with a sketch of an idea: that evaluative content itself may well extend beyond pro and con, and even beyond pro-in-a-way and con-in-a-way. Concentration on these ideas may help us to make further progress on understanding the thick, and the thin.[34]

References

Blackburn, Simon (1992) 'Morality and Thick Concepts: Through Thick and Thin', *Proceedings of the Aristotelian Society, Supplementary Volume* 66: 285–99.

Dancy, Jonathan (1995) 'In Defense of Thick Concepts', in Peter A. French, Theodore E. Uehling, and Howard K. Wettstein (eds.) *Midwest Studies in Philosophy* XX: 263–79.

—— (this volume) 'Practical Concepts'.

Dworkin, Ronald (1972) 'The Jurisprudence of Richard Nixon', *The New York Review of Books* 18: 27–35.

—— (2011) *Justice for Hedgehogs* (Cambridge, MA: Harvard University Press).

Elstein, Daniel and Thomas Hurka (2009) 'From Thin to Thick: Two Moral Reductionist Plans', *Canadian Journal of Philosophy* 39: 515–35.

Gibbard, Allan (1992) 'Morality and Thick Concepts: Thick Concepts and Warrant for Feelings', *Proceedings of the Aristotelian Society, Supplementary Volume* 66: 267–83.

Hare, R. M. (1952) *The Language of Morals* (Oxford: Clarendon Press).

Hart, H. L. A. (1961/1994) *The Concept of Law* (Oxford: Clarendon Press).

Kirchin, Simon (ms) *Thick Evaluation*.

Lukes, Steven (1974) *Power: A Radical View* (London: Macmillan).

Rawls, John (1971) *A Theory of Justice* (Cambridge, MA: Harvard University Press).

Ryle, Gilbert (1966–7) 'Thinking and Reflecting', in 'The Human Agent', *Royal Institute of Philosophy Lectures*, i (London: Macmillan). Reprinted in his *Collected Essays 1929–1968*, ed. Julia Tanney (London: Routledge, 2009), 479–93. [Page references to the Tanney collection.]

—— (1968) 'The Thinking of Thoughts: What Is 'Le Penseur' Doing?' University Lectures, 18, University of Saskatchewan. Reprinted in his *Collected Essays 1929–1968*, ed. Julia Tanney (London: Routledge, 2009), 494–510. [Page references to the Tanney collection.]

Tanney, Julia (2009) 'Foreword' in Gilbert Ryle, *Collected Essays 1929–1968*, ed. Julia Tanney (London: Routledge), vii–xix.

—— (2010) 'Gilbert Ryle', *The Stanford Encyclopedia of Philosophy* (Winter 2009 Edition), Edward N. Zalta, (ed.) [online] <http://plato.stanford.edu/entries/ryle/> accessed 28 November 2012.

[34] Thanks to Tim Chappell, Miranda Fricker, Adrian Moore, Debbie Roberts, Julia Tanney, Pekka Väyrynen, and an anonymous referee for comments on an earlier version of this paper.

Tappolet, Christine (2004) 'Through Thick and Thin: *Good* and its Determinates', *dialectica* 58: 207–21.

Williams, Bernard (1985) *Ethics and the Limits of Philosophy* (London: Fontana).

—— (1993) *Shame and Necessity* (Berkeley, LA: University of California Press).

—— (1996) 'Truth in Ethics', in Brad Hooker, (ed.) *Truth in Ethics* (Oxford: Blackwell), 19–34.

—— (2002) *Truth and Truthfulness* (New Jersey: Princeton University Press).

Zangwill, Nick (this volume) 'Moral Metaphor and Thick Concepts: What Moral Philosophy Can Learn from Aesthetics'.

5

It's Evaluation, Only Thicker

Debbie Roberts

The correct picture, I think, as I will try to explain later, is not that there are two 'really' distinct elements which by pseudo chemical reaction somehow become indistinguishable from each other. There are no elements at all, in any normal sense.[1]

5.1 Introduction

Are thick concepts evaluative? More precisely, are thick concepts such as GENEROUS, GAUCHE, GRACEFUL and GAUDY evaluative *in the same way* that thin concepts like GOOD and BAD are evaluative?

Orthodoxy has it that evaluation must be positive or negative; it must have a *pro* or *con* flavour. This translates naturally into the thought that any evaluation, to be evaluation, must have a thin evaluative element. If you evaluate something you must, the thought goes, be evaluating it as good in some respect or to some extent, or bad in some respect or to some extent. According to the orthodoxy then, to be evaluative, thick concepts must have a link to thin evaluation.

It is commonly assumed that thick concepts are evaluative, and that they are evaluative in the same way that thin evaluative concepts are. That is, it is commonly assumed that thick concepts have evaluative *content* that is asserted in utterances employing the terms that express these concepts, and that the evaluative nature of thick terms is a matter of their sense and reference.[2] What marks the thick out from the thin, on this story, is that whereas thin concepts have *only* evaluative content, the content of thick concepts can be characterized as a *combination* of evaluative and non-evaluative

---

[1] Dancy (1995), 268.
[2] It is also commonly assumed in the literature on the thick that semantic content and conceptual content match up. This assumption is hardly innocent and an important question to address is whether this is the case. I don't address this question here though.

content.[3, 4] Traditionally, then, the view has been that the link to thin evaluation that makes thick concepts evaluative is provided by the evaluative element of their content.

But the assumption that thick concepts have evaluative content at all has been challenged.[5] There are, after all, other ways that a link to thin evaluation could obtain, besides semantically or conceptually. Those who challenge the Content view argue that the evaluations that thick terms can be used to convey (or the evaluations 'most closely associated' with thick terms) are located not in what is strictly *said* in an utterance employing a thick term but in some other aspect of what is communicated.[6] They defend a pragmatic account of the evaluative nature of the thick.

As things stand, if we were to map out the possible positions on the evaluative nature of the thick the first item to set down would be the orthodox view of evaluation applied to the thick: that the evaluative nature of thick terms and concepts can be characterized as 'good (bad) in some way' or 'positively (negatively) evaluable in some respect'.[7] After this, the divide would be between Content views on the one hand and Pragmatic views on the other, since they disagree about where the evaluative elements is to be found—in the content of the concept, or elsewhere.

The aim of this paper is to argue that this map needs to be redrawn to leave space for a third alternative, which I term the 'Inclusive' view. The motivation for introducing this view is the thought that we should not let our taxonomy rule out possible views before they have been properly investigated.

For many of the examples of concepts standardly held to be thick (for example GAUCHE, GRACEFUL, GAUDY, DAINTY, LEWD, RAUCOUS, SUBTLE, TACKY, and CRUDE) a plausible case can be made that they do not encode particular thin evaluations in their content. This suggests that the question of whether some behaviour is raucous (or lewd, tacky, or crude) is a separate question from whether that behaviour is in that respect good to some extent or bad to some extent; to be approved of or disapproved of. Moreover, some have argued that thick virtue and vice concepts like INTEGRITY, GENEROUS, KIND, and CRUEL do not encode any

---

[3] I have simplified things slightly here. Thin concepts are usually characterized as having only *or mostly* evaluative content, usually to signal that the difference between thick and thin concepts may be one of degree rather than kind.

[4] I should make clear that I mean the traditional, content view that I am describing here to encompass both 'disentangling' and 'anti-disentangling' accounts of the thick. Anti-disentanglers typically accept that the evaluative nature of the thick is at least partially given by the pro (con) flavour of the content. They just think that this evaluative element of the content of the concept cannot be separated out in analysis from the non-evaluative element. This is how disentanglers tend to represent the anti-disentangling view; see Blackburn (1992) and Elstein and Hurka (2009). This seems to me to be a fair characterization of the accounts found in Williams (1985), Putnam (2002), Taylor (2003), and Wiggins (1998), as well as that expressed in Harcourt and Thomas (this volume). It is less clear what McDowell's view is, and Dancy explicitly rejects this sort of characterization.

[5] Notably by Blackburn (1992) and (1998), Väyrynen (2012), and Eklund (2011).

[6] See Väyrynen (2012), 4. Both Blackburn and Väyrynen concentrate their accounts on (so-called) thick *terms*. For their conclusions to be true of thick concepts, the assumption discussed in n. 2 would have to be true.

[7] See Väyrynen (2012), 4.

particular thin evaluation in their content either, and that the terms expressing such concepts may even in some cases be used in a neutrally descriptive way.[8] Even if we accept these arguments, as with the prior set of examples we might nonetheless be reluctant to hold that these concepts are not inherently evaluative. We might be reluctant to hold, that is, that such concepts are not themselves evaluative as a matter of sense and reference.

Such reluctance may or may not be justified. This paper explores the possibility that it is justified by making space for an alternative, third category in the taxonomy of accounts of the evaluative nature of the thick. This alternative rejects the orthodoxy that to be evaluative as a matter of content a concept must have thin evaluative content. It can be summed up as the claim that thick concepts have only a single 'element', if it makes sense to talk of elements at all, and that that element is evaluative.

I suspect, given the ubiquity of the orthodox view of evaluation, that this alternative will be difficult to see. Accordingly, I will start in section 5.2 in by setting out some of the main features of the position and by sketching in some background intended to bring it into relief. One of these main features is that the view is committed to a non-reductive (Content) account of thick concepts (I explain this below). Such accounts usually employ John McDowell's disentangling argument in their defence. I argue that we need to be careful to distinguish two separate 'disentangling arguments' found in McDowell's work and put to service in the literature on the thick. Once these two are separated out, it can be seen that the non-reductivist *need not* adopt the orthodox view of evaluation. The Inclusive view offers an alternative account of what it is for a concept to be evaluative; this is that a concept is evaluative in virtue of ascribing an evaluative property. In section 5.3 I deal with initial objections to this claim. In section 5.4 I discuss certain features, including essential contestability, which paradigmatic evaluative concepts exhibit. These features are not what *make* these concepts evaluative but they do, I argue, set constraints for an account of evaluative properties. Section 5.5 sketches one possible such account which allows that paradigmatic thick properties are evaluative just as much as thin evaluative properties are. We should conclude, then, that the Inclusive view is a live alternative to both Content and Pragmatic accounts of the thick.

My aim here is merely to make a case for the Inclusive view being a live option and to show the form it can take.[9] I do not defend it here. But I take it if I am successful in showing that it is a live option, then this will be of significance for the debate about the thick.

---

[8] See for example Blackburn (1992), 286–7, Dancy (1995), §V and (2004), 121, Swanton (2001) and (2003), 48. This point raises the question about the relation between semantic and conceptual content. Again, see n. 2.

[9] It is useful to say something here about what the scope of the account is intended to be. I do not claim, at the outset, that the account will accommodate every term that has been put forward as an example of a thick term. As others have pointed out, it may be that there is no one-size-fits-all account that accommodates all these terms. The Inclusive view makes claims about what a concept must be like to count as a genuinely thick concept. While I think a case can be made that this account fits certain concepts that are cited as paradigm examples of the thick, there may be others that it does not fit and thus these others will not count as thick on this view. (Perhaps more interestingly, the account may label as thick certain concepts that have not typically been cited as examples of thick concepts. Whether it is plausible to think of these concepts as thick will depend on whether it is plausible to think of them as evaluative.)

5.2 Disentangling two disentangling arguments

The Inclusive view includes elements of both the Content and the Pragmatic views. From the former, the Inclusive view takes the claim that thick concepts are evaluative as a matter of content, and from the latter the claim that there is no element of thin evaluation in the content of thick terms or concepts.

On the Inclusive view, *evaluation drives the extension* of thick terms. This is the idea that the extension of a thick term cannot be determined without making some evaluations, for to know the extension of a thick term, one has to appreciate its evaluative point.[10] That evaluation drives extension for thick terms can be explained, on the Inclusive view, by the fact that thick evaluative concepts and properties are *non-evaluatively shapeless*.[11] Evaluative concepts and properties are non-evaluatively shapeless if the *real similarity* across cases of the concept's correct application, or instantiations of the property, is evaluative, not non-evaluative.

The Inclusive view is a non-reductivist, Content view of the thick.[12] Non-reductivists are sometimes characterized as holding that the evaluative and non-evaluative elements that make up thick conceptual content cannot be 'disentangled' in analysis.[13] But, according to the Inclusive view, this characterization is faulty from the beginning: it is true that one cannot analytically reduce a thick concept to a thin evaluative component (or components) and a non-evaluative component, but this does not license the assumption that these *two* kinds of element are nonetheless somehow *initial* ingredients in an indissoluble amalgam that is thick conceptual content.

However, once we make that assumption, it is difficult to see how the evaluative nature of the thick could be given by anything other than a thin evaluative element (or elements), regardless of whether that element can be separated out by analysis or not.[14] Something that contributes to the pressure to hold that non-reductivists must claim that two sorts of elements are *combined* in thick conceptual content is a combination of two distinct 'disentangling' arguments found in McDowell's work. These two arguments are not carefully distinguished in the literature on the thick.[15] However, once

[10] See for example Williams's influential discussion in Williams (1985), 140–2. This claim is widely regarded as plausible. By itself, however, it is not sufficient for a non-reductive account of thick concepts. See Elstein and Hurka (2009) and Roberts (2011).

[11] The notion of non-evaluative shapelessness figures widely in the metaethical literature. For a recent discussion see Kirchin (2010).

[12] Elstein and Hurka (2009) introduce the reductive/non-reductive terminology to this debate. A reductive view holds that thick conceptual content can be analytically reduced to some combination of thin evaluative and non-evaluative content. A non-reductive view denies this is possible.

[13] For example, Blackburn (1992), 298–9.

[14] As Elstein and Hurka (2009) suggest with their second pattern of analysis for thick terms, there could be more than one thin evaluative element. For simplicity's sake I mostly phrase things such that it seems that the characterization I am objecting to has it that only one thin element is present in thick content, but nothing hangs on this.

[15] In the literature, reference is made to McDowell's point against disentangling, or the disentangling argument. Sometimes this is cited as appearing in McDowell (1978) and (1979), for example in Williams (1985), 141 n. 7, and sometimes it is cited as appearing in McDowell (1981), for example in Elstein and Hurka (2009), 519 n. 7. Sometimes it is cited as appearing in both, for example, Putnam (2002), 38. I argue that the disentangling argument in the two former articles is distinct from the one in the latter.

they are, we can see that the non-reductive view need not be construed as the claim that two elements, thin evaluative and non-evaluative content, are inextricably entangled in the content of thick concepts.[16]

'The Disentangling Argument', as it is referred to in the literature on the thick, is supposed to be what the non-reductivist takes to show that the evaluative and non-evaluative elements that make up thick conceptual content cannot be 'disentangled' in analysis. I will label this the 'indissoluble amalgam of two elements' conclusion. Of the two disentangling arguments both found in McDowell's work and referred to in the literature on the thick, neither supports (nor even purports to support) the 'indissoluble amalgam of two elements' conclusion. But the combination of these two arguments might be taken to support this conclusion. It is helpful to note that McDowell accepts a distinction between *evaluations* and *directives or deliberative (or practical) judgments*.[17] On the face of it, evaluations may have some link with action, but if they do it is not a direct and straightforward link. The latter have a direct and straightforward link with action. They are all things considered judgments about what one ought to do/must do/would be best to do in a particular case.

The first set of anti-disentangling remarks can be found in McDowell's 'Are Moral Requirements Hypothetical Imperatives?' and 'Virtue and Reason'.[18] These anti-disentangling remarks concern *directives*. McDowell is concerned to elucidate the nature of moral requirements through an examination of the state of mind and motivations of the virtuous person. The first kind of entanglement is the entanglement, according to McDowell, *in a virtuous person's conception of her situation* of cognition and will.

According to this first disentangling argument, these elements cannot be separated out into a neutral conception of the facts on the one hand and an independently intelligible desire on the other. The virtuous person's conception of the circumstances, according to McDowell, thus cannot be shared by someone who sees no requirement to act as the virtuous person does.

Importantly, this argument concerns directives and *not* evaluations, and the entanglement of cognition and will, as I have said. It thus does not by itself license the 'indissoluble amalgam of two elements' conclusion. For that conclusion is a conclusion about *evaluations* and the entanglement of evaluative and non-evaluative elements of *content* in one kind of evaluation, that is, thick evaluation.

---

[16] Those who defend *reductive* Content views are required to adopt the orthodox view of evaluation, and it would seem that defenders of the Pragmatic view are as well. I have argued elsewhere that the non-reductivist *cannot* adopt the orthodox view of evaluation and remain a non-reductivist in the relevant sense (that is, someone who holds that the content of a thick concept cannot be analytically reduced to some combination of thin evaluative and non-evaluative content). See Roberts (2011).

[17] McDowell (1985), 110 n. 4. The distinction comes from Wiggins (1998), 95–6. It does not obviously correspond to a distinction between the evaluative and the deontic, but nor is it straightforwardly the same as the distinction between the contributory and the overall. The category of evaluations is supposed to include both the thin and the thick, at least this is so working from the examples given. But neither McDowell nor Wiggins uses the thick/thin terminology.

[18] McDowell (1978) and (1979).

The second set of anti-disentangling remarks does concern evaluations rather than directives. In addition, the focus of these remarks is not restricted to the *virtuous* person's conception of the situation. This argument is to be found in McDowell's 'Non-Cognitivism and Rule-Following'.[19] But this set of anti-disentangling remarks does not license the indissoluble amalgam of elements conclusion either.

McDowell's aim here is to undermine the plausibility of holding that value experience involves two separable elements: detection of a non-evaluative property in the world, on the one hand, and an evaluative response to that property, on the other. McDowell argues that because it is plausible to think that evaluative concepts and properties are non-evaluatively shapeless (in the sense specified above), it is reasonable to be sceptical that we can always separate out non-evaluative classifications corresponding to the evaluative classifications made by evaluative concepts. Instead, because of shapelessness, we should hold that one could not identify the extension of an evaluative concept without adopting the *relevant evaluative point of view*.[20]

Although McDowell's aim in this second disentangling argument is to argue that competence with an evaluative concept cannot be disentangled (into sensitivity to a non-evaluative feature of the world on the one hand, and a propensity to a certain attitude on the other) his argument is not, or not merely, about the meaning of evaluative terms or the content of evaluative concepts. He takes the argument to undermine a view that he thinks R. M. Hare and J. L. Mackie both share, that to undermine the view that for any evaluative term there must be a corresponding non-evaluative classification. Hare's version of this view was that for any evaluative term there must be a corresponding value-neutral classification that is a part of the meaning of the evaluative term (the 'descriptive' meaning). But Mackie's view was that, whilst there must be such a non-evaluative classification, this is no part of the meaning of an evaluative term.[21]

The point of this disentangling argument is *not* that cognition and will are entangled. (McDowell does of course argue for this further claim, but elsewhere and independently.) The point here is that *evaluative properties are genuine features of the world* just as much as non-evaluative properties are. This second disentangling argument thus does not support the 'indissoluble amalgam of two elements conclusion' either. If this disentangling argument supports any entanglement thesis, it is that fact and value are entangled. But this is an unhelpful slogan. The argument does not purport to establish that two things are entangled. Rather, it purports to show that one kind (the evaluative) that we started off assuming did not also belong another kind (the factual), is indeed of that kind.

---

[19] McDowell (1981).

[20] Despite the fact that this is often taken to be an argument particularly about thick concepts, McDowell does not make the thick/thin distinction. This set of anti-disentangling remarks is meant to hold equally for both thick and thin evaluations. It should be noted that McDowell phrases things more cautiously than I have here.

[21] McDowell (1981), 143–6, especially notes 4, 5, 7, 8, and 10.

These two disentangling arguments are combined if we assume that McDowell means the same thing by 'the virtuous person's conception of the situation' and 'the evaluative point of view required for competence with an evaluative concept'. To illustrate this, consider McDowell's example of someone who does not really know what it means for someone to be shy and sensitive:

In urging behaviour one takes to be morally *required*, one finds oneself saying things like this: 'You don't know what it means that someone is shy and sensitive'. Conveying what a circumstance means, in this loaded sense, is getting someone to see it in the special way in which a *virtuous* person would see it....Failure to see what a circumstance means, in the loaded sense, is of course *compatible with competence*, by all ordinary tests, with the language used to describe the circumstance.[22]

According to McDowell, the virtuous person's conception of the situation when she recognizes a moral requirement includes her will being influenced in a certain way. That is, it includes 'seeing' the action as to be done or not to be done where part of that 'seeing' is achieved by her will being influenced in a certain way. It is natural to think that the virtuous person has either a pro or con attitude to the action. The virtuous person's conception of the situation when she recognizes a moral requirement thus contains a thin evaluation. The bully who teases the shy and sensitive individual doesn't see this moral requirement, for he does not share the virtuous person's conception of the situation, and so does not have the (morally) correct pro and con attitudes to the situation.

If we do not distinguish between 'the virtuous person's conception of the situation' and 'the evaluative point of view required in order to be able to discern whether or not an evaluative concept applies', then it looks like the evaluative point of view required in order to be able to discern whether or not an evaluative concept applies must also contain a particular thin evaluation. And so, if the bully describes her actions as good-for-being-cruel, we are led to say of her that she is not competent with the concept CRUEL because she fails to make the ethically correct thin evaluation. And this last looks like an implausible thing to say if it turns out, as is not difficult to imagine, that this bully is very adept at sorting the cruel from the not cruel, and is by all ordinary tests competent with CRUEL.

Thankfully, the non-reductivist does not have to say that the bully is not competent with CRUEL, (or SHY or SENSITIVE, for that matter). According to the Inclusive view, we

---

[22] McDowell (1978), 21–2 (my italics). For discussion, see for example Blackburn (1998), 92–104, and Gibbard (2003), 108–11. Blackburn structures his discussion of McDowell as if the purported entanglement of belief and desire in the virtuous person's conception of the situation is meant to plug a hole Blackburn finds in the rule-following argument. This is the gap Blackburn finds in the move from the claim that evaluation drives extension to the claim that this supports a genuine 'perception' or sensitivity to a property that has cognitive status. Blackburn is correct that there is this gap. But McDowell's argument is not structured like this; it is the shapelessness claim that is supposed to support both these things. Blackburn does not explicitly claim that the two arguments I have identified are the same, but he does talk of only one kind of disentangling/entanglement. (Blackburn recognizes that shapelessness is playing an important role in McDowell's argument, but says he can see no reason why, if shapelessness is the case, this supports there being a 'shapely' property.)

should not assume that 'the virtuous person's conception of the situation when she recognizes a moral requirement' should be equated with 'the evaluative point of view required to discern whether or not an evaluative concept applies'. It is very plausible that being competent with an evaluative concept, which on this view is a matter of discerning whether an evaluative property is present, is distinct from seeing that there is a *requirement* to act in a certain way.[23]

There is a question, then, even by McDowell's own lights, as to how we are to construe value experience that is not a matter of a virtuous person recognizing a requirement to act. However, whatever McDowell's own view is, the key point now is that the non-reductivist about the thick can accept the second disentangling argument without accepting the first.

This is the route that the Inclusive view takes. Given this, one need not accept that being competent with an evaluative concept involves one's *will* being influenced, in either a pro or con way. All one accepts, by accepting this second disentangling argument, is that evaluative concepts and properties are non-evaluatively shapeless, that evaluation thus drives extension for evaluative terms, and that evaluative properties are genuine features of the world.

Thus, on the Inclusive view competence with an evaluative concept does not *necessarily* involve making a thin evaluation.[24] Recognizing that an action is raucous (or lewd, tacky or crude) is a separate question from whether that behaviour is in that respect good to some extent or bad to some extent; to be approved or disapproved of. One can thus say that the bully from the case above is perfectly competent with the concept CRUEL for she is able to reliably identify which actions have the genuine evaluative feature of being cruel. This ability does not necessarily involve making a particular thin evaluation, for she, who has in general a pro-attitude to cruel actions, can reliably identify them just as well as us who in general have a con-attitude to such actions.[25]

This means that the Inclusive view can endorse arguments put forward by defenders of Pragmatic views of the thick, if the conclusions of these arguments are construed in a particular way: that there is no element of thin evaluation (separable or not) in the content of thick terms and concepts. These arguments point to data involving the use of thick terms concerning patterns of agreement and disagreement, objectionable thick terms, variability of the evaluative valence of thick terms, and the way in which building the thin element into the content of thick terms disables a certain kind of ethical criticism.[26]

---

[23] This will not be the case on McDowell's own view, at least for some evaluations, because McDowell accepts the doctrine of the unity of the virtues. But McDowell also seems to allow that non-virtuous people can be competent with evaluative concepts.

[24] It does, of course, if the concept in question is a thin evaluative concept, though she need not hold that making a thin evaluation is a matter of one's will being influenced.

[25] It does not necessarily involve making a thin evaluation, let along making a particular thin evaluation, if arguments about the variable evaluative valence of thick concepts show that these concepts can also have a neutral evaluative valence.

[26] See Blackburn (1992) and (1998), and Väyrynen (2009b), (2011), and (2012). I will not rehearse these arguments here, suffice to say that holders of the Inclusive view can accept them as convincing, if the conclusion is framed in the way shortly specified.

What the Inclusive view disputes and the Pragmatic view holds, is that these arguments signify that thick concepts are not themselves inherently evaluative. We now need to move on to the question of what, according to the Inclusive view, it is for a concept to be inherently evaluative.

5.3 What makes a concept evaluative?

The Inclusive view proposes that a concept is evaluative in virtue of ascribing an evaluative property. By itself, this is not a very satisfactory answer to the question of what makes a concept evaluative since we immediately confront the problem of what it is for a property to be evaluative.[27] It is, however, a good place to start. Two immediate objections must be confronted and replies to these objections, particularly the second, help to flesh out the proposal.

The first objection is that, according to the above proposal, on antirealist views there are no evaluative concepts. But this does not amount to a serious objection. Error theorists can be easily accommodated for, we need only add that the evaluative property that the evaluative concept purports to ascribe may not exist.[28]

Furthermore, expressivists can stomach talk of evaluative concepts and properties perfectly well.[29]

The second objection to the proposal comes from Matti Eklund.[30] He argues that the proposal can at most be a necessary condition for what it is for a concept to be evaluative, but it cannot be sufficient. Eklund conveys his objection using two thought-experiments. He asks us to imagine two different alien linguistic communities. In the first, the alien community introduces a word—'thgir' into their language that is stipulated to stand for the property that our 'right' stands for. But, says Eklund, this community does not in any way use 'thgir' evaluatively. He says:

> In this case 'thgir' stands for the same property as our 'right' does, a property which in fact is evaluative, but there is no reason to hold that the predicate is (positively) evaluative.[31]

In the second case, Eklund asks us to imagine that the alien community is a community of Martians hostile to humans. They too introduce 'thgir' into their language, and

---

[27] And the question of what it is to *ascribe* an evaluative property, as I point out below.

[28] Or they may exist, but be uninstantiated.

[29] However, if it should turn out that the Inclusive View is more at home within a certain kind of realist view, I do not think this should be seen as too damaging. After all, the proposal is put forward as a substantive view about what makes concepts evaluative, in opposition at least to the orthodox view discussed above. Given the ground that different metaethical positions are fighting over, it should not be surprising that a possible view of the nature of evaluation turns out to be parochial in some sense. Sturgeon (2009) makes a parallel point about different metaethical accounts of supervenience.

[30] Eklund (this volume). Although Eklund does not put the proposal in terms of ascription as I have, but in terms of an evaluative concept being evaluative in virtue of standing for an evaluative property. This difference is relevant to the upcoming discussion.

[31] Eklund (this volume), 164.

stipulate that it stands for the property that our right stands for, but they use 'thgir' to express a negative evaluation. If this is possible, he argues, then we should conclude that our concept RIGHT standing for the particular property it does is not sufficient to make RIGHT a positively evaluative concept. Moreover, he claims, if this can happen with 'right' it can happen with all other evaluative terms.

The first thing to say in response to these thought experiments is that Eklund clearly assumes the orthodox view of evaluation: on his view for a term, concept or property to be evaluative is for it to be positively or negatively evaluative. Given that I am questioning whether the orthodoxy is the only possible view of the nature of evaluation, an objection that assumes it is can legitimately be discounted for present purposes.

However, there is more that can be said in response to this second objection that will turn out to be helpful in setting out the Inclusive view. 'Right', we can say, is clearly an evaluative term, and we can assume that it is evaluative as a matter of content.[32] This much is not in question. But is it thus the case that the defender of the proposal that a concept is evaluative in virtue of ascribing an evaluative property is committed to holding that 'thgir' in each of the two alien communities is an evaluative term that ascribes an evaluative property? It seems to me that it is plausible to say that the aliens' term 'thgir' does not *ascribe* the property of rightness, but ascribes the property of being whatever our RIGHT ascribes. I am not suggesting that the property of rightness and the property of being whatever our right ascribes are not the same property. So there is a sense in which 'thgir' *stands for* the property of rightness. But these different ways of picking out the property are importantly different.

We can introduce a refinement to the initial proposal that a concept is evaluative in virtue of ascribing an evaluative property. This refinement is the claim that a concept is evaluative in virtue of directly ascribing an evaluative property. As I am conceiving of it a concept directly ascribes a property if (and only if) what it directly ascribes is the essence of that property. By 'directly ascribes the essence' of a property I mean that it directly ascribes what unifies the instances of property, or what constitutes the real similarity shared by all its instances.[33] A concept can *stand for* that essence—without directly ascribing it—if it latches on to the relevant property by one of its accidental, non-essential features.

Intuitively, by ascribing the property of being whatever our RIGHT ascribes, the alien communities are not directly ascribing the essence of rightness. This thought is made more plausible if we consider that the alien communities in the thought experiments above have to stipulate that their term 'thgir' is to pick out whatever our 'right' picks out. 'Thgir' is explicitly parasitic upon our predicate 'right' and the concept RIGHT it expresses. According to the Inclusive view, it would have to be. On this view, evaluation determines extension in the case of evaluative concepts, because evaluative concepts and properties are non-evaluatively shapeless. The real similarity that unifies different

---

[32] I'm here following Eklund's usage of 'evaluative' which encompasses normative terms in general.

[33] We could call this the 'real definition' of the property. See Wedgwood (2007), 139–41. I am here in agreement with Kit Fine's view, as is Wedgwood, that a modal definition of essence is incurably problematic. Instead, I follow Fine in understanding essence as real definition. See Fine (1994) and (1995).

instantiations of the property is evaluative. The aliens *could not* therefore introduce the term 'thgir' to stand for the property that our 'right' ascribes except parasitically. In other words, 'thgir' cannot directly ascribe the real similarity between different instances of rightness. It only pick outs this real similarity indirectly or derivatively. Hence, the property 'thgir' stands for is an evaluative property, but 'thgir' is not itself an evaluative predicate, and nor is THGIR an evaluative concept.

We need now to consider when it is correct to say that a concept directly ascribes an evaluative property, that is, under what conditions it is correct to say that the content of the concept represents the essence of the property directly or amounts to a real definition of the property. It is not plausible to say this in cases where the property picked out by a concept can be ontologically reduced. For example, what water *is* is H_2O; this is the essence, or real definition of water. Given plausible assumptions about the content of the concept WATER, this concept does not ascribe the property of H_2O.

However, evaluative properties, according to the Inclusive view, cannot be ontologically reduced. The Inclusive view is consistent with an ontological dependence thesis that states that evaluative properties depend on non-evaluative properties since this view is consistent with holding that the features that make actions right on a case-by-case basis are non-evaluative features. Because of shapelessness, however, it will not be the case that in any particular instance the non-evaluative features making an action right are the *property* of rightness. The defender of the Inclusive view is thus committed to denying that the long *disjunction* of all the non-evaluative features of different instances of rightness constitutes the property of rightness, and likewise for any evaluative property. And this is a perfectly respectable view of properties.[34]

If we follow Kit Fine in holding that the notion of one property (rightness, in this case) ontologically depending on other properties is the real counterpart to the nominal notion of one term being definable in terms of other terms, then we can say that on the Inclusive view the real definition of rightness (or of any evaluative property) cannot be given wholly in terms of non-evaluative properties.[35] And so, on this view, evaluative concepts ascribe evaluative properties since the content of the concept gives us the real definition of the property.

5.4 Marks of evaluative concepts

The next step in spelling out the view that thick concepts are inherently evaluative despite having no thin evaluation in their content, would seem to be to spell out what it is for a property (more specifically, the real definition of a property) to be evaluative.

---

[34] See for example Armstrong (1978), chapter 14, Majors (2005), Oddie (2005), chapter 6, and Suikkanen (2010). The claim here is that there is no type-identity in the case of evaluative properties and their non-evaluative realization bases. I argue below that there is no token-identity either.

[35] See Fine (1995), 275. As Wedgwood points out, a real definition need not be non-circular. Wedgwood (2007), 140.

The Inclusive view does not challenge a standard view of concepts and properties: that concepts are at the level of sense and properties at the level of reference. But in the case of evaluative concepts, as we saw in the previous section, the claim is that evaluative properties are exactly as evaluative concepts represent them as being, for the content of the concept tells us what the real definition of the property is. Investigating the nature of evaluative concepts, then, should tell us something about the nature of evaluative properties.

In this section I briefly outline a number of features, or marks, of evaluative concepts. The significance of these features will be discussed in more detail in section 5.5. I argue that, given what the Inclusive view holds about the relation between evaluative concepts and properties, these features operate as constraints on what can count as an adequate account of what makes a property evaluative.

Note that my claim is not that the features that I list in this section are what *make* a concept evaluative. What makes a concept evaluative is that it ascribes an evaluative property. In fact, I think the direction of explanation is the reverse: what *explains* the features that I discuss in this section is that the concepts in question are evaluative; it is their evaluative nature that gives rise to these features.

5.4.1 *Essential contestability*

A feature of paradigmatic evaluative concepts, such as GOOD, BAD, RIGHT, and WRONG, is that they are *essentially contestable*.[36] If a concept is evaluative, then it is essentially contestable.[37] There is not a great deal of literature on essential contestability, and the notion is neither well understood nor, perhaps, well labelled. In particular, it is not clear why or in what way such concepts are *essentially* contestable. For the most part, I am here merely appealing to the phenomenon which some have used this label to refer to, though some of what I say below may have a bearing on why it makes sense to use this label. But first, what is this phenomenon?

Concepts that are essentially contestable are concepts that *characteristically*, rather than just conceivably, admit of substantive disagreement.[38] With a conceivably contestable concept, under normal conditions there is no substantive disagreement or competing conceptions of the content of the concept. Conceivably, such disagreement may occur.[39] With essentially contestable concepts, such disagreement is characteristically present. Furthermore, disputes concerning an essentially contestable concept cannot be resolved by further empirical discovery or by legislating a solution, as disputes involving merely conceivably contestable concepts can.

---

[36] This notion was first introduced by Gallie (1955–6), although he wrote of essentially contes*ted* concepts.

[37] A concept being evaluative is sufficient for it being essentially contestable, though it may not be necessary: there may be non-evaluative concepts that are essentially contestable.

[38] See Hurley (1989), chapter 3, especially 46–50. According to Hurley, this is the defining feature of essentially contestable concepts.

[39] We might think that all concepts are conceivably contestable. Hurley (1989), chapter 3, argues that this is not so, and that there are some concepts (specific sensory concepts like RED for example) that if someone were to exhibit strange ways of going on in applying this concept, she would not share our concept of RED.

Given that essentially contestable concepts are concepts that characteristically admit of substantive disagreement, they are concepts that characteristically sustain competing conceptions of what the concept is a concept of. Where there is genuine essential contestability, there is a strong intuition that these are indeed competing conceptions of the same concept, and that rival users are not simply talking past each other. Think of the debate between Rawls and Nozick over DISTRIBUTIVE JUSTICE. It is typical, in the discussion of examples of essentially contested concepts, to note that the grounds upon which users apply the concept, which may be complex, typically admit of rival descriptions. Users recognize that their use can be contested, and are able to offer reasons for their use against others, which may include reasons for why their description of the grounds ought to be preferred.

It is sometimes said that with such concepts that what is essentially contestable is *what something has to be like* in order to merit the application of the concept.[40] I propose that this should be interpreted as the claim that what is essentially contestable in the case of essentially contestable concepts is whether a particular set of lower-level features give rise to the real similarity or essence of the property in question.

On the Inclusive view, what enables this essential contestability in the case of evaluative concepts is that no non-circular real definition of an evaluative property is available. It is thus never the case that a particular set of lower-level features necessarily gives rise to an evaluative property. I discuss this is more detail below.[41]

5.4.2 *Substantive disagreement*

Evaluative concepts characteristically admit of substantive disagreement. In particular, it seems possible that evaluative disagreement can persist even if the disputants agree on all relevant non-evaluative features present in a particular case.[42] That genuine evaluative disagreement can survive comprehensive agreement about the non-evaluative in this way is not surprising if evaluative concepts are essentially contestable in the way outlined above. For what is contestable is precisely whether the lower-level features here present give rise to the essence of the property in question.

5.4.3 *Open questions*

As Frank Jackson points out, the flip side of the intuition that genuine evaluative disagreement can survive comprehensive agreement about the non-evaluative is the intuition that drives the open question argument. This is the intuition that it is an open question whether, once all the non-evaluative information is in, whether something really is good (or whatever the evaluative property in question is). This, in turn, is closely related to the

---

[40] Wiggins (1998), 198, Dancy (1995), 266.

[41] In some cases, that essentially contestable concepts are contestable in this way gives rise to substantive disagreements where the disagreement is over what the real definition of the property in question is. In my view the disagreement between Rawls and Nozick can be explained in this way.

[42] Jackson (2008), 75.

claim that there is a gap between the non-evaluative and the evaluative, in the sense that no amount of information about the non-evaluative facts of a situation licenses a deductive conclusion about the evaluative facts. Again, this is just as it should be if it is essentially contestable whether a particular set of lower-level non-evaluative features give rise to the real similarity required if the evaluative property is to be here instantiated.

5.4.4 *Anthropocentricity*

Evaluative concepts are anthropocentric concepts. By 'anthropocentric concept' I mean a concept that is intrinsically linked to human concerns and purposes.[43] One way to cash this out is to say that such a concept could not be grasped by a being that did not share (or imaginatively attempt to share) in characteristic human concerns. Not sharing in these concerns, such a being would be unable to appreciate the point of view from which it makes sense to group the items to which the concept applies together. More specifically, in the context of this discussion, we can say that not sharing in these concerns makes it the case that the being cannot discern the real similarity that groups these items together.

5.5 Evaluative dependence

We now come to the question of what it is for a property to be evaluative, according to the Inclusive view. The account of what it is for a property to be evaluative is an account of what it is for the real definition, or essence, or the real similarity that unifies instances of the property, to be evaluative. On this view there is a close relation between evaluative concepts and properties effected by the fact that the real definition of an evaluative property is given by the content of an evaluative concept. The account of evaluative properties must therefore allow for each of the features of evaluative concepts listed in the previous section. It is in this sense that these features function as constraints on an account of evaluative properties on the Inclusive view.

5.5.1 *Shapelessness and multiple realizability*

On the face of it, the non-evaluative shapelessness of evaluative properties shapelessness looks like a local instance of the phenomenon of multiple realizability. Multiple realizability, in slogan form, is the phenomenon of sameness through difference: sameness in type through differences in the lower level conditions that give rise to instances of that type.[44] The classic example of a multiply realized property is pain, but multiple realizability is arguably true of many paradigmatic non-evaluative concepts. It is also used to

---

[43] This intrinsic link to human concerns and purposes is sometimes said to hold generally for essentially contestable concepts, and is supposed to explain the intuition that naturalistic concepts could not be essentially contestable. See for example Gallie (1955–6), Dancy (1995), Wiggins (1998), 318.

[44] Funkhouser (2007), 1. Funkhouser argues that the realizing relation that exists between a type and its lower-level conditions is importantly different from the specification relation that exists between a determinable and its determinates.

argue for their irreducibility. Merely pointing to shapelessness and the irreducibility of evaluative properties is thus not sufficient to characterize what it is that makes them *evaluative*.

One way to see this is to note that merely pointing to non-evaluative shapelessness does not explain why it should be essentially contestable whether a particular set of lower-level features here instantiates the relevant evaluative property. The non-evaluative shapelessness of evaluative properties is consistent with the claim that evaluative properties are *dependent* on non-evaluative properties, and thus that particular instantiations of these properties are grounded in lower-level non-evaluative properties. Why, then, could a full characterization of a situation in non-evaluative terms not settle the question of whether an evaluative property is there instantiated? Why should this be essentially contestable and thus potentially a matter of substantive disagreement?

I will return to these questions in a moment. First, consider this is a distinct matter from something else that the Inclusive view holds, that the real definition of an evaluative property cannot be wholly non-evaluative. (This was the point about ontological non-reduction I made above). This is something that is claimed on the basis of the non-evaluative shapelessness of evaluative properties. And it seems that the Inclusive view can offer this (that the real definition of an evaluative property cannot be wholly non-evaluative) as the explanation for the intuition behind the open question argument.[45]

However, to return to the above questions, we are now concerned with *token instances* of the evaluative property, and how it is that lower-level features can give rise to an instance of the evaluative property in such a way that it is nonetheless essentially contestable and thus open to substantive disagreement whether or not the property obtains, even if the parties have all the relevant information regarding what non-evaluative features are present. To deal with this issue we need to consider the relation that obtains between an instance of an evaluative property and the lower-level features that give rise to it.

5.5.2 *The making relation*

The non-evaluative shapelessness of evaluative properties puts paid to any type-type reduction of the evaluative to the non-evaluative, according to the Inclusive view. Despite the fact that it is consistent with this view that evaluative properties ontologically depend upon lower level-properties, this view also holds that there is no hope of token-token reduction in the case particular instantiations of evaluative properties.

An action is bad, for example, *in virtue of* other features that it has: causing pain, for example. On the Inclusive view, this feature not only ontologically grounds the

---

[45] If a conception of a concept, for example JUSTICE, is understood to be a candidate real definition of the property of justice, on the inclusive view no wholly non-evaluative such conception is possible, and neither is a non-circular conception possible.

property of badness but it also explains it.[46] But, on the Inclusive view holds that the realization relation between the badness and the causing pain is not a *determination* relation.[47] For it to be the case that this instance of causing pain *necessitates* the property of badness, a number of other features would have to obtain. Intuitively, the painfulness is responsible for the badness in a more robust sense than any of the other features of the case (such as the day of the week). For any particular instantiation of an evaluative property, the Inclusive view has it that on a determination account the grounding base would come out as too coarse-grained. Indeed, on this view it is plausible that to necessitate the instantiation of the evaluative property, the base would have to be widened out to include the whole world.

On the Inclusive view, only some parts of this base (in the example above, the causing pain) are *normatively* crucial to the property's being instantiated.[48] The other features of this base are not responsible for the instantiation of the evaluative property; they do not *make* the action bad (or whatever the evaluative property happens to be).

This kind of making relation, in the case of a token instance of an evaluative property, does not look like it will bear the weight of a reduction; it does not seem that it will be plausible to claim that the badness is *identical* with the causing pain, in the case discussed above, though it is its causing pain that makes the action bad, and explains its badness. I am not sure of this, but it seems to me that if it were the case that there was token-token identity here, given the account of the relation between concepts and properties on the Inclusive view, it would seem unlikely that it could be essentially contestable whether or not the evaluative property is instantiated.

5.5.3 *Anthropocentricity*

It is perhaps possible that there will be non-evaluative properties that are both multiply realizable and where the realization relation in a particular instance is the same kind of making relation as that just discussed. On the Inclusive view, evaluative properties have a further feature and that is the feature of anthropocentricity. This feature is to be understood in a particular way.

I said above that evaluative concepts are anthropocentric concepts. By 'anthropocentric concept' I meant a concept that is intrinsically linked to human concerns and purposes. I said that one way to cash this out is to say that such a concept could not be grasped by a being that did not share (or imaginatively attempt to share) in characteristic human concerns because such a being could not discern the real similarity that groups

---

[46] For a useful discussion of different kinds of in virtue of claims in metaethics, see Väyrynen (2009a). Väyrynen terms the kind of in virtue of claim that I am concerned with here a 'crucially in virtue of' claim.

[47] See, for example, Dancy (2004), 41 and 79–80, and Zangwill (2008).

[48] For a discussion of this notion of the normatively crucial see Väyrynen (2009a), 296–7. This is meant to contrast with the claim that an evaluative property obtains in virtue of the entire grounding base; we may restrict our focus to salient features of this base but this restrictions does not reveal that these features are metaphysically or normatively more crucial to the instantiation of the property. We single them out merely for pragmatic reasons.

these items together. The suggestion now is that what explains this is that the evaluative properties *themselves* are intrinsically linked to human concerns and purposes; the real definition of an evaluative property includes such a concern. One way that this could be the case would be if these properties were response-dependent properties. But we need not tie the Inclusive view to such an account. Another proposal is that we cash out this intrinsic link to human concerns and purposes in terms of importance or *mattering*. We might do this in terms of how evaluative properties characteristically generate reasons (though without further contextual information we will be unable to say what reasons are generated or for whom).[49]

That evaluative properties might themselves be intrinsically linked to human concerns and purposes (in terms of importance or mattering) explains why disputes about whether the non-evaluative features of a particular case instantiate a particular evaluative property (whether a particular set of lower-level features give rise to the real similarity or essence of the property in question) cannot be resolved simply by agreeing to some arbitrary definition.

5.6 The thick

The aim of this paper was to introduce an alternative view of the evaluative nature of thick concepts. This alternative rejects the orthodoxy that to be evaluative as a matter of content a concept must have thin evaluative content. On the Inclusive view, evaluative concepts are evaluative in virtue of ascribing evaluative properties. A concept ascribes a property if the real definition of the property is given by the content of the concept. A property is evaluative, on this view, if it is shapeless with respect to its grounds (and so the real definition of an evaluative property cannot be wholly non-evaluative); if in each token instance of the property a certain kind of making relation holds between the property instance and its grounds; and if the property is anthropocentric, in the sense discussed above. In addition, it is essentially contestable whether or not a particular set of lower-level features gives rise to the essence or real similarity that unifies instances of the property in question.

On the Inclusive view, irreducible thickness is characterized as meeting these criteria. Thus, on this view thick concepts are inherently evaluative in virtue of ascribing thick evaluative properties.

A thick concept (for example, TACTFUL) applies to an object in virtue of its having features of a certain sort. We may be able to give a rough purely non-evaluative characterization of the sort these features belong to in advance, but there is no lower-level non-evaluative shape for the concept. The concept will, however, have a shape at the higher level (all instances of tactfulness will be tactful, for example). There will be no non-circular real definition of the property however (that is, that does not involve

---

[49]   See Williams (1985), 140. These need not be restricted to practical reasons.

tactfulness). The real definition of the property is given by the content of the concept. In addition, in any particular instance of tactfulness, the lower-level features that make the action tactful will on this view be normatively crucial grounds for the property that give rise to its instantiation but do not determine or necessitate it. And, according to the Inclusive view, thick properties are properties intrinsically linked to human concerns and purposes. Furthermore, it is essentially contestable whether or not any particular set of non-evaluative, lower-level features gives rise to the essence or real similarity that unifies the property in question.

Given this, thick concepts ascribe evaluative properties. If this is the case then, according to the proposal defended above, thick concepts are inherently evaluative.

5.7 The conclusion

The aim of this paper was to reveal the space for, and sketch, an alternative view of the evaluative nature of thick concepts, one that rejects the orthodox notion that to be inherently evaluative a concept must have thin evaluative content.

To achieve this I explained what might motivate such a view before giving an alternative account of what it is for a concept to be evaluative. The Inclusive view, as I have called it, is the view that thick concepts meet the criteria set out in this account.

Much more work needs to be done of course, both in fleshing out the details of this view of the evaluative more generally, and in defending the Inclusive view in particular. However, I hope to have shown that it is at least a live option to the Content and Pragmatic views of the thick discussed at the beginning of this paper.

References

Armstrong, David (1978) *Universals and Scientific Realism, ii: A Theory of Universals* (Cambridge: Cambridge University Press).

Blackburn, Simon (1992) 'Morality and Thick Concepts: Through Thick and Thin', *Proceedings of the Aristotelian Society, Supplementary Volume* 66: 285–99.

—— (1998) *Ruling Passions* (Oxford: Oxford University Press).

Dancy, Jonathan (1995) 'In Defense of Thick Concepts', in Peter A. French, Theodore E. Uehling, and Howard K. Wettstein (eds.) *Midwest Studies in Philosophy* 20: 263–79.

—— (2004) *Ethics Without Principles* (Oxford: Oxford University Press).

Eklund, Matti (2011) 'What Are Thick Concepts?', *Canadian Journal of Philosophy* 41: 25–50.

—— (this volume) 'Evaluative Language and Evaluative Reality'.

Elstein, Daniel and Thomas Hurka (2009) 'From Thick to Thin: Two Moral Reduction Plans', *Canadian Journal of Philosophy* 39: 515–35.

Fine, Kit (1994) 'Essence and Modality', *Philosophical Perspectives* 8: 1–16.

—— (1995) 'Ontological Dependence', *Proceedings of the Aristotelian Society*, 95: 269–90.

Funkhouser, Eric (2007) 'A Liberal Conception of Multiple Realizability', *Philosophy Compass* 2: 303–15.

Gallie, W. B. (1955–6) 'Essentially Contested Concepts', *Proceedings of the Aristotelian Society* 56: 167–98.

Gibbard, Allan (2003) *Thinking How to Live* (Cambridge, MA: Harvard University Press).

Harcourt, Edward and Alan Thomas (this volume) 'Thick Concepts, Analysis, and Reductionism'.

Hurley, S. L. (1989) *Natural Reasons: Personality and Polity* (Oxford: Oxford University Press).

Jackson, Frank (2008) 'The Argument from the Persistence of Moral Disagreement' *Oxford Studies in Metaethics* 3: 75–86.

Kirchin, Simon (2010) 'The Shapelessness Hypothesis', *Philosophers' Imprint* 10: 1–28.

Majors, Brad (2005) 'Moral Discourse and Descriptive Properties', *Philosophical Quarterly* 55: 475–94.

McDowell, John (1978) 'Are Moral Requirements Categorical Imperatives?' *Proceedings of the Aristotelian Society, Supplementary Volume* 52: 13–29.

—— (1979) 'Virtue and Reason', *The Monist* 62: 331–50.

—— (1981) 'Non-Cognitivism and Rule-Following', in Stephen Holtzman and Christopher Leich (eds.) *Wittgenstein: To Follow a Rule* (London: Routledge and Kegan Paul), 141–62.

—— (1985) 'Values and Secondary Qualities' in Ted Honderich (ed.) *Morality and Objectivity* (London: Routledge and Kegan Paul), 110–29.

Oddie, Graham (2005) *Value, Reality, and Desire* (Oxford: Oxford University Press).

Putnam, Hilary (2002) *The Collapse of the Fact/Value Dichotomy and Other Essays* (Cambridge, MA: Harvard University Press).

Roberts, Debbie (2011) 'Shapelessness and the Thick', *Ethics* 121: 489–520.

Sturgeon, Nicholas (2009) 'Doubts about the Supervenience of the Evaluative', *Oxford Studies in Metaethics* 4: 53–90.

Suikkanen, Jussi (2010) 'Non-Naturalism: the Jackson Challenge', *Oxford Studies in Metaethics* 5: 87–110.

Swanton, Christine (2001) 'A Virtue Ethical Account of Right Action', *Ethics* 112: 32–52.

—— (2003) *Virtue Ethics: a Pluralistic View* (Oxford: Oxford University Press).

Taylor, Charles (2003) 'Ethics and Ontology', *Journal of Philosophy* 100: 302–20.

Väyrynen, Pekka (2009a) 'Normative Appeals to the Natural', *Philosophy and Phenomenological Research* 79: 279–314.

—— (2009b) 'Objectionable Thick Concepts in Denials', *Philosophical Perspectives* 23: 439–69.

—— (2011) 'Thick Concepts and Variability' *Philosophers' Imprint* 11: 1–17.

—— (2012) 'Thick Concepts: Where's Evaluation?' *Oxford Studies in Metaethics* 7: 235–70.

Wedgwood, Ralph (2007) *The Nature of Normativity* (Oxford: Oxford University Press).

Wiggins, David (1998) *Needs, Values, Truth*, 3rd edn. (Oxford: Oxford University Press).

Williams, Bernard (1985) *Ethics and the Limits of Philosophy* (London: Fontana).

Zangwill, Nick (2008) 'Moral Dependence', *Oxford Studies in Metaethics* 3: 109–27.

6

On the Nature and Significance of the Distinction between Thick and Thin Ethical Concepts

Michael Smith

Bernard Williams famously distinguishes 'thin' from 'thick' ethical concepts.[1] Examples of the former include the concepts of *goodness, badness, rightness, wrongness*, and *obligatoriness*. Examples of the latter include not just nice concepts like *justice, fairness*, and *kindness*, but also nasty concepts like *chastity, sluttiness,* and *poofiness*. The nature and significance of this distinction has long been a matter of dispute. Here I focus on two issues concerning the nature of the distinction, issues that bear directly on the distinction's significance.

Imagine someone who says to someone who is evidently heterosexual, 'You're a poof!' Or imagine someone who says of a man who takes no account of the fact that others may be especially sensitive, and so suffer hurt feelings when he engages them in conversation, 'He is being unfair!' Absent any further details, these claims should be dismissed as misapplications of the concepts in question. Whatever else we might think of those who call people 'poofs', someone's being evidently heterosexual makes it impossible for him to be correctly described as a 'poof'. And while insensitivity to the feelings of others may indicate that someone is unkind or crass, it isn't something in virtue of which he could correctly be called 'unfair'. Such uses of these concepts may of course be justified on other grounds. Perhaps they are being used as metaphors, or they are an attempt to subvert some social practice, or perhaps some other feature of the context makes their use felicitous. On their face, however, such uses are misapplications plain and simple.

Cases like these underscore a deep truth about the application of the thick ethical concepts. Their application requires that those to whom the concepts are applied have certain non-ethical features rather than others. Their application is thus 'world-guided', as Williams puts it. The first issue to be addressed is whether this is a *difference* between thick ethical concepts and thin ones. Are thick ethical concepts world-guided in some way in which the thin are not? Answering this question requires us to

---

[1] Williams (1985), 140–2, 150–2.

do two distinct things. We must first spell out what it is about thick ethical concepts that explains their world-guidedness, and we must then ask whether thin ethical concepts are similar to the thick in this respect. To anticipate, it turns out that the very feature of thick ethical concepts that explains the non-ethical constraint on their application is a feature of thin ethical concepts as well. The upshot is that all ethical concepts, even the maximally thin ones, turn out to be a little bit thick. They are all world-guided.

The second issue concerns the order of definition or analysis. Should we analyse the thick ethical concepts in terms of the thin, or the thin in terms of the thick, or should we simultaneously define thick and thin ethical concepts in terms of each other, perhaps along with their relations to other concepts? Perhaps the best-known answer to this question is R. M. Hare's.[2] Hare thinks that the thick ethical concepts can all be given a two-part definition. For example, whatever non-ethical features are such that people's being unkind is a matter of their having those non-ethical features—call these features X, Y, Z—Hare thinks that the claim that someone is unkind means that they have X, Y, Z and their having those features is bad. Others, like Williams, seem to think that the order of definition goes in the other direction.[3] Someone's being bad (say) means nothing over and above his instantiating certain negative thick ethical concepts: his being unkind, or unfair, or cowardly, or whatever. Again, to anticipate, the correct answer to this question turns out to be closer to Hare's than to Williams's. Once we have analyses of the maximally thin thick ethical concepts, we can use them to analyse the rest of the thick ethical concepts.

Once we appreciate that and why these two issues have to be resolved in these ways, it will become clear that the significance of the distinction between thick and thin ethical concepts is not so easy to assess. On the one hand, since all ethical concepts are a little bit thick, it follows that there isn't any distinction to be drawn between them, and hence nothing whose significance we can assess. There is only a distinction between the maximally thin thick ethical concepts and the not-maximally thin thick ethical concepts. On the other hand, since we can define the rest of the thick ethical concepts in terms of the maximally thin ones, it also follows that the maximally thin thick ethical concepts have a significance that is over and above that of the rest of the thick ethical concepts. Their significance lies in the fact that they are definitionally prior.

Before confronting these two issues, however, it will be helpful if we step back and settle the answer to a question that lurks in the background of all discussions of thick and thin ethical concepts. What makes a concept an ethical concept, as opposed to a non-ethical concept? Equipped with an answer to this question, it will be much easier to frame the discussion of the two issues we have identified, and to see why proper responses are the ones suggested.

---

[2] Hare (1952) and (1963).   [3] Williams (1985), 130.

6.1 What makes a concept an ethical concept?

Though no account of what makes a concept an ethical concept will be completely uncontroversial, I suggest that we work with an account that builds on a distinction made by Thomas M. Scanlon. According to Scanlon, there is a distinctive class of mental states, the judgement-sensitive attitudes, which comprises all and only those attitudes 'for which reasons can sensibly be asked or offered'.[4] In terms of this distinction, my suggestion is that a concept is an ethical concept if and only if, if someone believes that that concept is instantiated, then that person is committed to believing that there is a reason for a certain sort of the judgement-sensitive attitude. Let me explain this suggestion in greater detail.

According to Scanlon, judgement-sensitive attitudes are those:

That an ideally rational person would come to have whenever that person judged there to be sufficient reasons for them, and that would, in an ideally rational person, 'extinguish' when that person judged them not to be supported by reasons of the appropriate kind.[5]

Reasons 'of the appropriate kind' are reasons in the 'standard normative sense', which Scanlon explains by way of a paradigm example: the considerations that support the truth of our beliefs. These are the paradigmatic example of reasons in the standard normative sense because, insofar as we are rational, we acquire and maintain our beliefs when we judge there to be considerations that support the truth of what we believe, and we lose beliefs when we judge there to be no such considerations. Beliefs are thus judgement-sensitive attitudes *par excellence*. But belief is not the only judgement-sensitive attitude, or so Scanlon tells us. Intention, desire, hope, fear, admiration, respect, contempt, indignation, and a range of other attitudes as well, are all judgement-sensitive attitudes, as he sees.[6] These mental states are all judgement-sensitive attitudes because they too are sensitive to our appreciation of reasons in the standard normative sense for acquiring them, maintaining them, and getting rid of them.

The relevant contrast is with mental states that do not come and go according to our assessment of the reasons for and against them. Dizziness is an obvious such example, as we don't have reasons in the standard normative sense at all for being dizzy.[7] But another less obvious example might be perceptual appearances like its seeming to us that the lines in the Müller-Lyer illusion are different lengths. Such perceptual appearances, like all perceptual appearances, can be more or less faithful to reality—that is, they can get things wrong—but it doesn't follow from this that they are sensitive to the considerations that bear on whether or not they get things wrong. Even when we know that the lines in the Müller-Lyer illusion are the same length, the appearance of their being the different lengths remains stubbornly in place.

---

[4] Scanlon (1998), 20.   [5] Scanlon (1998), 20.
[6] Scanlon (1998), 20–1.   [7] Compare Thomson (2008), 208.

What exactly it means for non-belief attitudes like intention, desire, hope, fear, admiration, and the rest to be supported by reasons in the standard normative sense, a sense explained by having us focus on the case of the considerations that support the truth of our beliefs, is a matter of some dispute. Scanlon thinks that it requires us to posit a *sui generis favouring* relation in terms of which we can explain both reasons for beliefs and reasons for these other judgement-sensitive attitudes: reasons are those considerations, whatever they are, that favour our having judgement-sensitive attitudes.[8] Others think that we can explain reasons for these non-belief states in terms of reasons for belief in particular.[9] More specifically, they think that reasons for non-belief mental states are considerations that support the truth of the belief that the correctness condition of the relevant non-belief mental state obtains. Reasons for desiring are considerations that support the truth of the belief that the thing desired is desirable; reasons for admiring are considerations that support the truth of the belief that the thing admired is admirable; and so on. For present purposes, we do not need to decide between these ways of spelling out the idea of a reason in the standard normative sense. It suffices that some such story can be told.

Moreover, what exactly it means for any of these judgement-sensitive attitudes to be supported by reasons in the standard normative sense, as distinct from their being supported by reasons in the sense of its being good to acquire them, is also a matter of some dispute. Many think that the best way to explain this difference is to appeal to whatever the correct account of reasons in the standard normative sense is.[10] As they see things, we can explain what its being good to have some judgement-sensitive attitude amounts to in terms of the existence of reasons in the standard normative sense for wanting to have that judgement-sensitive attitude. The distinction, in other words, is that between there being reasons in the standard normative sense for having some judgement-sensitive attitude and there being reasons in the standard normative sense for wanting to have that judgement-sensitive attitude. For present purposes, I propose that we simply assume that this way of making the distinction is correct. Nothing will turn on this in what follows, however.

As they see things, we can explain what its being good to have some judgement-sensitive attitude amounts to in the following terms. Its being good is a matter of there being reasons in the standard normative sense for wanting to have that judgement-sensitive attitude. Given that these non-belief attitudes all seem either to be or to entail a desire of some sort—an intention seems to be, inter alia, the desire that the desirer himself performs some action available to him; hope seems to be, inter alia, the desire that things turn out a certain way; fear seems to be, inter alia, the desire that one or one's associates be out of harm's way; and so on—the suggestion can be simplified. A concept is an ethical concept, I suggest, if and only if, if someone believes that that concept is instantiated, then that person believes that there is a reason for him to

---

[8] Scanlon (1998), 17.   [9] Thomson (2008), 130.
[10] Parfit (2011), vol. 1, Appendix A.

desire that the world be a certain way. As the examples help make plain, there is no assumption the world could be that way without standing in a certain relation to the desirer himself—in other words, the desire may have *de se* content, or it may have *de dicto* content—and nor is there any assumption that the option of making it that way is available.

This suggestion should sound at least somewhat familiar. The signature doctrine of moral rationalism is, after all, that facts about what agents morally ought to do are just facts about what they have reasons to do, and hence that beliefs about moral obligations are beliefs about what agents have reasons to do. If, as Scanlon suggests, facts about what agents have reason to do are just facts about what they have reasons in the standard normative sense to intend to do, and if intention is just a kind of desire, then we can generalize the rationalist's signature doctrine as follows.[11] An ethical fact, whether thick or thin, is just a fact about what there is reason to desire: facts about what's morally obligatory are facts about what there is reason to desire to do of the options available; facts about what's good are facts about what there is reason to desire be the case; facts about what's bad are facts about what there is reason to be averse to, or to desire not be the case; facts about justice and fairness are a subspecies of facts about what there is reason to desire be the case; and so on.

But though I have no objection to this generalization of the signature doctrine of moral rationalism to cover all ethical facts, I don't myself think that it constitutes, all by itself, a story of what makes a concept an ethical concept. Consider, for example, the most straightforward way of turning it into a story of what makes a concept an ethical concept. A concept is an ethical concept, the idea would be, if and only if facts about that concept's instantiation entail the existence of reasons for corresponding desires. The difficulty with this idea is that it doesn't tell us why those ethical concepts that are *uninstantiated* are ethical concepts. Think once again about the concept of *poofiness*. The concept of *poofiness* is an ethical concept, indeed a thick ethical concept, but it isn't the case that facts about this concept's instantiation are facts about the reasons that there are to (say) be averse to people on account of their being homosexual. This isn't the case because there are no such facts. A story about what makes a concept an ethical concept must therefore allow for the possibility that such concepts are not instantiated. Ethical concepts that are not instantiated include all the nasty thick ethical concepts: *poofiness, sluttiness, chastity*, and so on. These concepts are not instantiated for the simple reason that their instantiation would require there to be reasons for desiring that there aren't. The proper theory of these is an error theory. My suggestion, by contrast, is tailor-made to avoid this difficulty. Since what makes a concept an ethical concept is the fact that someone who believes that that concept is instantiated believes that there is a corresponding reason for desiring, the concept of *poofiness* counts as an ethical concept simply in virtue of the fact that someone who believes of certain people that they are poofs thereby believes that there are reasons to be averse to them on account of their being

[11] Scanlon (1998), 21.

homosexual. The fact that their belief makes a false presupposition about the reasons that there are is neither here nor there.

Note that this suggestion is also similar to, though importantly different from, a similar proposal from Williams. Williams tells us that the distinctive feature of thick ethical concepts, and hence by implication thin ethical concepts too, is that they have a general connection with reasons for action.

> If a concept of this kind applies, this often provides someone with a reason for action, though that reason need not be a decisive one and may be outweighed by other reasons...Of course, exactly what reason for action is provided, and to whom, depends on the situation, in ways that may well be governed by this and by other ethical concepts, but some general connection with action is clear enough.[12]

Williams's proposal should sound familiar, as it is very like that of the moral rationalist's. This should, however, give us pause for thought, as throughout his career Williams was famously opposed to moral rationalism.

As Williams sees things, all reasons for action are what he calls 'internal reasons', where an agent has an internal reason to act in some way just in case she would be motivated to act in that way if she were to deliberate correctly.[13] Correct deliberation, for Williams, is a matter of making sure that the elements in one's 'subjective motivational set' (or 'S', as he terms it)—we can think of all these as one's desired ends—are determinate; getting these desired ends to cohere with each other in a manner suited to their satisfaction over time; using one's imagination to make sure that desire satisfaction really would be the result of the attempt to satisfy them; and, finally, taking the means to satisfy these desired ends in the light of knowledge of what those means are. What an agent would be motivated to do after deliberating correctly, as Williams conceives of correct deliberation, and hence what she has reason to do, is therefore relative to her S: that is, relative to what her antecedently desired ends are. The contrast with what she morally ought to do thus could not be starker. When we say to a man who is cruel to his wife that he morally ought to treat her better, he does not refute us simply by pointing out something that may already be evident, namely, that he has no desire that would be satisfied by treating her better. But that is precisely how he refutes the claim that he has a reason to treat her better, according to Williams.

Williams's idea that facts about reasons for action are relative to antecedently desired ends also sets claims about reasons apart from claims couched in thick and thin ethical terms. He tells us, for example, that it would be apt to make all of the following claims about a man who is cruel to his wife, some thick and some thin:

> That he is ungrateful, inconsiderate, hard, sexist, nasty, selfish, brutal, and many other disadvantageous things. I shall presumably say, whatever else I say, that it would be better if he were nicer to her.[14]

---

[12] Williams (1985), 140.   [13] Williams (1981).
[14] Williams (1995), 39.

But as before, if his desired ends are sufficiently horrible and ingrained, Williams admits that, as he sees things, the husband may have no reason to be grateful, or to be considerate, or to treat her better. As he puts it,

I say, 'You have a reason to be nicer to her'. He says, 'What reason?' I say, 'Because she is your wife.' He says—and he is a very hard case—'I don't care. Don't you understand? I really do not care.' I try various things on him, and try to involve him in this business; and I find that he really is a hard case: there is nothing in his motivational set that gives him a reason to be nicer to his wife as things are.[15]

The hard case he imagines is appropriately describable in thick and thin ethical terms, but Williams thinks that he does not have corresponding reasons for action because he would not have corresponding desires if he were to deliberate correctly. Whatever he has in mind when he says that there is a general connection between the application of thick and thin ethical concepts and reasons for action, Williams therefore most certainly isn't suggesting that someone who is appropriately describable in thick or thin ethical terms has corresponding reasons. So what does he have in mind?

Here is the passage in which Williams hints at how he would develop his view if he were to spell it out fully:

It may well be that 'thick' ethical concepts are, to an adequate degree, both 'world-guided' and 'action-guiding'. People who use a given concept of this sort will find their application of it guided by their experience, and also accept that it gives them reasons for or against various kinds of action. Then this disposition will figure in their S, in rather the same way as the disposition to avoid the poisonous or the disgusting may figure in it.

But this does not mean that a speaker who does use a given concept of this kind (*chastity* is an example that focuses the mind) can truly say that another agent who does not use the concept has a reason to avoid or pursue certain courses of action in virtue of that concept's application. To show this, the speaker would need to show that the agent has reason to use that concept, to structure his or her experience in those terms. That is a different and larger matter; all the work remains to be done.[16]

Though Williams does not elaborate further, his idea here seems to be that the role of ethical concepts as such is to make salient to users of those concepts features that bear in some very direct way on what they have reason to do. Just as different people have reasons to act in different ways, depending on their antecedently desired ends, so, according to Williams, different people have reasons to use different ethical concepts, depending on their antecedently desired ends, because different ethical concepts make salient different features of their circumstances. His strategy is to turn this feature of ethical concepts into an account of what makes a concept an ethical concept because of its connection to reasons for action.

Imagine someone who conceptualizes his experience in terms of the concept of *chastity*. Williams's idea seems to be that, for such a person, whether or not women are

[15] Williams (1995), 39.   [16] Williams (1995), 37–8.

restraining their sexual behaviour will be a very salient feature of their circumstances. Who would have a reason to make that feature of their circumstances salient? His answer is: those who desire that women restrain their sexual behaviour. Such people have a reason to *use* the concept of *chastity*, and they have corresponding reasons for action, but all this is consistent with others who have no such desire having no such reasons. The connection that Williams sees between ethical concepts and reasons for action is thus mediated by such reasons as they have to use ethical concepts. To put Williams's idea in our terms, a concept is an ethical concept if and only if those who have reasons to use that concept have corresponding reasons for action, and hence, given the general connection between reasons for action and reasons for intention, if and only if they have corresponding reasons for intention. To return to the example of chastity, what makes this an ethical concept isn't anything about our use of the concept, and it isn't anything about the reasons had by those to whom the concept is applied, but is rather the fact that those who have reasons to use the concept of chastity have corresponding reasons for intention.

Williams's proposal differs from ours in several respects, two of which are worth emphasizing. First of all, unlike ours, Williams's proposal tells us that what makes the concept of chastity an ethical concept is the fact that there are certain people, namely those who have reasons to use that concept, who in fact have reasons for corresponding intentions: reasons to intend to (say) restrain women's sexual activity. Our suggestion has no such upshot. What makes the concept of chastity an ethical concept, according to our suggestion, is the fact that those who believe that certain women are chaste *believe* that they have reasons to have certain intentions, or to desire that the world be a certain way, not that they really do have such reasons. The second difference is that Williams's proposal tells us that there is a connection between ethical concepts and corresponding reasons for intentions in particular, rather than reasons for desiring that the world be a certain way. Our suggestion, by contrast, allows that though certain ethical concepts have a connection with reasons for intention, other ethical concepts have no such connection, though of course they do have a connection with reasons for desires. In order to see how this second difference makes a difference, consider some examples.

Consider the thin ethical claim that it would be better if, in the natural order of things, not as a result of anyone's intervention, good people flourished and bad people suffered. Or consider the thick ethical claim that it would be fairer if, in the natural order of things, not as a result of anyone's intervention, natural disasters were the burden of all equally, not the special burden of only some. Not only would the truth of such claims not require anyone to have the option of doing something to make things other than the way they are, the truth of such claims rules out the possibility of there being such reasons for intention. This creates a difficulty for Williams's proposal, as it seems incapable of explaining what makes it the case that those who have a reason to use these concepts in this way—the concept of betterness and fairness without any tie to reasons for intentions—are using ethical concepts at all, given that they plainly are not being used to make salient a feature of an agent's circumstances that is relevant to what he has reason to intend to do. Our suggestion, by contrast, faces no such difficulty. For our suggestion is simply that, if someone believes that it would be better if, in the natural order of things, not as a result of anyone's intervention, good people flourished and bad people suffered, or if he believes that it would be fairer if, in the natural order of things, not as a result of anyone's intervention, natural disasters were the burden of all equally, not the special burden of only some, then he believes that he has reasons to prefer that the world be these ways. The fact that he has no reasons to intend anything is irrelevant.

To sum up, our suggestion is that a concept is an ethical concept if and only if, if someone believes that that concept is instantiated, then that person believes that there is a reason for him to desire that the world be a certain way. It might be objected that this suggestion entails, implausibly, that philosophers like Williams who deny that there is a quite general conceptual connection of the kind Scanlon proposes between ethical concepts and reasons for desires are thereby precluded from possessing any ethical concepts. But the objection is based on a misunderstanding of the debate between rationalists and anti-rationalists. At least as I understand it, these theorists are offering competing accounts of the nature of not just ethical *facts*, but also ethical *beliefs*. Philosophers like Williams, who believe that certain acts are kind and others are cruel, may well therefore be led by their anti-rationalism to deny that they believe that the agents of those acts have reasons to desire to act in corresponding ways, but they are wrong. Their anti-rationalism leads them to misdescribe the contents of their ethical beliefs. They do believe that the agents of kind acts and cruel acts have reasons to desire to act in corresponding ways, it is just that they don't believe that this is what they believe.[17]

6.2 Ethical concepts, moral concepts, and world-guidedness

Before using this account of what makes a concept an ethical concept to give an account of what makes thick ethical concepts world-guided, it will be helpful to remind ourselves of what Hare has to say about the thin ethical concepts. Once we have Hare's account of the thin ethical concepts before us, it will be clear that the thin ethical concepts are world-guided in exactly the same way in which the thick ethical concepts are world-guided. In what follows we will focus on what Hare has to say about the thin ethical concept of an obligation, but there is nothing special about this thin ethical concept. We could have chosen any of the thin ethical concepts to make the point.

Suppose that A says to B, 'You ought to ϕ'. Hare thinks that in saying this, A may or may not be expressing an ethical belief. His basic idea, one that permeates all of his work

---

[17] For more on this issue, see my disagreement with David Brink about whether different philosophers' metaethical views should be read into the content of those philosophers' first-order moral beliefs in Smith (1997), 107–8.

in ethical theory, is that A expresses an ethical belief only if A's grounds for saying that B ought to ϕ is his commitment to some universal principle.[18] A expresses a non-ethical belief, by contrast, if his grounds for saying that B ought to ϕ has nothing to do with a universal principle, but instead turns essentially on facts about some particular. Imagine, for example, that A says B ought to give him some money. If A's grounds for saying that B ought to give him some money is that his doing so would make A richer—perhaps A is a robber—then A's grounds essentially involve a particular, namely, the effect of B's giving money to A on satisfying *A's* desire for money. But if A's grounds for saying that B ought to give him some money is that his doing so would repay a debt, then A's grounds do not essentially involve any particular. His claim is rather grounded in the universal principle that people ought to repay their debts.

Adapting this to our account of what makes a concept an ethical concept, we can put the point schematically as follows. If Hare is right, then when A says to B, 'You ought to ϕ', A expresses a belief about the instantiation of an ethical concept only if:

(i[universal]) A believes that there is some subset, C, of the universal features of the circumstances in which B finds himself; and
(ii[universal]) A believes that being in C is a reason for anyone who finds himself in those circumstances to desire that he ϕs.

If these conditions are not met, then A doesn't express an ethical belief at all. Moreover, since Hare thinks that a similar universality condition applies to the other thin ethical concepts as well, it follows that, if he is right, then what makes beliefs about their instantiation ethical beliefs is that versions of (i[universal]) and (ii[universal]) are true of them too.

Hare himself thinks that there are further conditions on the application of the thin ethical concepts. For example, he thinks that for a claim about what ought to be done to be an ethical judgement, that judgement must entail commitment to an imperative, and the agent's commitment to that imperative must be overriding.[19] Whether or not we would take issue with these further conditions on the application of an ethical concept, it is virtually universally agreed that he is right that for a judgement to be an ethical judgement, that judgement must universalizable. Nor is this surprising. The concept of an ethical claim just seems to be the concept of one that gives no privilege to any particular over any another, and the deeper explanation of this, if our suggestion is along the right lines, is that *reasons* must be universal features. The difference between the robber and someone who thinks B ought to repay his debts, in other words, is that though they both desire B to give them money, only B has that desire *for a reason*.

Assuming that thin ethical concepts really are subject to the universalizability condition, two important and related conclusions follow. The first is that there is a sense in which even the thin ethical concept of an *obligation* is world-guided. The worldly condition takes the form of a constraint on the sorts of considerations that people can believe

---

[18] Hare (1952), (1963), and (1981).   [19] Hare (1981).

provide reasons for desires to do things when they think that there are ethical obligations, a constraint that we can specify in non-ethical terms. These considerations, it turns out, must all be *universal* features of the circumstances in which those obligations are had. The concept of universality is not itself an ethical concept, however. Non-universal features of circumstances—features that concern the particulars involved—cannot be believed to be the features that provide reasons for desires. But though there is this constraint on the sorts of considerations that can provide reasons for desires, the constraint doesn't wholly determine what those considerations are. The considerations must be a subset of the universal features, but it is left open which subset. Moreover, since as I said it is somewhat arbitrary that we have chosen to focus on the thin ethical concept of *obligation*, we should suppose that the rest of the thin ethical concepts are subject to a similar universalizability condition. There is therefore a sense in which all the thin ethical concepts are world-guided.

The second conclusion is a corollary of this. When A says 'B ought to φ' and D denies this, we must sharply distinguish between two very different possibilities. One is that A and D have a substantive ethical disagreement about what B ought to do. Their disagreement is substantive when they both meet conditions ($i^{universal}$) and ($ii^{universal}$), but they believe that a different subset of the universal features of B's circumstances provide reasons for B's desires about what to do. The mere fact that A and D share the thin ethical concept of *obligation*, and have ethical beliefs about what B's obligations are, thus doesn't guarantee that they will have the same conception of what B's obligations are. A's and D's conceptions of B's obligations turn instead on which subset of universal features they believe provide B with reasons to desire.

The other possibility, however, is that A and D are not having a substantive disagreement at all, but are rather having a merely verbal disagreement. Their disagreement is merely verbal when one of them is making an ethical judgement and the other isn't. This would be the case if (say) A meets conditions ($i^{universal}$) and ($ii^{universal}$), but B doesn't. Imagine, again, that when A says 'B ought to φ', he is simply applying the universal principle that people ought to repay their debts, whereas when D denies this, he is a robber who thinks that B should give all his money to him. A's use of the word 'ought' is the application of an ethical concept, whereas D's isn't: D's claim simply reports what B needs to do in order to satisfy D's desire for money. What makes this the case is the fact that their judgements are grounded in worldly features that we can discriminate between in non-ethical terms. The features that ground A's judgement are a subset of the set of universal features, whereas the features that ground D's judgement concern a particular, namely, D himself. A's and D's judgments could therefore both be true.

So far we have asked what's required for a concept to be an *ethical* concept. Let's now turn to ask what might turn out to be a slightly different question. What makes a concept a *moral* concept? For example, what has to be true for someone's claims about another's obligations to be claims about their *moral obligations*? Hare's own view is that the three conditions already described suffice: judgements of moral obligation are universalizable, prescriptive, and overriding. He therefore sees no difference between ethics and morality. But whatever Philippa Foot thinks is required for ethical obligation, she plainly thinks that Hare's account is inadequate as an account of moral obligation.

> Some philosophers [argue] that a man can choose for himself, so long as he meets formal requirements of generality and consistency, what his ultimate moral principles are to be; while others insist that certain criteria of good and evil belong to the concept of morality itself. The first, or formalist, position seems to me indefensible, implying as it does that we might recognize as a moral system some entirely pointless set of prohibitions or taboos, on activities such as clapping one's hands, not even thought of as harmful, aggressive, treacherous, cowardly by the community in which the prohibitions exist. A moral system seems necessarily to be one aimed at removing particular dangers and securing certain benefits.[20]

Foot's objection here is that the principle that people ought to clap their hands in circumstances where their doing so will do nothing to remove harms or secure benefits is perfectly universalizable, but that that plainly doesn't suffice for it to be moral principle. Nor is the problem that we have taken no account of prescriptivity or overridingness. The problem is rather that, for a principle to be a moral principle, and hence to give rise to moral obligations, the principle must concern itself with acts that have something to do with removing harms or securing benefits.

Is Foot right? Remember that earlier it seemed incoherent to suppose that someone was making an *ethical* judgement if their judgement wasn't based on a universal principle. For Foot to be right, it would have to be similarly incoherent to suppose that someone has a belief about what people *morally* ought to do if he supposes that that has nothing whatsoever to do with removing harms and securing benefits. For reasons I will explain presently, I am not sure that this is incoherent. But whether or not Foot is right isn't really relevant to the present concern. What's relevant is rather what follows on the supposition that she is right. So, suppose now that Foot is right. What minimal revision to conditions ($i^{universal}$) and ($ii^{universal}$) would we be forced to make in order to turn our earlier Harean account of what makes a concept an ethical concept into an account of what, as Foot sees things, makes a concept a moral concept?

When A says to B, 'You ought to ϕ', we would have to suppose that A expresses a belief about the instantiation of the concept of *moral obligation* only if:

($i^{universal/harms/benefits}$) A believes that there is some subset of the universal features of the circumstances in which B finds himself, features having something to do with removing certain sorts of harms and securing certain sorts of benefits: call these circumstances '$C^{universal/harms/benefits}$'; and

($ii^{universal/harms/benefits}$) A believes that being in circumstances $C^{universal/harms/benefits}$ is a reason for anyone who finds himself in those circumstances to desire that he ϕs.

---

[20] Foot (2002), 6–7.

If these conditions are not met, we would have to suppose, then A isn't expressing a belief about moral obligation at all. Moreover, we would also be forced to suppose that similar conditions apply to the application of the other thin moral concepts, concepts like *moral rightness, moral wrongness, moral goodness*, and *moral badness*. The thin moral concepts as such would have to be such that believing that they are instantiated in certain circumstances is a matter of believing that some more restricted subset of the universal features of the circumstances, a subset having to do with the harms and benefits that arise, provides a reason for having some appropriate desire about what is to be the case in those circumstances.

If this is right, then note that two conclusions follow, conclusions that are very similar to those that followed from the constraint of universalizability in the ethical case. Focus again on the thin concept of moral obligation. The first is that there is also a sense in which the concept of moral obligation is world-guided, indeed *more* world-guided than the ethical concept of what ought to be done. Imagine, for example, that A says 'B morally ought to clap his hands' and that D denies this. If A believes that B's clapping his hands in his circumstances has nothing whatsoever to do with removing harms and securing benefits, then what he says is false for conceptual reasons. This is because the circumstances that A thinks provide B with a reason to desire to clap his hands have a feature characterizable in non-ethical and non-moral terms—the feature of being in circumstances in which B's clapping his hands would have nothing whatsoever to do with removing harms or securing benefits—that precludes them from being the sorts of circumstances which, even if they did provide B with reasons for desiring to clap his hands, are such that their providing B with reasons to desire to clap his hands makes it the case that B morally ought to clap his hands.

Of course, if these circumstances are still characterizable wholly in universal terms, then it may yet be true that B *ethically* ought to ϕ. Though it might initially sound fanciful to suppose that this is so, it isn't hard to imagine situations in which it at least some people might well think that it is so. Imagine, for example, that B's clapping his hands will in some miraculous way preserve a species from extinction, but neither the act of species preservation, nor the allowing of species extinction, has any effect on harms or benefits. Perhaps the species would have died out harmlessly, but, if it did, its ecological niche would have been occupied by a new species that would have brought about harms and benefits that are the same as those that would have obtained if the species had been preserved. The only difference made by B's clapping his hands, in other words, is the existence, rather than the non-existence, of the species itself. In these circumstances, it is easy to imagine that a radical environmentalist might think that B has a reason to desire to clap his hands, and hence believe that he ought to do so. But given that we have stipulated that this feature of B's circumstances has nothing whatsoever to do with removing harms or securing benefits, the claim that B *morally* ought to clap his hands in these circumstances is false on conceptual grounds. We may, however, still suppose that the radical environmentalist believes that B *ethically* ought to clap his hands.

(It should now be clear why I said that I am not sure that Foot is right. For the example of the radical environmentalist puts pressure on the idea that it is incoherent to suppose that someone has a belief about what people *morally* ought to do if he supposes that what they morally ought to do has nothing whatsoever to do with removing harms and securing benefits. The idea that radical environmentalism of the kind described is an ethical view, but not a moral view, seems more like a stipulation about how to use the words 'ethical' and 'moral', not an a priori truth about either ethics or morality. At this stage I am therefore inclined to side with Hare rather than with Foot. The ethical concept of obligation *is* the moral concept of obligation, and the only conceptual constraint on the concept of obligation is the constraint of universalizability.)

The second conclusion is a corollary of this. When A says, 'B ought to clap his hands' and D denies this, we must sharply distinguish between two very different possibilities. One is that A and D have a substantive moral disagreement about what B ought to do. Their disagreement is a substantive moral disagreement when they both meet conditions ($i^{universal/harms/benefits}$) and ($ii^{universal/harms/benefits}$), but they believe that a different subset of the universal features of B's circumstances having something to do with removing harms and securing benefits provide B with reasons to desire to clap his hands. Perhaps A is a utilitarian and D is a deontologist. The mere fact that A and D share the thin concept of *moral obligation*, that they use the word 'ought' to express this concept, and that they both have beliefs about what B's moral obligations are, thus doesn't guarantee that they will have the same conception of what B's moral obligations are. A's and D's conceptions of B's moral obligations turn instead on which subset of universal features having to do with removing harms and securing benefits they believe provide B with reasons to desire.

The other possibility, however, is that A and D are not having a substantive disagreement at all, but are rather having a merely verbal disagreement. Their disagreement is merely verbal when one of them is making a moral judgement and the other isn't. This would be the case if (say) A meets conditions ($i^{universal/harms/benefits}$) and ($ii^{universal/harms/benefits}$), but B's merely meets ($i^{universal}$) and ($ii^{universal}$). Think again about the possibility that A is a radical environmentalist in the circumstances we imagined above, and suppose that D is a utilitarian in those same circumstances. A's use of the word 'ought' is the application of the concept of ethical obligation, not the concept of moral obligation, whereas D's use of 'ought' is the application of the concept of moral obligation. What makes their disagreement merely verbal is thus the fact that their judgements are grounded in differently worldly features, features that we can distinguish between in non-ethical terms. The features that ground A's judgement are a subset of the universal features, but features that have nothing to do with removing harms or securing benefits, whereas the universal features that ground D's judgement do have something to do with removing harms and securing benefits. This explains why their judgements could both be true together.

Let me sum up the discussion thus far. We've spent some time discussing Hare's suggestion that thin ethical concepts are universalizable, and Foot's suggestion that thin moral concepts aren't just universalizable, but must have something to do with removing harms and securing benefits, and we have seen how we can build these insights into our account of what makes a concept an ethical concept. In doing so we have learned that, if Foot is right, then we may have to distinguish sharply between the *thin ethical* concepts, on the one hand, and the *thin moral* concepts on the other. We could do this by acknowledging that there is a sense in which, though both the thin ethical concepts and the thin moral concepts are world-guided, the thin moral concepts are more world-guided than the thin ethical concepts. In other words, a more demanding worldly condition must be satisfied for a thin moral concept to be applicable. Finally, we have seen that satisfying these worldly conditions, worldly conditions that are themselves characterizable in non-ethical and non-moral terms, doesn't wholly determine which features someone who applies these concepts believes to provide reasons for desiring. The worldly condition narrows the set of features that can be believed to provide reasons, but doesn't wholly determine it.

With this discussion of thin ethical and thin moral concepts under our belt, let's now turn to consider the thick ethical concepts. What is it about the thick ethical concepts that makes them world-guided? The best place to start in providing an answer to this question, I think, is with the exemplary work done by Daniel Elstein and Thomas Hurka.[21] Elstein and Hurka's aim is to show that thick ethical concepts can all be given a reductive two-part analysis in the spirit of Hare's two-part analysis. Of course they don't analyse every thick ethical concept. Instead they illustrate their general strategy of analysis by working through an example, specifically the concept of distributive justice. Their claim, which they leave as a homework task for those who doubt them, is that similar analyses can be given of all the other thick ethical concepts.

Here is the passage in which Hurka and Elstein explain the difficulty to be faced in providing such a reductive analysis.

Consider the term 'just' in the specific sense used in discussions of distributive justice. And imagine two people who disagree about the ground of distributive justice, one saying that just distributions of, say, happiness are equal distributions, while another says they are distributions proportioned to people's merits, which may be unequal. If the reductive view had to use a fully determinate two-part analysis of 'distributively just', it would have to say these two people use different concepts of justice. For the egalitarian, 'x is just' means 'x is an equal distribution and is good for being so', while for the desert-theorist it means 'x is a distribution proportioned to merit and is good for being so'. It would not follow that the two cannot disagree about distributive justice, since the claims their concepts imply about the ground of goodness in distribution contradict each other. But in debating the justice of a particular distribution they could not be disagreeing about whether a single concept applies to it, since they use different concepts. But does it not look as if they are in disagreement about the application of a single concept? And is an analysis not preferable that allows this?[22]

The problem they describe was the main problem faced by the two-part analyses Hare himself offered. Hare thought that all thick ethical concepts could be analysed into a

---

[21] Elstein and Hurka (2009).   [22] Elstein and Hurka (2009), 521–2.

non-ethical component and a thin ethical component. Moreover, he thought that the non-ethical component had to be a specification of the non-ethical features in virtue of which the thin ethical concept that figures in the ethical component of the analysis is instantiated. Thus, for example, if Hare were to provide an analysis of the concept of distributive justice, then, given that he is a utilitarian, he would have said that 'x is just' means 'x is a distribution in which individuals are satisfied according to the principle of utility and is good for being so'. What's crucial here is that the first component of the analysis tells us everything about the distribution in virtue of which it is good: it is, in Elstein and Hurka's terms, 'fully determinate'. And the trouble they see with this is that it makes it impossible for an egalitarian or a desert-theorist's use of the expression 'x is just' to have the same meaning. For they don't believe that a distribution is good for being one in which individuals are satisfied according to the principle of utility. An egalitarian and a desert-theorist cannot express their disagreement with each other by using a single concept of justice.

Elstein and Hurka go on to explain how we can provide a reductive two-part analysis of thick ethical concepts that doesn't face this problem.

We can construct such an analysis if we ... give 'distributively just' an only partly determinate descriptive component. Then 'x is distributively just' will mean something like 'There are some properties X, Y, and Z (not specified) that distributions have as distributions, or in virtue of its distributive shape, such that x has X, Y, and Z, and X, Y, and Z make any distribution that has them good'. This analysis certainly places significant restrictions on the extension of 'distributively just'. If someone says an act of generously helping a stranger is distributively just, she is misusing the concept, because only distributions can be just in this sense. And if she calls a distribution just because it was brought about by generous actions, she is likewise misusing the concept, because only a distribution's properties as a distribution can bear on its justice. But these restrictions do not completely determine the concept's extension, and in particular do not determine whether it contains equal distributions or ones based on desert. That depends on which properties of distributions are in fact good-making ... To know the intended extension of 'distributively just' as used by some person or community, it is not enough to know the descriptive part of that term's meaning; we must also know what evaluations they make, that is, which properties they take to make extensions good. And to know the term's actual extension, we must know which properties in fact make distributions good.[23]

The crucial feature of Elstein and Hurka's analysis of justice, unlike the earlier two-part analysis, is that the non-ethical component is not fully determinate. It constrains, but doesn't wholly determine, the features in virtue of which the thin ethical concept that figures in the ethical component is instantiated. The attraction of this less determinate analysis is that it is therefore an analysis of a concept that could be shared and used by an egalitarian, a desert-theorist, and a utilitarian alike, a concept that they could use to express their disagreements with each other about what makes a distribution just. For though they disagree about the grounds of goodness in a distribution, they can also

---

[23]   Elstein and Hurka (2009), 522.

agree that there is no conceptual barrier to supposing that something is just on different grounds, so long as those grounds have something to do with the distributive shape of the thing that is being judged to be just.

Elstein and Hurka's analysis of justice can easily be reformulated in our terms. So reformulated, and taking into account what we learned from our discussion of Hare, the idea would be that when A says to B, 'x is just', A expresses a belief about the instantiation of the thick ethical concept of distributive justice only if:

(i$^{universal/distributive\ shape}$) A believes that x has, among its universal features, a distributive shape, and he further believes that that distributive shape has a further feature F; and

(ii$^{universal/distributive\ shape}$) A believes that the fact that x's distributive shape has feature F is a reason to desire that x has that distributive shape.

It thus isn't a requirement on anyone's having a belief about the justice of some state of affairs that the feature of the distributive shape that they believe provides reasons to desire that that state of affairs obtains is the very same as the one everyone else who has beliefs about justice believes provides such reasons. It is sufficient that they believe that the reason-providing feature is some feature or other of the distributive shape of the state of affairs. A and B can therefore disagree with each other about whether x is just, precisely because they disagree with each other about which specific feature of the distributive shape provides reasons for desiring that that state of affairs obtains.

On the assumption that the concept of justice is a *moral* concept, then, if what Foot says is right about the analysis of moral concepts, our analysis of justice requires further amendment. When A says to B, 'x is just', A expresses a belief about the instantiation of the thick *moral* concept of justice only if:

(i$^{universal/harms/benefits/distributive\ shape}$) A believes that x has, among its universal features that have something to do with harms and benefits, a distributive shape, and he further believes that that distributive shape has feature F; and

(ii$^{universal/harms/benefits/distributive\ shape}$) A believes that the fact that x's distributive shape has feature F is a reason to desire that x has that distributive shape.

In other words, if Foot is right, then one has a fully-fledged moral belief about the justice of some state of affairs only if one believes that the feature of its distributive shape that provides one with a reason has something to do with harms and benefits. But as is I hope clear, it is far from obvious that this is correct. Those who reject all forms of welfarism— for example, those like Rawls who think that justice concerns the distribution of primary goods (primary goods, remember, are all-purpose means like opportunities, the social bases of self-respect, and the like), rather than the distribution of welfare—deny that just distributions need have anything to do with harms and benefits.[24] Since it doesn't seem incoherent to suppose that these theorists are right, it seems to me that we should there-

---

[24] Rawls (1971).

fore stick with our original reformulation of Hurka and Elstein's analysis, the one that insists merely that the feature of distributions has to be a universal feature. In other words, we should suppose that the ethical concept of justice *is* the moral concept of justice.

Note that our original reformulation of Hurka and Elstein's analysis explains why the thick ethical concept of justice is world-guided. The concept is world-guided because a worldly condition must be satisfied by the considerations that someone who employs the concept thinks provide reasons for desire, a worldly condition that we can describe in non-ethical terms. These considerations must be *universal,* and they must have something to do with a *distributive shape.* The upshot is that if someone applies the concept of justice to something in virtue of something other than its distributive shape, then that person is making a straightforward conceptual error. Their use of the concept doesn't satisfy the worldly condition. For example, imagine a disagreement between an environmentalist who says of a certain distribution 'x is just' and an egalitarian who says 'x is unjust', but suppose further that the radical environmentalist's grounds for desiring that that distribution obtains is the fact that it is one in which a certain species is preserved. This disagreement is purely verbal. Something can only be just if it the feature that provides a reason for desiring it is a universal feature that has something to do with a distributive shape. But if an egalitarian says 'x is just' and a desert-theorist says 'x is unjust', then this is a substantive disagreement. It is a substantive disagreement because they both believe that the considerations that provide reasons to have desires concerning x are universal features having something to do with x's distributive shape, it is just that they disagree about which such features provide such reasons.

What's much more striking about this analysis of the thick ethical concept of justice, however, is the fact that it has exactly the same form as the earlier analyses of the thin ethical concepts inspired by Hare. Thick and thin ethical concepts both turn out to be world-guided, and the explanation of their being world-guided is exactly the same in each case. The world-guidedness of an ethical concept, whether thick or thin, is a matter of there being a constraint on the considerations that those who employ the concept believe to provide reasons for desiring, a constraint that, so far at any rate, we have been able to describe in non-ethical terms. In the case of the thin ethical concepts, the constraint is that those features must be universal, and in the case of the thick ethical concept of justice, the constraint is that those features must be universal and have something to do with distributive shape. In order to complete our homework task, all we need to do is to work through the remaining thick ethical concepts and identify the constraints on the reasons for desires that they are believed to provide.

Moreover, just to keep the record straight, note that if we were to do this then we would discover that such constraints *are not* always describable in non-ethical terms. For example, Elstein and Hurka ask us to:

Consider the virtue of integrity. It is a morally good trait that involves, roughly, sticking to one's ideals and projects despite temptations or distractions. But not any fidelity to a project counts as integrity. Someone who persists in building his beer-mat collection despite the rise of Nazism around him and the temptation to fight against it would hardly be described as acting with integrity. The reason is that only fidelity to good or important goals counts as integrity. An initial analysis of 'x is an act of integrity' therefore runs something like 'x is good, and x involves an agent's sticking to a significantly good goal despite distractions and temptations, where this property makes any act that has it good', and where the second 'good' indicates an embedded evaluation. Given this analysis, we can only know what counts as integrity if we know which goals are independently good, and there can be disputes about this. Consider a pope who remains faithful to the views on homosexuality and the ordination of women that he and his church have long held, despite calls from modernizers within and outside the church for change. Supporters of traditional Catholic teaching may say his resistance to reform shows integrity; those who reject that teaching will not.[25]

Certain thick ethical concepts are thus such that some of the believed constraints on the features that provide reasons for desire are themselves only describable ethically.

In our terms, Elstein and Hurka's suggestion can be recast as follows. When A says 'B has integrity', A has a belief about B's *integrity* if and only if:

(i[universal/temptation-imperviousness/ideals]) A believes that B has, among his universal features, some universal features having something to do with sticking to his ideals and imperviousness to temptations: call these features 'G'; and

(ii[universal/temptation-imperviousness/ideals]) A believes that B's ideals are themselves aimed at things that have some universal feature that provides reasons to desire that those things obtain; and

(iii[universal/temptation-imperviousness/ideals]) A believes that G plus the fact that B's ideals are themselves aimed at things that have some universal feature that provides reasons to desire those things, provides reasons to desire that B sticks to those ideals and remains impervious to temptations.

In order to fully understand the world-guidedness of the thick ethical concept of integrity, it is therefore crucial that we appreciate that ethical considerations can themselves serve as reasons for desires.

We began this paper with two questions. The first was whether thick ethical concepts are world-guided in some way in which the thin are not. We have now answered this question and we have done so by doing two distinct things. We first gave an analysis of the thin ethical concepts and saw that there is a sense in which they are world-guided. We then gave an analysis of the thick ethical concepts and saw that they too are world-guided, indeed, world-guided in the very same sense in which the thin ethical concepts are world-guided. The world-guidedness of an ethical concept, whether thick or thin, has turned out to be a matter of there being a constraint on the sorts of considerations that those who employ the concept believe to provide reasons for desiring. The upshot is thus the one anticipated at the very beginning. There is no distinction between thick and thin ethical concepts in terms of world-guidedness. All ethical concepts, even the maximally thin ones, turn out to be a little bit thick.

---

[25] Elstein and Hurka (2009), 526.

6.3 Thick ethical concepts, thin ethical concepts, and the issue of definitional priority

Let's finally turn to a brief discussion of the second question with which we began. Should we analyse the thick ethical concepts in terms of the thin, or the thin in terms of the thick, or should we simultaneously define thick and thin ethical concepts in terms of each other, perhaps along with their relations to other concepts?

It might be thought that the answer to this question has already been given. For haven't we seen that the thin ethical concepts—*obligatoriness, rightness, wrongness, goodness,* and *badness*—are all defined in terms of the existence of some universal features that provide reasons for desiring, and haven't we seen that the thick ethical concepts are all simply definable in terms of some further restriction on these reasons for desiring? So haven't we already seen that the thick ethical concepts are indeed to be defined in terms of the thin ethical concepts? But tempting though this line of thought may be, we shouldn't go along with it straight away. The line of thought starts from the observation that the features that provide reasons for desires must themselves be universal. But since instantiating a thick ethical concept is itself a universal feature, it follows that the observation doesn't rule out the possibility that the universal features that provide reasons for desires are always further restricted in the way in which some thick ethical concepts are restricted. The question remains whether this is so and, if it is, whether it follows that we can define the thin ethical concepts in terms of the thick (or, perhaps, simultaneously define them in terms of each other).

What exactly such a definition would look like isn't something that anyone has fully spelled out, at least to my knowledge. Susan Hurley has, however, done us the great service of describing the idea in broad outline.

A feature common to many philosophical accounts of ethical concepts is that the general concepts, *right* and *ought*, are taken to be logically prior to and independent of the specific concepts, such as *just* and *unkind*. According to such accounts, the general concepts carry a core meaning... that also provides the specific concepts with reason-giving status... I shall refer to accounts that take the general concepts in some category to be logically prior to and independent of the specific as *centralist*.[26]

The tempting line of thought just described is an instance of centralist thinking. As Hurley goes on to point out, however, this isn't the only possible view.

Non-centralism about reasons for action rejects the view that the general concepts *right* and *ought* are logically prior to and independent of specific reason-giving concepts such as *just* and *unkind*. Instead it may take the identification of discrete particular values as a starting point, subject to revision, and give an account of the interdependence between the general concepts and the specific concepts. Coherentist views provide an example of non-centralism. According to such a view, to say that a certain act ought to be done is to say that it is favoured by the best account of the relationships among the specific values that apply to the alternatives in question.[27]

---

[26] Hurley (1985), 56.   [27] Hurley (1985), 56.

A specification of how the reason-providing universal features associated with thin ethical concepts are further restricted may therefore itself derive from an account of the way in which different thick ethical features present in a situation relate to each other: that is, it may be an account of the normative significance of the various thick ethical features vis-à-vis each other, something that is in turn fixed by (say) the best theory of their relations.

The concept of an act's being obligatory in certain circumstances, according to non-centralism, is thus the concept of an act's having the thick ethical feature, or combination of features, that has the greatest normative significance in those circumstances, and this in turn is a concept which someone believes to be instantiated when he believes that that act has whichever thick ethical feature, or combination of thick ethical features, has the greatest normative significance in those circumstances. Someone who believes that an act is obligatory will therefore believe that the universal feature that provides a reason for desiring in those circumstances is further restricted in whatever way the concepts of those thick ethical features are restricted. But note that non-centralism itself takes no stand on whether we can define the thick ethical wholly independently of the thin ethical concepts because, for all that it tells us, defining the normative significance of the thick ethical concepts in terms of each other may require further appeal to the thin ethical concepts. In this way non-centralism allows that the thin ethical concepts may be simultaneously defined in terms of each other.[28]

Note that there are two readings of non-centralism. According to the *de re* reading, there is a distinctive set of thick ethical features that have a certain normative significance vis-à-vis each other in various circumstances—for short, let's just suppose that these are exhausted by justice and kindness—and we define the thin ethical concepts in terms of these features (and perhaps vice versa). To be obligatory is by definition to be either just or kind. This in turn has implications for what it is to believe that an act is obligatory. According to the *de re* reading, there is a distinctive set of thick ethical features that have a certain normative significance vis-à-vis each other in various circumstances—justice and kindness—such that, when someone believes that an act performed in those circumstances is obligatory, he believes that that act has those thick ethical features.

According to the *de dicto* reading, the thin ethical concepts are to be defined in terms of some set of thick ethical features that have a certain normative significance vis-à-vis each other in various circumstances, but that set of thick ethical features is left unspecified. To be obligatory is by definition to have some thick ethical feature or other. When someone believes that an act performed in certain circumstances is obligatory, he therefore believes that there is some set of thick ethical features that have a certain normative significance in those circumstances, and that the act has those thick ethical features. The *de dicto* reading thus allows people to have beliefs about obligatoriness based on their *false* beliefs about the thick ethical features that there are. It allows, for example, that the homophobe can have beliefs about what's obligatory based on his beliefs about 'poofs',

---

[28] Compare Hurley (1985), 58.

as he would put it. It simply requires that, to have a belief about what's obligatory, he has to believe that the act has *some* thick ethical features. The *de re* reading doesn't allow this.

When Hurley suggests that we can define the thin ethical concepts in terms of the thick (and perhaps vice versa), she certainly seems to have the *de re* reading in mind. But given what this tells us about what it is to believe an act to be obligatory, we must surely conclude that non-centralism is false on the *de re* reading. The homophobe who says, 'Homosexuals ought to be shunned!' does not believe, of the thick ethical features of justice and kindness, that shunning homosexuals has *those* features. He believes that not to shun homosexuals would be 'poofy', as he would put it, and he may readily grant that this has nothing whatsoever to do with its being unjust or unkind. This simplifies our discussion, for it leaves us with non-centralism on the *de dicto* reading. The question we must ask about the doctrine on this reading isn't just whether it is plausible, but whether it is an alternative definitional doctrine to centralism at all. Let's start with whether the doctrine is plausible.

On the *de dicto* reading, there is no constraint at all on the thick ethical features that non-centralism insists are definitive of obligation. What's true by definition is simply that an act's being obligatory is a matter of its having some thick ethical features or other. When someone believes an act to be obligatory, he therefore believes that this is so because of the presence of some thick ethical feature or other. Accordingly, it might be thought that non-centralism on this reading is manifestly implausible. For think again about the radical environmentalist who believes that someone ought to clap his hands because he will thereby preserve a species, and suppose further that the radical environmentalist believes this because of the loss of value that the extinction of a species would represent. He has a belief about the obligatoriness of acting to preserve the species, it might be thought, but he doesn't believe that any thick ethical feature is present. This seems to be a counterexample to non-centralism on the *de dicto* reading, or so it might be thought.

But I am not so sure about this, as on plausible assumptions, the radical environmentalist clearly does believe that a not-maximally-thin thick ethical feature is present. For we have seen that a not-maximally-thin thick ethical concept is just a concept whose application requires a further constraint on the sorts of considerations that provide reasons for desiring, over and above being universalizable, and the radical environmentalist does believe that such a concept is instantiated, as he believes that the universal feature of causing species-preservation provides a reason for desiring to clap hands. Of course, the radical environmentalist's language may not include a word whose dedicated role is to express this concept, and we may have no such word either. Perhaps the best either of us can do is to talk about how the following universal feature of state of affairs—the feature of that-state-of-affairs-having-the-universal-feature-of-being-one-in-which-a-species-is-preserved—provides a reason to desire that that state of affairs obtains. But this is neither here nor there. The important point is simply that this is what it is to believe that a thick ethical feature is present.

The real question, I think, is therefore not whether non-centralism so understood is plausible, but whether it is an alternative definitional doctrine to centralism at all. Given that the truth of non-centralism on the *de dicto* reading is entailed by the truth of centralism, myself I think it follows that it is not. Rather, as we have just seen, what it means for acts to have some thin ethical feature is for them to have *some subset* of universal features that provide reasons for desiring, and, on the *de dicto* reading of non-centralism, this is exactly what it means for some thick ethical feature to be present. Non-centralism on the *de dicto* reading is just centralism described in other terms. The upshot, I think, is that we therefore should go along with the tempting thought outlined at the very beginning of this section. The thick ethical concepts can indeed all be defined in terms of the thin because the thin ethical concepts are all defined in terms of the existence of some universal features that provide reasons for desiring, and the thick ethical concepts are all defined in terms of some further restriction on these reasons.

6.4 Conclusion

I said at the outset that the significance of the distinction between thick and thin ethical concepts is not easy to assess. I hope that it is now clear why this is so. Since all ethical concepts are a little bit thick, it follows that there isn't really any distinction to be drawn between them. There is only a distinction between the maximally-thin thick ethical concepts and the not-maximally-thin thick ethical concepts. However, since we have also seen that we can define the rest of the thick ethical concepts in terms of the maximally-thin ones, it follows that the maximally-thin thick ethical concepts have a significance that is over and above that of the not-maximally-thin thick ethical concepts. Their significance lies in the fact that they are definitionally prior to the not-maximally-thin thick ethical concepts.[29]

References

Elstein, Daniel and Thomas Hurka (2009) 'From Thick to Thin: Two Moral Reduction Plans', *Canadian Journal of Philosophy* 39: 515–35.

Foot, Philippa (2002) 'Morality and Art' in her *Moral Dilemmas—and Other Topics in Moral Philosophy* (Oxford: Oxford University Press), 5–19. First published in *Proceedings of the* British Academy 56 (1970), 131–44. [Page references to her collection of essays.]

Hare, R. M. (1952) *The Language of Morals* (Oxford: Clarendon Press).

—— (1963) *Freedom and Reason* (Oxford: Clarendon Press).

—— (1981) *Moral Thinking* (Oxford: Clarendon Press).

---

[29] Earlier versions of this paper were presented at *Thick Concepts*, University of Kent, Canterbury, England, July 2009; the Australasian Association of Philosophy Annual Conference, Melbourne University, June 2009; and Rice University, January 2010. I am grateful for all of the helpful comments I received on these occasions, but especially for those received from Simon Kirchin and the skeptical audience at Rice. Thanks also to two anonymous referees for OUP.

Hurley, S. L. (1985) 'Objectivity and Disagreement', in Ted Honderich (ed.) *Morality and Objectivity* (London: Routledge and Kegan Paul), 54–97.

Parfit, Derek (2011) *On What Matters: Volume One* (Oxford: Oxford University Press).

Rawls, John (1971) *A Theory of Justice* (Cambridge, MA: Harvard University Press).

Scanlon, Thomas M. (1998) *What We Owe to Each Other* (Cambridge, MA: Harvard University Press).

Smith, Michael (1997) 'In Defence of *The Moral Problem*: A Reply to Brink, Copp and Sayre-McCord' in *Ethics*, Symposium on Michael Smith's *The Moral Problem* 108: 84–119.

Thomson, Judith Jarvis (2008) *Normativity* (Chicago: Open Court).

Williams, Bernard (1981) 'Internal and External Reasons', in his *Moral Luck* (Cambridge: Cambridge University Press, 1981), 101–13. First published in Ross Harrison (ed.) *Rational Action: Studies in Philosophy and Social Science* (Cambridge: Cambridge University Press, 1979), 17–28. [Page references to 1981 version.]

—— (1985) *Ethics and the Limits of Philosophy* (London: Fontana).

—— (1995) 'Internal Reasons and the Obscurity of Blame' in his *Making Sense of Humanity* (Cambridge: Cambridge University Press, 1995), 35–45. First published in William J. Prior (ed.) Reason and Moral Judgment, Logos, 10 (1989). [Page references to 1995 version.]

7

Disentangling Disentangling

Simon Blackburn

The issue of 'thick' words has had a prominent place in discussions in moral philosophy, for at least twenty years. I have myself attempted a discussion of them, on several occasions.[1] Indeed, I am not sure that I can say much more than I have said already. I am prompted to try, however, by Hilary Putnam's collection of papers, *The Collapse of the Fact/Value Dichotomy*, and specifically the title essay. Here, the thickness of some evaluative terms is the central lever used to dislodge the dichotomy and to precipitate its advertised collapse. The question I shall address is whether this lever is rigid enough to perform this job, or indeed whether the collapse of the dichotomy, as Putnam conceives of it, is better effected by other means. But the interest is wider than that, for Putnam is of course not alone. He himself makes handsome references back to Iris Murdoch and John McDowell, while he also salutes the tradition of American pragmatism as containing precursors.

Indeed, I suspect it is fairly orthodox to suppose that the thickness of some terms, and the impossibility of disentangling an evaluative and a descriptive component out of them, is an ingredient in things that many of us wish to applaud: the demise of positivism and its contempt for value theory, the resurgence of first-order ethics as a subject, the parallel resurrection of political philosophy, and, as Putnam stresses, the demise of *homo economicus* and the resurgence of pluralistic accounts of the good in writers such as Martha Nussbaum and Amartya Sen. Those like myself, who are unconvinced by the use made of disentangling, must stress and stress again our attachment to these civilized things if we are to get a hearing.

7.1 Loving thick concepts

Thick terms then, have taken up the moral high ground. My problem is with whether they should have. First, however, we should understand a distinction that is frequently ignored, between a strong and a weak sense of the idea of disentangling thick terms.

---

[1] See Blackburn (1981), (1992), and (1998), 92–104.

One sense would require that the extension of the term is one thing, given by a purely descriptive concept, while the other dimension (usually an evaluative one) simply attaches to what is thereby described. This is roughly the case with, for instance, terms of racial or national abuse: the members of the race or nation are identifiable in empirical terms, and the abuse added. The extension can be identified independently of the 'evaluation' (or abuse). As far as I am aware, nobody now thinks that this model applies to interesting candidates for thickness, such as 'cruel' or 'courageous'.

However there is a much more interesting, but weaker sense of disentangling, in which it is still an open question whether such terms can be disentangled. In this sense, the claim is that there are two vectors or dimensions in question, but that they interact. Most obviously, the evaluative element can help to determine what is put into the extension. So, for instance, you do not call someone 'pig-headed' unless you wish to imply a criticism of them, and this fact goes some way into determining who is so-called. The descriptive dimension is that of being resolute or firm, disinclined to change your mind under discursive pressure from others; the other dimension is that of being so *unduly* or inappropriately. The term signals both things, but there is no identifying its extension without employing the evaluative side. There is still disentangling, since there are so clearly two different vectors, and there is predictably going to be disagreement over when 'unduly' kicks in. One man's admirable resolution is another man's pig-headedness. So the descriptions and the valuations interact, and only when they harmonize, in one mind or another, will the term get used. Clearly the common argument that there is no determining the extension of any particular term without deploying an evaluation (or piggy-backing on an evaluation that one does not share) is of no force whatsoever against this view, since it simply seizes on exactly what the view describes.

We now need to be clear about the distinction between thick concepts, as they are understood by those hostile to disentangling, and the same phenomenon described differently. Thickness is a term of art, and it should surely strike us as odd that Bernard Williams needed to find a term for what he was aiming at, when on the face of it perfectly good words existed already. Ordinary people talk of loaded words or loaded descriptions. I believe, as everyone does, that many words are loaded, and loaded with many different things. I am more troubled with the idea that they introduce a unitary concept and hence that we cannot disentangle or usefully separate the different dimensions in the one term. The important point is that the idea behind thick concepts is that a candidate, such as 'chaste' or 'courageous', *simply does the one thing*. If we like to think in these terms, we could say that it ought to get no more than a homophonic entry in a truth theory that fully exhibits the structure of our language and our doings: 'X is courageous' is true in English if and only if X is courageous. I shall talk of thick concepts as the advertised product of this way of looking at things.

To illustrate that this point is not well understood, I can summon a crude claim that I heard recently (far too crude for Putnam himself, I hasten to add). The claim was that expressivists such as Allan Gibbard and myself as well as precursors such as R. M. Hare or

C. L. Stevenson, commit the 'fallacy' of failing to recognize that a word can do two things at once: both describe and evaluate. The irony in this is that the truth is, obviously enough, exactly the reverse. It is lovers of thick concepts who deny that there are two things we are doing. They say that we are doing the one thing, describing something as courageous, for example. Expressivists recognize that there are two activities going on and that we manage to do both things at once. In fact, there are many more than two things to do, since positive or negative evaluations make up only one of the kinds of stance that we may wish to communicate. Furthermore lexical choice is but one kind of instrument for expressing a practical stance. Intonation and emphasis are more flexible and often equally powerful. Consider how many ways I might say, 'He admires Broadway musicals'—amusedly, incredulously, contemptuously, reassuringly, condescendingly, and so on and so on, and sometimes in combination—which is why there may be more than two things being done. 'Tell all the truth but tell it slant', said Emily Dickinson, 'success in indirection lies' and she was right that the slant can be indicated in the most subtle and indirect ways. We may be more successful if the load can be spread across a whole speech, as in Antony's deliberately back-firing eulogy for Caesar.

The everyday metaphor of a loaded description makes salient the idea that a load is something that is put upon something else, and that can equally be taken off. Things can be said in derogatory ways, but rephrased to avoid the derogation. Lovers of thick concepts have to resist the view that this is typically the case, and we come to their reasons in due course. But the issue is whether we should see the unitary, thick concept as fundamental, or the idea of a loaded way of describing things, where the load plays a role in determining which things are so described, but where the load can also in principle be shed.

Before coming to the arguments, let me cast an eye over the consequences. My heresy has always been this: thinking in terms of thick concepts does a disservice to ethics. It discourages critique. I have made this point before with the example of a group happy in the habit of appraising women as cute.[2] We may want to say that there is something wrong with them, along the lines of this: they admire and respond excitedly (or perhaps enviously, if they are women) to the non-threatening, infantile, subservient self-presentations that some women consciously or unconsciously adopt. Theirs is a group amongst whom women are successful by presenting themselves as there to be patronized, like pets or babies (which themselves are frequent terms of endearment). And that, we say, is bad.

Now this critique involved disentangling. It involved separating the features picked upon—the subservience and the rest—and the reactions of admiration and appreciation that they elicit from the group, and then finding it abhorrent that those features generated those reactions. It would be all right, or at least better, if other features such as intelligence and wit generated those reactions, or if the same features of infantile self-presentation generated other reactions, such as compassion or a desire to educate.

[2] Blackburn (1998), 101–4.

While the group is unselfconscious, it may not realize what it is doing by deploying the vocabulary. It can come as a surprise to people to learn of the practical atmosphere surrounding a term. This is why consciousness-raising is a task. But if it comes as an uncomfortable surprise, then thanks to lovers of thick concepts, our group can mount a defence. The critique only worked by disentangling. But, they may complain, ours is a thick concept. And then comes a litany: to call someone cute, in our whirl of organism or form of life, is not to stitch together a distinct fact and a distinct attitude. It is instead to respond seamlessly to the world, only using a full human sensibility. When young men and women grow into our way of life, they acquire a second nature, a receptivity to a certain kind of woman, the cute ones, and the property that distinguishes them, cuteness. When success arrives one has become receptive to cuteness, indeed, one simply observes it. It is a salient and welcome part of the *Lebensweld*. Furthermore when you saw us as admiring and appraising favourably, and even choosing cute partners, you misdescribe our reactions. Our reaction, if you call it that, is really *sui generis*. It is simply that which is demanded or merited by cute women. If you wanted a term for the reaction, we would have to make one up. But that may go too far: better to stick with the cognitive success that understanding of cuteness denotes. Above all, nothing here has anything to do with projecting or gilding or staining—the usual expressivist metaphors—but simply with appreciating cuteness as it demands.

And having got this far our group may then go on the offensive: perhaps the supposed critique only appeals to reductionists or to the scientistic, or to exiles from this way of life, and therefore need not be heard at all. We don't listen to critiques mounted from delusive Archimedean points outside the social world we inhabit! You cannot criticize our singing unless you have learned our songs. Or, they may insinuate that we only reject thick concepts if we misunderstand the actual phenomenology: the way cuteness involves no kind of inference, but a simple single experience, whose content is describable in no other terms.[3]

I take it as obvious that this 'defence' against the original critique does not work. The force of our critique has not been blunted. But the question for anyone tempted to be a lover of thick concepts is—why not? If our critique worked by disentangling, but disentangling is not to be done, then our critique depends on a false account of the phenomenon.

Examples such as this abound. One I like is the way the historian Quentin Skinner gives a lucid and convincing account of the social and economic changes at the end of the sixteenth century and how they led to contests over such terms as 'vocation', 'calling', 'dedication', and others, previously cemented to specifically religious practices, but increasingly coopted by the rising mercantile classes to defend and give value to their economic activities.[4] Skinner's diagnosis would be impossible if all we saw was a cultural

---

[3] A similar attack is made, in a similarly futile way, by philosophers trying to attack Hume's theory of causation, and many other naturalistic projects.

[4] Skinner (2002), chapter 8. I discuss this example further in Blackburn (2008).

change in which words which once expressed one concept began to express a different one. The whole point is that it is the positive evaluative direction that makes it worth trying to stretch the application of the terms to cover activities to which nobody, previously, would have thought of applying them. It is this constancy of positive evaluative direction that anchors the whole diagnosis.

It is instructive here to compare, as Putnam does, the reception of thickness in moral theory with that of similar doctrines in the philosophy of science. Suppose we fasten upon four episodes, some of which Putnam also highlights.[5] There is, with Quine, the collapse of the analytic-synthetic dualism and the substitution of general holism. There is, with Goodman, the general failure of 'algorithmic' confirmation theory. There is, with Sellars, a collapse of the observation/theory distinction. And there is, with Kuhn, the growing stress on 'extrinsic' factors as determinants of the fate of theories, where extrinsic denotes social and cultural factors outside the textbooks, but that play a surprisingly large role in determining what gets into the textbooks.

Clearly, these four episodes played a role in generating a crisis in the philosophy of science, as well they might have done. This crisis was not just the overthrow of some parochial 'positivist' model of how science is to be described. The grave problem was the far-reaching threat to many of the cherished notions attaching to science: by the 1970s or so rationality, objectivity, observation, or falsification, and commensurability had been made problematic, each in turn.

At first sight it is strange, therefore, that ethical theory took the other tack, supposing that the parallel themes that surround the emphasis on thick concepts, far from undermining rationality, objectivity, commensurability and the rest, liberated them. Whereas the four episodes I mentioned threatened to take science off its pedestal, parallel themes were taken to elevate ethics onto one. This must surely prompt us to ask why ethics is supposed to be able to profit from the very complexities that seemed to diminish science?

The thought, clearly, must have been that once science had been properly cut down to size, ethics resurrected itself from the dustbin into which the positivist account of science had thrust it. If *that's* what observation, confirmation, theory, rationality, or even truth, come to in science, goes the thought, then we can have them all in ethics. What seems to have impressed lovers of thick concepts less than it should have was the question of what you do with them when you have them: whether the prize is won in name only. For if science's pedestal was ground down by removing everything previously comprehended under the idea of *authority*, it is no great trick for ethics to jump up to the same height.

Putnam does not directly address the question of whether thickness discourages critique. But he very strongly implies the reverse, that only thickness protects and enables various kinds of subtle and civilized ethics. His particular illustration is the 'capabilities'

---

[5] For Quine, see, for example, Putnam (2002), 9–11; for Kuhn, see n. 41 on 25 and surrounding discussion in the main text.

approach of Sen, which argues that welfare economics needs to recognize that the freedom of members of a society to enjoy valuable human functioning is the prime measure of the value of their social set-up.[6] As Sen has shown, such a measure fits uneasily with anything like classical utility, or indeed anything indexed by simple economic measures. It sits badly as well with the classical measure of well-being in terms of desire satisfaction, since as Aldous Huxley showed in *Brave New World*, and as Sen also stresses, the absence of unsatisfied desire may itself be the result of the adaptation of desire to subordination or deprivation. Putnam believes that the collapse of the fact-value dualism helps Sen's project: he describes himself as 'providing a philosophy of language that can accommodate and support' this kind of economic and ethical thought.[7]

However, it is harder to see why this should be accepted. Putnam's stated reason is that the terms in which this thought must be conducted are themselves entangled: he cites terms such as 'valuable functioning', 'functioning a person has reason to value', 'well nourished', 'premature mortality', 'self respect', and 'ability to take part in the life of the community'.[8] He is perfectly correct that these terms involve valuations. In a warrior society death in battle in the late teens might not count as a premature death whereas in ours it would. In a traditional society, a disenfranchised woman might count as taking part in the life of the community, whereas in ours she would not, and so on. But this does not address the question of why these valuations require thick concepts rather than loaded terms, or indeed whether they actually require either. For we can say well enough what Sen approves of and what he regrets, and what he would have us approve of in the way of progress and what he would not. Hence Putnam actually evades the question that he ostensibly raises, of whether Sen's approach is compatible with Sen's own prescriptivism, expressed in the earlier paper to which he refers.

Putnam is certainly correct that Sen's approach, like any substantial ethic, can only be supported if there is space for substantial, rational, discussion of values.[9] He reminds us of the melancholy fact that some positivists, particularly in the 1930s, denied that there was space for such discussion. His particular example is the economist Lionel Robbins, who indeed seems to have made hair-raising pronouncements of just this kind.[10] A. J. Ayer and perhaps Rudolf Carnap could be put in the dock beside him. But for seventy years since then, and for two thousand years before then, other theorists have taken great care to acknowledge that discussion of attitudes and stances is fundamentally important. (Think of Plato on love and desire. It is arguably only scientism of just the kind that Putnam deplores that could think such discussion as other than important.) Indeed expressivists claim that they have a particular insight into *why* discussion of these things is important. It is important because when you change someone's mind about a value,

---

[6] Putnam (2002), 46–64. See, for example, Sen (1987).

[7] Putnam (2002), 64.

[8] Putnam (2002), 63.

[9] But only a weak sense of 'rational'—what I call a Hume-friendly sense—is necessary. In this sense, rational discussion of an end or a value will proceed in the light of other ends or other values. It will not take off from a Kantian landscape of pure rationality informed by no aims, no concerns, and no desires.

[10] Putnam (2002), 53–4. See Robbins (1932).

you change their stance towards the world, and that will typically change what they do and what they support and what they regret and what they campaign for. It changes their way of being in the world, for better or worse.

Not only is discussion important, but there are better and worse ways of conducting it, and it is the good ways that are collected under the umbrella 'rational'. Manipulation, concealment, evasion, fantasies, arguments *ad hominem, ad baculum*, and the rest are bad. Addressing peoples' concerns, unveiling the truth, testing commitments against cases, sketching analogies, expanding open-mindedness, and so on are good. Can expressivists draw the distinctions here? Certainly. Even when the aim of discussion is to change the other person's mind (which is not always the case), it is not true that the end justifies any means. Only some means are compatible with respect for the other person. Changing the other person's mind—changing their stance towards the world—is a fine art, but expressivists as much as anyone else can distinguish between my bringing it about that someone wants something by deception and manipulation, and bringing it about by revealing truths about it that, in one's own eyes, ought to impress the subject favourably.[11] It is the same with valuations and appraisals. Furthermore, the 'Neurath's boat' account of the epistemology of such processes, which Putnam implies is the private property of lovers of thick concepts, is in fact common property. Just as readily as lovers of thick concepts, those who prefer an approach in terms of load and attitude can agree on a holistic, anti-foundational, fallible, coherentist method of aiming at virtuous equilibrium.

For these reasons, then, we should resist any general tendency to believe that love of thick concepts abets the authority of ethics, or helps us to understand the relationship between different ethical perspectives or different ways of living. Indeed, as my first example shows, we should believe exactly the reverse, that emphasis on indissoluble thick concepts only engenders a creeping complacency, a separation of those with whom we can talk from those whom we cannot, and an easy excuse for turning our backs on the latter, excising them from the sphere of discourse.

Putnam, clearly, does not fear these worrying consequences. Before discussing Putnam directly, however, I shall outline some of the issues on which I have previously taken a stand.

7.2 Representation and attitude

I am inclined to distinguish between attitudes, or other stances towards things, and representations of how things stand. I think there are a number of reasons for doing this. The simplest, and certainly the motivation that has received most prominence in these debates, derives from Miss Anscombe's celebrated 'direction of fit' metaphor.[12] Representations of how things stand must fit the world whereas it is the world that must fit, or

---

[11] I fear that Williams's notorious distinction between internal and external reasons has clouded counsel here. I say more about this in Blackburn (1998), 264–6.

[12] See Anscombe (1957).

be desired to fit, or be regretted for not fitting, our attitudes. The distinction is traditional: what a person believes and what he desires, for example, have always been held to be two different things. This is not undermined by the allegedly Aristotelian thought that liking or desiring something is the same as believing it good, since that equation can be read more as a comment on believing good than on liking, as it was by Hobbes, for example.

This might sound uncontroversial, but 'cognition' has imperialistic ambitions. Even emotions have been described as nothing more than cognitions. I resist those ambitions. To take an uncontroversial (so far as I know) example, suppose I describe someone who has just received a surprise as confused, or having his head in a whirl. I am not describing his beliefs, but his difficulty in coming to beliefs. Being unable to stabilize or settle upon some beliefs is a distinct state, and distinctly described by saying that an agent has his head in a whirl. It is the most dreadful dogma that all that can be said about an agent's mental state is sayable in terms of the content of their beliefs—having your head in a whirl is a counterexample. Equally when I say that someone likes Broadway musicals, with contempt, surprise, amusement, fear, or cunning in my voice, I make public facts about myself, but not by voicing further beliefs. Rather, I put into the public domain my practical or emotional take on the one belief.

Employing the distinction between attitudes and beliefs does, of course, open me to the demand to say something about representation itself. This I am happy to do: representations play a distinctive role in the explanation of success in action. When I token to myself a sentence such as 'The university library is over there' I am typically successful, if I act upon it, because the university library is over there. No explanation of my success that failed to mention the library would do. Similarly if I talk of things having a property I am typically successful, when I act upon such a representation, because the property is instanced in some case or in some pattern of cases.

Some might scent an opening here. Why not extend the account to cover representations of things being good or right? Might we not say that actions derived from tokens of sentences such as 'That is the right thing to do' are typically successful, when they are, because whatever was picked out *was* the right thing to do? My answer to this is complex. I admit that in some circumstances we can say this. But I deny that they form a pattern. If our interest is explanation, we will reject such explanation in favour of ones that look at the underlying circumstances. As Jeremy Waldron pointed out to me when discussing Nick Sturgeon's example, we could say, casually as it were, that the Donner party died because Passed Midshipman Woodward was no damned good.[13] But we couldn't say it as anything except a summary or slogan, where what was summarized would be a much more complicated history told in quite other terms. There would be no interesting commonality between an explanation of the fate of the Donner party, and an explanation of the fate of the British Labour Party, although each could be told in terms of individual people being no damned good.

---

[13] The example is from Sturgeon (1985), 64.

This is where thick terms first make their appearance. For if we advance explanations using such terms, interesting commonalities may indeed emerge. If the Donner party perished specifically because Passed Midshipman Woodward was pig-headed, and the Labour Party perishes because Gordon Brown is pig-headed, we do have a common pattern, and one which has been exemplified and repeated throughout human history. Indeed, this repeated pattern will be the reason why vices get their bad name, and virtues get their good names, names which, in Hume's terms, force an avowal of their merits. The rationale for having a word like 'pig-headed' lies largely in the characteristic way in which projects fail when people are insufficiently attentive to other things than whatever they hold onto, blindly, given the evidence and the stakes.

So do the representative credentials of thick terms simply declare themselves, given this account? Not unless we have taken a prior stance on the issue of disentangling. For we do not know yet what is doing the explaining. 'Pig-headed' is indeed a loaded term. Was the load an integral part of the explanation? Was it essential to the history that we tell it with the term 'pig-headed' carrying its evaluative charge? On the face of it, we can imagine the same history of how the Labour Party perished written in terms of Gordon Brown's capacity for conviction and indifference to other peoples' attempts to reason with him, without at all committing ourselves on whether these traits (or for that matter the demise of the Labour Party) are good things or not. We would not have to choose the overtly loaded vocabulary. Perhaps the load does none of the explanatory work. If an executive explains his success at getting cheap raw materials by boasting that they are supplied by—and then uses a derogatory term, say for the nationality of his suppliers— his explanation is no better than if he said that they were supplied by the people of that nationality, but his way of presenting the explanation is nastily overloaded.

Often, however, because of the way in which the load drives the extension, it may be harder to get rid of the particular term. Suppose, carelessly, we thought that 'acolyte of X' was simply a derogatory term for 'student of X'. We might then suppose that there is no difference between explaining why Y was at the conference by saying that Y is one of X's students, or by saying that Y is an acolyte of X. This is wrong, because the derogation points to something specific that is corrupt or wrong about the relationship between X and Y, something beyond Y just being a student of X, and it may be just this that explains why Y is at the conference. It is not because Y learns from X, or X is Y's professor, but because of the extent of Y's devotion, or the nature of X's acceptance of that devotion. But of course, we can get past the loaded vocabulary as we say this: indeed, I just did. (I return later to the reasonable suspicion that something thick or loaded still remains.)

So far we have learned that, as far as critique goes, thinking in terms of loaded terms is better than loving thick concepts, and so far as representation goes, there is no problem about maintaining the non-representative or non-receptive nature of the loads which we make our descriptions carry.

There is another moral to this brief account of representation. One of Putnam's most effective strategies is to claim that the breakdown of the fact-value distinction is to be expected, given modern pessimism about ever finding a substantive concept of a fact. It is only, he implies, if we are wedded to the old eighteenth-century conception of a fact as something that can be pictured, or perhaps to some equally discredited positivist successor, that can any longer sustain the distinction.[14] But I deny that this is so. For our brush with representation shows that whether or not we see a stance as representational is tied in with our best accounts of explanation (in particular, the explanation of success of action based upon it). There is no reason why an approach based on such a notion should not certify a representation/stance distinction without in any way inheriting empiricist or positivist simplicities, and for that matter without in any way trespassing upon modern deflationism about the concept of a fact.

7.3 Thickness and the fact-value distinction

Putnam has several reasons for thinking of many words as thick. The most prominent is supposed to start from the premise he attributes to Iris Murdoch and John McDowell, that when a term involves an evaluative element (if, indeed, it is permissible for lovers of thick concepts to put it that way) there is no saying just which things the term applies to without either sharing, or at least appreciating, the evaluative outlook of those who use it.[15] But as we have seen, any intelligent notion of the way terms are loaded admits and explains exactly the same phenomenon.

If a term is loaded, the load can well play a role in determining the extension. You do not call someone pig-headed unless you have an unfavourable take on the way he forms or maintains his convictions. If I cannot cotton on to the contours of your favourable and unfavourable takes on such things, indeed I cannot predict who you will call pig-headed. Similarly if I cannot understand your sense of humour I will not be able to understand why you laugh at some things and not at others. If queer things make you panic, I cannot predict when you will do so. I do not know what sets you off. But this is no argument that what happens when you *are* set off is that you do no more than make a representation of a feature of things. Nor is it an argument for denying that on any particular occasion on which you are set off there is something to which you were responding, even if across the board the class of things that elicit this response is what I called 'shapeless'—sharing no significant commonality except that they so strike you.

We can, of course, go on to discuss whether you *should* be set off as you are, either whether it is a case of evaluation, or of humour, or of emotion, or of any other stance. We want to know whether we should be like-minded. But this is no argument that in being like-minded we are simply describing or representing the world in the same way, as opposed to the much more natural way of putting it, which is that we are reacting to it in the same way, or adopting the same stance towards it.

Some words that are alleged to be thick have quite a flexible relationship with any particular attitude or stance. Sometimes at any one time, a variety of attitudes and stances

[14] Putnam (2002), 20–3.
[15] Putnam (2002), 37–8. He references the papers in Part II of McDowell (1998) and Murdoch (1970).

may attach to one word. (No one attitude is attached to English words for place of origin, like 'Geordie' or 'Scouse', although their use is a signal that some attitude or other is in the offing. It might be affection, or contempt, or something else again.) Sometimes the load is more a matter of 'passing theory' or context and purpose than it is of standing theory or semantic convention. I myself have difficulty hearing 'courageous' as inevitably admiring. After all many values are contested, and we have to be able to say what we are contesting and what the rivals are bargaining for. Other words slip off one load, and begin to bear others. This was the moral of Skinner's slice of history. Words are often ready to be decoupled from particular stances with which they have been associated—witness the political ambition of many marginalized groups to 'reclaim' the vocabulary that expressed their marginalization. But you can only decouple what was coupled in the first place. To revert to my original metaphor, you can only unload something that was loaded. But for the lover of thick concepts there can be no such ambition. All you can do is junk one term, and replace it by an (accidentally? unfortunately?) homologous one.

Going onto the offensive, we might raise nasty questions about the identity criteria for thick concepts. When do they arise, and when do they go out of use? I have illustrated this with the example of a group who begins to find fat unattractive, and to use a sneery intonation to express their derogation of it.[16] 'He is fat↓' they say, in that contemptuous tone. Have they acquired the new thick concept yet? Presumably not: it was not a conceptual advance but a social dislike that originated their doings. Suppose now a piece of vocabulary arrives to do what the intonation did: they find the word 'gross', just as ageists find 'wrinklies' and philistines call people like us 'eggheads' and we call them 'yobs'. Was this the conceptual advance? Again, there is no reason so to describe it. When things get better and the social divide loses its significance, there is no conceptual loss, just an emotional gain.

Putnam's other main argument is more original, and I would like to close by considering it. He introduces it by quoting the famous passage with which Quine finishes his essay 'Carnap and Logical Truth':

The lore of our fathers is a fabric of sentences. In our hands it develops and changes, through more or less arbitrary and deliberate revisions and additions of our own, more or less directly occasioned by the continuing stimulation of our sense organs. It is a pale grey lore, black with fact and white with convention. But I have found no substantial reasons for concluding that there are any quite black threads in it, or any white ones.[17]

Putnam quotes with approval Vivian Walsh's addendum, that the composite may as well be red with values, but they too will be spread over the web, making it always pinko-grey.[18] In other words, what we say must always be an indissoluble compound of fact or observation, conceptual or theoretical take on that fact, and the values infusing that choice of fact or way of taking it.

---

[16] See both Blackburn (1992), 290, and (1998), 94ff.
[17] Quine (1963).
[18] Putnam (2002), 30. See Walsh (1987).

Putnam is careful here, since he himself has denied some of the excesses that Quine prompted. He does not oppose limited use of an analytic/synthetic distinction, for instance in cases of definitional abbreviation (which Quine himself allowed to be intelligible, as was pounced upon by P. F. Strawson and Paul Grice). He now expresses himself by denying an analytic synthetic dualism or dichotomy, an unbridgeable gulf between things of one kind and things of the other, with implications for the way they should be treated, and still more for the questions it is worth asking. For one of the effects of Quine's work was to stop us from asking how the analytic and the synthetic are distributed, for instance over Newton's three laws of motion. The whole has empirical significance, but how the empirical and the definitional are distributed ceases to be of concern. It is not, as the positivists would have had it, a sign of confusion or insufficient analysis, but a sign of health, that we cannot say what is definition and what is doctrine. Similarly in the case of values, which is why Putnam's essay and book are called *The Collapse of the Fact/Value Dichotomy*, not ...*of the Fact-Value Distinction*.

This raises many questions, as of course Quine's own attack does. It is not really clear what the metaphor of everything having a tinge of pink comes to when, for instance, we reel off unloaded descriptions of the external world. I shall return to this in the context of Putnam's insistence on the pervasive presence of epistemic norms that enable us to make even the most flat and unloaded of descriptions. But meanwhile there is a different question. How much does Walsh's extension undermine what anybody sensible might want from a fact-value *distinction*? Those who have wanted such a distinction have not typically demanded that evaluation and appraisal, what I have called the load, be allocated precisely to particular words or sayings. For Quine, the impossibility of saying that one sentence represents convention and that another sentence represents fact was of paramount importance, because the single sentence is the only possible candidate for analyticity. But for most defenders of a fact-value distinction, such as Hume, it is simply does not have to be true that it is a single sentence that carries the load of value, any more than it had to be one sentence of Antony's speech that contained its overall intention.

Let me illustrate with a closely parallel example. Suppose I believe in a distinction, or even a dichotomy, between describing a natural scene on the one hand, and expressing nostalgia for a lost childhood on the other. And now suppose I come across a poem which clearly does both, but where in some sense the load of nostalgia is spread across the whole poem. No bit of the poem is white with pure description, and no bit is red with nothing but nostalgia, but the whole effect is undeniably pink. Does this undermine my distinction, or even dichotomy? Surely not. It is simply no part of the interest or propriety of the distinction that the load must be carried by a precisely determinate word or phrase or other trope. Perhaps it was done by a tiny accumulation of hints and choices nudging the mood as the poet wished. Similarly we can be sure that a drawing of a politician by some cartoonist is derogatory, without needing to say which bit does the trick. As critics, or as emulators, we will want to discover how the thing is managed. But as consumers we can just remain pleased or shocked that it was. By saying that there is a fact-value distinction, or equally a geography-nostalgia distinction, we need mean no more than that there is a feat to be managed. The load must be placed somewhere, and skill lies in knowing how best to place it.

Hence, used for this purpose, Walsh's extension of Quine's metaphor misfires. The analytic-synthetic distinction, in Quine's view, is *intrinsically* tied to distributing meanings to sentences one at a time. But the fact-value distinction, like the geography-nostalgia distinction, is not. It really *does not care* how the evaluative load is distributed.[19]

Similarly suppose we allow that there may be no such thing as a purely neutral description of a scene. There may always be pink in the offing. Would this undermine a geography-nostalgia distinction? No, because the geography may be whatever is left after we ignore the different kinds of pink it comes in. If one book describes the noble elevation of the Alps, and another describes their menacing grandeur, the Alps and their height are what are left if we abstract from the difference. If what is left still shows tinctures of pink, we can repeat the process as often as we need.

We do not actually need to worry whether we ever arrive at pure white. This picks up the point left dangling above, the fear that if there is always pink remaining, the process of peeling off layers of it is somehow futile. I follow Nietzsche in reversing the issue. There can be a point in a process if something is achieved at each stage of the process, not only if there is an end-point; something like a limiting frequency or descriptions asymptotic to pure white in the long run. One might even suggest that the fact-value distinction is best conceived as a methodological recommendation—the way to approach individual issues in particular contexts, when disentangling needs to be done before we can make any progress.

The point is parallel to one frequently made in the philosophy of science. The Sellarsian idea of all observations being theory-laden only unsettled the idea that science is responsible to observation for a very short time. For it was rapidly realized that this responsibility is only threatened if the theory that loads the observation is the very theory that is under test, and this need not be the case. When it is not the case, theory can still be confirmed or undermined by independent observations: ones that themselves require no standpoint on the theory itself, whatever other cognitive baggage it takes in order to make them. Similarly here. If we discuss, say, whether a death is premature or not, and someone suggests that this is so whenever the subject is healthy at the time, their contribution is not nullified by the fact that 'healthy' itself carries a shade of pink. Provided soldiers and victims of car accidents can be agreed to be previously healthy, which they can, then the suggestion delineates at least a class of premature deaths.

Perhaps Putnam need not oppose that, nor we him. We can meet Putnam halfway. As I have described, he is conciliatory about distinctions but harsh about dichotomies or dualisms. His purpose is to rescue intelligent ethical thought, argument about ends as well as

---

[19] As far as the philosophy of language goes. Practically there may be advantages one way or another: for instance, intonation is more readily deniable than vocabulary, which is why PC bans on vocabulary can backfire. Antony could disown the intended effects of his speech.

means. Putnam wishes to make room for what he sees as an insight of Murdoch, that there can be an expansion of our understandings given by increasing attention to things like courage and justice, or cruelty or harm.[20] The positivists such as Robbins were blind to this possibility: the other side of their fact-value dichotomy was occupied by nothing but a dustbin.

If that was the dichotomy or dualism, then good riddance to it indeed. And we can also applaud one of Putnam's strategies for getting rid of it, which is to point out the way in which things on the good side of the divide, such as scientific theories, only get there with the aid of things from the dustbin: epistemic values and stances on things like plausibility, simplicity, economy, and even probability. Conviction, or cautious acceptance, or skepticism, are themselves stances, as are explanatory preferences or taste in theoretical avenues. I too think it is good for theoretical scientists that they realize their dependence on epistemic values and choices, and it was bad of positivism to disguise it from them. Here a note of caution is appropriate, however. For it is one thing to point out the pervasive presence of epistemic values in determining what we believe. It is another thing to say that those values pervade the content of what we believe. The pink does not seep into what we say, even if it plays a role in getting us to say it. Robert Millikan had to make choices and deploy values to arrive at a measure for the charge on the electron, but it makes no sense to suppose that the fact that the charge on the electron is around $1.60217733 \times 10^{-19}$ coulombs inherits those choices and values. Some say that Millikan had to be self-confident and even a little bit devious to get the results of his classic paper, but the charge on the electron is neither self-confident nor devious.

Putnam is certainly right that we can increase our understanding of all kinds of human phenomena by all kinds of traditional humane and literary studies. We learn more of what cruelty might be from Henry James, or more of what bigotry might mean from Salman Rushdie. Political hypocrisy is revalued by Machiavelli and integrity by Rousseau. Do-gooding itself is rendered ambivalent by Dickens. Simple-minded words of praise and blame give way to nuance and qualification and judgment. In other words we learn—and it is indeed learning—to contour the directions of our praise and approval and admiration, or of our contempt or discomfort or disgust. It deserves to be called learning because at the end of it we are better than we were at the beginning, even if we cannot prove this to those who remain differently minded.

All that I hold is that in context, and for the purpose of enabling discussion and critique to go forward at any particular junction, the right methodological route is to distinguish as well as we may. We advance one step of fact at a time, distilling the residue of disagreements of value as far as we can, until if we are lucky (but only if) any that remain prove slight or tractable.

It is sometimes thought that the expressivist concentration on attitude at the expense of representation is some kind of denial that in these areas learning and understanding can increase. This was no part of Plato's view, or Hume's view. It is no part of my view, and I think it should be no part of anybody's.

---

[20] Putnam (2002), 40.

References

Anscombe, G. E. M. (1957) *Intention* (Oxford: Blackwell).

Blackburn, Simon (1981) 'Rule-Following and Moral Realism', in Stephen Holtzman and Christopher Leich (eds.) *Wittgenstein: To Follow a Rule* (London: Routledge and Kegan Paul), 163–87.

—— (1992) 'Morality and Thick Concepts: Through Thick and Thin', *Proceedings of the Aristotelian Society, Supplementary Volume* 66: 285–99. Reprinted in Blackburn (2010), 129–46.

—— (1998) *Ruling Passions* (Oxford: Oxford University Press).

—— (2008) 'The Absolute Conception: Putnam vs. Williams', in Daniel Calcutt (ed.) *Reading Bernard Williams* (London: Routledge), 9–23. Reprinted in Blackburn (2010), 245–61.

—— (2010) *Practical Tortoise Raising* (Oxford: Oxford University Press).

McDowell, John (1998) *Mind, Value, and Reality* (Cambridge, MA: Harvard University Press).

Murdoch, Iris (1970) *The Sovereignty of Good* (London: Routledge and Kegan Paul).

Putnam, Hilary (2002) *The Collapse of the Fact/Value Dichotomy and Other Essays* (Cambridge, MA: Harvard University Press).

Quine, W. V. (1963) 'Carnap and Logical Truth' in Paul Arthur Schlipp (ed.) *The Philosophy of Rudolf Carnap* (LaSalle, IL: Open Court), 385–406.

Robbins, Lionel (1932) *On the Nature and Significance of Economic Science* (London: Macmillan).

Sen, Amartya (1987) *On Ethics and Economics* (Oxford: Blackwell).

Skinner, Quentin (2002) *Visions of Politics* (Cambridge: Cambridge University Press).

Sturgeon, Nicholas (1985) 'Moral Explanations' in David Copp and David Zimmerman (eds.) *Morality, Reason, and Truth* (Totowa, NJ: Rowman and Allanheld), 49–78.

Walsh, Vivian (1987) 'Philosophy and Economics' in John Eatwell, Murray Milgate, and Peter Newman (eds.) *The New Palgrave: A Dictionary of Economics* (London: Macmillan), 861–9.

8

Thick Concepts and Underdetermination

Pekka Väyrynen

8.1 Introduction

What is supposed to be distinctive of "thick" concepts relative to "thin" concepts in ethics and aesthetics is that thick concepts somehow "hold together" evaluation and non-evaluative description, whereas thin concepts are somehow more purely evaluative or normative.[1] This seems to capture an intuitive contrast between thick concepts, such as those expressed by terms like *rude, brutal, graceful*, and *kind*, and thin concepts, such as many concepts expressed by terms like *wrong, good*, and *impermissible*. Even if causing offense is both rude and bad, only *rude* seems to require as a matter of meaning that things falling under it must have something to do with causing offense; the meaning of *bad* generates no such constraint, since many bad things have nothing to do with causing offense. Thick terms and concepts seem to bear some broadly conceptual connections to some fairly concrete sort of non-evaluative descriptions.

What is more controversial is whether thick terms and concepts bear similar conceptual relations to evaluation. (By "evaluations" I mean claims or information with evaluative content, not mental acts of evaluation.) No doubt *rude* is typically used to convey negative evaluation, where "convey" is an umbrella term for different means (such as content, presupposition, or implicature) by which utterances can transfer information. Just what kind of failure of understanding would be manifested by someone who has caused offense but fails to grasp the kind of negative evaluation that is typically conveyed by calling something *rude* depends precisely on just how thick terms and concepts are related to the evaluations they may be used to convey. The standard view is that evaluation is built into the meaning (sense, semantic content) of utterances involving thick terms and concepts as much as the non-evaluative descriptions that they entail are so built. The alternative is that evaluations are some weaker, perhaps broadly pragmatic

[1] For discussion of whether the distinction between thick and thin epistemic concepts is analogous, see Väyrynen (2008).

implication of utterances involving thick terms and concepts. Such views are currently in the minority.

This paper takes a step in defense of such rival views. Certain features of how thick terms and concepts combine evaluation and description are widely taken to support a semantic view of the relationship between thick terms and concepts and evaluation. I'll focus specifically on the idea that the non-evaluative aspects of their meanings underdetermine their extensions. If they do, then what, if not evaluation, could help to determine the extensions of thick terms and concepts? And how, if not by belonging to their meanings, could evaluations drive their extensions? What I'll argue is that the relevant kind of underdetermination of extension can be expected to arise irrespective of whether the relationship between thick terms and concepts and evaluation is semantic or conceptual and can be explained without that supposition. If that is correct, the underdetermination phenomena I'll discuss cannot be used to support a semantic view of the relationship between thick terms and concepts and evaluation.

8.2 Extension and evaluation

Everyone agrees that thick terms and concepts can be used to convey both non-evaluative description and evaluation. Most writers across various other party lines presume that this is because both aspects are built into the meanings of thick terms and concepts. Information that is "built into" the meaning of a term is to be understood as including the semantic and conceptual entailments of sentences involving those terms. Assigning non-evaluative information of this kind to thick terms and concepts explains why it is semantically permissible to apply thick terms and concepts only to certain non-evaluatively constrained types of things. For instance, *cruel* can apply only to things that have to do with causing suffering.

The view that evaluation is similarly built into the meanings of thick terms and concepts is often simply assumed as common ground in discussions of other issues about thick terms and concepts, such as the issue of "disentanglement" or "separability." This is the issue of whether thick terms and concepts represent some kind of irreducible fusions of evaluation and description or whether their evaluative and non-evaluative aspects are somehow separable.[2] It is, all the same, a controversial view, especially when taken as a fully general view about thick terms and concepts. This class is usually introduced ostensively by listing some paradigmatic examples, such as *cruel, courageous, generous, greedy*, or those at the beginning of this paper. But already the characterization and the scope of the relevant class are matters of dispute.[3] Some philosophers also argue

---

[2] For discussions of this issue, most of which assume the standard view, see for example Foot (1958), McDowell (1981), Williams (1985), Hurley (1989), Blackburn (1992), Gibbard (1992), Dancy (1995), Elstein and Hurka (2009), Kirchin (2010), and Roberts (2011).

[3] For problems with existing characterizations of what thick concepts are, see Scheffler (1987) and, especially, Eklund (2011). Regarding the scope of the class, there are disputes as to whether ethnic slurs or other sorts of pejorative expression should be counted as thick concepts, and even whether such terms as *unchaste* and *cruel* are significantly alike.

that in fact thick terms and concepts, or at least a very wide range of the paradigmatic examples of them, aren't inherently evaluative in meaning but merely are typically used in ways that convey evaluation.[4] Finally, tacit assumptions to the effect that thick terms and concepts form a uniform class are common in the literature, but such assumptions are rarely defended explicitly and by no means obviously true. It cannot therefore be simply assumed that evaluation is in general built into the meanings of thick terms and concepts.

The view that evaluation belongs to the meanings of thick terms and concepts is often supported by claiming that evaluation "drives the extension" of thick terms and concepts.[5] This former claim may be stated as follows:

> *Extension* The extensions of thick terms and concepts (relative to context) are determined in part by global evaluations.

The extension of a term can be understood as the set of all and only the things that satisfy the term.[6] The qualification "relative to context" will be discussed shortly. The phrase "global evaluations" also requires explanation, regarding both what makes some information evaluative to begin with and what the restriction "global" means.

It is controversial what evaluation is. I'll assume that evaluation is somehow positive or negative in flavor. More precisely, I'll understand evaluation as information to the effect that something has (or lacks) merit, worth, or significance (that is, a positive or a negative standing) relative to a certain kind of standard, namely one that grounds claims of merit, worth, or significance.[7] It is, in brief, information that something is good, or bad, in some way. Being intrinsically good and being instrumentally good, being morally good and being aesthetically good, being good for having features F, G, H, and being a good instance of a kind K, are all ways of being good in the relevant sense. This characterization focuses my discussion on the relationship of thick terms and concepts to evaluations of their instances as good, or bad, in some way.

The restriction to "global" evaluations is meant to focus my discussion on the issue of whether the meaning of *courageous*, for instance, builds in the condition that accepting certain risks of harm for the sake of good goals is good in a certain way, not whether it entails that things falling under it involve accepting certain risks of harm for the sake of

---

[4]　See Hare (1952), chapter 7, and (1981), 17–18, 73–5, Blackburn (1992), and Väyrynen (2012).

[5]　See for example Foot (1958), McDowell (1981), Williams (1985), Blackburn (1992), Gibbard (1992), Elstein and Hurka (2009), Kirchin (2010), and Roberts (2011).

[6]　There is a wrinkle here. It is often not clear in the literature on thick terms and concepts whether extension is understood to be the set of things that actually satisfy the term or the set of the actual and possible things that fall under it. Of these two notions, the latter is more closely aligned with such things as meanings and properties. Thus, insofar as Extension is supposed to bear on the meanings of thick terms and concepts, it may be more charitably understood as concerning this latter notion of extension.

[7]　This characterization derives in part from Williams (1985), 125. It takes no stand on whether the evaluative aspects of thick terms and concepts are irreducible to thin evaluations. The mere appearance of the word *good* or *bad* isn't enough to make the evaluation it expresses thin. Consider predicates like *a good philosopher* or *good with children*.

goals whose value is greater than the badness of the harm.[8] The latter evaluation involves evaluative notions that are prior to and independent of *courageous*. Whether φ-ing involves good goals and bad risks can and must be settled prior to settling whether φ-ing is courageous. So the crucial issue whether thick terms and concepts have any *distinctive* significance to evaluative thought and judgment turns specifically on their relationship to global evaluations.[9] The sort of idea that Extension is meant to convey is that the extension of *courageous* is driven in part by some conception (perhaps difficult to articulate) of when and why it is worthwhile to accept a risk of harm for the sake of something valuable. Actions of this general type simply don't count as courageous unless they are thereby good in some way, unless there is some kind of reason to perform them or the like.

Typical arguments for Extension trade on common intuitions about when speakers are engaged in genuine agreement or disagreement about evaluative and normative matters and not merely talking past one another.[10] Consider disputes about distributive justice. Thrasymachus holds (or at least could hold) that distributive justice is conformity to what is in the ruler's interest regarding distributions, while Nozick holds that it is conformity to entitlement and Rawls holds that it is conformity to his two principles of justice.[11] These features of distributions sometimes come apart, so not all three parties can be right about what distributions count as just. But parties to such disputes typically take themselves to be addressing a common topic. Their disagreement about the extension of *distributively just* seems univocal. This cannot be explained by whatever overlap there may be in their conceptions of distributive justice. A better candidate for what ties their dispute together might rather seem to be the assumption that just distributions are distributions with those features, whatever they may be, which make distributions good in a certain way. Their disagreement concerns what the relevantly good-making features of distributions in fact are. This is to treat evaluation as driving the extension of *distributively just*.

I'll briefly register some general concerns about this kind of argument before focusing on other issues. The concern can be illustrated by recalling that Thrasymachus is contemptuous of justice (which he, again, conceives of as what is in the ruler's interest),

---

[8] These evaluative conditions illustrate the distinction between what Daniel Elstein and Thomas Hurka call "global" and "embedded" evaluations. See Elstein and Hurka (2009).

[9] The exception to this is the view that thick terms and concepts are evaluative in some *sui generis* sense in which evaluation need be neither positive nor negative in flavor. I'll set these views aside here; but see Kirchin (this volume) and Roberts (this volume).

[10] A different argument for Extension can be found in Dancy (1995). He infers Extension from his argument that the evaluative and non-evaluative aspects of thick terms and concepts are irreducibly inseparable. The discussion to follow is relevant to this argument as well, since the argument operates with the background presumption that the meanings of thick terms and concepts involve evaluation.

[11] See Plato, *Republic*, Book I, Rawls (1971), and Nozick (1974). I am of course taking liberties in representing Thrasymachus' view as an account of specifically distributive justice. More generally, whether the view described in the text provides the best textual interpretation of Thrasymachus' position in the *Republic* is irrelevant to the illustrative use to which I put the example here. All that is required is that the view is coherent.

but he clearly means to be talking about the same subject as those who praise justice as a virtue and reject his account of it. In other words, it seems that there can be genuine disagreement about what distributions count as just among people who disagree as to whether just distributions are thereby good in a certain sort of way. If that is right, then it cannot be a conceptual constraint that the specific property of distributions, whatever it may be, which is the stuff of distributive justice must be relevantly good-making. As Nicholas Sturgeon notes:

> We have ... many cases in which it is enormously plausible to regard a disagreement as genuine, as focused on a single topic, but in which the dispute is anchored *neither* in a shared set of basic standards *nor* in a shared disposition to (for example) praise justice and condemn injustice.[12]

One general concern about arguments from the conditions of genuine disagreement to Extension is therefore that we often appear to take sameness of topic to be preserved across a broader range of disagreements than these arguments appear to allow.[13]

Another general concern is that what counts as genuine disagreement is itself a controversial topic. It may be unduly narrow to think of disagreement over an utterance as concerning the truth or correctness of its content. Utterances carry many kinds of information beyond the content of the sentence uttered, such as various presuppositions and implicatures. Each of these could potentially underlie a dispute between speakers.[14] The intuition that the speakers are disagreeing can therefore often be explained in a way that doesn't constrain the meanings of the expressions involved or impact their extensions. But in that case it is unclear to what extent intuitions about when speakers are engaged in genuine (dis)agreement about normative or evaluative matters are reliable guides to the meanings or extensions of the terms in which the (dis)agreement is framed. This is but a special case of the general phenomenon that our intuitions about what is said by our utterances may be based on more than what is linguistically determined. The difference between information that is linguistically encoded in the meaning of an expression and information that speakers associate in other ways with its utterances may not always be psychologically salient. Judgments from ordinary speakers may thus fail to match with the distinctions that matter to assignments of meaning or extension.

These general observations generate a further concern about arguments from disagreement to Extension. Intuitions of disagreement are guided in part by how individuals apply and withhold terms. What we have just noted is that patterns of application and withholding may be sensitive not only to the meaning of a term and one's view of its extension but also to various non-semantic factors. If one withholds the application of a term to something, this can be either because one thinks it doesn't fall under the term or because one recognizes that although it falls under the term, applying the term to it would

---

[12] Sturgeon (1991), 22; cf. Blackburn (1991), 4–5.

[13] Another general issue here is just to what extent genuine disagreement over a topic requires shared content among claims about the topic.

[14] For discussion, see Sundell (2011).

be misleading or conversationally inappropriate in some way.[15] If so, patterns of application and withholding for a term may diverge from its extension, including even the extension intended in a stable and cohesive community of users. Thus, even if the application and withholding of thick terms and concepts is sensitive to evaluation, this may well be explicable without treating evaluation as a semantic feature of thick terms and concepts.

I'll bracket these general concerns about Extension for now. Let's instead ask how Extension is supposed to be related to the view that evaluation belongs to the meanings of thick terms and concepts. For the purposes of my discussion this view can be formulated as follows (with elaboration to follow shortly):

Semantic View The semantic meanings of thick terms and concepts involve global evaluations.

While Semantic View entails Extension, the converse isn't true. Linking Extension to claims about the meanings of thick terms and concepts requires further assumptions about how extension relates to meaning.

The nature of meaning is a controversial topic in its own right. But one uncontroversial point is that one cannot use extension to guide views on the identity of concepts: two thinkers can have the same concept but different views concerning its extension, as in our example of distributive justice. Thus, the more closely the meanings of linguistic expressions are related to concepts, the more careful one should be with using extension to guide views about the meaning of an expression or concept identity.[16] Thick terms and concepts are no exception. All that I'll assume about meaning itself is the fairly standard idea that the meaning of an expression or a sentence imposes a set of constraints on what any literal use of it expresses in all normal contexts.[17]

Care is all the more due insofar as meaning may underdetermine extension. Sometimes input from context is needed as well. The meanings of such context-sensitive expressions as indexicals, for instance, don't alone determine their referents on particular occasions of use, since they have different referents in different contexts. The aspect of meaning that remains constant across the different occurrences of context-sensitive expressions in normal contexts is their "character"—a function from contexts to contents.[18] A general mark of context-sensitive expressions is that

---

[15] For instance, global evaluations might function in typical conversational contexts as background assumptions. If so, they might influence patterns of application and withholding by making only those things conversationally salient which conversational participants treat as admissible candidates for satisfying the relevant evaluation.

[16] The relationship between thick terms and concepts is usually unclear in the literature. A common tacit assumption seems to be that the meanings of thick terms are more or less the same as the concepts they express. (Perhaps the assumption is that terms *have* meanings whereas concepts *are* meanings.) This may be a significant simplification; perhaps, for instance, linguistic meaning is less fine-grained than concepts, in which case the relationship might well be one-to-many rather than one-to-one. See also §§8.4–8.5 this volume.

[17] See for example King and Stanley (2005), as well as Soames (2008), who thinks more strongly that such constraints exhaust semantic meaning. My purposes don't require this latter assumption.

[18] For the notion of character, see Kaplan (1989).

their characters deliver different contents in different contexts. Their extensions vary relative to context.

This suggests the following general view about the connection between the literal meanings of expressions and their extensions:

Meaning-Extension Link Meaning determines extension (relative to context).

I'll take up the issue whether and how thick terms are context-sensitive in sections 8.4–8.5. (Alert readers will notice that I am speaking only of thick terms, and not of thick concepts, as context-sensitive. That is because the label doesn't apply unproblematically to concepts.)[19] But first I want to ask how Meaning-Extension Link is supposed to apply to thick terms and concepts.

The case of Thrasymachus, Rawls, and Nozick suggests that people whom we have no reason to regard as linguistically or conceptually defective can each be talking about distributive justice while failing to share a basic set of standards about what counts as just in distributions of benefits and burdens. Presumably one can then know what *distributively just* means without knowing what things are distributively just, just as one can know what *now* means without knowing to what time it refers in a given context. (Similarly, one can know what *morally good* means without knowing which things are morally good.) How then does meaning determine the extensions of thick terms and concepts?

The question seems to get an elegant solution from Semantic View if we assume Extension. Glossed in terms of the notion of the character of an expression, Semantic View says that the functions from context to content that determine the extensions of thick terms and concepts relative to context involve global evaluations. If Extension is true, then the extension of *distributively just* (relative to context) is most plausibly (given the possibility of genuine disagreement about its extension) taken as driven by substantive evaluative facts about which specific features of distributions are good-making. But Semantic View doesn't require those facts to be involved by having them be built into the meaning of the term. What needs to be built into the meaning of *D is distributively just* is only that *D* has those features, whatever they may be, which make distributions good in the relevant way.[20] This is one way for the meaning of *distributively just* to "involve" the sorts of global evaluations facts which, if Extension is true, are most

---

[19] There are two options regarding how to talk about concepts corresponding to context-sensitive expressions. One option is that if a term like *tall* is context-sensitive with respect to what height counts as tall, then there is no such thing as *the* concept of tallness. There is only the contextually salient concept of tallness, selected from a wide range of more specific concepts given the semantic content of *tall* relative to context. The other option is that there is such a thing as the concept of tallness but it is a Kaplanian character. In the case of *tall*, this function returns no content independently of context and returns different contents in different contexts, thereby helping to specify various specific concepts. This is the sense in which one might talk of "the concept I" if one were so inclined in the case of the first-person pronoun. (Characters resemble concepts in that each is usually located closer to sense than reference.) My present purposes don't require a choice between these options.

[20] See the analysis of *distributively just* in Elstein and Hurka (2009), 521.

plausibly taken to determine its extension. But it seems to explain how one can know what *distributively just* means without knowing which features of distributions in fact are relevantly good-making, and thus how genuine disagreement about its extension, based on disputes about what these features are, is possible.[21] If only one knew which features of distributions in fact are relevantly good-making, one could then figure out which distributions in fact count as just.

This argument for Semantic View raises two issues. Is Semantic View really part of the best explanation of how the extensions of thick terms and concepts are determined? Is Extension itself true, or might the considerations used to support it have some other explanation? I'll focus on a further assumption behind the argument which bears on both issues.

8.3 Underdetermination and evaluation

The best-explanation argument from Extension to Semantic View outlined above involves a significant presumption. It follows from Extension that the non-evaluative (and embedded evaluative) aspects of the meanings of thick terms and concepts underdetermine their extensions. But if meaning determines extension (relative to context), then what other further factor but global evaluations could be involved in determining the extensions of thick terms and concepts?

The underdetermination claim that can thus be used to motivate Extension may be stated as follows:

> *Underdetermination* Even the strongest non-evaluative descriptions and embedded evaluations that are built into the meanings of thick terms and concepts underdetermine their extensions (relative to context).

If Underdetermination were false, then there would be no reason to accept Extension, and hence the argument for Semantic View as part of the best explanation of Extension would fail to get off the ground. If, however, Underdetermination is true, that isn't yet enough to motivate that argument for Semantic View. Underdetermination would also be true either if extension (relative to context) were in general underdetermined by meaning or if the meanings of thick terms and concepts *in toto* underdetermined their extensions (relative to context) irrespective of whether their meanings build in evaluation. The presumption behind the best-explanation argument from Extension to Semantic View is therefore that Underdetermination is true specifically in virtue of how global evaluations are involved in their meaning and determination of extension. I'll argue that this presumption isn't needed to explain Underdetermination.

This presumption depends in part on Meaning-Extension Link. Meaning-Extension Link allows that sentences may underdetermine propositional interpretation without

---

[21] This brackets the earlier general concern about arguments for Extension that are based on univocality intuitions concerning disagreements about extensions.

contextual supplementation when they involve context-sensitive expressions. Context-sensitive expressions include indexicals and demonstratives but may range far more widely, from quantifiers to gradable adjectives to certain verbs.[22] But the presumption is false if linguistic meaning underdetermines extension even relative to context in certain other ways. A particularly stark challenge to Meaning-Extension Link comes from the views of those linguists and philosophers of language who think that the meanings of linguistic expressions systematically underdetermine the contents of utterances, far beyond the gap present in ambiguity, polysemy, and context-sensitivity. Perhaps the meanings of expressions are contextually adjusted to conversational needs through various pragmatic processes that endow expressions with contextual senses, and therefore extensions, which are distinct from their literal meanings.[23] Or perhaps most linguistic expressions have no stable or determinate meanings and determining what counts as an instance of a predicate is in large part a matter of exercising general-purpose abilities that aren't specifically linguistic, and a matter that is systematically up for debate and negotiation in particular conversational situations when different potential assignments of meaning are available.[24] These views imply that extension is in general underdetermined, perhaps radically, by the literal meanings of expressions.

In what follows I'll bracket these kinds of general issues to focus specifically on thick terms and concepts. The assignment of semantic values to sentences involving thick terms and concepts isn't insulated from various more innocent forms of underdetermination. It can be widely agreed that meaning often fails to determine definite semantic value without some help from context, and similar phenomena arise in the case of concepts. If whatever individuates a concept specifies or otherwise determines its content, then the information encoded in its content will typically underdetermine just what entities fall under the concept.[25] Many people have a concept MOUNTAIN that underdetermines just which landforms fall under it (this isn't to say that a determinate technical concept isn't possible!), a concept VEHICLE that doesn't settle whether a Jeep that constitutes a war memorial statue

---

[22] It matters to Meaning-Extension Link that many of these further cases are controversial. One example is nominal restriction. Modifiers can receive different interpretations depending on what noun they modify. For instance, *huge* can involve a claim about large physical size (*a huge tree*) or the holding of the nominal predicate to a high degree (the more natural reading of *a huge Époisses enthusiast*). This is also true of many uses of *good* and *bad*. The implications of nominal restriction for Meaning-Extension Link depend on how meaning interacts with interpretation relative to context. According to typical forms of semantic contextualism, for instance, nominal restriction engages a contextual parameter that is part of the meaning of the adjective. But according to minimal semantics and many forms of truth-conditional pragmatics, the difference in interpretation is a result of pragmatic processes like enrichment which are underdetermined by meaning. (See, respectively: King and Stanley (2005); Bach (2001) and Cappelen and Lepore (2004); and Carston (2002) and Recanati (2004) and (2010).) These latter views aren't hospitable to Meaning-Extension Link.

[23] See for example the truth-conditional pragmatics of Carston (2002) and Recanati (2004) and (2010) and the lexical pragmatics of Blutner (1998).

[24] See for example the dynamic lexicon view of Ludlow (2008); cf. Larson and Ludlow (1993), von Fintel and Gillies (2011) and Rayo (forthcoming).

[25] This may or may not be due to whatever corresponds to context-sensitivity in the case of concepts.

falls under the rule *No vehicles in the park*, and a concept ATHLETE that doesn't specify whether only humans or also non-human animals engaged in sport fall under it.[26] Which way our concepts should go might be up for debate, not something determined by the concepts themselves.

To see how this goes in the case of thick terms and concepts, consider that a sentence like *x is selfish* entails, as much as a matter of meaning as anything does, at least that *x* manifests some kind of preference for the agent's own happiness or other interests ("happiness," for short) over a greater contribution to the happiness or interests of others. What its meaning, whether evaluative or not, doesn't seem to specify is just how much greater the happiness for others must be relative to the happiness for the agent in order for *x* to count as selfish. Although most people don't think that (other things being equal) spending £100 on a new pair of shoes instead of donating the money to famine aid is selfish, although the latter would benefit others more, it seems that they can fully coherently ask themselves, in a moment of doubt before clicking "Buy now," whether it really is selfish after all. The non-evaluative descriptions that are aspects of the meaning of *selfish* seem only to restrict its application to things with non-evaluative features of a certain generic type, namely bringing about one's own happiness over a greater happiness for others when the latter meets some unspecified differential threshold θ, not to determine any specific property of this type. The question I am addressing is what follows from this sort of phenomenon.[27]

What I'll argue is that insofar as Underdetermination is true of thick terms and concepts, this is an instance of a kind of underdetermination of their extensions (relative to context) by their meanings *in toto* which is exhibited by certain kinds of non-evaluative context-sensitive terms and can therefore be expected to arise irrespective of whether Semantic View is true. I'll also argue that, given the range of contextual factors that are eligible to enter into determining the extensions of thick terms and concepts, Extension is unlikely to hold across all contexts. My conclusion will therefore be that if there is a good argument for Extension or Semantic View as a general thesis about thick terms and concepts, it won't come from Underdetermination.

8.4 Underdetermination and gradability

I'll begin by arguing that the paradigmatic examples of thick terms and concepts express gradable notions and explaining how the kind of context-sensitivity that is characteristic of gradable expressions bears on Underdetermination, Extension, and Semantic View.

Many thick terms and concepts are gradable: they express qualities of which things can have more or less and can thus be used to order the things under discussion.

---

[26] The last two examples are due to Hart (1958) and Ludlow (2008), respectively. They show that this kind of underdetermination doesn't reduce to vagueness.

[27] The phenomenon itself is well discussed by Elstein and Hurka (2009).

Adjectives are one standard way to express gradable notions. Many thick terms are adjectives that exhibit syntactic marks of gradability. They admit of comparatives: things can be *more frugal* or *more courageous* than others, *less cruel* or *less generous* than others. And they take degree modifiers: things can be *very* industrious, *somewhat* tacky, *extremely* frugal, and so on. But gradability isn't a property of adjectives alone. One person can be *more of* a jerk than another, or a *heavier* smoker than another, one can regret some things *more than* others or regret them *very much*, just as a person can be an *outright* idiot or an *absolute* genius and an attempt at a clever joke can be a *total* failure.[28] And expressions that aren't syntactically gradable might still be semantically linked to scales of measurement in the way gradable expressions are. Insofar as thick terms and concepts are gradable, some of their features might be explicable as features of gradable expressions in general. The question will be how their gradability bears on Semantic View.

According to the standard treatment of gradable adjectives, their semantic interpretation involves three operations: determining a dimension (the quality of which there can be more or less), computing a scale (an ordering with respect to the dimension) and computing a standard (a value on the scale that is high enough to count).[29] For instance, *tall* orders things according to their (ascending) height. This analysis makes straightforward sense of comparatives: *A is taller than B* can be analyzed as saying that the value *A* takes on the scale of tallness (which is something like *A*'s degree of height) exceeds the value *B* takes on the scale of tallness. The positive form is usually treated as implicitly comparative: *A is tall* can be analyzed as saying that the value *A* takes on the scale of tallness exceeds the contextually determined threshold for counting as tall. The standard will be such that the objects of which the positive is true "stand out" in the context of utterance relative to the relevant measurement.[30]

We can accordingly distinguish at least three issues concerning the interpretation of gradable thick terms like *courageous*, *cruel*, and *selfish*:

---

[28] I am not suggesting gradability as a diagnostic for thick terms and concepts. For instance, *morally good* is a gradable expression but is typically classified as thin. Moreover, some thick concepts may lack gradable expressions; *murder* doesn't seem to be a gradable term but some think that murder is a thick concept. Focusing on gradability works here as a heuristic guide.

[29] Any respect in which two things may be compared may qualify as a standard in the relevant sense. It needn't be evaluative in the sense discussed earlier in §8.2.

[30] This sketch draws primarily on the degree-based analysis in Kennedy (2007) and Glanzberg (2007). Earlier degree-based accounts of gradability include Cresswell (1977), von Stechow (1984), and Bierwisch (1988a), (1988b), and (1989). Such accounts can treat gradable adjectives and their comparatives either as measure *functions* from individuals to values on a scale or as *relations* between individuals and such values. There is also room for debate about whether scale values are to be understood as abstract objects or not, as degrees or intervals, and so on. A degree-based analysis is most naturally understood as requiring that the comparative generate a total ordering (Kennedy 2007). But this seems too strong as a general requirement on scale structure (van Rooij 2011).

The main alternative to a degree-based analysis is to analyze gradable adjectives as simple predicates whose extension varies with respect to a contextually determined comparison class. See Klein (1980); cf. Ludlow (1989). One worry here is that there seems to be no reason why a standard should have to be based on a comparison class. See DeRose (2008).

- *Standards:* What degree of courageousness (etc.) is minimally sufficient to count as satisfying *courageous* (etc.), and hence determines its extension, relative to context?
- *Dimensions:* What counts as courage (etc.)? What is the quality of which there may be more or less, or a lot or little?
- *Scale structures:* What counts as more (or less) courageous (etc.) than what? What determines how two objects are related on the scale?

We can further ask how these issues bear on Extension and Semantic View. The issue of how the meanings of thick terms and concepts are related to dimensions will occupy section 8.5. Issues about scale structure are the least central to my present concerns and will appear mainly in notes. How the meanings of thick terms and concepts are related to standards is the clearest of the three issues, so I'll discuss it first.

Gradable expressions are generally context-sensitive with respect to the standard. For instance, Amy may count as tall in a discussion of ballerinas but not in a discussion of basketball players. So the extension of *tall* varies with context. Many thick terms are context-sensitive in this way. What counts as satisfying *generous*, for instance, is different when millionaires and paupers are in question.[31] Help from context is required to set the standard. There is no such thing as the set of generous things, except relative to context.[32] Thus, insofar as positive constructions involving thick terms vary in extension from one context to another because they make reference to a degree that exceeds a contextually specified standard, this delivers Underdetermination. But that will hold irrespective of whether thick terms are inherently evaluative in meaning, and so explaining it doesn't require Semantic View.

One might nonetheless think that in fact the contextually supplied standards for satisfying thick terms are determined in part by evaluation. This would support at most Extension. It wouldn't support Semantic View because not all literal uses of gradable expressions in normal contexts make reference to a degree that exceeds a contextually specified standard; at most their positive forms do.[33] Such reference is therefore not encoded in the meanings of gradable thick terms. But even the case of Extension is unclear. Context-sensitive expressions differ with respect to whether their meanings specify what contextual inputs are relevant to determining their semantic values. It is therefore an open question whether it is built into the meanings of thick terms that global evaluation plays (or doesn't play) such a role.

---

[31] Some may be inclined to think that if something displays the property T measured by a thick term *T* to any degree, then it is automatically an instance of *T*. They should note that something can have a value on the scale of T-ness without counting as T. Such sentences as *He couldn't muster up enough courage to save his comrades* seem to make perfect sense. Compare *tall*: some degrees of tallness (that is, values on the dimension of ascending height) qualify as short in some contexts.

[32] This makes some writers' focus on what it takes to "master the extension" of a thick concept, in a way that enables ones to apply it correctly to new cases, seem ill-conceived. This focus can be seen in, for example, McDowell (1981), Williams (1985), Dancy (1995), Kirchin (2010), and Roberts (2011).

[33] Each of *Bill is tall*, *Bill is taller than Ted*, and *Bill is as tall as Ted* contains the adjective *tall*, but neither of the latter two constructions (the comparative and the equative) makes reference to a degree that exceeds a contextually specified standard; only the positive construction does so. See Rett (2008).

This complication arises because we must distinguish semantics from "metasemantics". The job of semantics is to specify what kind of meaning each sentence has as some compositional function of the semantic values of the constituents of the sentence.[34] This calls for an assignment of semantic values relative to contexts. The job of metasemantics is to say how constituents wind up having the semantic values they do—how context fixes a particular value for an expression in context. The semantics of context-dependent parameters is simply that they are set to values by context. Such issues about the interpretation of gradable adjectives as how the standard is computed, and on the basis of what sorts of rules and contextual inputs, are metasemantic in this sense. So is, therefore, the issue whether evaluation plays a standard-setting role.

Context-sensitive expressions differ with respect to how direct their metasemantics is. One example of a fairly direct metasemantics are pronouns like *he* and *she*. Their metasemantics involves pronoun resolution rules, which help determine to which individual a pronoun refers in a particular context. These rules might direct us, for instance, to the speaker's referential intentions to determine semantic value. In general, how context manages to set the values of contextual parameters is something that may be constrained, but is typically not fully determined, by the meaning of the expression in question.

The meanings of gradable expressions generally show few restrictions on how the value of the standard parameter may be set, beyond there having to be some appropriately salient factors in the context. For instance, speaker intentions may be neither necessary nor sufficient for setting it, although they often play a role; some speakers' intentions may be too idiosyncratic relative to the presuppositions shared by other speakers or the broader structure or aims of the discourse.[35] Working out the standard value from context may require taking into account a range of factors which may combine in complex ways. Factors that may in general play a role in semantic interpretation include: salient properties of the context; the denotations of the expressions involved; whatever intentions and interests to compare and classify speakers and hearers might have, plus coordinating intentions; the structure of the discourse in which the utterance appears; and a rule that Christopher Kennedy calls the "principle of interpretive economy," which requires making as much use as possible of the (conventional) meanings of expressions in computing what a sentence expresses in context.[36] There is no reason in advance to think that gradable thick terms will differ from other gradable expressions in this respect.

All this matters here because if the meanings of gradable expressions don't generally specify the contextual factors that determine the standard, then nothing about

---

[34] Semantics that is "descriptive" in this sense may be distinguished from accounts of the factors (such as inferential role, causal-historical profile, or whatnot) in virtue of which particular expressions have the semantic properties they do. This is sometimes called "foundational semantics," but sometimes it, too, is called metasemantics. I won't follow this usage.

[35] Glanzberg (2007), 24.   [36] See Kennedy (2007) and Glanzberg (2007).

gradability gives us grounds to think that the meanings of thick terms specify that global evaluations must play a role in setting the standard relative to context. Global evaluations might play no role, or they might play a role sometimes but not always, depending on context. This raises a challenge to the claim that the meanings of thick terms involve global evaluations in their interpretation.

Let's use *selfish* to illustrate how thick terms might not specify as a matter of semantic rule that global evaluations play a standard-setting role. Impartialists in ethics think that preferring n units of happiness for oneself over $n^{\star}$ units of happiness for others is wrong whenever $n^{\star} > n$, whereas those who advocate agent-centred prerogatives think that it is wrong only when $n^{\star}$ exceeds some higher threshold θ above n. They agree that selfishness is gradable. But, for all that is at issue between them as regards wrongness, they needn't disagree over whether choosing ten units of happiness for oneself over eleven units of happiness for others is selfish.[37] Agent-centrists could agree that it is selfish, but permissibly so. Or, impartialists could agree that it isn't selfish, but judge it to be wrong even so. This would be enough to explain how they can use the term *selfish* univocally despite their disagreement over wrongness, without treating the meaning of *selfish* as necessarily co-opting global evaluations.

What if impartialists and agent-centrists *did* take the moral sticking point to concern which acts are selfish? In that case their disagreement would be about how something must rate on the metric of happiness differential to count as selfish—that is, about the standard for counting as selfish. Would this kind of disagreement require global evaluations to play a role in determining the standard, as a matter of semantic rule or not?

Nothing in the semantics of gradability *rules out* that global evaluations can enter into determining the degree exceeding which counts as selfish in context. If impartialists and agent-centrists want to couch their dispute as concerning which specific property of preferring one's own happiness over a greater happiness for others counts as selfishness relative to context, then they can agree for the purposes of conversation that the stuff of selfishness is, for instance, those preferences for one's own happiness over a greater happiness for others which are wrong *according to the correct moral standards, whatever they are*. This kind of broadly objectivist presumption could well be salient in typical moral contexts.[38]

But equally nothing in the semantics *requires* that global evaluations play a standard-setting role in the interpretation of thick terms.[39] As far as I can tell, it is semantically permissible to take social convention rather than morality to determine what counts as

---

[37] This departs from the stipulation in Elstein and Hurka (2009), 522, to whom I owe the example.

[38] Thanks to Janice Dowell for this point. It may not be the only way to model how sameness of topic is preserved.

[39] It also seems that in certain contexts at least standards concerning such thin notions as wrongness *cannot* play a standard-setting role with respect to *selfish*. Whenever a selfish act must have whichever specific feature of preferring one's own happiness over a greater happiness for others that makes acts wrong, an act cannot be wrong *in virtue of* being selfish. For in that case a selfish act is trivially a wrong act, and it seems that if *A*s are trivially *B*s, then something cannot be a *B* in virtue of being an *A*. Similarly, the judgment that the act is wrong couldn't be justified by saying that it is selfish, if it can only count as selfish to begin with if it is wrong.

selfish in some contexts, or for psychologists studying self-regarding and other-regarding behaviors to set an operational standard of selfishness without being guided by global evaluations. All that the semantics requires is that there be some degree of concern for one's own happiness over a greater happiness for others which exceeds a contextually determined standard. The rest depends on matters that aren't in general settled by the meanings of thick terms. So nothing here implies that the meanings of gradable thick terms in general involve global evaluations in determining the contextually specified standard; nothing here supports even Extension as a general thesis about thick terms and concepts.

So far I have argued that many thick terms express gradable notions, and that because such expressions are context-sensitive, their extensions are underdetermined by their meanings *in toto*, irrespective of whether their relationship to evaluation is semantic. I also argued that nothing in the context-sensitivity of gradable expressions shows that global evaluations are required in determining the contextually supplied standards for counting as satisfying thick terms. We have yet to see anything about Underdetermination that would support either Extension or Semantic View as a general thesis about thick terms and concepts.

At this point it is natural to wonder why the sort of underdetermination that would best support Semantic View or even Extension should concern the contextually specified standard. For instance, although Nozick and Rawls can agree that distributive justice is gradable, their disagreement isn't about how just a distribution has to be to count as just. Rather it is about what feature of distributions is the stuff of distributive justice. This points to a different possible form of underdetermination having to do with the dimensions associated with thick terms and concepts:

> *Underdetermination+* The non-evaluative aspects and embedded evaluative aspects of the meanings of thick terms and concepts underdetermine the metric on which such a term grades things (relative to context), not just the value on the metric needed to make the grade which determines the term's extension (relative to context).[40]

Underdetermination+ implies that the non-evaluative and embedded evaluative aspects of the meaning of *courageous*, for instance, underdetermine what counts as courage—the quality of which there may be more or less, (not) enough or too much, very much and so on, and different amounts of which may be enough in different contexts to count as courageous. This couldn't be explained in terms of gradability, since gradability only requires that the (more or less complex) qualities or properties ascribed by thick terms may be realized to different degrees. Thus, insofar as Underdetermination+ is what is typically going on in cases where evaluation might be regarded as driving the extensions of thick terms, that cannot be explained by gradability as such either.[41] This seems right.

---

[40] I use the word "metric" to refer to dimensions to capture the phenomenon of multidimensionality that I'll discuss shortly.

[41] Thanks to Daniel Elstein for emphasizing the points in this paragraph.

Not all thick terms and concepts exemplify Underdetermination+ with equal plausibility, however. Underdetermination+ isn't plausibly true of *selfish*, for instance. The semantic clause that selfish acts somehow involve preference for the agent's own happiness or interests over a greater contribution to other people's happiness or interests (where "somehow" signals that the happiness differential threshold θ is left semantically unspecified) underdetermines the extension of *selfish*. But that clause is enough to generate a multitude of such comparative facts as that preferring ten units of happiness for oneself over twenty units of happiness to others is more selfish than preferring it over eleven units of happiness to others and as selfish as preferring five units of happiness for oneself over fifteen units of happiness for others. Such comparative and equative facts are enough to generate a scale of selfishness. Since a scale is an ordering along a dimension, those facts are enough to determine a metric of selfishness without global evaluation. So Underdetermination+ isn't plausible with respect to *selfish*. It is at most plausible with respect to some restricted set of thick terms and concepts. I'll now turn to discuss what Underdetermination+ shows in cases where it seems plausible.

8.5 Explaining Underdetermination+

Underdetermination+ makes a claim about how the metrics along which thick terms and concepts measure things are determined. To assess this we need to know how the properties ascribed by gradable expressions are in general determined. Semantic theory doesn't much care about how or why different gradable expressions differ in the ways they do.[42] The standard analysis of gradable adjectives takes no stand on what properties are scaled by a particular scale, what contextual factors qualify as inputs for computing the scale, and what computational rules must be taken into account and how these must be weighed in fixing the values of such contextual parameters as the standard. All it requires is that there *be* a scale and standard somehow to be computed from context; determining these is, again, the job of metasemantics.

The fact that *tall, frugal, cruel*, and *good* are used to measure different qualities is due to differences in their conventional meanings. (This point reflects the principle of interpretive economy mentioned earlier.) How fully their meanings determine the associated dimensions varies from case to case. In some cases the dimension is conventionally fixed; examples include *tall* (ascending height), *young* (descending age), and *cheap* (descending cost). The same applies to comparisons and the corresponding scale structure: whether one thing is taller, heavier, younger, or cheaper than another is usually clear. In other cases, however, meaning underdetermines the metric. For instance, *good* and *bad* require help from context to determine a respect of comparison, such as being good at cooking or with children, or what is a good government policy for higher education.

---

[42] Main exceptions concern certain structural features of scale structure, such as the distinction between "absolute" and "relative" gradable adjectives; see Kennedy (2007).

Even fixing a respect of comparison may, however, underdetermine the relevant property. For instance, the qualities measured by *a good philosopher*—such as perhaps insight, creativity, clarity, and rigor, among others—may themselves be unclear or controversial. It may similarly be unclear or controversial how the corresponding scale is structured, due to the possibility of disputes about who is a better footballer or a cook than who, which are based on disagreements about what the qualities to be measured are or their relative importance.

These complications arise clearly in the case of "multidimensional" notions, such as what is a good philosopher. Many gradable expressions grade things along multiple dimensions in one and the same context and the degree to which things possess the quality measured by the expression depends somehow, on the basis of some kind of combinatorial function, on separate orderings along these multiple dimensions. Getting a metric along which things are graded requires such a function.[43] For instance, whether somebody is more philosophically talented than somebody else depends, somehow, on separate orderings along such dimensions as insight, creativity, clarity, rigor, and more, and how painful something is depends, somehow, on the intensity and the duration of pain. Just how the various dimensions are to be combined is often not clear. So multidimensionality tends to complicate the determination of both scale structures and the metrics along which things are graded.

I'll now argue that the meanings of multidimensional thick terms and concepts *in toto* tend to underdetermine their extensions relative to context. The argument will apply even to their comparatives, because one factor in play will turn out to be variation in combinatorial functions. This is important because the comparatives of unidimensional gradables are typically not context-sensitive. The extension of *taller than* doesn't vary with context. The upshot will be that if Underdetermination+ is true of thick terms and concepts, this will be so for reasons that hold irrespective of whether the relationship between thick terms and concepts and evaluation is semantic. Thus Underdetermination+ fails to support Semantic View. As before, global evaluations may play a role in determining the extensions of thick terms and concepts, but there is no reason why they need to. Underdetermination+ therefore fails to support Extension as a general thesis.

As with Underdetermination, there are various general views about word meaning that could be used to make the kind of point I am seeking to make about Underdetermination+. For instance, various people argue that word meanings are systematically underdetermined by what is common coin among speakers and protean beyond certain fairly minimal constraints.[44] This fits with the observation that the shared meaning of thick terms and concepts tends to consist in various hints and clues. Witness such typical lexical

---

[43] The relevant metrics, and locations in them, can be represented using n-dimensional vectors, where the combinatorial function is a mapping from such vectors to degrees, positions, or values on a scale; see Benbaji (2009), 321–3. Formulating such vectors can be a real challenge.

[44] See for example Blutner (1998), Carston (2002), Ludlow (2008), von Fintel and Gillies (2011), and Rayo (forthcoming).

entries as *disposed to inflict suffering, indifferent to or taking pleasure in another's pain or distress* in the case of *cruel*; *lacking consideration for others, concerned chiefly with one's own personal profit or pleasure* in the case of *selfish*; *having or showing a tender and considerate and helpful nature* in the case of *kind*, and *not deterred by danger or pain; strength in the face of pain or grief* in the case of *courageous*.[45] It might be thought to be up to conversational participants to deploy further cognitive resources to flesh out these largely non-evaluative clues in some way that is appropriate to their discourse situation. This might involve selecting meanings from a pre-existing stock of different possible senses or generating them anew.

Thick terms operate primarily in domains which we regard as normatively significant. Ascriptions of justice and cruelty, for instance, aren't usually neutral with respect to what is good or bad, but are at least normally taken to ascribe good-making and bad-making features that are connected to reasons for action. It would then be no surprise if conversational partners often relied on global evaluations to flesh out contextual meanings for thick terms even if the relevant global evaluations weren't contained in their meanings. Insofar as our evaluative outlooks tend to overlap, it would also be no surprise if evaluation commonly guided us to certain particular sharpenings among the many available. There would, however, be nothing privileged about those sharpenings.[46] They would come about through various general norms that regulate how word meanings are negotiated and sharpened against conversational purposes and context, through having the views of particular speakers expressed and debated, and on that basis accepted, rejected, or modified.[47]

Nothing in this shows more than that thick terms can be loaded with evaluation in particular discourse situations. There is no reason why fleshing out a meaning that works for a discourse situation would have to involve global evaluation. In some discourse situations the extension of a thick term may be driven by global evaluation, but in others global evaluation will have to be trimmed off for conversational coherence and progress to be possible. An example would be a discussion of how we should respond to international terrorism in which someone claims that we should respond to it with focused brutality.[48] Such a speaker may be misguided but seemingly doesn't have to be conceptually confused. It won't do to interpret *brutal* as building in negative global evaluation in such a discourse situation. Nothing in this kind of general picture portrays evaluation as something contained in the meanings of thick terms.

My purposes don't, however, require any such general view about word meaning. The example concerning approval of focused brutality, for instance, can stand on its

---

[45] See for example *The Oxford English Dictionary* or WordNet 3.0 (a lexical database for English accessible at <http://wordnet.princeton.edu/>, accessed 1 April 2012).

[46] There would, accordingly, be no privileged concept CRUEL, SELFISH, or COURAGEOUS that could somehow override various factors that bear on deciding how to sharpen the corresponding terms relative to conversational goals, interests, and context.

[47] See for example Ludlow (2008), 125–6. Also metasemantic decisions as to what contextual factors to take into account in semantic interpretation are often subject to debate and negotiation. See Glanzberg (2007) and Sundell (2011).

[48] This example was relayed to me by Nicholas Sturgeon many years ago. A real-life example reported to me by Remy Debes speaks to the same point, namely the comment, "Don't change this beautiful and brutal sport" made in a discussion of whether increased concussion risks in (American) football should lead to changes in the rules of the game.

own. Moreover, I'll now argue that the constraints on literal uses of multidimensional terms in normal contexts tend to underdetermine the metrics along which things are graded, and thereby their extensions relative to context. This will support Underdetermination+ in the case of multidimensional thick terms and concepts irrespective of whether their relationship to global evaluation is semantic.

How bald someone is depends on both the number of hairs on his scalp and the distribution of hairs on it. How painful something is depends on both the intensity and the duration of pain. The extent to which something is bald or painful is some combinatorial function of separate orderings on the relevant dimensions. But the relative weighting of these dimensions, and hence the resulting combinatorial function, can vary with context. The shape of this function will be constrained by whatever formal properties the resulting ordering of objects is desired to have.

Whatever shape such functions take, it seems rare for them to be specified as a matter of meaning or even linguistic practice. How the various dimensions are to be weighted against one another often depends on context. Although a person with a greater number of hairs on his scalp usually counts as less bald than a person with fewer hairs on his scalp, this isn't so when the former's hairs are distributed on his head very unevenly in one big tuft.[49] Or consider *painful*. Day 1 has a longer duration of pain of lower intensity; Day 2 has short durations of pain of higher intensity. Thus Day 1 ranks higher in the duration of pain but Day 2 ranks higher in the intensity of pain. Which is more painful of the two? The answer may vary with context even if Day 1 is stipulated to have a greater total amount of pain, let alone if the total amounts are stipulated to be equal. The extension of *more painful than* may vary with context in this way because the dimensions of intensity and duration may be weighted differently in different contexts. And the question of which is more painful appears to have no answer unless some idea of how intensity and duration are to be weighted against one another is supplied. If so, then not only the positive construction *D is a painful day* but also the comparative construction *D1 is a more painful day than D2* may vary in extension relative to context. It is exceedingly difficult to see facts about which dimensions we take into account in which contexts as determined by meaning or linguistic practice.[50] I conclude that the meanings of multidimensional gradable expressions *in toto* only require that there *be* a metric along which things are graded and tend to underdetermine the metric.

Thick terms seem no different. What counts as courageous, for instance, is some function of the likelihood and (relative) value of the goods to be achieved by action,

---

[49] See Wasserman (2004), 396.

[50] The points in this paragraph are further reinforced by the observation that in some contexts one of the dimensions may even drop out of the comparison as irrelevant to the conversational purpose. We often don't focus on all dimensions when evaluating comparatives, and often focus just on dimensions along which things differ and ignore those along which they don't. See for example Benbaji (2009) and van Rooij (2011).

the likelihood and (relative) disvalue of the harms risked by action, confidence, and resistance to fear and so on. Competent speakers know that the meaning of *courageous* permits greater feelings of fear the greater the danger, at least provided that the expected gains of going ahead are greater than its expected harms. They also know that absolute fearlessness or confidence in the face of a high probability of a grave injury in pursuit of something barely worthwhile is reckless or foolhardy, not courageous. And they know that fearfulness in the face of a low probability of grave injury in pursuit of something highly worthwhile is cowardly, not courageous.[51] But even if these are stable constraints on what literal uses of *courageous* express in normal contexts, it is exceedingly hard to believe that meaning or linguistic practice specify much further which dimensions are to be taken into account and how the relevant dimensions are to be weighted in a particular context, or otherwise specify how changes along each contextually relevant dimension are related to changes of location in the multidimensional property space out of which the relevant metric is constructed. They seem not to determine the relevant combinatorial function much beyond requiring that there be one and placing some loose constraints on it. Surely *courageous* is also not an isolated case.

What does all this mean for the relationship between thick terms and concepts and evaluation? It is consistent with this argument that some thick terms and concepts contribute evaluative properties as dimensions and even that some of them do so as a matter of meaning. I see no a priori argument to the contrary. But as with the case of standards, nothing in the semantics of thick terms in general requires global evaluations to play a role in specifying the metrics along which multidimensional thick terms grade things. Factors that determine them seem not to be stable across the literal uses of thick terms in normal contexts in the way they should be if they were built into meaning. Whether, and how widely, global evaluations play a role in determining those metrics are primarily

---

[51] Many issues concerning scale structure arise here. One is whether thick terms impose scales that are continuous with the scales imposed by their antonyms, where they have one. It is by no means clear how such clusters as *brave, bold,* and *courageous* relate not only to *cowardly, timid,* and *fearful* but also to *reckless, foolhardy,* and *rash.* How to analyze those virtue terms that have two different kinds of vice terms as their negative counterparts is an important issue. Depending on how this plays out, *courageous* may not be semantically well represented as denoting a mean between cowardice and recklessness in the sense that it maps its arguments onto intervals on a scale which lie between intervals to which *cowardly* and *foolhardy* map their arguments. We might not want to analyze the relevant metric so that foolhardy things rank higher than courageous things on it. Foolhardy things may display greater confidence in the face of danger and fear than courageous things, but this isn't the same as having a greater degree of courage than courageous things. If *courageous, cowardly,* and *foolhardy* don't impose a scale on the same dimension, then they are to be represented as operating on different (albeit related) scales. If they do, then the issue will be how to represent the scales imposed by *courageous, cowardly,* and *foolhardy* as scales on the same dimension. It doesn't seem that either cowardly or foolhardy things have in any systematic way more or less of the same quality than the other. Irrespective of how *cowardly* and *foolhardy* compare to one another, it also isn't clear how to represent them relative to the standard for counting as courageous. A further issue will be how to analyze such sentences as *A is as cowardly as B is foolhardy* in terms of degrees on the same dimension. All these issues deserve more attention.

questions about contexts and metasemantics. Since contexts are contingent entities, there seems to be no reason to think in advance that global evaluations must always be a relevant factor. Because all these considerations arise from reflection on multidimensional gradable terms in general, they imply that Underdetermination+ has nothing in particular to do with how thick terms and concepts combine description and evaluation. The exception would be cases where global evaluations are built into the meanings of thick terms and concepts. Whether isolated cases of this kind would be able to carry any significant broader metaethical consequences is a complicated issue which I cannot address here. But since exceptions are sometimes best left as spoils to the victor, the question merits attention.

I conclude that insofar as Underdetermination+ holds for thick terms and concepts, that is generally because the meanings of multidimensional thick terms *in toto* underdetermine the metrics along which things are graded. This account is simpler and based on more general principles than the explanation that the meanings of thick terms fully determine those metrics by co-opting global evaluations that complement the non-evaluative aspects of their meanings in determining them. The explanation I have developed works irrespective of whether the relationship between thick terms and concepts and evaluation is semantic. Therefore Underdetermination+ doesn't support Semantic View as a general thesis about thick terms and concepts. It doesn't even support Extension. For although global evaluations may play a role in determining the extensions of thick terms relative to context, nothing in the semantics forces this.[52]

This explanation of Underdetermination+ has broader dialectical significance. Consider, for instance, cases where global evaluation seems to drive the extensions of thick terms and concepts. If Underdetermination+ can be explained without appealing to Extension, then attempts to explain these cases as cases where patterns of application and withholding are influenced by non-semantic or conversational factors cannot be dismissed out of hand.[53]

The sort of explanation I have developed also undercuts certain arguments regarding the putative implications of the underdetermination phenomena discussed in this paper. Allan Gibbard, who explicitly allows that there might be non-evaluative constraints on a thick concept, claims that statements that predicate thick concepts of things don't have "enough of" descriptive meaning that, in some combination with evaluative meaning, can yield the full meaning of the statement. In thick concepts, "descriptive and evaluative components intermesh more tightly than that."[54] Jonathan Dancy similarly claims that the non-evaluative aspects of the meanings of thick terms and concepts determine only the range or domain in which they operate, but no content that could stand alone in semantic evaluation.[55] For instance, describing courage as "something to do with

---

[52] Moreover, as mentioned earlier in n. 39, there seem to be contexts where at least certain kinds of evaluations don't, or even can't, play such a role.

[53] I alluded to the availability of such explanations in §8.2.

[54] Gibbard (1992), 277–8.   [55] Dancy (1995), 275–7.

confidence, resistance to fear and danger," or lewdness as "something to do with sexual display, something to do with mockery" doesn't determine a meaning or content for *courageous* or *lewd*. But all that one needs to do to explain why such general characterizations underdetermine a content that can stand alone in semantic evaluation is to point out that they try to characterize terms that are context-sensitive in abstraction from any particular context. The indeterminacy of characterizations that merely specify the various dimensions shows neither that evaluation belongs to the meanings of thick terms and concepts nor even that it drives their extension. (Dancy uses their indeterminacy explicitly to argue for Extension.) If *courageous*, for instance, is multidimensional, then we shouldn't expect to be able specify in the abstract how its various dimensions are to be combined and weighted in particular cases.

I am therefore underwhelmed by arguments for Extension or Semantic View that are premised on the observation (pressed by both Dancy and Gibbard) that linguistic convention and practice attach no sharp non-evaluative properties to thick terms and concepts. That is generally not the case with context-sensitive terms, especially if they are multidimensional. It is also useful to note that views that deny Extension and Semantic View aren't committed to being able to specify or characterize the properties ascribed by thick terms and concepts in "thickness-free" terms. If the meaning of *selfish* doesn't build in global evaluation, then *selfish* itself ascribes non-evaluative properties in contexts where it takes such properties as its semantic values. But, like a wide range of ordinary terms, both evaluative and not, *selfish* may have no informative analysis in independently intelligible *selfish*-free terms. Similarly, a term like *courageous* might easily lack any accurate *courageous*-free correlate irrespective of whether its relationship to the global evaluations it may be used to convey is semantic.

8.6 Conclusion

I have argued that insofar as the non-evaluative aspects of the meanings of thick terms and concepts underdetermine their extensions, this is due to their meanings *in toto* and can be expected to arise irrespective of whether their relationship to global evaluations is semantic. Considerations of underdetermination fail therefore to support the hypothesis that their meanings in general build in global evaluations, and support the hypothesis that their extensions are driven by global evaluations at most with respect to certain contexts.

I wish to close by noting that thick terms and concepts may be quite diverse in their relationship to evaluation. For all I have argued here, some may bear a semantic relationship to global evaluation, but we have yet to see any good reason to make such semantic posits across the class of thick terms. The issue would be an empirical question about the meanings of particular thick terms, in the way questions about semantic posits generally are questions about the meanings of particular linguistic expressions. The construction of the metrics along which things are graded may be guided by evaluation, but it may not, depending in part on whether a thick term is multidimensional and in part on context. The standard for making the grade on the metric may be driven by evaluation, but again it may not, depending on context. And so on. Further dimensions of diversity may well come into view in future inquiry.

The lack of a one-size-fits-all account of thick terms and concepts would have important ramifications all by itself. The greater the room for differences in the sorts of respects just enumerated, both across different thick terms and concepts and across different contexts of their use, the harder it is to see why the global evaluations that thick terms and concepts may be used to convey should in general be treated as built into their meanings. The extant literature on thick terms and concepts conspicuously fails to entertain the possibility that diversity among thick terms and concepts goes deep but has no systematic theoretical upshot. This is beginning to look like a serious possibility.[56]

References

Bach, Kent (2001) 'You Don't Say?' *Synthese* 127: 11–31.

Benbaji, Yitzhak (2009) 'Parity, Intransitivity, and a Context-Sensitive Degree Analysis of Gradability', *Australasian Journal of Philosophy* 87: 313–35.

Bierwisch, Manfred (1988a) 'Tools and Explanations of Comparison—Part 1', *Journal of Semantics* 6: 57–93.

—— (1988b) 'Tools and Explanations of Comparison—Part 2', *Journal of Semantics* 6: 101–46.

—— (1989) 'The Semantics of Gradation' in Manfred Bierwisch and Ewald Lang (eds.) *Dimensional Adjectives: Grammatical Structure and Conceptual Interpretation* (Berlin and Heidelberg: Springer-Verlag), 71–261.

Blackburn, Simon (1991) 'Just Causes', *Philosophical Studies* 61: 3–17.

—— (1992) 'Morality and Thick Concepts: Through Thick and Thin', *Proceedings of the Aristotelian Society, Supplementary Volume* 66: 285–99.

Blutner, Reinhard (1998) 'Lexical Pragmatics', *Journal of Semantics* 15; 115–62.

Cappelen, Herman and Ernest Lepore (2004) *Insensitive Semantics* (Oxford: Blackwell).

Carston, Robyn (2002) *Thoughts and Utterances* (Oxford: Blackwell).

Cresswell, Max (1977) 'The Semantics of Degree' in Barbara Partee (ed.) *Montague Grammar* (New York: Academic Press), 261–92.

Dancy, Jonathan (1995) 'In Defense of Thick Concepts', in Peter A. French, Theodore E. Uehling, and Howard K. Wettstein (eds.) *Midwest Studies in Philosophy* XX: 263–79.

DeRose, Keith (2008) 'Gradable Adjectives: A Defence of Pluralism', *Australasian Journal of Philosophy* 86: 141–60.

Eklund, Matti (2011) 'What Are Thick Concepts?' *Canadian Journal of Philosophy* 41: 25–49.

Elstein, Daniel and Thomas Hurka (2009) 'From Thick to Thin: Two Moral Reduction Plans', *Canadian Journal of Philosophy* 39: 515–35.

Foot, Philippa (1958) 'Moral Arguments', *Mind* 67: 502–13.

[56] Many thanks to Matti Eklund, Daniel Elstein, Simon Kirchin, Debbie Roberts, an audience at University of Leeds and two reviewers for the press for helpful comments on earlier versions of this material. Work on this paper was supported by the Arts and Humanities Research Council (UK) under grant agreement AH/H038035.

Gibbard, Allan (1992) 'Morality and Thick Concepts: Thick Concepts and Warrant for Feelings', *Proceedings of the Aristotelian Society, Supplementary Volume* 66: 267–83.

Glanzberg, Michael (2007) 'Context, Content, and Relativism', *Philosophical Studies* 136: 1–29.

Hare, R. M. (1952) *The Language of Morals* (Oxford: Clarendon Press).

—— (1981) *Moral Thinking* (Oxford: Clarendon Press).

Hart, H. L. A. (1958) 'Positivism and the Separation of Law and Morals', *Harvard Law Review* 71: 593–629.

Hurley, S. L. (1989) *Natural Reasons: Personality and Polity* (Oxford: Oxford University Press).

Kaplan, David (1989) 'Demonstratives' in Joseph Almog, John Perry, and Howard Wettstein (eds.) *Themes from Kaplan* (Oxford: Oxford University Press), 481–563.

Kennedy, Christopher (2007) 'Vagueness and Grammar: The Semantics of Relative and Absolute Adjectives', *Linguistics and Philosophy* 30: 1–45.

King, Jeffrey and Jason Stanley (2005) 'Semantics, Pragmatics, and the Role of Semantic Content', in Zoltán Szabó (ed.) *Semantics Versus Pragmatics* (Oxford: Oxford University Press), 111–64.

Kirchin, Simon (2010) 'The Shapelessness Hypothesis', *Philosophers' Imprint* 10: 1–28.

—— (this volume) 'Thick Concepts and Thick Descriptions'.

Klein, Ewan (1980) 'A Semantics for Positive and Comparative Adjectives', *Linguistics and Philosophy* 4: 1–45.

Larson, Richard, and Peter Ludlow (1993) 'Interpreted Logical Forms', *Synthese* 96: 305–55.

Ludlow, Peter (1989) 'Implicit Comparison Classes', *Linguistics and Philosophy* 12: 519–33.

—— (2008) 'Cheap Contextualism', *Philosophical Issues* 18: 104–29.

McDowell, John (1981) 'Non-Cognitivism and Rule-Following', in Stephen Holtzman and Christopher Leich (eds.) *Wittgenstein: To Follow a Rule* (London: Routledge and Kegan Paul), 141–62.

Nozick, Robert (1974) *Anarchy, State, and Utopia* (New York: Basic Books).

Plato, *Republic* (several editions).

Rawls, John (1971) *A Theory of Justice* (Cambridge, MA: Harvard University Press).

Rayo, Agustín (forthcoming) 'A Plea for Semantic Localism', *Noûs*.

Recanati, François (2004) *Literal Meaning* (Cambridge: Cambridge University Press).

—— (2010) *Truth-Conditional Pragmatics* (Oxford: Clarendon Press).

Rett, Jessica (2008) 'Antonymy and Evaluativity', in Masayuki Gibson and Tova Friedman (eds.) *Proceedings of SALT (Semantics and Linguistic Theory) 17* (Ithaca, NY: CLC Publications), 210–27.

Roberts, Debbie (2011) 'Shapelessness and the Thick', *Ethics* 121: 489–520.

Scheffler, Samuel (1987) 'Morality Through Thick and Thin: a Critical Notice of *Ethics and the Limits of Philosophy*', *Philosophical Review* 96: 411–34.

Soames, Scott (2008) 'Drawing the Line Between Meaning and Implicature–and Relating Both to Assertion', *Noûs* 42: 440–65.

Sturgeon, Nicholas L. (1991) 'Contents and Causes: A Reply to Blackburn', *Philosophical Studies* 61: 19–37.

Sundell, Tim (2011) 'Disagreements about Taste', *Philosophical Studies* 155: 267–88.

van Rooij, Robert (2011) 'Measurement and Interadjective Comparisons', *Journal of Semantics* 28: 335–58.

Väyrynen, Pekka (2008) 'Slim Epistemology with a Thick Skin', *Philosophical Papers* 37: 389–412.

Väyrynen, Pekka (2012) 'Thick Concepts: Where's Evaluation?' *Oxford Studies in Metaethics* 7: 235–70.

von Fintel, Kai and Anthony Gillies (2011) '"Might" Made Right' in Andy Egan and Brian Weatherson (eds.) *Epistemic Modality* (Oxford: Oxford University Press).

von Stechow, Armin (1984) 'Comparing Semantic Theories of Comparison', *Journal of Semantics* 3: 1–77.

Wasserman, Ryan (2004) 'Indeterminacy, Ignorance and the Possibility of Parity', *Philosophical Perspectives* 18: 391–403.

Williams, Bernard (1985) *Ethics and the Limits of Philosophy* (London: Fontana).

9

Evaluative Language and Evaluative Reality

Matti Eklund

9.1 Introduction

What is the *evaluative* (or the *normative*—I will here discuss these things together, under one general label)? There are two questions here. One is what it is for a *property* or a *fact* to be evaluative (as opposed to, e.g., simply being something we value or disvalue). Another is what it is for a *linguistic expression* or a *concept* to be evaluative (again as opposed to, e.g., simply being something which stands for something we value or disvalue, or being something we use to recommend or warn). Let us call the former *the property question* and the latter *the concept question*.

It is possible to adopt a *dismissive* view on both these questions, and say that properties and concepts are not in themselves evaluative. All there is to it is that there are some properties or facts that we tend to value, and some expressions that we tend to use for evaluative purposes. Speaking of the properties or expressions themselves as evaluative is to mistake for a feature of them what is merely something that has to do with us. However, I will here for argument's sake mostly assume that there are things which are evaluative in the ways gestured at, and discuss how this is best construed.

Another kind of dismissive attitude toward the questions is that of the sort of non-reductivist who holds that even if there is something that distinguishes evaluative properties and facts, and something that distinguishes evaluative concepts, it is simply not possible to say what is distinctive about the evaluative. While perhaps this view should not be ruled out, I will attempt to be constructive. Moreover, we will see that there are non-reductivist views on which constructive remarks can be made regarding our questions.

I will often simply talk about predicates and the concepts they express, assuming that the lessons of the discussion of predicates carry over to linguistic expressions of other kinds. Moreover, I will often speak of linguistic expressions rather than concepts. The reason is that I will occasionally bring up the question of whether the evaluativeness of a predicate is a matter of sense or reference or instead of something like conventional implicature; and on one entrenched way of talking about concepts, the concept expressed by the predicate is not itself evaluative in the latter case. Throughout I will assume that the predicates concerned stand for properties. In so doing I set aside prominent versions of expressivism, as well as the Geach-Thomson view that "good" only ever functions as a predicate modifier.[1]

While I will not defend any particular view on either the property question or the concept question, I will close the paper by highlighting a couple of views on the evaluative which, whatever in the end their proper fate, are rendered more salient by some central points made in the present discussion.

There are different kinds of evaluative expressions, and one can reasonably suspect that they can be importantly different, so that we shouldn't assume that the same view on what makes an expression evaluative applies to all. There are many different distinctions within the class of evaluative expressions that can be proposed, but let me here use a fairly coarse-grained classification of evaluative expressions as *thin* ("good," "bad," "right," "wrong," "ought"), *thick* ("brutal," "generous," "lewd," "courageous"), and *epithets* ("nigger," "kike," "fag"). In provisionally drawing these distinctions, I do not mean to imply that by the end of the day all the distinctions between these classes of expressions and concepts will prove especially important. More importantly, perhaps, I do not mean to commit to the claim that all these expressions should in the end count as evaluative. One might for example be skeptical as to whether the so-called thick expressions really are evaluative.[2] For most of the discussion I will speak as if they are, but at appropriate points skepticism will be brought up.

9.2 The metaphysical view on the concept question

Let us start with the concept question. More specifically, consider what I will call the *metaphysical* view on the concept question: the view that a predicate is positively (negatively) evaluative by virtue of standing for a property which is itself positively (negatively) evaluative. A consequence of the metaphysical view is that any predicate which stands for the same property that a given positively (negatively) evaluative predicate stands for must itself be positively (negatively) evaluative. Sometimes the metaphysical view is simply accepted as a matter of course. In a recent survey article, Stephen Finlay writes, "On a realist view of normativity, a concept or word is normative in virtue of being about a normative part or feature of the world—a normative fact, entity, property, function, or relation. . . . For realists, normativity is in the first place something metaphysical, and only derivatively a feature of normative thought and discourse."[3] Finlay notes that antirealists may tell a different story. But I think Finlay is mistaken already about what should be said about a realist standpoint. The metaphysical view faces problems which should make even a realist want to reject it.

---

[1] See for example Geach (1956) and Thomson (2008).

[2] See for example Blackburn (1992).

[3] Finlay (2010), 334. While Finlay's concern is with the "normative," I presume someone with Finlay's view of what realism entails would say the same thing about the broad category I here call the "evaluative."

Some might be inclined to think that Finlay may be trivially right, for he could simply use "evaluative concept" to mean *concept that stands for an evaluative property*. If someone wishes to use "evaluative concept" that way, there need be nothing that prevents her from so using it. But as is clear from Finlay's restriction to realist views, this is not Finlay's usage (else Finlay should hold open that on antirealist views there just are no evaluative concepts).

Sometimes authors are happy to go back and forth between talking about concepts and talking about properties, apparently not drawing any significant distinction between the two. Such authors would see the metaphysical view as a mere truism. But in this discussion I will draw a sharp distinction between concepts and properties, of a kind that should be familiar. Properties are something objects have; concepts are representational, and stand for properties. Different concepts may stand for the same property. Given this distinction, to say that a property is evaluative is to say that it has a certain metaphysical characteristic; but to say that a concept is evaluative is rather somehow to say something about how the property is presented. But then the metaphysical view should immediately seem suspect: no matter how metaphysically special evaluative properties may be, these properties can be represented in different ways. This will underlie the specific arguments I go on to give against the metaphysical view.

The way I propose to speak of evaluative concepts and properties fits how concepts and properties are spoken of elsewhere in the philosophical literature. Here is an illustration. One reasonable, whether or not correct, view in the philosophy of mind is the reductionist view that mental properties are identical with physical properties. If this view is correct, then, for example, the property of having one's C-fibers firing is a mental property. But it would be odd to say that the concept *having one's c-fibers firing* is a mental or psychological concept. The natural thing to say given this view is that one psychological concept and one physical concept pick out one and the same property, which is both mental and physical.

The metaphysical view is arguably not true of epithets. On one popular view, to use an epithet for a given group of people effectively amounts to using a non-evaluative word, "——" ("black," "jew," and so on), but with a negative or contemptuous tone of voice; it is only that the negativity is conventionally associated with the word. Less metaphorically put, the evaluation can be held to reside not in what is *said*, in Paul Grice's favored sense, but in some other feature of how what is said is communicated. Perhaps there is a negative conventional implicature: the speaker's use of the epithet conventionally implicates that the speaker has a negative attitude toward ——s. Epithets then stand for the same properties as their non-loaded counterparts. But then their evaluativeness is not simply a matter of what property they stand for. Call the kind of view on epithets just sketched *the tone view*.[4]

---

[4] "Tone" is the common English rendering of Frege's "*Färbung*" (literally: coloring). Frege held that "horse" and "nag" have the same sense but still differ in tone.

Conventional implicature is a linguistic phenomenon, and anyone who defends a conventional implicature view on the evaluativeness of slurs or any other linguistic expressions faces questions about the employment about the corresponding concept in thought—surely it seems one can use slurs in thought and still one would thereby think whatever negative thing is associated with the slur. For relevant discussion see Williamson (2009), 154f.

The tone view can be resisted. One might instead hold that an epithet stands for a property different from one its neutral counterpart stands for—perhaps something like ___-and-therefore-worthy-of-contempt. This property would in all the ordinary cases be uninstantiated: no one is worthy of contempt on account of being a ___. And even should the tone view be correct, one can reasonably maintain that this counterexample to the metaphysical view relies on facts specific to the case of epithets, and does not generalize to other types of evaluative expressions. Maybe different views on what it is for an expression to be evaluative are true of different classes of evaluative expressions. A restricted version of the metaphysical view might be that predicates that are, so to speak, *evaluative by virtue of sense* are so by virtue of standing for evaluative properties.

Turn then to a different argument against the metaphysical view. Suppose that an alien linguistic community introduces into their language a word—"thgir"—with the stipulation that "thgir" is to stand for *the property that our "right" stands for,* but this community does not in any way use their word "thgir" evaluatively. (We might tell different stories about why that would be so. But one possibility is that they might just not have understood that our "right" is evaluative.) In this case, "thgir" stands for the same property as our "right" does, a property which in fact is evaluative, but there is no reason to hold that the predicate is (positively) evaluative. If this can happen with respect to a thin term like "right," one can present similar examples with respect to arbitrary thin and thick terms.

The friend of the metaphysical view might suggest that because of how "thgir" is used in the alien community, it in fact stands for a different property than our term "right" stands for, the explicit stipulation to the contrary. But the alien community, as described, can certainly have the description "the property ascribed by 'right.'" Why should they not also be able to introduce a predicate ascribing this property? ("Let 'thgir' ascribe the property ascribed by 'right.'")[5]

Some might be inclined to think that if "right" and "thgir" stand for the same property, they must be synonymous, so if one is evaluative then so is the other. But even if the synonymy claim can be defended—and clearly this is far from obvious—this is not sufficient for the metaphysical view. One might also take the lesson to be that we should adopt a *dismissive* view: a predicate with this meaning shared by "right" and "thgir" can be used to evaluate or fail to be so used, but the meaning is not itself evaluative.

To stress, and to relate back to Finlay's remarks, none of the problems with the metaphysical view is in itself a problem with realism. One possible view is that all that the problems point to is that there can be a kind of mismatch between a language's predicates and what properties in the world really are evaluative. That view is perfectly compatible with—indeed, as formulated it *requires*—that some properties are in and of themselves evaluative; and that is a hallmark of realism about the evaluative.

---

[5] When being careful I will keep talking about what is "ascribed," not what is denoted. The terminology is from Jackson (1998), 119 n. 10. It is trivial that any property we can use an expression to *denote*, we can denote in purely descriptive terms. (Consider "the property I am currently thinking about.")

9.3 The deflationary view on the concept question

Where should we turn after having rejected the metaphysical view? A natural suggestion to turn to is:

(D)   A predicate F is positively (negatively) evaluative just in case "x is F" conceptually entails "x is [to that extent] good" ("bad")

Maybe a distinction should be drawn between conceptually entailing something about goodness/badness and conceptually entailing something about rightness/wrongness. Such distinctions are orthogonal to my present concerns. But I do bother with the "to that extent." One might reasonably be concerned that positive (negative) thick concepts may be true of some behavior which is all things considered pretty bad (good). The "to that extent" is there to ward off this kind of concern.

"Thgir" does not present a problem for (D). Even if "thgir" and "right" ascribe the same property, so necessarily something is thgir if and only if it is right, one can maintain that "x is thgir" does not *conceptually* entail "x is right" or "x is good."

There is a certain kind of deflationist view on the concept question, according to which for a concept to be evaluative just is for it to stand in the right entailment relations to the concept *goodness* or the concept *badness*. Merely to accept (D) is not immediately to subscribe to this deflationary view. But unless the friend of (D) subscribes to this view, it is unclear in what sense she is offering an account of what it is to be evaluative. What is special about the deflationary view is its insistence that (D), or something like it, provides a *full* explanation of what it is to be evaluative. This is what makes the view a genuinely *deflationary* view. For any predicate F, we can define a notion, "F-ish," such that a predicate G is F-ish just in case "x is G" conceptually entails "x is F." While such notions can be defined they do not generally carve out classes of predicates in any interesting way.

If the tone view on epithets is correct, (D) is false as it stands. But again, epithets are special, so one might anyway prefer the more restricted:

(D')   A predicate F is positively (negatively) evaluative *as a matter of sense* just in case "x is F" conceptually entails "x is [to that extent] good" ("bad").

However, also thick concepts present potential problems. Let an evaluative concept be *objectionable* iff, roughly, its use in some sense presupposes a false evaluative claim. Many epithets are objectionable. The point is also sometimes made that there appear to be objectionable thick concepts. Allan Gibbard has prominently argued that "lewd" expresses an objectionable thick concept, for its use presupposes a false negative view on overt displays of sexuality.[6] Whether or not Gibbard is right about this specific example, surely the phenomenon of objectionableness cannot reasonably be denied.[7] (Here are

---

[6] Gibbard (1992). Of course this is a much simplified account of what use of "lewd" signals.

[7] See my (2011) and Väyrynen (2009) for more on objectionable thick concepts. Gibbard (1992) also argues that the phenomenon obtains by considering a fictional example, "gopa," meaning roughly *glorious killing*.

other candidates for objectionableness: "chaste" may be thought to falsely presuppose that abstaining from sex is in and of itself good; and "(sexually) perverted" may be thought to falsely presuppose that sex has some particular purpose such that sex which doesn't serve that purpose is thereby bad. It is perhaps not surprising that the examples are all terms pertaining to sexual morality.)

What should be said about the *extension* of an objectionable thick concept? One possibility is that if a concept is objectionable, then it is *empty*; another possibility is that even if a concept is objectionable, it is actually true of pretty much what it would be true of if it weren't—its objectionableness effectively doesn't matter to its extension. Let us say that on the second hypothesis, objectionable thick concepts *misevaluate*, the idea behind the label being that if an evaluative concept is true of things that do not "fit" the evaluation associated with the concept, it misevaluates. It can be that I should agree that such-and-such behavior is lewd, even while I should not agree that the behavior is in any way *bad*.

Although I cannot mount a full defense here, my view is that objectionable thick concepts misevaluate.[8] Here is the most straightforward argument for this. Surely, whatever else may be true of the concepts perverted, lewd and chaste—in particular, even if these are objectionable concepts—behaviors which would paradigmatically be regarded as perverted or lewd or chaste do occur, and when one considers the question of how one would answer if forced to answer the question of whether the behaviors are or are not perverted (lewd, chaste, and so on) one will intuitively have to answer in the positive. (One may wish to *avoid using the words*, in light of what use of these words would convey, but that is different.)

If objectionable thick concepts are evaluative but misevaluate, there can be behaviors which are, say, lewd or perverted, but which are not *bad*. If thick terms are evaluative as a matter of sense, they then present counterexamples to (D'). A friend of (D') can attempt to respond that if objectionable thick concepts misevaluate, that just shows that a tone view is true of them. I believe that someone inclined to take this route will face an uphill battle: paradigmatic thick concepts are sufficiently similar in behavior to thin concepts that it is hard to maintain that a tone view is true of the thick concepts but not the thin. But I may be wrong. (After all, some theorists do appear happy to discuss epithets and thick concepts together, not drawing much of a distinction between the two cases.)[9] Another possible response is that the so-called thick evaluative terms are not really evaluative after all.[10] A problem for both these suggestions is that, as is often remarked, there seems to be a spectrum between the thin and the thick concepts rather than a simple dichotomy.[11]

In fact, misevaluating thick concepts also present a further problem for the metaphysical view: a misevaluating thick concept can be positively (negatively) evaluative even while the *property* it stands for is not in fact so. The same possible ways out are available for the friend of the metaphysical view as for the friend of (D').

---

[8] See my (2011).
[9] See for example Blackburn (1984), Elstein and Hurka (2009), and Scanlon (2003).
[10] See Blackburn (1992).
[11] See Scheffler (1987).

The phenomenon of misevaluating thick concepts must not be confused with another supposed phenomenon which also threatens to pose problems for (D'). Some writers have insisted that many thick concepts do not have invariant evaluative valence, but instead have *variant valence*: for example, that while it may perhaps *typically* be the case that something's being a courageous thing to do counts in its favor, sometimes this can count against it. One may try to *contain* this by saying that even if x's being courageous is *in and of itself* something that is good-making, this feature can in *combination* with x's other features make x less good than it would otherwise be. But *suppose* the phenomenon of variant valence obtains and cannot be contained in this way: for some instances of, say, courage, not only make the possessor less good than the possessor would otherwise be, in combination with some of the possessor's other features, but they are not even in and of themselves something good. This presents a possible problem for (D'). But we must be careful here. Bearing in mind the concepts/properties distinction, there are two different variant valence-theses:

(i) For some property that a thick concept stands for, sometimes this property is a good-making (bad-making) feature of what has it and sometimes not.

(ii) Some thick concept C is such that sometimes to say "___ is C" is to say something positive (negative) about ___ and sometimes not.

It is possible, for example, that (i) is true but (ii) is not: that while something's having the property in question isn't always a good-making feature, to say of it that it is "C," where C is a thick concept which stands for the property, is always to say something positive about it.

The thesis that is of relevance to (D') is (ii). It would be natural for someone subscribing to (ii) and who holds that thick concepts satisfying (ii) are evaluative to reject (D'): these thick concepts do not stand in simple conceptual relationships to the concepts *goodness* and *badness*. The examples used to motivate variant valence in the first instance justify (i). And (i) can be true without (ii) being so: even if a property has variant valence, a concept ascribing the property can unfailingly present it in a positive light, as it were.

Even if (ii) presents a problem for (D'), the friend of (ii) can in principle accept a different kind of deflationary view. For example, it can be maintained to be evaluative is just to be one of the predicates on a big list: there is nothing deeper that unites these predicates; not even their conceptual entailment relations to the concepts *goodness* and *badness*.[12]

My own view, moreover, would be that if some, or all, thick concepts really verify (ii)—and this cannot be explained as simply due to pragmatic factors—then we should simply question whether these concepts really are evaluative. Recall the possibility of a dismissive view.

---

[12] For this kind of list view, see Jackson (1998), 120. However, Jackson's motivations for accepting such a view are different.

None of the problems presented shows that (D) and (D') *must* be rejected. Even if the tone view of epithets is accepted, that only casts doubt on the fully general (D); (D') is a natural revision. Misevaluating thick concepts, if there are any, cast doubt on (D') only on the assumption that thick concepts are evaluative as a matter of sense. As for variant valence, I have just outlined my preferred response. But it cannot be doubted that (D) and (D') are both problematic.

9.4 The affective view on the concept question

A third view on the concept question is the *affective* view, according to which the contents of evaluative concepts are such that their use is tied to the *expression of an attitude* or perhaps to *recommending* or *prohibiting*. I will avoid the disjunctive formulation and instead speak only of attitude-expression, sliding over distinction between different versions of the affective view which might for other purposes be very important. While non-factualist views are based on an affective answer to the concept question, one can very well accept the affective view without being a non-factualist.

The affective view evades the problems facing the views earlier considered. "Thgir" fails to be positively evaluative despite standing for the property of rightness, since its use doesn't serve to express an attitude. Objectionable thick terms express attitudes even if they do so objectionably. The affective view also promises to trace a significant distinction in a way a deflationary view does not. I find the affective view attractive, in part because of how it deals with the examples discussed, even though I will go on to mention important problems.

There are many clarificatory questions that can be raised about the nature of the attitude-expression at issue. I will pause only on such clarificatory questions as are relevant for present purposes. One question regarding the affective view concerns how to conceive of the attitude expressed. A *coarse-grained* view would be that there are only two attitudes for evaluative expressions to express, *positive* and *negative* ("pro" and "con"). A more *fine-grained* view would make more fine-grained distinctions between the evaluations associated with different terms. The attitude that "beautiful" expresses is different from that which "tasty" expresses; and these two are in turn quite different from the attitude that "good" expresses. I favor the latter view. One intuitive way of motivating this stance is to consider the possibility of two coextensive predicates, where one is used for positive aesthetic evaluation and the other for positive moral evaluation. A proponent of the coarse-grained view on attitude-expression would have to say that the predicates mean the same. While there need be nothing strange about such a view from a perspective according to which the evaluative use of a predicate is not something which makes the predicate itself evaluative, the view should seem strange from the perspective we are currently exploring, according to which some predicates are in and of themselves evaluative. Why should not the kind of evaluativeness then also be a matter of the meaning of the predicate? However, a problem in using this kind of example to pose problems for the coarse-grained view is that the friend of the affective view can in principle maintain that it is just not possible for two predicates to relate to each other this way, for the evaluative differences between the predicates necessitate differences in extension (that, as we might put it, *evaluation is extension-determining*). I will soon return to this concern. For now, let us take the point against the coarse-grained view on board.

Some well-known issues prominently discussed in the literature present potential problems for the affective view. Let me briefly mention these issues and the nature of their relevance. I will however not comment further on them, for the literature on them is already huge and I rather wish to focus on complications that are less widely recognized. First, there are *embedding problems*, such as famously brought up by the Frege-Geach problem for non-cognitivism. Even if "right" serves to express an attitude when used in sentences of the form "x is right," it is hardly so used in "if ϕ-ing is right then getting your little sister to ϕ is right." Yet "right" obviously expresses the same thing as used in both contexts. Second, even setting embedded occurrences to the side one may think that evaluative terms are not always affectively used. Thick terms certainly can be used in ways apparently contrary to their intuitive valence. Blackburn's example "last year's carnival wasn't lewd enough" makes the point well.[13] More generally, it has been argued, for example by appeal to the "amoralist," that one can felicitously use even thin terms without expressing attitudes.[14]

The affective view, as so far characterized, can be fleshed out in different ways, depending on how one sees the attitude as expressed. On one way of fleshing it out, expressing an attitude is a matter of *conventional implicature*; on another way of fleshing it out, when an evaluative predicate expresses an attitude that a non-evaluative co-extensive counterpart does not, that is because the predicates differ in *sense* although they stand for the same property. A friend of the affective view need not decide between these ideas. It is consistent with the affective view that some evaluative expressions work one way and some work another way.

On an affective view, an evaluative expression serves both to stand for a property and to express an attitude, and the property that the expression stands for does not determine what attitude the expression expresses (for if it did we would be dealing with a version of the metaphysical view). One might then naturally suspect the following two claims to be true given an affective view:

($) For each property P that an evaluative predicate can stand for, there are different possible evaluative predicates F1 and F2 standing for P such that F1 and F2 do not express the same attitude.

($$) For each attitude A that an evaluative predicate can express there are different possible evaluative predicates F1 and F2 expressing A such that F1 and F2 do not stand for the same property.

---

[13] Blackburn (1992), 296.   [14] See for example Brink (1989).

I want to discuss some issues related to ($$). Let me call what is envisaged in ($$) *variability*. In what follows I will discuss the relation between the affective view and variability.

On the coarse-grained view on attitude-expression, ($$) is trivial and uninteresting, since there are only two attitudes for evaluative predicates to express, positive and negative. But recall that I want to focus on a fine-grained view on attitude-expression. Given that the property the predicate stands for does not explain the attitude expressed given an affective view, ($$) can be suspected to be true on an affective view even given the fine-grained view on attitude-expression.

If variability indeed obtains, then we are faced with the following situation. There is a possible predicate, call it "right★," *evaluatively* like our "right"'—expressing the same (fine-grained) attitude—but which stands for a different property and has a different extension. This sort of thing which may be natural to expect in the case of thick terms. But as I will argue, certain puzzles arise if this generalizes also to thin terms.

The phenomenon I am talking about may seem strange; if so, all this means is that the affective views committed to variability are committed to the possibility of something strange. Below I will turn to some specific views of this kind.

An immediate reaction may be that the speakers using "right★" must in some way be importantly mistaken, even if they are completely clear about what is indeed right★: they are evaluating, in the way we evaluate what is right, what has a different property. They are, one might want to say, evaluating non-right things in the way right things ought to be valued.

But *we* would seem the same way to *them*. They can give the following speech: "Those people [that is, *us*] are importantly mistaken even if they are clear on what is indeed 'right.' They are evaluating, in the way we evaluate what is right★, what has a different property. They are, one wants to say, evaluating non-right★ things in the way right★ things ought to be valued." (Or *ought★* to be valued; see below.) And the situation is *symmetric*, so their speech should seem as reasonable as ours.

Seeing this symmetry, one can say to oneself: So, there are many possible predicates which are evaluative in the way "right" is evaluative. Some such predicates are such that their users are somehow mistaken in letting a predicate standing for the property this predicate stands for be evaluative in the way that "right" is. The important question is which of these predicates one *ought* to use for these purposes. Maybe it is *our* "right" one ought to use, but this cannot be blithely assumed. We must figure out whether it is so.

But there is a glaring problem regarding such an inquiry. When one states what the inquiry concerns, one says that it concerns what notion of "right" one *ought* to use, but "ought" is itself an evaluative term, and the same phenomenon arises for "ought" as arises for "right." The fact that the phenomenon arises also for "ought" means that speakers using different sets of evaluative terms, with different extensions, will in effect ask different questions.[15] One question asks which "right" one *ought* to use, another asks which "right" one *ought★* to use, etc. (And while one might find a formulation which

---

[15] Thus in the envisaged speech two paragraphs back, we should think of them as asking what notion of "right" *ought★* to be used rather than what notion of "right" *ought* to be used.

avoids "ought" specifically, any alternative formulation of what the inquiry concerns will have to employ some evaluative term or other, so the underlying problem remains.) An inquirer using our "ought" will conclude in favor of one of the "ought"-concepts; an inquirer using one of the alternative oughts might conclude in favor of another. On the one hand, one wants to say that there is a further question as to *which one of these "oughts" one ought to use* in an inquiry like the one sketched. On the other hand, variability does not entail that there is no fact of the matter as to which "ought" one *ought* to use; variability just means that there is another "ought" one *ought** to use, and so on. Perhaps one can sum things up by saying that our would-be inquirer is concerned with which one of the oughts is *privileged*.

There are three different reactions one might have to the predicament our inquirer is in. One might think that the absurd questions that arise show that there is something wrong with any view committed to variability, for example with affective views thus committed; that there is a privileged ought of the kind our inquirer seeks; or that the idea of a privileged ought is a non-starter. I will not seek to adjudicate which one of these reactions is the most reasonable. Whichever reaction is right, there is something *seemingly* absurd about the difficulties encountered. One natural reaction is that something has gone wrong somewhere when issues like the ones I have described these past few paragraphs arise. It may help to compare some views from the literature, to see that the puzzles presented by variability really are genuine, at least in that there are natural and prominent affective views given which variability obtains.[16]

Scott Sturgeon is naturally taken to defend an affective view.[17] He discusses the problem arising from the fact that the following is an inconsistent triad of initially plausible claims:

(a) Cognitivism: normative sentences take cognitivist psychology.
(b) The link thesis: there's an internal link between normative judgment and desire-like elements of mind.
(c) Humeanism: belief- and desire-like elements of mind can always be pulled apart.

Non-cognitivists give up (a). Those who defend cognitivism give up (b) or (c). Sturgeon thinks that once we clearly distinguish between concepts and properties, and keep in mind that content can be talked about as either coarse-grained or fine-grained, the conflict can be resolved. (Of course the coarse/fine distinction concerning content is distinct from the coarse/fine distinction I earlier drew concerning attitudes.)

For example, the link thesis is false when content is individuated in a coarse-grained way: there is no property ϕ such that whenever a thinker judges *that a is C*, for any concept C which stands for ϕ, something about desire is entailed. But when content is

---

[16] Puzzles related to what I have called variability are also discussed, from a different perspective, in my (forthcoming).
[17] Sturgeon (2007).

individuated in a fine-grained way, the link thesis can still be true: there can be a concept C of F such that whenever a thinker judges *that a is C* something about desire is entailed. Correspondingly, Humeanism has two readings. Under one it is the thesis that coarse belief and desire are two-way disentangleable; under the other it is the thesis that finely individuated belief and desire are two-way disentangleable. Here the "coarse" thesis can be argued to be true, while the "fine" one is false. For every property φ there is a concept C such that one can believe *that a is C* without this being at all linked to desire; but for all that, it could be that there is a concept C of φ such that believing *that a is C*—as it were, believing under that mode of presentation that a is φ—is linked to desire. Sturgeon's response to the problem, then, is to maintain cognitivism together with the "fine" link-thesis and "coarse" Humeanism.

I find this attractive. But what exactly would the fine-grained concept with a link to desire be like? Sturgeon cannot explain the nature of the concept simply by appeal to what property it stands for—that would entail that all concepts of a given property have the same link to desire—along the lines of a metaphysical view. Instead all he says are things like:

Normative concepts are themselves individuated not only by their semantic values but also by volitional elements which manifest conceptual content...On such an "affect conceptualist" approach to normative judgement, the concept *OUGHT* used in your judgement requires for its manifestation [in "base case judgement"] a *bona fide* desire concerning its non-normative content.[18]

Nothing here suggests how *alternative* semantic-value-plus-volitional element combinations would be ruled out. There will be natural psychological or sociological explanations of why we have the evaluative concepts we have, but even so there are other concepts one *could* employ, and variability arises.

Turn next to David Copp's account.[19] Copp defends what he calls *realist-expressivism*. This is an at bottom realist view coupled with the idea that use of evaluative expressions serves to express an attitude, through a mechanism like conventional implicature.[20] The view is an affective view. Copp sees a need to provide a link between the truth-conditional contents of evaluative predicates and the conventional implicatures associated with these predicates. He proposes that to say that something, φ-ing, is "wrong" is to say that there is a "relevantly justified or authoritative" standard which prohibits φ-ing. This is supposed to explain the implicature, for if I say that according to some justified or authoritative standard, φ-ing is prohibited, it is only natural that I thereby should somehow convey the attitude that I am in favor of the standard. Copp thus apparently seeks to avoid variability: the property the predicate stands for explains what attitude is expressed.

---

[18] Sturgeon (2007), 580.

[19] Copp (2001). My discussion parallels that of my (forthcoming).

[20] Copp is non-committal as to whether the phenomenon he is concerned with deserves exactly the label "conventional implicature." In his (2009) follow-up article, he coins the label "simplicature." These details will not matter to my discussion of Copp.

However, here is a problem with Copp's story. It is crucial to Copp's story that what is said is that according to some *justified or authoritative* standard, φ-ing is prohibited. If what was said was only that according to some standard satisfying some *purely descriptive* condition φ-ing is prohibited, the connection between content and implicature would not be so readily explained. But what Copp says goes for "right" and "wrong" goes for "justified" too, assuming he means to account for evaluative language more generally, for "justified" is also an evaluative expression. So to declare something "justified" is to say that it has such and such a property and moreover to express an attitude about this. Once we keep this in mind, Copp's account of the connection between content and implicature can be seen to be problematic. For the truth-conditional content of "φ-ing is wrong" is then just that there is some *F* standard which prohibits φ-ing, where F simply states the truth-conditional content of "justified."[21]

Suppose Copp had tried to "explain" the connection between truth-conditional content and implicature as follows: "Someone who says 'φ-ing is wrong' is saying that φ-ing is *wrong*, and why would she say *that it is wrong* unless she was against φ-ing? So it is only to be expected that the speaker implicated that she has that attitude." This story should not carry conviction, given, precisely, that what makes "wrong" evaluative on Copp's account is not a matter of its truth-conditional content but a matter of implicature. Copp's actual explanation is more complex, as Copp further analyzes the talk of rightness and wrongness in terms of what a justified or authoritative standard permits or prohibits, but Copp's explanation of the connection between truth-conditional content and implicature fails for the same reason that the simpler explanation does.

Variability arises naturally given an affective view. But is there a way for the friend of the affective view to avoid variability? Briefly: in principle, yes. Ralph Wedgwood's (2001) view, whatever else its virtues and vices may be, at least promises to avoid these difficulties.[22] Wedgwood proposes a certain form of conceptual-role semantics for evaluative terms. He focuses on a particular predicate, intuitively meaning something like "ought all things considered to prefer," whose semantic value is conceived of as completely determined by its *action-guiding role*; its role in *practical reasoning*. More precisely, what Wedgwood proposes is that the predicate is governed by the following basic rule:

Acceptance of "B(x, y, me, t)" commits one to having a preference for doing x over doing y at time t.[23]

Further, the semantic value of this predicate is, Wedgwood argues, the four-place relation between x, y, z, and t, if any, which is such that "it is correct for z to prefer doing x over doing y at t and a mistake for z to prefer doing y over doing x at t if, and only if, x, y,

---

[21] Copp also uses "authoritative." But while this introduces some complications it does not affect my criticism. Either "authoritative" too is an evaluative term and then what is said in the text applies to it too, or it is not evaluative but just expresses that a norm is in play without in any sense endorsing it, in which case it does not explain the conventional implicature.

[22] Compare too Wedgwood's more recent (2007). The account in (2007) is slightly different from that of (2001) but not in any way that matters to present concerns.

[23] Wedgwood (2001), 15.

z, and t stand in that relation."[24] The preference is correct if and only if it is in accordance with the goal of practical reasoning; and it is a substantive question if there is such a goal and, if so, what the goal is.[25] On Wedgwood's view, a term's evaluativeness lies in its action-guiding role; and any term with the action-guiding role that "B(x, y, z, t)" has must have the same extension as "B(x, y, z, t)." While Wedgwood's view isn't a metaphysical view, Wedgwood can still deny variability, at least for maximally thin predicates like "B(x, y, z, t)," fully characterized by their roles in practical reasoning.[26]

On Wedgwood's theory, evaluation is extension-determining in the way earlier characterized. On the views for which variability arises, evaluation is not extension-determining. Earlier I distinguished between the fine-grained and coarse-grained views on attitude-expression. I gave an argument against the coarse-grained view but noted that this argument could be resisted if one held that evaluation is extension-determining. I further noted that variability only clearly arises given the fine-grained view on attitude-expression. Now I can add that the views for which variability seems prima facie to be a problem are views on which it is at best unclear whether evaluation is extension-determining, so it is doubtful whether this way out is open for the friends of these views.

In general terms, here is what is going on with Wedgwood's view. Wedgwood holds that there is a class of evaluative predicates such that what makes them evaluative—their conceptual role—also is extension-determining. Yet his view is not metaphysical in the sense earlier characterized: there can be non-evaluative predicates which stand for the same properties as these evaluative predicates do. Rather, Wedgwood's view most plausibly seen as affective: what is special about evaluative predicates concerns their role in practical reasoning.

9.5 The property-presentation view on the concept question

When introducing the affective view, I said that it deals well with the problems faced by the metaphysical view and by (D) and variants, and is motivated by how it deals with these problems. But there is also a potentially importantly different kind of view for which the same can be said.

Earlier I noted that similar considerations as were used against the metaphysical view show that the analogue of the metaphysical view is not correct when it comes to the question of what makes a concept psychological. One might furthermore be skeptical of the plausibility of a deflationary view on this question, thinking that the psychological

---

[24] Wedgwood (2001), 18.

[25] Wedgwood (2001), 20.

[26] I anticipate the objection that "correct," a normative term, is used in the theory of how the semantic value of "B(x,y,z,t)" is determined, and if there are different notions of correctness, we still face variability. But even in the worst case, this *at most* shows how there *can* be variability even given Wedgwood's account. All I am concerned to show in the text is how one in principle can avoid variability by taking evaluation to be extension-determining.

concepts do form a genuine kind. But it is absurd that an analogue of the affective view should be the correct account of what makes a concept psychological. Rather, some-how or other, what makes a concept psychological is that, some way or other, it *presents* the property it stands for as being of a certain kind—*as being psychological.*

The analogue of this in the case of the concept question is that what makes a concept evaluative is that it presents the property it stands for as evaluative. That slogan, as far as it goes (I don't pretend it is very clear), is compatible with an affective view. But it can also be understood as it is understood in the case of the psychological, not as indicating any kind of affective view but as indicating what type of property it is the concept presents the property it stands for as being. Call this non-affective view *the property-presentation view.* This view promises to avoids the problem presented by "thgir," and the traditional problems for the affective view. But what does "presenting as evaluative" come to exactly? Some questions one may raise here are general, and concern generally what it is for a concept to present a property it purports to ascribe as being of a certain kind. While the problems may be significant, let me here set aside such perfectly general questions, which could equally well be asked concerning, for example, psychological concepts. There are more specific questions that may be raised concerning the property-presentation view. Is the property-presentation view best understood to entail that all evaluative concepts stand for evaluative properties or not? If it does, then problems for (D') such as what to say about objectionable thick concepts are equally problems for the property-presentation view. If it does not, then the property-presentation view is impor-tantly different from its supposed analogue in the case of psychological concepts, for one would be hard pressed to find a non-empty psychological concept that fails to stand for a mental property.

9.6 Selectively dismissive views

One reaction one might have given the problems faced by the different constructive answers to the concept question, is that a dismissive attitude should simply be adopted toward this question. While we can sometimes use some expressions and concepts to evaluate, speaking of some expressions and concepts as in and of themselves evaluative is misguided. Importantly, however, that does not mean that one must adopt a dismissive attitude toward the metaphysical question. One can say that the only things properly called evaluative are properties; there is no reasonable notion of evaluativeness that prop-erly applies to concepts.

Conversely, for example the friend of the affective view on the concept question might in principle just reject the property question. She might insist that there is no significant difference in the kinds of properties that descriptive and evaluative predicates stand for: the linguistic or conceptual evaluative/descriptive distinction after all con-cerns only how properties *are conceptualized.* When we speak of properties themselves as evaluative, we are treating what is properly a feature of expressions as a property of what the expressions stand for. This view—let us call it the *presentationalist* view (the reason being that on this view, evaluativeness is strictly only a feature of how properties are conceptualized and not of the properties themselves)—is an interesting view in its own right. It problematizes the question of what moral realism should be taken to be. On the one hand, it is a realist view, in that it is a view on which evaluative sentences are mind-independently true and false, and some atomic evaluative sentences are true. On the other hand, someone whose metaphysics is like that of the paradigmatic moral antireal-ist should agree that there can be predicates that function like evaluative predicates do on the view we are currently considering: they ascribe plain vanilla descriptive proper-ties but, as it were, present these properties in a particular positive or negative light.

Interesting though presentationalism may be, I will not here pause on it. As we will see, even the friend of the affective view can in principle agree that there is a significant evaluative/descriptive distinction at the level of properties; and what I want to do is to investigate what this distinction might be like. Only toward the end will I make a few further remarks on presentationalism.

9.7 The property question

Turn now to the property question: what is it for a property to be evaluative? One sim-ple suggestion is:

(P1)   An evaluative property is a property that can be ascribed with an evaluative predicate.[27]

But (P1) actually faces a host of potential problems. None of them is lethal, but together they illustrate that (P1) is incompatible with many other reasonable views. First, when we take into account epithets and objectionable thick concepts we should be open to the possibility of evaluative predicates standing for non-evaluative properties. Second, on any version of the affective view that allows for variability even when it comes to the thin, (P1) threatens to mas-sively overgenerate also in the case of thin predicates. (For on such an affective view, there are alternative thin predicates standing for different properties.) Third, (P1) immediately rules out the presentationalist view, but that view, whatever its fate, is surely a coherent option. Fourth, (P1) is incompatible with any view on the concept question which picks out evaluative predi-cates in terms of evaluative properties, such as the metaphysical view and arguably also the property-presentation view. In sum, (P1) is in conflict with a large variety of views.

A more promising view may be:

(P2)   Property ϕ is positively (negatively) evaluative iff for all x, if x is ϕ then necessarily x is [to that extent] good (bad).

(P2) deals nicely with examples like "thgir." To be thgir is to be right, even if "right" is evaluative and "thgir" is not. The property of being thgir is an evaluative property (even

---

[27] The idea is common. A recent discussion where it receives expression is Streumer (2011), esp. 326.

if the "thgir"-users may be unaware of the fact that it is). That consequence sounds correct to me. (P2) also deals well with objectionable thick concepts. An objectionable thick positively (negatively) evaluative concept may stand for a property that fails to be positively (negatively) evaluative.

However, (P2) might be thought too permissive. One might want to leave room for there being a purely descriptive property ϕ such that something's being ϕ necessitates this thing's having an evaluative property. But by (P2), ϕ is then an evaluative property after all. This may be unwanted. Someone who finds (P2) too permissive might try to appeal to the distinction between *essential* features on the one hand and merely *metaphysically necessary* ones on the other. The essential features of something are those of its necessary features which make this something what it is. A well-known example, due to Kit Fine, is that while it is a metaphysically necessary feature of Socrates that he is a member of his singleton set, this is intuitively not an essential feature of Socrates.[28] Given this distinction one can say that some properties ϕ are such that it's an essential feature of ϕ that if something is ϕ then it is good (bad), while others fail to be such even though necessarily, if something is ϕ then it is good (bad). The evaluative properties can be identified as the ones in the former category.

Even if (P2), or a version modified as suggested, can be argued to be extensionally adequate, it may be regarded as being too deflationary. For any property ϕ, we can define a notion of being ϕ-ish such that a property ψ is ϕ-ish if (it is an essential feature of ψ that) something's being ψ necessitates its being ϕ. Compare above remarks on the deflationary view on the concept question.

What might a suitable non-deflationary view be like? One view is the non-reductionist view which maintains that the evaluative properties form a significant metaphysical kind but which eschews any sort of informative characterization of what makes a property evaluative. This view may well be correct. But I don't have much to say about this possibility. Another type of non-deflationary view focuses on *motivation*. There are two different kinds of view of this general type. On one kind of view, evaluative properties are such that recognition that they are instantiated is somehow in and of itself motivating. On another kind of view, evaluative properties are such that recognition of their being instantiated *ought* to be motivating. While there is much to say about these views, let me here be brief. The former kind of view is implausibly Panglossian. The latter kind of view is in effect non-reductive in its talk of what *ought* to motivate.

Yet another type of non-deflationary view takes a leaf from Wedgwood's account. Let a predicate be *Wedgwoodian* if its reference is fully determined by its conceptual role in practical reason, along the lines of how the reference of "B(x,y,z,t)" above is determined. (The "along the lines of" is vague and a proper account would need to be more precise.) Then consider the following suggestion:

(P3)   Property ϕ is positively (negatively) evaluative iff it can be ascribed using a Wedgwoodian predicate.

---

[28] Fine (1994).

(P3) is like (P1) except that evaluative predicate (P3) speaks of Wedgwoodian predicates rather than evaluative predicates. If Wedgwood's general semantic theory is attractive, then (P3) may likewise be attractive. But it is reasonable to speculate that it has the consequence that there are relatively few evaluative properties: that relatively few properties can be picked out by Wedgwoodian predicates.

9.8 Thick properties

Just as one might want to call some properties evaluative, one might want to call some properties descriptive. Indeed, I have employed such formulations, which are rather natural, above.[29] One cheap way of characterizing what it is a for a property to be descriptive, given an account of what it is for a property to be evaluative, is just to say that for a property to be descriptive simply is for it *not to be evaluative*. But this threatens to lead to problems elsewhere.

Since early on, I have spoken of thick terms and concepts. Some authors speak also of *thick properties*.[30] Sometimes I suspect that this is a mere mistake, and that authors who speak this way simply do not distinguish carefully between concepts and properties. But suppose we take the idea of thick properties, as opposed to thick concepts, seriously. How are we to understand it?

Thickness gets characterized in different ways. But on one prominent way of characterizing thickness, the thick somehow merges the descriptive and the evaluative. However, how is this merging to be understood in the case of properties? If the descriptiveness of a property is identified with its non-evaluativeness, then no property can be both evaluative and descriptive; but then, among other things, thick properties cannot be both evaluative and descriptive.

If the friend of the idea of thick properties holds that properties have some sort of *structure*, whereby they can have other properties as *constituents*, she can say that what is special about thick properties is that they have both descriptive and evaluative constituents. But if she does not hold that properties are thus structured—and certainly the idea of structured properties is controversial (and should be controversial even if there are structured *predicates* and *concepts*)—she is forced to find some alternative account of descriptiveness.[31]

---

[29] As indicated by my tentative formulations, one may think that "descriptive" does not apply to properties. I will here attempt to be constructive, even if such doubts are reasonable.

[30] See for example Dancy (1993), and McNaughton and Rawling (2000).

[31] Some prominent authors who speak of the thick hold that while the thick in some sense has descriptive and evaluative elements, these elements cannot be "disentangled." I find this talk of what can and cannot be disentangled somewhat dark. But whatever it means, one may think that if thick properties have the kind of structure here envisaged, the descriptive and evaluative elements can be "disentangled" after all.

Incidentally, as we distinguish between the idea of thick concepts and thick properties, we should also distinguish between different entanglement theses. One entanglement thesis is that the descriptive and evaluative elements in thick concepts cannot be disentangled; another entanglement thesis is that the descriptive and evaluative elements in thick properties cannot be disentangled.

Here is one characterization that allows for this: a descriptive property is one that can be ascribed by a purely descriptive predicate. In the first instance, this only pushes the problem back, as it relies on the notion of a descriptive predicate. But suppose that we understand a descriptive predicate to be one whose reference is determined in a way that is fully *non*-Wedgwoodian, that is, whose reference is not in any way determined by anything which makes the predicate evaluative. Then if we combine this with the characterization (P3) of what it is for a property to be evaluative, we allow for a property to be both descriptive and evaluative.

However, this makes it too easy for a property to be descriptive. Does any property fail to be descriptive, given this characterization? Recall "thgir" from above. Even the property of rightness can be ascribed by a fully descriptive predicate.

9.9 Specificity

The characterization of the thick in terms of the merging of descriptive and evaluative aspects is not the only kind of characterization one finds in the literature. Sometimes the thick is simply described as something which is more *specific* than the thin. In the case of concepts, this becomes something along the lines of:

(TC)   A positively (negatively) evaluative concept C is a thick concept just in case "___ is C" conceptually entails "___ is [to that extent] good" ("___ is [to that extent] bad"), but not vice versa.

Misevaluating objectionable thick concepts present counterexamples to this principle. But appeal to specificity could still help characterize what a thick evaluative property is. Maybe the following holds:

(TP)   A positively (negatively) evaluative property ϕ is thick if, necessarily, if ___ is ϕ then ___ is [to that extent] good (bad), but not vice versa.

(As in the discussion of what makes a property evaluative, one might worry that this criterion is too liberal, and want to turn to a notion of essence to correct this.) An objectionable positive (negative) thick concept may then fail stand for a positively (negatively) evaluative thick property. This seems correct, as I have earlier stated.

Variant valence of properties, discussed above, would present a problem for (TP). To repeat, the relevant variant valence thesis is:

(i)   For some property that a thick concept stands for, sometimes this property is a good-making (bad-making) feature of what has it and sometimes not.

If (i) is true and some property which verifies it is evaluative, then (TP) is false. On the other hand, to relate to a consideration from the discussion of variant valence of concepts, if (i) is true, then one may be skeptical of the idea that a property verifying it is evaluative, as opposed to, say, merely being a property which tends to have evaluatively significant consequences. With dismissive views on the property and concept questions a real option it cannot be blithely assumed that seemingly evaluative properties and concepts really are so.

9.10 Some views made salient

My main concern here has been to draw attention to some problems when it comes to characterizing what it is for a predicate or a property to be evaluative. I will not commit myself to any positive view. But let me conclude by highlighting two somewhat different views which, whatever their proper fate, are made more salient by some of the distinctions drawn.

The first of these views is what I earlier called presentationalism. According to presentationalism, the affective view is the correct view on the concept question, and the property question is misguided, for evaluativeness is a feature of predicates and not properties. Some properties are such that some predicates that stand for them also serve to express attitudes or guide action. But while there will be a historical explanation of which properties we have such predicates for, in a deeper sense this is arbitrary. We could have had such predicates for quite different properties. Given presentationalism, the phenomenon of variability is not a *problem*—as it might appear to be on other views—so much as a *basic fact*. It is logically completely arbitrary what properties are picked out by evaluative predicates, and it is this arbitrariness that underlies variability.

The second view is what we may call the *generalized Wedgwoodian view*. This view too is based on adherence to the affective view on the concept question. But on this view, the reference of some possible evaluative predicates—the "thinnest" ones—is wholly determined by their evaluative role, and some properties are distinguished by the fact that they can be picked out by such predicates. Those properties are evaluatively special, so the view serves to distinguish a special class of properties. The general Wedgwoodian view avoids the problem of variability. Wedgwood has his own way of spelling this all out, but the general strategy is independent of the details of Wedgwood's own project.

References

Blackburn, Simon (1984) *Spreading the Word* (Oxford: Clarendon Press).
—— (1992) 'Morality and Thick Concepts: Through Thick and Thin', *Proceedings of the Aristotelian Society, Supplementary Volume* 66: 285–99.
Brink, David (1989) *Moral Realism and the Foundations of Ethics* (Cambridge: Cambridge University Press).
Copp, David (2001) 'Realist-Expressivism: A Neglected Option for Moral Realism', *Social Philosophy and Policy* 18: 1–43.
—— (2009) 'Realist-Expressivism and Conventional Implicature', *Oxford Studies in Metaethics* 4: 167–202.
Dancy, Jonathan (1993) *Moral Reasons* (Oxford: Blackwell).
Eklund, Matti (2011) 'What Are Thick Concepts?' *Canadian Journal of Philosophy* 41: 25–49.

——— (forthcoming) 'Alternative Normative Concepts', *Analytic Philosophy*.

Elstein, Daniel and Thomas Hurka (2009) 'From Thick to Thin: Two Moral Reduction Plans', *Canadian Journal of Philosophy* 39: 515–35.

Fine, Kit (1994) 'Essence and Modality', *Philosophical Perspectives* 8: 1–16.

Finlay, Stephen (2010) 'Recent Work on Normativity', *Analysis* 70: 331–46.

Geach, Peter (1956) 'Good and Evil', *Analysis* 17: 32–42.

Gibbard, Allan (1992) 'Morality and Thick Concepts: Thick Concepts and Warrant for Feelings', *Proceedings of the Aristotelian Society, Supplementary Volume* 66: 267–83.

Jackson, Frank (1998) *From Metaphysics to Ethics* (Oxford: Clarendon Press).

McNaughton, David and Piers Rawling (2000) 'Unprincipled Ethics', in Brad Hooker and Margaret Little (eds.) *Moral Particularism* (Oxford: Oxford University Press), 256–75.

Scanlon, T. M. (2003) 'Thickness and Theory', *Journal of Philosophy* 100: 275–87.

Scheffler, Samuel (1987) 'Morality Through Thick and Thin: A Critical Notice of *Ethics and the Limits of Philosophy*', *Philosophical Review* 96: 411–34.

Streumer, Bart (2011) 'Are Normative Properties Descriptive Properties?', *Philosophical Studies* 154: 325–48.

Sturgeon, Scott (2007) 'Normative Judgement', *Philosophical Perspectives* 21: 569–87.

Thomson, Judith Jarvis (2008) *Normativity* (Chicago: Open Court).

Väyrynen, Pekka (2009) 'Objectionable Thick Concepts in Denials', *Philosophical Perspectives* 23: 439–69.

Wedgwood, Ralph (2001) 'Conceptual Role Semantics for Moral Terms', *Philosophical Review* 110: 1–30.

——— (2007) *The Nature of Normativity* (Oxford: Clarendon Press).

Williamson, Timothy (2009) 'Reference, Inference, and the Semantics of Pejoratives', in Joseph Almog and Paolo Leonardi (eds.) *The Philosophy of David Kaplan* (Oxford: Oxford University Press), 137–58.

10

There Are No Thin Concepts

Timothy Chappell

This democratized self which has no necessary social content and no necessary social identity can then be anything, can assume any role and take any viewpoint, because it *is* in and for itself nothing.[1]

The locals' statements imply something that can be put in the observer's terms and is rejected by him: that it is *right,* or *all right,* to do things he thinks it is not right, or not all right, to do. Prescriptivism sees things this way. The local statements entail, together with their descriptive content, an all-purpose *ought.* We have rejected the descriptive half of that analysis—is there any reason to accept the other half?[2]

There are no thin concepts. Or almost none. And those that there are are like the higher-numbered elements in the periodic table, artefacts of theory which do not occur naturally and which, even once isolated, are unstable under normal conditions; they may have some theoretical interest, but we should expect far less of them than many theorists do. Let me explain.

On the usual story, thick concepts are moral concepts in which a descriptive aspect or component and an evaluative aspect or component are somehow, perhaps inextricably, combined. Examples are concepts such as LIE, COURAGE, PROMISE, CHASTITY, COURTESY, BRUTALITY, IRREVERENCE. Thin concepts are supposed, by contrast, to be concepts without this descriptive side: purely evaluative moral concepts. RIGHT, GOOD, OUGHT are standard examples.

Derogatory terms such as 'Yid' and 'Kraut' and 'Limey' are often supposed to express thick concepts of exactly the same kind as CRUEL and JUST and CHASTE, that is simple amalgams of a neutral description and a negative evaluation. I think this is a mistake. Other derogatories may of course have had other histories; but *these* derogatories—which are among the examples most discussed—came into being when some group,

---

[1] MacIntyre (1981), 32.   [2] Williams (1985), 145–6.

wanting to outgroup some other group, looked for a jeering name to call them. The name needed to allude to some (supposedly) embarrassing (alleged) fact about the out-grouped group (that they say the German word *Jude* in a funny way, or that they eat a lot of sauerkraut or limes); and it needed to do so contemptuously. If we accept anything like the amalgam analysis of these derogatories, then we have to say that they originated as compounds, not of a neutral description and an evaluative tone, but of a caricature and an evaluative tone. The genesis of paradigm thick concepts such as CRUEL and JUST and CHASTE is plainly quite different both from these cases and from cases, if there are any, to which the standard amalgam analysis does in fact apply. The idea that the paradigm thick concepts are essentially parallel to either sort of derogatories is false, and it creates nothing but muddle.

Another parallel often alleged to the ethical thick concepts is 'Boche'. In a well-known discussion Michael Dummett made a different proposal about this case from either of the two analyses of pejoratives just mentioned.[3] He proposed that to apply the concept BOCHE is to say of someone that he is German, and 'as a consequence of this application' is 'barbarous and prone to cruelty'. This sounds like a nesting of two thick concepts within a third, and in more recent work by Brandom and Boghossian the nest-ing has become more explicit.[4] They offer a proposal about the inferential role of the concept BOCHE: to use the concept, they suggest, is to accept the inference-rule 'X is German *therefore* X is cruel'.

It is a remarkable feature of this discussion that it never quite becomes clear whether '*the* concept BOCHE' is supposed to be a concept in the French language, or the English, or both. (Dummett l.c. discusses the possible 'addition of the term "Boche" to *a* lan-guage'.) In a sense it doesn't matter, because the Brandom-Boghossian analysis is just plain wrong about either language.[5] Five minutes on www.wikipédia.fr establishes that '*Le mot [boche]…sera surtout popularisé par les poilus dans les tranchées de la Grande Guerre, sans qu'elle soit systématiquement empreinte d'animosité*' [Above all, the word *boche* will have been popularized by the ordinary soldiers in the trenches of the Great War, *without being systematically loaded with hostility.*[6]] Likewise in English I can describe some-one as a Boche without committing myself thereby even to the conversational implica-ture that I don't like him, let alone to the logical implication that he is cruel or barbarous. I can, for a start, use the term jocularly; isn't *most* slang jocular, even when it sounds (or indeed is) pejorative?

Perhaps philosophers who consider the French term *les rosbifs* will solemnly conclude that francophones cannot use it without incurring a logical commitment to the

---

[3] Dummett (1973), 454.

[4] Brandom (1994), 126, Boghossian (2003).

[5] It is less clear what to say about Dummett's analysis, especially given that he seems to offer the example tongue in cheek.

[6] <http://fr.wikipedia.org/wiki/Boche>, retrieved on 7th October 2011; emphasis added. Other online sources say similar things. Richard Cobb, in his wonderful social history of the First World War (Cobb 1983), notes that the inhabitants of the Pas de Calais were known to other Frenchmen as *les boches du Nord*, 'the *boches* of the North'. Does that mean other Frenchmen inferred that they were cruel?

proposition that the English, despicably, eat beef. If we want to avoid such unpromising conclusions, we need to be more careful with our data. In particular we need to keep in view the distinctions, obvious and familiar though they are, between meaning, use, tone, context, association. After all, even 'Bannockburn' and 'Agincourt' are, at the level of *meaning,* simply place-names.[7]

As well as these doubts about some typical examples of the supposed data on which the main parties to the mainstream discussion of thick and thin concepts have chosen to rely, two doubts of a more a priori sort about the usual story also arise pretty quickly. As we may put them, we can doubt whether there are thin *concepts;* we can doubt, too, whether there are *thin* concepts. Maybe nothing could fit the specification of thinness as pure evaluation and still genuinely be a concept: that is the first doubt. Or maybe the usual examples of thin concepts, though they are concepts, are thick concepts not thin ones: that is the second doubt. I have both doubts.

The first doubt arises in its most familiar form in the context of the expressivist account of the nature of evaluation. (It has another, less obvious manifestation, which we'll come to later.) Of course it is not only expressivists who are typically 'separationists', believers in the disentanglability of the thick and the thin. As Elstein and Hurka observe, separationists can be prescriptivists or cognitivists as well, and if so their accounts of the thin will of course be different.[8] But since expressivism faces particular, and instructive, difficulties at this point, I begin with those.

Expressivists take evaluation to be a matter, not of attempting to say how things are evaluatively, but of expressing our evaluative attitudes. (Contrast Mackie-style error theorists, for whom evaluation *is* a matter of attempting to say how things are evaluatively; but an attempt that always fails, that always ends up with a description of how things aren't, because there *are* no ways 'things are evaluatively'.) We do not seem to be enunciating a concept when we say, 'Hurrah!', or 'Boo!', but rather a reaction. If we think that the description and evaluation parts of any thick concept are as thoroughgoingly disentanglable as expressivists claim, then we are likely to find that once we have separated off the descriptive part of the thick concept, there is nothing *conceptual* left for the evaluative 'part' of it to be. A fortiori, when we are dealing with thin 'concepts', where the evaluative part is all there is to the 'concept', we won't find anything genuinely conceptual at all.

Expressivists might rejoin that 'Hurrah!' and 'Boo!' are reactions—the reactions corresponding most closely to the two thin concepts *good* and *bad* respectively—but suggest that what is conceptual is anything that fits the schema 'such as to prompt an N-reaction'. When someone says something X is good, he means that X is such as to prompt a hurrah-reaction. And that (they might suggest) is the structure of the thin concept GOOD.

---

[7] It is no good replying, 'Whatever! Some examples *do* fit the amalgam analysis. Let's talk about those'. I don't deny that *some* fit it. The point is that lots of other examples *don't* fit it, and that any discussion of pejoratives and/or of thick concepts that aims at generality cannot simply ignore those other examples.

[8] Elstein and Hurka (2009).

One problem about this is that typically act-expressivists do not in fact propose that 'X is good' should be understood in this concept-friendly way as 'X is such as to prompt a hurrah-reaction'.[9] Typically[10] they propose that it be understood more attitudinally, as 'Hurrah (X)!' This makes their current keenness to go for a more conceptual and less attitudinal understanding of 'X is good' to fit their needs in the present context look decidedly ad hoc.

Secondly, whichever we pick out of 'Hurrah (X)!' and 'X is such as to prompt a hurrah-reaction', we still need to ask: Is this supposed to be the correct expressivist analysis of *X is good,* or of *X is right?* Expressivists seem to lack a principled reason for choosing here. As they also do if we ask whether 'Boo (X)!'/'X is such as to prompt a boo-reaction' is supposed on their view to stand for *X is bad,* or for *X is wrong.* Where, come to that, has *ought* got to in this story? At this point the expressive resources of expressivism are strikingly, well, thin.

Talking of expressive resources, the work that 'Hurrah!' and 'Boo!' do in our ordinary (English) language seems pretty clear. But (to make a third point) neither of them, *pace* the expressivists, does anything specially *moral.* As used outside moral theory, 'Hurrah!' does not express moral approval, as such, at all, nor 'Boo!' moral disapproval. On the lips of ordinary people, 'Hurrah' expresses something more like a sense of glory.[11]

In real life, when people do their mundane moral duty by, say, paying their taxes or writing their Christmas thank-you letters, our response is not 'hurrah' (not even a bit; not even sotto voce). These are morally positive actions, but there isn't even a hint of glory about them. Conversely, there are many things that do make us shout 'hurrah', many instances of glory, which are not so much morally negative as never normally evaluated at all...glory is a kind of *radiance.* There are actions, events, objects, people even, that have a kind of glow or aura about them, that are 'lit up from within' or that 'light things up'; it is this radiance that makes them hurrahable.[12]

---

[9] 'Act-expressivist' is (so far as I know) a coinage of my own here. The term is intended as analogous in meaning to 'act-utilitarian'. The idea is that expressivists can direct their attitudes either at individual items (acts, attitudes, events, states of affairs, etc.) or at general rules (or other general items). Those who go the latter way are rule-expressivists, of whom Allan Gibbard is the paradigm example; his own name for his view is of course 'norm-expressivism'. The problem I state here is tailored, as stated, to act-expressivism. With suitable retailoring, however, the same problem can be stated for rule-expressivism.

[10] As remarked in the previous note, there are different versions of expressivism on the market; I don't claim that the criticisms I offer here are guaranteed to bite against *all* versions of expressivism. I do claim that they bite against all *typical* and *basic* versions of expressivism.

Anecdotally speaking, I find that contemporary expressivists' *viva voce* expositions of their view are usually closer to what I am calling the typical and basic version than their written expositions are. Whether the expressivists come closer to saying 'what they really mean' *viva voce* or *ex libris* is an interesting question. I won't try to answer it here.

[11] Even in saying this there is a large risk of over-simplifying; the expressive resources of our exclamatory language are very rich indeed. In the case of 'Hurrah!' we should distinguish, for a start, between genuinely cheering—making the noise that is conventionally transcribed as 'Hurrah!'—and deliberately pronouncing the word 'Hurrah!'. The latter is nearly always an ironic or partly ironic speech-act. (Cf. the differences between tittering and pronouncing the word 'Tee-hee', between screaming and saying 'Eek!', and between yawning and saying 'Yawn!'.) Naturally, then, the range of things that evoke the pronouncing of 'Hurrah!' is different from the range that evokes a true cheer. And likewise for 'Boo!'

[12] Chappell (2011), 108.

The thinness of the expressivist's resources is all the more striking because of the contrast with the richness of the resources available in our language for the more or less completely pure expression of attitudes. Though any list derived from ordinary language is likely to be a mixed bag, it does seem that 'Yuck',[13] 'Wow', 'Yummy', 'Grr', 'Aww', 'Gah', 'D'oh', 'Der', 'Tch', 'Tut tut', 'Sheesh', 'Bah', 'Meh', 'Bof' (this one is a loan-word, or loan-noise, from French), 'Allez-op' (French again), 'Oy vey' (Yiddish), 'ô papaî' (classical Greek), 'Eheu' (Latin), 'Alas' (poetese), 'Ach' (Scots), 'Tee-hee', 'Pah', 'Pshaw',[14] 'Pfft', (raspberry noise), 'Cor', 'Phwoar', (groan), (sigh), 'Ulp', 'Phew', 'Whew', 'Er', 'Um', 'Humph', 'Hmm', 'Ho hum', 'Gnnng', 'Aha', 'Oho', 'Oi', 'Oof', 'Freeow', 'Whee', 'Yowsa', 'Oops', 'Bleh', 'Tsssh' (as in the cymbal noise), 'Boom boom', 'Ta daa', 'Wahey', 'Crikey', the wide and interesting range of swear-words that is available in English[15], and equally for all I know in other languages, 'Hup', 'Waah', 'Ouch', 'A pa pa pa paa' (as in 'hands off!'), 'Woot woot', 'Ooh', 'Aah', 'Aargh', 'Eeek', 'Yawwn', '*Yess*', '*Nooo*', and many other exclamations all do little or nothing except express attitude.

In striking contrast to this rich variety of expressive exclamations, our language has *no* naturally occurring exclamations which correspond at all closely to GOOD/BAD (or RIGHT/WRONG, come to that). I think there is a simple reason for this, namely that the contents of GOOD/BAD and RIGHT/WRONG are not representable by exclamations at all. If so, then typical expressivism crucially misrepresents the key facts about ordinary language of which it most regularly avails itself. To do what expressivist metaethicists routinely do, and press-gang 'Hurrah'/'Boo' into correspondence to GOOD/BAD, is to distort the meanings on both sides of the equation.

The alleged equation is often presented in a rather tongue-in-cheek way, as if it were an amusing approximation to a more precise equivalence between exclamations and moral predicates that we all understand really. But really, we don't. The original joke has got itself widely accepted in metaethics, perhaps is not even heard as a joke any more. But for the reasons just given, it has still never been justified. We should refuse to be fobbed off with prestidigitation and patter.

Even if we waive these last points about what 'Hurrah' and 'Boo' actually mean, still—fourthly—saying, 'X is such as to prompt a hurrah-reaction' is obviously ambiguous in a familiar way: between 'X is such as to *merit* a hurrah-reaction' and 'X is such as to *evoke* a hurrah-reaction'. The former is, as people like to say, evaluative, or about reasons; the latter is, as they like to say, descriptive, or about causes. If the expressivist takes the descriptive alternative, he seems to lose his grip on the *normativity* of ethics: ethics is supposed to be about what we *should* think, do, or feel, not merely about how we *do* think, act, or feel.

---

[13] On which, see Kelly (2011).

[14] See Hacking (1999), x.

[15] For some more of the detail about these words, see Zangwill (this volume). It is a platitude that different swear words (whether they are exclamations, adjectives, or nouns) express different types of reaction: for instance, in British English 'Bugger!' is typically a reaction to an unkind event, 'Bastard!' to an unkind person. Different swear words also register different levels of reaction; roughly, the ruder the word, the stronger the feeling.

Whereas if he takes the evaluative alternative, it seems that he cannot say, 'X is good' without saying that there is a hurrah-reaction to X to which he himself has a hurrah-reaction (to which in turn he has a *further* hurrah-reaction?). This seems overly complicated. It also sounds like the start of a vicious regress.

Mind you, something like the same ambiguity just noted in 'such as to prompt a hurrah-reaction' is there in 'good' itself. I can say, 'John is good' unironically, as a participant myself in the normal practice of using 'good' as a term of commending description; or I can say it simply in order to describe or predict that those who participate in this practice of using 'good'—who do not necessarily include me—will use it of John.[16] Compare 'beautiful', which can also be used in this latter, predictive-descriptive way.[17] When a film mogul says that some film star is beautiful, he can just mean, and in practice often does, that she has the kind of appearance which (the mogul predicts) the film-going public as presently disposed and constituted will admire and find attractive. He need not at all mean that *he* admires her or finds her attractive. (Perhaps she's not his type. Perhaps she's not his gender.) Or again, a sufficiently crass consequentialist might have no interest whatever in justice for its own sake, yet still have a use for sentences such as 'Hanging innocent men to prevent riots is unjust' inasmuch as they pick out the generally-accepted descriptive content of (IN)JUSTICE.

This moves us from wondering whether there are thin *concepts*, to wondering whether there are *thin* concepts. The flexibility just noticed between 'distanced' and 'undistanced' uses is supposed to be one of the hallmarks of the thick concepts. But what we have just seen is that clear examples of such flexibility can be found equally easily in uses of undisputedly thick concepts and of allegedly thin concepts. It is no harder to contrast distanced and undistanced, involved and ironic, commending and merely descriptive, uses of BEAUTIFUL and JUST than it is of GOOD. Relative to this sort of distancing, the thick and the allegedly thin concepts seem to be on *exactly the same footing*.

Here it is instructive to compare the ways in which we might make sense of moral concepts from another society. Is the Japanese concept of GIRI, for example, a thin moral concept or a thick one? (I will not attempt here to answer the further question whether GIRI—or anything else—is usefully described even as a *moral* concept; but not because I have no doubts about that.)[18] On the one hand, certainly it is (so I gather) most natural to translate 'right' and 'wrong' from English into *giri* terms in Japanese. On the other, consider this:

---

[16] I am far from being the first to notice the possibility of a merely descriptive use of GOOD, RIGHT, OUGHT. That possibility seems to furnish an immediate refutation of the fairly widely-held thesis that these 'thin moral concepts' have evaluation—that is, the speaker's own evaluation—as an essential part of their meaning.

[17] If there are any thin concepts in aesthetics, perhaps BEAUTIFUL is one of them. Or is BEAUTIFUL parallel to JUST—thick, but not that thick, with AESTHETICALLY GOOD/BAD/RIGHT as the paradigm thin aesthetic concepts? If so, that is more grist to the mill of the present argument: these allegedly thin aesthetic concepts look vulnerable to analogues of the points I make here against MORALLY GOOD etc. as thin concepts. If we insist on the analogy, we will also, I predict, find ourselves facing intractable problems about AESTHETIC OUGHT. However, this is another story.

[18] On this, see Chappell (2009).

It is not an easy task to translate (yet explain) Japanese morals and emotions. Giri, what this feature is based on, does not have a clear English translation. The birth of the concept of giri occurred during the feudal period in Japan, and holds the highest regard in human relationships...The most basic definition one can give giri is a debt of gratitude and a self-sacrificing pursuit of their happiness...Giri also has a very strong presence in Japanese business. To a foreigner, it can been seen as irrational and against the principles of Western business...The Japanese business perspective is not the pursuit of individual gain, but one of support and respect for human relationships. This leads to mutual support in the work place instead of inter-office competition and mistrust of one's contemporaries. Giri does have its downside too. Organized crime, the yakuza, who are among the anti-modern and anti-rational nationalist in Japan, interpret giri to include acts of violence. This is, of course, giri taken to its furthest extreme and is not readily tolerated in Japan.[19]

In the light of such remarks, nothing seems more obvious to us than that the Japanese talk of 'giri' is the deployment of a thick concept. As Abe shows, GIRI has an evaluative side, but it also has a strong and detailed descriptive side. It has a whole variety of historically particular and socially situated implications and applications which together enable us to say a great deal about the factual content of GIRI. It is up to us too whether we accept the social and cultural institution of GIRI or reject it. There is nothing incoherent in the idea of some alien (whether territorial or planetary) having a perfectly good 'anthropological' grasp on what exactly GIRI comes to or demands in any particular situation, without his being at all inclined to engage in non-ironic or undistanced uses of giri-talk.

So is GIRI a thick concept? But if we look at our own society from a Japanese point of view, exactly the same sort of reasoning shows that the anglophone concepts RIGHT, WRONG and GOOD, BAD are thick concepts too. To repeat, the case for counting GIRI as thick is (a) because it has strong descriptive content, (b) because giri is clearly indexed to a particular society, sociology, and history, and (c) because it is possible to understand and engage in *giri*-talk in a distanced or ironic way, and without endorsing it. But all three of these points apply to RIGHT, WRONG, GOOD, BAD, OUGHT. Perhaps it is harder for us than for Japanese observers, given our sheer familiarity with our own concepts, to see this point. Perhaps we suffer from a touch of unspoken cultural chauvinism: '*Our* moral concepts can't be just another interesting specimen in the museum of anthropology, as GIRI is; after all, our moral concepts are *right!*' And perhaps we are too monocularly concerned with phenomena specific to our own language, English. But if you want to tell whether something you want to say really makes sense, it is nearly always instructive to try and say it in another language.

It is only our lack of analytical distance on our own key moral concepts that makes them seem anything other than thick to us. One anglophone author who famously manages to get some of this analytical distance is Elizabeth Anscombe. In 'Modern

---

[19] Namiko Abe, 'Giri—moral obligation', [online] <http://japanese.about.com/od/japaneseculturl /a/071497.htm> accessed 28 November 2012.

Moral Philosophy', she concluded that MORALLY GOOD, RIGHT, and OUGHT are all, just as I have been arguing here, extremely particular and indeed peculiar historical products.[20] As Anscombe shows in detail, OUGHT does not refer simply to demandedness, period. As much as the Japanese GIRI and the Chinese TAO[21] and the Polynesian TAPU[22] and the ancient Hebrew TSEDEK[23] and the classical Greek THEMIS (and so on), it refers to a particular *kind* of demandedness. To state again the three key characteristics of thick concepts, this kind of demandedness is (a) full of descriptive implications both about what it is to make such a demand and about what it is to fulfil it,[24] (b) clearly indexed to a particular sociology and history, and (c) such that it forms a particular social institution of moral demand that we can easily distance ourselves from, use merely ironically, or

---

[20] Anscombe (1958a). Actually Anscombe denies that OUGHT expresses any concept at all—she takes it to be a word of 'mere mesmeric force'. As it happens I disagree with her about that—I think OUGHT does express a concept, though probably one that we are better off without. For present purposes I can simply conditionalize on her denial, and just say that *if* OUGHT expresses any concept, then it expresses a thick one, not a thin one.

[21] 'Not to discriminate "this" and "that" as opposites is the very essence of *Tao*. "This" and "that" are both alternately right and wrong. The right is an endless change. The wrong is also an endless change. One should not keep up endless debate with the person who maintains a definite idea of right and wrong, but should stand in the centre of the circle and let others alone ...the Sage harmonises the systems of right and wrong, and rests in the evolution of nature.' Yu-lan Fung (1983), vol.1, 233.

[22] 'In Māori and Tongan tradition, something that is *tapu* or *tabu* is considered inviolable or sacrosanct. Things or places which are *tapu* must be left alone, and may not be approached or interfered with. In some cases, they should not even be spoken of...There are two kinds of *tapu*, the private (relating to individuals) and the public *tapu* (relating to communities). A person, an object or a place, which is *tapu*, may not be touched by human contact, in some cases, not even approached. A person, object or a place could be made sacred by *tapu* for a certain time....A violation of *tapu* could have dire consequences, including the death of the offender through sickness or at the hands of someone affected by the offence. In earlier times food cooked for a person of high rank was *tapu* ...Burial grounds and places of death were always *tapu*, and these areas were often surrounded by a protective fence.' <http://en.wikipedia.org/wiki/Tapu_(Polynesian_culture)> accessed 22 November 2012.

[23] 'The Hebrew word for righteousness is *tseh'-dek*, tzedek, Gesenius's Strong's Concordance 6664—righteous, integrity, equity, justice, straightness. The root of *tseh'-dek* is *tsaw-dak*' ...upright, just, straight, innocent, true, sincere. It is best understood as the product of upright, moral action in accordance with some form of divine plan.' <http://en.wikipedia.org/wiki/Righteousness> accessed 22 November 2012.

[24] Anscombe's remarkable 'On Brute Facts' (1958b) is a study of the institutional and contextual preconditions for applications of *ought*. It is also an independent original statement of the idea of thick properties from the Murdoch/Foot seminars where Williams says he got the idea. (It does not seem irrelevant to point out that Anscombe was very close philosophically and personally, especially at that time, with both Foot and Murdoch—and far from close with Williams, who often displays a marked reluctance to cite her at all.)

Anscombe's key claim in 'On Brute Facts' is that there is a relation that she calls *brute relativity*: facts x y z are brute relative to fact p when p is true 'in virtue of' x y z. So for example—her example—the grocer has delivered my potato order in virtue of the fact that he has brought 50lbs of Maris Pipers to my house and left them in my porch; and I owe the grocer £2 in virtue of the facts that I ordered 50lbs of potatoes, and he has delivered them. Anscombe makes it plain in her opening sentence that she thinks brute relativity is interesting not just in such humdrum cases of financial obligation as this, but also in ethics in general. Surely one thing she has in mind is the thought that *oughts* apply in virtue of the facts that are brute relative to them. So, for example, if I owe the grocer £2, that fact will normally be brute relative to my having an obligation to pay him £2. (It must be relevant here that *ought* is historically the subjunctive of *owe*.) Or again, if I typically toss aside my rifle and run away when the enemy advance, that fact will normally be brute relative to my being a coward. And with this last example, the sense in which Anscombe's study of brute relativity is a study of the relations of 'thicker' to 'thinner' concepts should become quite obvious.

describe without at all endorsing it. That, after all, is precisely what Nietzsche does with GUT and BÖSE in *Beyond Good and Evil*. Indeed it is what undergraduate relativists do by insisting, as they often do, on writing the words *good* and *right* consistently in shudder-quotes.

Mightn't someone object that (a) doesn't apply to the paradigm thin concepts, because RIGHT, WRONG, GOOD, BAD, OUGHT have no descriptive implications? But they do. If I say, 'John is a good person', or that he has done the right thing or what he ought in some context, then you immediately get at least *some* idea of what sort of person John is or of what he has done, even if your idea is both defeasible (I, the speaker might have odd views about RIGHT or GOOD or OUGHT) and full of disjunctions (perhaps John is good in respects X, Y, and Z, which is what I have in mind, even though he obviously isn't in respects A, B, and C). The situation is not essentially different from how things are if you tell me, 'John is cruel' or 'John has acted justly (or graciously) in some context'. Here too what you say gives me *some* idea of the sort of person John might be, or the sort of thing that John might have done in that context, though of course the idea I get is vague, and there are possible defeaters.

There seems to be no serious analytical difference between RIGHT, GOOD, OUGHT and CRUEL, JUST, GRACIOUS. The former three may be vaguer and more general thick concepts than the latter three, but that is no reason for denying that any of these six is a thick concept. After all, CRUEL is vaguer and more general than BRUTAL, which in turn is vaguer and more general than SADISTIC. Nonetheless CRUEL is a standard example of a thick concept, and so is BRUTAL.

We touch here on one standard motivation for the belief that there are thin concepts, namely the stacked type-instantiation relations that hold between many moral properties. Thus (I suppose) SADISTIC instantiates BRUTAL, which instantiates CRUEL, which instantiates BAD. Obviously there *are* such stacked relations in our moral vocabulary. It is also pretty clear that BAD, GOOD, RIGHT, WRONG form termini of such stacked relations. That makes these concepts general in an interesting way. It does not make them thin concepts, because (as we've seen) they still have (a) descriptive content, (b) cultural loading and societal specificity, and (c) flexibility with respect to irony and distancing. Nor would the fact, if it were a fact, that all other moral concepts were evidentials, and only BAD, GOOD, RIGHT, WRONG were verdictives. For this is not in fact a fact—all sorts of terms besides those four can very easily be verdictives: 'That was so boorish/petulant/pompous/mean-spirited of you'; 'That was so thoughtful/witty/inventive/charming of you'. The evidential/verdictive distinction is simply a separate distinction from the thick/thin distinction. So again is the prescriptive/evaluative distinction. What Anscombe in 'On Brute Facts' characterizes as the relation of being brute relative to, and what Nick Zangwill usefully characterizes as the 'because-relation' of 'moral dependence', is or are different again.[25]

---

[25] Anscombe (1958b), Zangwill (2008). This depends on whether Anscombe's brute-relativity relation is the same as Zangwill's because-relation—a question which I leave to another time.

'So' (someone might interject here) 'you admit that there are degrees of thickness/ thinness, that some concepts are *relatively* thin, relatively free of descriptive loading, compared to others. Why isn't that all we need? Why not take thinness to be a matter of degree, and reserve the name "thin concepts" simply for the ones most towards the thin end of the spectrum? In which case, isn't your denial that there are thin concepts exposed as a merely terminological point?'

Terminological perhaps, but not *merely* terminological. Sometimes a thorough clean-out of our terminology is the best, maybe even the only, way to stamp out a persistent mistake. So here, I think, 'the relatively general and unspecific moral concepts' is a better name for GOOD, OUGHT, and RIGHT than 'the relatively thin moral concepts', because it does not allow us so easily to slip back into the mistaken idea that any concepts are absolutely thin, or thin *simpliciter.*

But *is* that idea mistaken? Here is another objection: 'You've just said that OUGHT expresses one particular kind of demandedness. Doesn't that imply that there is such a thing as *generic* demandedness? Isn't this generic demandedness precisely an absolutely or purely thin concept? And wouldn't—to put it roughly—GENERIC COMMENDEDNESS be the purely thin concept that corresponds to GOOD?'

The quick answer to these questions is Yes; that's why I began by saying that there are *almost* no pure thin concepts. If there are any, then, I suggest, there are exactly two.[26] These are the two just mentioned—GENERIC DEMANDEDNESS and generic commendedness.[27]

GENERIC DEMANDEDNESS is reflected (but *not* simply reproduced) in our culture's RIGHT and OUGHT; GENERIC COMMENDEDNESS is reflected (but *not* simply reproduced) in our culture's GOOD. However, as I said at the outset, these 'pure thin concepts', although theoretically available at least in principle, for example by stipulating them into existence, are unstable in isolation, and therefore less useful to ethicists than is often supposed.

The point to keep in mind here is that GENERIC DEMANDEDNESS and GENERIC COMMENDEDNESS are not naturally occurring concepts. Of course it is possible for us simply to *stipulate* that we are going to talk about completely pure demandedness or commendedness in some theoretical context; and then, by definition, it will indeed be these two concepts that we are talking about.[28] But for one thing, as already noted, when I use these purely evaluative concepts, I will still not necessarily be expressing *my own* evaluations: I can still say that something is generically demanded, while distancing

---

[26] Assuming, that is, that we don't count their negations as separate concepts. (But why should we?)

[27] A different and perhaps commoner taxonomy, which I believe Simon Kirchin endorses, would enumerate two basic thin concepts, generic PRO and generic CON. I am suspicious of this, because I think 'generic PRO' is either a confusion of demand and commendation, or it is a way of smuggling the decidedly thick idea of APPROVAL into the discussion. (For the thickness of APPROVAL, cf. Foot (2002), 190–1: 'It is no more possible for a single individual, without a special social setting, to approve or disapprove than it is for him to vote'.) Meanwhile CON is (so far as I can see) simply meant as the negation of PRO, and therefore shares its faults.

[28] I am grateful to Laurence Goldstein, Philip Ebert, and Colin Johnston for pushing me on this point.

myself from the whole idea of being generically demanded. And for another: between any such theoretically-stipulated moral concept and any naturally occurring moral concept there is a great gulf fixed. We cross it at our peril—yet all too often we cross it without even noticing. So we easily arrive at the claim that GENERIC DEMANDEDNESS just *is* OUGHT/RIGHT, or that GENERIC COMMENDEDNESS just *is* GOOD. This is *too* easy. It is like seeing that *something* in my own moral psychology opposes my self-interested tendency to prefer telling a lie and not being hanged to refusing the lie and being hanged, and concluding that the only thing that this self-interest-opposing something could possibly be is Pure Practical Reason. This, to put it crudely, is one heck of a leap.

Within the context of any actual society, there is no such thing as an intelligible concept of demandedness or commendedness without some minimally intelligible account of *why* whatever it is we are talking about is demanded or commended.[29] In any particular society or situation such an account will typically be spelt out in great detail. But with these spellings-out comes thickness: every such articulation is a particular historical and social reality with its own particular descriptive implications, and as such rejectable by anyone who chooses to take an ironic or distanced stance on it. The 'pure thin concepts' of GENERIC DEMANDEDNESS and GENERIC COMMENDEDNESS buy their purity at the cost of abstraction. Within the contexts and practices of any actual society, that means: at the cost of unintelligibility.

But why, we may ask in closing, would anyone have wanted there to be thin concepts in the first place?

One possible motivation is confusion or elision, deliberate or inadvertent, of the thick/thin distinction with all or some of the other distinctions noticed above: evidential/verdictive, particular/general, specific/vague, prescriptive/evaluative, and the two sides of the because-relation and the brute-relativity relation.

A second possible motivation is a hermeneutical thought. To interpret other people, especially people from very different and/or distant societies, don't we need some very general categories under which to classify their actions, if only as a starting-point? Certainly we do. But then there are large questions in the offing about what these very general categories are: for instance, whether they are natural or stipulated, and whether we in fact do better, at least for most hermeneutic purposes, to work with the natural categories rather than the stipulated ones. I am not attempting to answer those questions here; I am saying that they should not be ducked.

---

[29] Compare Philippa Foot's doctrine of internal objects (see her 'Moral Arguments' and 'Moral Beliefs' in *Virtues and Vices* (2002)): we cannot make sense of moral utterance as the prescriptivists and logical positivists wished to—simply as universalizable commendation of whatever one happens to find commendable. As a matter of logical grammar, not just anything can be intelligibly commended (even in a single case, never mind universalizably). We need to understand what is meant by suggesting that something is commendable; and to show what is meant by that suggestion, we have, Foot argues, to find a way of linking the commendation back to notions of human well-being and harm. I disagree with Foot that this is the *only* link we could make to give these notions intelligibility; I agree with her that *some* link is needed.

Third possible motivation: a view about practical inference. It might be thought that unless we have the thin concepts, we won't be able to use practical rationality to get ourselves going in action: 'Practical reasoning, if it is to reach the level of actual practicality, will have to route itself via RIGHT or OUGHT or the like. So we have to believe in the thin concepts, because without them we couldn't act on practical reasoning at all.'

This is just wrong. There are indefinitely many possible trains of practical reasoning that get along absolutely fine without RIGHT or OUGHT. For example:

1. It would be cruel for me to tell Joe about Moe, unless I had a special reason to.
2. But I don't (or: I do have a reason, but it's not special *enough*).
3. So I won't.

Is this bit of practical reasoning incomplete because it doesn't include the line 2a?

2a. It is wrong to do what is cruel unless you have a special (and special *enough*) reason.

No, it isn't. Indeed, not only is (1 2 3) fine as it stands and without adornment, there is also the risk that adornments like (2a) will lure us into further adornments. For just the same sort of thought as might prompt us to think that (1 2 3) does not make sense unless it is rewritten as (1 2 2a 3) might equally prompt us to think that (1 2 2a 3) needs supplementation by something such as

2b. I ought not to do what is wrong.

At worst, this kind of thinking pushes us into an Achilles-and-the-tortoise regress; at best, it adds unnecessary shuffles to our practical reasoning. Of course such shuffles might actually be present, in someone's real psychological processes; but that is not the point. The point is that they don't *have* to be in order for agents to get from thoughts to actions in a rational way.

A fourth possible motivation, somewhat related to the third, is a combination of what Susan Hurley calls 'centralism'[30] with what we may call ethical monoculturalism: the conjunction, that is, of the belief that in ethics it is a small range of strongly evaluative and very weakly descriptive concepts—RIGHT, GOOD, OUGHT—that 'run the show', with the belief—a belief which at any rate R. M. Hare[31] clearly held—that, really, it's the same show everywhere, or if it isn't it ought to be. Like Hurley, I believe that centralism belies, and where believed tends to impoverish, the richness of our ethical life. Like most people in our society, I believe that ethical

---

[30] Hurley (1992), chapter 1.

[31] Hare (1952). Hare is happy to entitle his most important book *The Language of Morals*. There and elsewhere, his assumption that there is just one such language, that it either is universal or only fails to be so through confusion or benightedness, and hence that there is just one thing worth calling 'the logic of OUGHT', is so pervasive that it is hard to isolate any one particular statement of it. In reality Hare's 'language of morals' is pretty clearly 1950s Oxford English. But to quote another 1950s Oxonian, 'We can ask why something called "moral language" should be expected to reveal anything reliable...Language consists in human practices; human beings...have suffered and do suffer from many illusions about the relation of value to the world and so forth; if language can embody or imply any propositions at all about such things, why should it not embody illusions?' Williams (1988), 188.

monoculturalism is both mistaken as a description of how things are, and, as a prescription for how things ought to be, really rather hard to tell apart from cultural imperialism.

The fifth and last possible motivation that I'll consider here is the idea that 'thinking in terms of thick concepts…discourages critique' (to quote Simon Blackburn, in this volume, section 7.1). Believing in thick concepts, according to him, makes it likelier (*statistically* likelier?) that you will uncritically accept the sort of reprehensible evaluations expressed in terms like 'cute', as used of grown women. Believers in CUTENESS, he predicts (*empirically* predicts?), will defend their attitudes by claiming that their practice of calling grown women cute is the deployment of a thick concept. They will claim, as he parodically puts it, that 'to call someone cute, in our whirl of organism or form of life, is not to stitch together a distinct fact and a distinct attitude. It is instead to respond seamlessly to the world, only using a full human sensibility'.[32]

Supposing someone has this reprehensible thick concept CUTENESS that Blackburn describes, how should we criticize her concept? Blackburn thinks we should criticize it by *disentangling* it. What he means by 'disentangling' is, he explains, a two-step procedure. First we separate out the descriptive feature from the evaluative reaction that it provokes, and then we come out with an evaluative reaction to the evaluative reaction: in the case of CUTE, 'that, we say, is bad'.

If this is what disentangling is as a form of critique of reprehensible thick concepts, then once more, the obvious thing to say about it is that it seems a bit, well, thin. 'Describing grown women as cute is bad': is that *all* we can say about it, on the evaluative side? Simply to say, 'using CUTE is bad' (or 'wrong', or even 'abhorrent', two other adjectives Blackburn deploys) is not much of an argument; it is hard to see why this sort of remark should be expected to impress the cultists of CUTE. But then, what more is there for an austerely thin ethicist to say, given that, *ex hypothesi*, he and his opponents agree about the descriptive facts?

What is remarkable is how much else Blackburn in fact finds to say:

> We may want to say that there is something wrong with them, along the lines of this: they admire and respond excitedly…to the non-threatening, infantile, subservient self-presentations that some women consciously or unconsciously adopt. Theirs is a group amongst whom women are successful by presenting themselves as there to be patronized, like pets or babies (frequent terms of endearment). And that, we say, is bad.[33]

The argumentative work done in this passage is done by thick concepts of Blackburn's own. There are three key ones, marked by the words 'infantile', 'subservient', and 'patronized'; it is arguable that further thick concepts are marked by 'non-threatening', 'admire', and 'respond excitedly' too. (Probably 'abhorrent' marks another thick concept as well. Perhaps even Blackburn's use of 'pets' and 'babies' here picks up or alludes to thick concepts.) Blackburn's official line, as we have seen, is that his is a disentangling argument. So presumably he thinks that he has managed

---

[32] Blackburn (this volume), 124.   [33] Blackburn (this volume), 123.

here to austerely separate out the descriptive from the evaluative, and that all of the concepts in this passage apart from WRONG and BAD are simply descriptive. But that, I submit, is obviously false, and false in Blackburn's own terms. It's not merely that INFANTILE, SUBSERVIENT, PATRONIZING mark moral concepts that *I* would count as thick: I, as we know, count every naturally occurring moral concept as thick. More than that, these are concepts that are bound to be counted as thick by any party to the debate, including Blackburn. It is these admittedly thick concepts, and not the allegedly thin concept BAD, that give Blackburn's argument against CUTE its bite.

The moral is that the concepts that Blackburn takes to be thin are not, as he claims, more useful to us in moral critique than the thick concepts; if anything, they are *less* useful. It goes without saying that we need to keep a critical eye on our own thick concepts, and indeed on others'. Still, the only effective way to criticize one thick concept is by deploying another thick concept, or group of concepts. And *malgré lui*, this is the way that Blackburn himself takes when criticizing CUTE.

What else would we expect? Do the theorists of the thin[34] suppose that thin concepts are a magic carpet that can whisk us off, above and beyond our own limited histories and cultures and the conditioned thick concepts that they leave us with, to the absolute and crystalline unconditioned certainty of the 'View From Nowhere'? Or that, unless we have some such magic carpet, the only alternative is a dreary, hermetic, self-regarding, and implicitly relativist traditionalism?

It is far too easy to talk about a separation between 'description' and 'evaluation' as if all the cultural baggage of our pasts attached only to the 'description' side of this dichotomy. But how many centuries did it take nature to breed a creature with the ability to do what *we* do, when we evaluate?

'Thin concepts' are dubious entities: there are serious doubts both about their conceptuality and about their thinness, and there is, confusions aside, not a great deal of obvious use for them in ethics or metaethics. The very idea that there could be a naturally occurring purely evaluative moral concept, with no descriptive content, no cultural setting, and no capacity for distanced or ironic use, is as chimerical as any other ahistorical illusion. Our concentration on thick and thin has distracted us from thinking about other interesting and important ethical distinctions—evidential/verdictive, evaluative/prescriptive, determinable/determinate, Zangwill's because-relation, Anscombe's brute-relative-to relation—which have something genuine and non-illusory on *both* sides of them. If these claims are right, then it is time for us to recognize, liberatingly I believe, that there are no thin concepts.[35]

---

[34] Blackburn finds it amusing to refer to theorists of the thick as 'thickies'. Perhaps the thickies should return the compliment with a joke of equal quality, by referring to his side of the debate as unrepentant thinners.

[35] This paper was presented to a helpful and lively audience in Stirling in October 2011; thanks to all participants. Especial thanks for their help to Philip Ebert, Laurence Goldstein, Edward Harcourt, Simon Hope, Colin Johnston, Alan Millar, Derek Parfit, Ben Saunders, David Smith, Alan Thomas, Naoko Yamagata, and, in particular, Simon Kirchin.

References

Anscombe, Elizabeth (1958a) 'Modern Moral Philosophy', *Philosophy* 53: 1–19.

—— (1958b) 'On Brute Facts', *Analysis* 18: 69–72.

Blackburn, Simon (this volume) 'Disentangling Disentangling'.

Boghossian, Paul (2003) 'Blind Reasoning', *Proceedings of the Aristotelian Society, Supplementary Volume* 77: 225–48.

Brandom, Robert (1994) *Making It Explicit* (Cambridge, MA: Harvard University Press).

Chappell, Timothy (2009) *Ethics and Experience* (London: Acumen).

—— (2011) 'Glory as an Ethical Idea', *Philosophical Investigations* 34: 105–34.

Cobb, Richard (1983) *French and Germans, Germans and French* (London: University of New England Press).

Dummett, Michael (1973) *Frege: Philosophy of Language* (London: Duckworth).

Elstein, Daniel and Thomas Hurka (2009) 'From Thick to Thin: Two Moral Reduction Plans', *Canadian Journal of Philosophy* 39: 515–35.

Foot, Philippa (2002) *Virtues and Vices*, 2nd edn. (Oxford: Oxford University Press).

Hacking, Ian (1999) *The Social Construction of What?* (Cambridge, MA: Harvard University Press).

Hare, R. M. (1952) *The Language of Morals* (Oxford: Clarendon Press).

Hurley, S. L. (1992) *Natural Reasons* (Oxford: Oxford University Press).

Kelly, Daniel (2011) *Yuck! The Nature and Moral Significance of Disgust* (Cambridge, MA: MIT Press).

MacIntyre, Alasdair (1981) *After Virtue* (London: Duckworth).

Williams, Bernard (1985) *Ethics and the Limits of Philosophy* (London: Fontana).

—— (1988) 'The Structure of Hare's Theory' in Douglas Seanor and Nicholas Fotion (eds.) *Hare and Critics: Essays on Moral Thinking* (Oxford: Clarendon Press), 185–98.

Yu-Lang, Fung (1983) *History of Chinese Philosophy*, tr. Derk Bodde (Princeton, NJ: Princeton University Press).

Zangwill, Nick (2008) 'Moral Dependence', *Oxford Studies in Metaethics* 3: 109–27.

—— (this volume) 'Moral Metaphor and Thick Concepts: What Moral Philosophy Can Learn From Aesthetics'.

11

Moral Metaphor and Thick Concepts: What Moral Philosophy Can Learn from Aesthetics

Nick Zangwill

There are limits to literal description. For example, when we describe inner experience, we often feel we need to employ metaphor because of a lack of an adequate literal mode of description. There is a reality there, but it outruns the literal modes of description that are at our disposal. The properties of inner experience, so it seems, can only be superficially described in literal terms and beyond that point must be non-literally described. In aesthetics, too, literal indescribability must be acknowledged. There is no way to do justice to many aesthetic properties of things without describing them using metaphors and other non-literal devices. There is no literal language available to describe such properties. Of course there are the purely evaluative words—'beauty', 'ugliness', 'aesthetic merit' or 'aesthetic demerit'—but they do not convey all that we want to convey. We want to convey the *specific* aesthetic character of things. For that we must use metaphor or other non-literal devices, including non-linguistic means, such as gestures.[1]

The same, I shall argue, is true in moral philosophy. I want to make a modest beginning thinking about this neglected aspect of our moral thought—moral metaphors. I want to develop the idea that there is literal indescribability in morality, which parallels the description of inner experience and aesthetic properties. Wittgenstein thought so.[2] For many years that puzzled me; but now I think there is something right in his idea. Wittgenstein constantly emphasized the ineffability of moral value. We certainly feel a lack of words in some morally dramatic cases. Wittgenstein also thought we should pass over moral value in respectful silence—but this is another matter: I don't see why we should if we can use metaphors that gesture towards what we have in mind so that others can understand, to an extent. What was Wittgenstein's problem with metaphorical descriptions?

I shall take ideas about metaphorical description from aesthetics and show how they apply in moral philosophy and articulate something close to what have been called

---

[1] See Zangwill (2011a).   [2] Wittgenstein (1965).

'thick' concepts. In this respect, moral philosophy can learn much from aesthetics. In the first two parts of this paper, I survey the situation in each of the two areas, before proceeding to see how attention to the use of metaphor in moral descriptions allows us to rehabilitate something like the idea of thick moral concepts, without the usual drawbacks associated with that idea.

11.1   Thickiphobia in moral philosophy

In moral philosophy in the 1980s and 1990s, many moral philosophers thought that what were called 'thick' moral concepts played an important role in moral thinking. Thick concepts were said to be those that are at once descriptive and evaluative. Standard examples that were given of these concepts were courage, kindness, cruelty, and rudeness, which were said to be used both to describe the world as well as to make an evaluation. For a long time, I did not merely reject this idea, I was actively hostile.[3]

Some of my reasons were theoretical: it seemed to me that the idea of thick concepts confused issues and allowed people to think that certain problems—especially the problem of the source of our right to make particular moral judgements—are not problems, when they are. (This leads to what Colin McGinn calls 'problem blindness', which is, he says, 'the worst fault a philosopher can have'.)[4] But I also thought that there was also more than a whiff of moral danger, of a moral dogmatism assumed by the person wielding such notions, which inoculates them against doubt. The step from (non-evaluative) fact to value is problematic and controversial, and not to be lightly skipped over, especially with the blithe assurance that doing so is part of the meaning of certain words or grasping certain concepts. This is a serious error, for we must not turn our face away from the *perilous abyss* between (non-evaluative) fact and value. Perhaps this was not Bernard Williams's own use of thick concepts.[5] He was appealing to them partly to show the diversity and complexity of moral thinking. Nevertheless, I think it is fair to say that this was not the norm among the defenders of thick concepts, who appealed to thick concepts in order to make life easier; in particular, they thought that the fact that they had descriptive content meant that moral judgements could be known in broadly empirical ways.[6]

Furthermore, what was said about the standard examples also seemed to me to be problematic. My view of courage, kindness, cruelty, rudeness, and the rest was that when people use these terms, there is usually only a 'conversational implication' that they are good or bad, and this is not a matter of their semantic content of words of the language, as the defenders of thick concepts think. It certainly seems that there are circumstances

---

[3] I hope I may be excused for this somewhat autobiographical way of introducing ideas, the point of which is to lead up to a certain change of mind whereby I apply ideas from aesthetics to moral philosophy.

[4] McGinn (1998), 2.

[5] Williams (1985).

[6] For example, see Foot (1958), and McDowell (1979) and (1996).

in which we apply the words without the evaluations that usually accompany them. Some defenders of thick concepts, such as Peter Goldie and Adrian Moore, notice the problem that one can apply these words without the usual evaluations.[7] Their response is to say that 'full' or 'proper' grasp of the meaning of words such as 'kindness' or 'cruelty' implies an evaluation. But the idea of a 'full' grasp of the meanings or concepts is a hypothetized state that we have no reason to believe in. How would it differ from the conjunctive state of ascribing a character trait plus an evaluation? So far as I can see this is merely a definitional attempt to save an implausible view.

I am also impressed with Williams's appeals to the variety and social variation of these concepts: his examples were piety and chastity. We may grasp these notions but withhold the evaluations in question. In my view, this shows, not that there is social variation in thick concepts, but that these concepts are not really thick.

Much was made in the literature of the fact that courage or whatever cannot be reduced to *other* psychological or physical characteristics—the so-called 'shapelessness' or 'disentangling' point.[8] But this does not begin to show that courage has any evaluative content. For it may just be a case of the irreducibility of one non-evaluative fact to another. If so, there is a no evaluative content to 'disentangle'.

The most sensible view of the standard examples—of courage, kindness and the like—is that they are in fact devoid of moral content. It is no trivial semantic claim that courage and kindness are good.[9]

For these reasons, I steered clear of these notions and from the entire debate over them, which seemed to me to be misguided.

11.2 Substantive aesthetic concepts, inexpressibility and metaphor

Let us now consider the situation in aesthetics. In the late 1950s and early 1960s there was an interesting debate about something like 'thick' aesthetic concepts—concepts, such as daintiness, dumpiness, elegance, delicacy, balance, and the like. This was pursued by the two greatest aestheticians of the post-war age, Frank Sibley and Monroe Beardsley.[10] (I recommend these writings to moral philosophers.)

My own approach, when I came to wrestle with the works of these philosophers, was to recognize the thick, but to prioritize the thin.[11] The view is that properties such as

---

[7] Goldie (2008) and Moore (2006).

[8] McDowell (1979).

[9] There are other kinds of examples of ways we talk in the course of moral evaluation. Simon Blackburn and Allan Gibbard have explored the words 'cute' and 'lewd'; Blackburn (1992) and Gibbard (1992). But it is unclear whether these are cases that confirm or disconfirm what the defenders of thick concepts want, which is the embedding of evaluation in the semantic content of the word, as opposed to merely being a predictable conversational implication in many usages.

[10] See Sibley (2001) and Beardsley (1982).

[11] See Zangwill (1995). See also Burton (1992).

daintiness, dumpiness, elegance, delicacy, and balance (I called them 'substantive' aesthetic properties) are *ways*—ways of being beautiful or ugly. A major bonus of this account is that we get for free an account of what unifies aesthetic judgments, which always remained a mystery on Sibley's view. Sibley's view was plagued by an infamous closed circle of aesthetic concepts, taste, and sensitivity.[12] Prioritizing beauty and ugliness solves this problem—for properties like delicacy are aesthetic properties in virtue of being ways of possessing beauty or ugliness, which are the central aesthetic properties, and there is an independent account of those.[13] As the excellent Clement Greenberg said 'The value judgment comes first'; thereafter one proceeds to give a further description, as a way of fleshing out, or rationalizing, the value judgment. There is, however, one difficulty with this kind of account. Jerrold Levinson argued, not unpersuasively, that this will not do in general because some substantive descriptions are value-neutral.[14] I offer a reply to Levinson at the end of this paper.

Roger Scruton—the leading aesthetician of our era, in my opinion—explored something that was present in Sibley and Beardsley, which they noted but did not make much of, namely the metaphorical nature of much aesthetic description. For example, it is common to describe music as 'delicate', 'balanced', 'sad', and surprisingly even 'high' and 'low' are examples. On this basis, Scruton, remarkably, fashioned a completely original argument against realism in aesthetics. The argument turned on what today we would classify as a broadly Davidsonian theory of metaphor, although Scruton's theory predated Davidson's by half a decade.[15] In Scruton's view, there is no metaphorical meaning. If so, words for emotion, motion, and height, used in 'substantive' or 'thick' musical descriptions, have the same meaning that they have in non-musical contexts. So they are not used to describe aesthetic properties of music in their literal senses. The words or sentences have no distinctive aesthetic sense. Therefore such descriptions do not describe aesthetic properties or facts—so argued Scruton.[16] His positive view is that aesthetic experience is an *imaginative* experience in which things are subsumed under nonaesthetic concepts without our believing that they genuinely apply to things. That, for Scruton, is the mental state that explains the point of the metaphor.

My response to this argument was to assert a sharp thought/talk distinction and say that we have aesthetic thoughts that lack literal expression and that lack literal expressibility. The metaphor 'makes us notice' (Davidson) aesthetic properties of things. There is metaphorical *talk* about things, but contra Scruton, there is no metaphorical *thought* and *experience*. To think that is to *assert* an imagination-based account of aesthetic thought, which would be question-begging. For the issue is just whether our thought is a matter of belief or imagination—beliefs about aesthetic properties, or the imaginative redeployment of nonaesthetic concepts to a new domain, that of music.[17] Thus an aesthetic

---

[12] See Kivy (1975).   [13] Zangwill (1998)   [14] Levinson (2001).
[15] Davidson (1978).   [16] Scruton (1974), 39–44, and (1997), 154.
[17] See Zangwill (1991) and (2010).

realist view can be defended, despite the prevalence of metaphorical aesthetic description.[18]

Now, it may be observed that I am up to my elbows in thick concepts in aesthetics, even though I grant them secondary status, while running as fast as I can away from them in moral philosophy. This seems odd. I have a negative attitude in one area but not in the other. Am I inconsistent? Given my views in aesthetics, why am I not happy to say that some thick moral notions describe ways of having moral value or disvalue?

What held me back was that the standard *examples* of thick concepts were concepts such as courage, kindness, and so on, and these I thought, are not good examples, for reasons given in the last section. But maybe we should not generalize on the basis of those dubious examples. As we shall see, there are better examples, embodied in metaphorical moral descriptions.[19]

11.3 Examples of moral metaphors: animal descriptions, swearwords, and gestures

We give plenty of moral descriptions of situations, people and actions in metaphorical terms. I shall give a number of examples.

Consider racial prejudices, which are moral views even though we might not concur. Racists and other prejudiced folk very often express their stronger views in medical or biological terms. The target population might be described as a virus, as a disease, as an illness, as a parasite, as vermin. (Hitler's *Mein Kampf* is a famous case in point.)[20] To reverse the example, in case we think that metaphor is the preserve of views of which we might disapprove: I remember a police chief being interviewed on television. He said, 'We must stamp out this racist poison'. I read the *Daily Mirror* (9th June 2009) describing the British National Party's views as 'having been dredged up from the sewer'. Any expression of a strongly held moral view will *bristle* with such metaphors. Consider 'poisonous gossip' or 'bestial murder'.

The point of giving such metaphorical descriptions, as I see it, is to describe the *manner*, or *way*, that a person or their actions possess moral value—where that is not a description of the natural features that are the thin-value-makers. Of course, metaphors may die. Perhaps 'bestial' used of a murder is metaphorical, but 'brutal' is now a dead metaphor. Nevertheless, in both cases we are thinking of ways of having moral value.

Much moral evaluation goes on by calling people *animals*—'dog', 'snake', 'cow', 'pig' . . . one could go on. These are thick moral descriptions! Many have standard thick meanings, in a sense. There is social variation in the thick *concepts* that are usually

---

[18] In aesthetics there are both metaphorically and non-metaphorically expressed substantive notions. There can be angry and elegant music; but 'elegant' is not a metaphor like 'angry', when applied to music. Both are *ways* of having aesthetic value or disvalue.

[19] I defend this general approach to metaphor in Zangwill (ms).

[20] For discussion, see Musolff (2007).

annexed to animal words. Being called 'donkey' in one country may translate into being a 'cow' in another country. (In Hebrew calling someone 'chicken' means little, but calling someone a 'rabbit' means what English speakers mean when they call someone a 'chicken'.) Translators have to know about these culturally local associations when they translate these words in their moral metaphorical use. Moralizing invokes a veritable bestiary! It is surprising that this has been overlooked in twentieth-century moral philosophy, which prided itself on its attention to moral language.[21] Once we step outside the study, lecture hall, or seminar room, we find that much moral discourse consists in giving animal descriptions of people and their actions and passions. Perhaps the 'language of morality', where that means those words whose the primary function is to make moral evaluations, does not include animal words, and is limited to 'duty', 'evil', 'virtue', and the like. And perhaps the original function of animal words is to talk about animals. Nevertheless, much of the language we in fact use in moral talk deploys animal words in a significant way, and so should be included in a study of the language that we use in moral descriptions.

Another prominent phenomenon of the language we use when making moral judgements is expletives and swear words. Examples are 'fuck', 'piss', 'arsehole', 'tosser', 'prick', 'bastard', and the interestingly strong, 'cunt'. Religious cultures often have rich traditions of religious swearing. Roman Catholics and Orthodox Christians have a particularly vivid discourse in the respect. There is the very common: 'Go fuck the virgin Mary!' for example. The Greek word or concept 'malakas' is notably rich. Literally it means 'masturbator' but it has a wide range of extended meanings and uses. One can even say that people have 'malakies' (the result of masturbating) in their heads. There is also the charismatic, 'Go and suck Saint Sebastian's balls!' said in some areas of Greece.[22]

Rude words and expressions are interesting. I say that if we are interested in moral thick concepts, then we do far better to leave behind the 'courageous' and the 'kind' and to focus on the 'arsehole' and the 'cunt'! Such uses of language are prevalent because of our *need*: our need to express the *ways* of value, which resist other modes of expression.[23]

In attempting to describe the indescribable, not only do we deploy non-literal language but we may also seek to convey what we want by non-linguistic methods. Moral philosophers have made it their business to study moral *language*. But what about rude *gestures*, such as putting two fingers in the air towards someone's face? Or one finger? Or shaking the wrist?[24] Do these not express thick concepts? Here is a rich field for moral enquiry.

---

[21] For example, in his (1952), Hare does not mention animal descriptions.

[22] Hill and Ottchen (1991)—*Shakespeare's Insults*—contains a wealth of creative and powerful descriptions, which convey moral or other thick normative thoughts.

[23] Stephen Pinker discusses swear words in chapter 7 of Pinker (2007). But I do not think he sufficiently probes the fundamental issue of why we employ swear words.

[24] This paper was originally given as a talk where I was able to demonstrate these gestures, with enthusiasm!

In all this it is vital to make the thought/language distinction. To illustrate this point, consider the word 'cunt', which is usually a severe, offensive, and very insulting thick moral description. The important thing is the thick *concept* in play. The mere *word* may be 'reclaimed', cleansed of the usual evaluation. For example, consider the *Cunt Coloring-in Book*; this is an American feminist book for girls/female children published in 1975. I brought a copy of this book at a Wisconsin feminist bookshop from the children's section. Each page displays a black-and-white line drawing of different female genitalia for the girls (female children) to colour in. (It is very 1970s American.) In the Foreword, it is written:

In the beginning we come from the cunt, not from some man's side; and we are washed in the water and blood of birth, not the spear-pierced side of some dying god. In the beginning women made pots and jars shaped liked wombs and breasts, and decorated with triangles, which were symbols of the cunt. So the first art was cunt art.[25]

Now perhaps the *word* 'cunt' can be used without its standard evaluation. Perhaps that can be 'cancelled'. The important thing however is the *concept* of cunt, of that which is thought when the word is used in standard very offensive and insulting sense. That concept is inexpressible except by means of metaphor or other non-literal modes of communication. It is a thick *concept*, however it is with the *word* 'cunt'. It is not my language, but suppose someone applies the word 'cunt' to someone they strongly disapprove of. Then the concept they deploy is not the same as that deployed by members of a Wisconsin feminist collective when they use the word 'cunt' as an 'affirmation', just as what we think when we use the word 'delicacy' in aesthetic concepts is not the same as what we think when we use the word 'delicacy' in nonaesthetic contents, as is shown by the fact that an aesthetically delicate vase may be physically sturdy.[26]

11.4 The limits to metaphorical moral description

Having drawn attention to metaphorical moral descriptions and inexpressibility, we should note that it should not be over-emphasized. Philippa Foot once attended a seminar on 'thick' concepts among other things given by my doctoral supervisor Ian McFetridge; and I remember her making the point that in many legal cases there is no room or need for endless redescription. This seems right. Consider, for example, an employee who embezzles some money. Where is the ineffability there? It is plain theft. The case might be straightforward, and we do not need subtle description to make sense of an evaluation. Another example is a charming elderly woman, who lived near me. She was in her 90s, impoverished, and living on her own. She was almost completely neglected by her comfortably-off daughter and even more comfortably-off grand-daughters, who lived nearby. There is no need for any sophisticated description or

---

[25] Corinne (1975).

[26] I resisted the temptation to call this paper 'Two Concepts of Cunt'!

intervening moral notions to reach a moral judgement. It is clear what the bad-maker is. Nevertheless, having made such an evaluation (remember Greenberg's dictum—'the value judgement comes first') our discourse would naturally extend to colourful metaphors in describing her daughter and granddaughters. ('How sharper than a serpent's tooth it is to have a thankless child!' were Lear's words (*King Lear*, Act 1, scene 4, 281–9).) Not all moral thinking employs metaphors; but we may often augment moral thought with them.[27]

Although not all moral description is metaphorical, metaphorical moral description is not a mere luxury or a disposable inessential ornament in moral thinking. It is an attempt to specify more about why a natural property is a bad- or good-maker. This is what we struggle to articulate when we strive to say the unsayable as best we can with non-literal modes of expression of various kinds. I have concentrated on metaphor but also wish to include the large variety of ways in which we communicate thick moral judgements non-literally, such as hand-gestures.[28]

This is not to express a general anti-theoretic view; there may be deeper accounts of the dependencies that we are committed to in ordinary moral or political thought.[29] Nevertheless at some point, when the question 'Why?' is asked, something is taken to be rock bottom, and we should resist being bullied into digging more. The rhetorical pressures towards consequentialism or Kantianism or whatever should be firmly resisted. When it comes to what is rock bottom for us, we may feel disgust or have feelings of quasi-religious awe, or use metaphors, and of course all these are fallible; but that does not mean they are to be shunned and replaced by abstract theory. A deeper moral theory need not always undergird moral feeling or intuition. The metaphors are there whenever we are at rock bottom. We would not have recourse to metaphor if we could give some further deeper moral principle. Metaphors reveal basicality.[30]

---

[27] It has been suggested to me that a corollary of what I am saying is that we should appeal to emotions in a central way in our understanding of our moral life. But I do not make moral emotions fundamental. Just as I prioritize the thin over the thick, so I prioritize moral judgement or belief over moral emotion. (Recall Greenberg's dictum, again.) Moral emotions are not ways of appearing morally. Moral emotions have moral content and are rationalized *by* moral beliefs, not vice versa. It is true that moral emotions often have a phenomenology that begs for metaphor if it is are to be described, and sometimes that phenomenology may be the source of the metaphors we use in moral descriptions. But this is not always the case.

[28] I would extend the point to political thought as well. In any moral or political outlook, we reach rock bottom, and then we have ultimate moral or political principles. When at that point we try to say more, we reach for metaphors, and these metaphors are revealing, not incidental; they reveal matters perhaps not fully present in the self-image of the outlook in question. For example, in many cases, a secular person will reach for semi-religious notions, such as sacredness, which they might express in metaphors of various kinds, even though they may disavow any religious influence or motivation if asked. Consider apparently secular liberal human rights. If we dig a little, we uncover religious or semi-religious ideas, which will come out in the metaphors deployed. According to Genesis, we are all equally 'in God's image'—a subtle, obscure, yet nonetheless powerful idea. Without this idea, it is very doubtful whether we would have any idea of secular liberal human rights. Reason does not get you there.

[29] For discussion, see Zangwill (2011b).

[30] I am not sure how far our overall moral outlook has a determinate structure, although it is structured to an extent. Such structure as there is, however, is revealed by metaphor.

11.5 Against epistemic thickness

So, thickness may be rehabilitated via metaphor and other non-literal devices. But it is crucial, if thick concepts are be rehabilitated, to deny that thick concepts function *epistemically*, as ways of reaching and supporting thin judgements. That was the main hope I believe underlying the interest in them in the 1980s. That interest was ill-motivated. But that does not mean we should dispense with thick concepts altogether.

There is a three-layered cake. Between thin and thick and base there are dependence relations. The beauty of a flower depends on its elegance, which depends on the configuration of petals, leaves, and so on. Similarly, evil depends on murder or poisonousness, which depends on non-moral natural (and non-thick) properties. (These dependencies need not generate modal or 'supervenience' relations.)[31] Having a thick property is a *way* of having a thin evaluative property, such as goodness or badness, rightness or wrongness.

Although there are dependence relations between each layer—in aesthetics, the non-aesthetic level is metaphysically basic and the thin depends on the thick—in our judgements, the thin has primacy over the substantive or thick. Those who make different thin judgements make different substantive ones. Similarly in morality, there are three layers: the evaluative, substantive or thick, and natural (in a broad sense of 'natural' in which God's psychological states are natural). There are dependencies between each layer. But the thin has primacy over the thick in our judgements. Different thick judgements flow from different thin judgements.

Once a thin judgement is made, a thick judgement may follow, not as an answer to the demand for justification, but as an answer to the question 'How?' It is a *rationalization*, not a *justification*. In some special cases there is an analytic link between thick and thin. An act is bad because it is murder, or a thing is beautiful because it is graceful. However, such a close analytic link means that is there is no non-circular justification. It is too close for that.

The legitimate use of thick concepts is in explication or amplification or rationalization, not justification; we are given more information about *how*, in what *way*, a thing has an evaluative property. The illegitimate use is as a crutch for the lazy moralist who says, 'This thing uncontroversially has these "thick" properties, therefore that supports its having its thin properties'. For example, suppose a person makes the thick judgement that Jews are snakes. This is not the *ground* for a negative (anti-Semitic) judgement, but depends on that thin judgement, in that it presupposes the thin judgement and also goes beyond it in being more specific. Compare Moses Maimonides on describing God: given that one believes in God's existence, one might go on to describe Him further, and to do that one will use metaphors, which will be more or less appropriate in the way that there are more or less appropriate metaphorical descriptions of music and pain.[32] However, metaphorical descriptions of God are clearly not evidence for His existence!

---

[31] See Zangwill (2008).   [32] See Maimonides (1958) and Zangwill (2009).

Given that thick judgements are not justifications, there might be thought to be a puzzle about moral change: how do thick judgements figure in the *revision* of moral judgements? With a shift in social attitudes we may come to use certain metaphors or cease to use them. This is because the thin value judgements associated with them changes too. But thick judgments are not an *engine* of change. Change in thick concepts follows in the wake of thin change. To some extent we revise our thin moral judgements so as to cohere with other thin moral judgements. But thick judgements are not a source of change of thin judgements, since they are post facto rationalizations, not justifications, for thin judgements. It is not that they are not at all involved in moral judgement change, but that their role is only to articulate and perhaps solidify thin change. Perhaps there are some unusual cases, where one feels uncertainty over a thin moral judgement, and one seeks a thick rationalization, which might be more or less convincing. If so, in that special kind of case, thick judgements could play a role in the modification of thin judgements. But then the weakness of the thin moral judgement played a role in allowing for the revolution by the thick lower orders.

11.6 Thick determinates and thin determinables

Lastly, there remain issues concerning the metaphysical structure of these properties. Addressing this will enable us to address Levinson's objection.

In aesthetics, there is a *three*-fold distinction among concepts of delicacy: firstly, there is ordinary *nonaesthetic* delicacy (the tendency to break); secondly, there is the *general aesthetic* notion of delicacy; and thirdly, there is the *specific aesthetic* notion of the delicacy of some vase or cloud. Let us label these with subscripts—delicacy$_{NA}$, delicacy$_G$, and delicacy$_S$.[33]

There is a hierarchy of properties in the world, between more general and more specific properties—that is, between more or less determinate properties. The world has specific properties, and more general properties. But the specific properties are metaphysically basic; the more general properties are had by things in virtue of their having the specific ones. For example, something is a thing in virtue of being an animal in virtue of being a dog in virtue of being a dachshund. The general nature of things flows from their particularity. Delicacy$_G$ is a *general* aesthetic property had by many different kinds of things—clouds, poetry, music, vases. By contrast, the delicacy$_S$ of a vase is not had by a cloud, although both are delicate$_G$. The vase may also be undelicate$_{NA}$, being sturdily built.

Levinson objected that some substantive aesthetic properties are not evaluative, whereas I claimed that substantive properties are always ways of possessing the thin aesthetic properties, beauty and ugliness.[34] This point needs to be addressed.

---

[33] The specific delicacy is not a trope, being multi-instantiable: a very similar cloud will share the same delicacy$_S$ unlike a vase, which may nevertheless share the same delicacy$_G$.

[34] Levinson (2001), 62.

As a preliminary, let us put to one side the sort of cases that Stephan Burton raised—of the delicacy of a triumphal arch, which is not good-making feature of it.[35] This is a matter of the fit of one aesthetic property—delicacy—with other aesthetic properties of the whole, or with the thing considered as a thing with a specific function, which is a special case.[36]

The reply to Levinson's objection, I propose, is this: I concede that delicacy$_G$ may be neutral, but the *specific* delicacy$_S$ of a Ming vase *is* always a specific way of having excellence. We have the concepts of both delicacy$_S$ and delicacy$_G$—we have specific and general aesthetic concepts of delicacy—and the specific notion does have intrinsic evaluative direction.

If we say this, it means that we are committed to recognizing thick concepts. They are concepts of features that are ways of being beautiful. Delicacy$_G$ is not; I concede that to Levinson. But the delicacy$_S$ of a vase or cloud *is* a way of being beautiful. It is a thick property. Moreover, our concept of it is a concept of a property that is a way of being beautiful. The *word* 'delicacy' does not pick out such a property. But the *concept* of delicacy$_S$ does do so, and a particular *use* of the word 'delicacy' may do so.

The same goes for metaphorical descriptions in morality. Suppose Suzie says that Jim is a 'pig' (greedy pig, chauvinist pig, selfish pig, or some other kind of pig). The specific pigginess of Jim is a *way* that he is bad. Perhaps the word 'pig' does not exactly express the specific property she has in mind on a particular occasion. What she has in mind is a specific thick property. She is thinking of that specific thick property in calling him a 'pig'. It is what she has in mind even though she cannot convey it unambiguously, although tone of voice and gesture may help. She is thinking something specific and she thinks that there is some specific property of Jim that she is trying to get at as best she can by using this figure of speech, together with non-verbal communication. She is trying to describe the indescribable—an aspect of the moral world that eludes our limited moral language. Hence the need for metaphor and other non-literal communicative means. They describe the ways of moral value.

11.7 Conclusion

It seems, then, that there are, after all, thick moral concepts and thick moral properties. We can embrace thick properties and thick concepts in moral philosophy as well as aesthetics—on three conditions: (1) that thick concepts are not supposed to function epistemically; (2) that we drop the poor examples—kindness, cruelty, courage, rudeness, and the like; and (3) that we explore metaphorical descriptions in moral philosophy, which are descriptions of ways, often inexpressible ways, in which things have moral values.[37]

[35] Burton (1992).   [36] Zangwill (1999).

[37] This paper was originally written for the 'Thick Concepts' conference in Canterbury. It was also delivered at Stockholm University, and at the Hebrew University of Jerusalem where I was a Lady Davis Fellow. Many thanks for discussion from the audiences on those occasions. Thanks also for comments from Simon Kirchin, Mathew Ratcliffe, and Andreas Pantazatos.

References

Beardsley, Monroe (1982) *The Aesthetic Point of View* (Ithaca, NY: Cornell University Press).

Blackburn, Simon (1992) 'Morality and Thick Concepts: Through Thick and Thin', *Proceedings of the Aristotelian Society, Supplementary Volume* 66: 285–99.

Burton, Stephan (1992) 'Thick Concepts Revisted', *Analysis* 52: 28–32.

Corinne, Tee (1975) *Cunt Coloring Book* (San Francisco, CA: Last Gasp), reprinted 1988.

Davidson, Donald (1978) 'What Metaphors Mean', *Critical Inquiry* 5: 31–47.

Foot, Philippa (1958) 'Moral Arguments', *Mind* 67: 502–13.

Gibbard, Allan (1992) 'Morality and Thick Concepts: Thick Concepts and Warrant for Feelings', *Proceedings of the Aristotelian Society, Supplementary Volume* 66: 267–83.

Goldie, Peter (2008) 'Thick Concepts and Emotion', in Daniel Callcut (ed.) *Reading Bernard Williams* (London: Routledge), 94–109.

Hare, R. M. (1952) *The Language of Morals* (Oxford: Clarendon Press).

Hill, Wayne and Cynthia Ottchen (1991) *Shakespeare's Insults* (Cambridge: Mainsail Press).

Kivy, Peter (1975) 'What Makes "Aesthetic" Terms Aesthetic?', *Philosophy and Phenomenological Research* 36: 197–211.

Levinson, Jerrold (2001) 'Aesthetic Properties, Evaluative Force, and Differences of Sensibility', in Emily Brady and Jerrold Levinson (eds.) *Aesthetics Concepts: Essays after Sibley* (Oxford: Oxford University Press), 61–80.

Maimonides, Moses (1958) *Guide for the Perplexed* (London: Dover).

McDowell, John (1979) 'Virtue and Reason', *Monist* 62: 331–50.

—— (1996) 'Two Sorts of Naturalism', in Rosalind Hursthouse, Gavin Lawrence, and Warren Quinn (eds.) *Virtues and Reasons: Philippa Foot and Moral Theory* (Oxford: Oxford University Press), 149–179.

McGinn, Colin (1998) *Knowledge and Necessity* (Oxford: Oxford University Press).

Moore, A. W. (2006) 'Maxims and Thick Ethical Concepts', *Ratio* 19: 129–47.

Musolff, Andreas (2007) 'What Role Do Metaphors Play in Racial Prejudice? The Function of Anti-Semitic Imagery in Hitler's Mein Kampf', *Patterns of Prejudice* 41: 21–43.

Pinker, Stephen (2007) *The Stuff of Thought* (London: Penguin).

Scruton, Roger (1974) *Art and Imagination* (London: Methuen).

—— (1997) *The Aesthetics of Music* (Oxford: Oxford University Press).

Sibley, Frank (2001) *Approach to Aesthetics* (Oxford: Oxford University Press).

Williams, Bernard (1985) *Ethics and the Limits of Philosophy* (London: Fontana).

Wittgenstein, Ludwig (1965) 'A Lecture on Ethics, *Philosophical Review* 74: 3–12.

Zangwill, Nick (1991) 'Metaphor and Realism in Aesthetics', *Journal of Aesthetics and Art Criticism* 49: 57–62. Reprinted in his *Metaphysics of Beauty* (Ithaca, NY: Cornell University Press, 2001), 166–75.

—— (1995) 'The Beautiful, the Dainty and the Dumpy', *British Journal of Aesthetics* 35: 317–29. Reprinted in his *Metaphysics of Beauty* (Ithaca, NY: Cornell University Press, 2001), 9–23.

—— (1998) 'The Concept of the Aesthetic', *European Journal of Philosophy* 6: 78–93. Reprinted in his *Metaphysics of Beauty* (Ithaca, NY: Cornell University Press, 2001), 24–42.

—— (1999) 'Feasible Aesthetic Formalism', *Noûs* 33: 610–29. Reprinted in his *Metaphysics of Beauty* (Ithaca, NY: Cornell University Press, 2001), 55–81.

—— (2001) *Metaphysics of Beauty* (Ithaca, NY: Cornell University Press).

—— (2008) 'Moral Dependence', in *Oxford Studies in Metaethics* 3: 109–27.

—— (2009) 'Music and Mysticism', *Research Journal of the Iranian Academy of Arts, Pazhoheshnameh* 12.

—— (2010) 'Scruton's Musical Experiences', *Philosophy* 85: 91–104.

—— (2011a) 'Music, Private Language and Essential Metaphor', *American Philosophical Quarterly* 48: 1–16.

—— (2011b) 'Cordelia's Bond', *Oxford Studies in Normative Ethics* 1: 143–65.

—— (forthcoming) 'Metaphor and Appropriaion', *Philosophy and Literature.*

12

Williams on Thick Ethical Concepts and Reasons for Action

Eric Wiland

It would be foolish to try to say exactly what Bernard Williams's greatest contributions to philosophy were. But I want to discuss the relations between two contenders: (1) the idea that your reasons for action always depend upon your pre-existing motives, and (2) the idea that moral philosophy would be more fruitful if its practitioners paid closer attention to thick ethical concepts. There is a tension between these two rather different ideas that I hope to tease out here.

My goal is to persuade you that REASONABLE is a thick concept. Even if I am successful, I realize that I will not have shown that REASON FOR ACTION is likewise thick. Explicating the connection between those two concepts is a task for another time. I am, for the sake of the present argument, just going to *assume* that some close connection can be forged: that if REASONABLE is thick, then so too is REASON FOR ACTION. Perhaps this assumption is unreasonable (ahem), but for now I will just echo the following thought from G. E. M. Anscombe: "Where we are tempted to speak of 'different senses' of a word which is clearly not equivocal, we may infer that we are in fact pretty much in the dark about the character of the concept which it represents."[1]

Williams, you'll recall, defended an internal theory of reasons for action, according to which if Owen Wingrave (the character of Williams's main example) has a reason to join the military, then joining the military serves some motive Owen already has. To say that Owen has a reason to join the military while acknowledging that joining it won't get him anything he wants is, according to Williams, mere bluff. Genuine reasons for action are thus related to an agent's desires.[2]

Williams also emphasized the importance of reflecting upon the ubiquity of thick ethical concepts in our practical thought. First, thick ethical concepts are world-guided. Judgments involving them are truth-apt; your thinking that some thick concept applies does not make it correctly applied. Second, thick concepts are evaluative, though we must be careful here. Even though thick concepts are evaluative, one can sincerely use a

---

[1] Anscombe (1957), 1.   [2] Williams (1981) and (1995).

thick ethical concept, and even appreciate and endorse the evaluative point of it, without wholeheartedly identifying with it: recall Augustine's sincere prayer for belated chastity. Third, thick concepts are, in some way that I need to articulate, culturally dependent.[3]

The term "culture" is of course rather vague. What is this culture on which thick concepts somehow depend? One way of cashing out this idea is to relate it to Williams's notion of the absolute conception of the world. Some concepts will figure in the absolute conception of the world: presumably, many concepts in physics, probably biology, possibly psychology, and so on. But other concepts will not appear in the absolute conception, or if they do, they will appear only in intensional contexts, for example, "some people believe in *voodoo*" and "they think that she is *treacherous*." To say that a thick concept is culturally specific is, among other things, to say that it will not appear in the absolute conception.

Thick ethical terms, then, are (1) somewhat objective, (2) evaluative, and (3) somewhat relative to a culture.

When Williams turned his attention from ethical action to reasons for action, however, his stance was very different. Whether it is correct for you to say that you have a reason to do something, for Williams, depends not simply upon whether your judgment represents the way the world is independently of you. It doesn't report an objective fact about the world you face. Instead, your judgment about what you have reason to do depends in the first place upon whether some possible action of yours fits well with your pre-existing motives. Your reasons for action are thus *not* significantly independent of what you want. They always depend upon your psychological makeup.

Williams's stance here is usually viewed by philosophers as the taking of sides in a debate about whether reasons for action are either subjectively grounded or grounded in the world. But Williams's own emphasis on thick ethical concepts points to a different way of viewing the ground of reasons for action: perhaps whether Owen Wingrave acts reasonably depends not so much (or at all) on what Owen wants, or the way the world is in itself, but upon cultural features.

There is a huge ambiguity in that last sentence, for there are (at least) two different ways cultural features might shape whether it is correct to say that Owen has a reason to V. First, one might think that whether Owen has reason to V depends upon features of the culture that *Owen* inhabits. Facts about his society may make it true that he has or has not reason to V. On this view, reasons for action track the mountains and valleys of the *agent's* cultural milieu.

But I don't think this view is correct, nor does it cohere well with Williams' view of the way thick ethical concepts work. Whether a thick ethical concept (courageous, chaste, cruel) can be correctly applied to someone depends not in the first place upon the culture of the person up for ethical evaluation. It depends upon the culture in which the concept has its home and its point. That is, while Hugh Hefner probably never finds himself operating with the concept CHASTE, the Pope still speaks the truth when he

---

[3] Williams (1985).

says that Hefner is not chaste. It doesn't have to be one of Hefner's concepts for the term to correctly apply to him. And such thick ethical terms can figure in sensible explanations of action: Hefner once had three girlfriends in part because he is not a chaste man.

Now if reasons operate the same way thick ethical terms do, then whether Owen Wingrave acts reasonably depends not in the first place upon Owen's culture, but upon the culture that gives the concept REASONABLE its point. And this, of course, is *our* culture. The mistake we and Williams make, I think, is that we typically fail to see that our concept of the reasonable is itself culturally peculiar. We wrongly assume it is timeless and universal.

The reasonable person standard governing appropriate care emerged specifically from English common law; it has not always existed, and it does not exist everywhere. We first see it in the case of *Vaughan v. Menlove* (1837), in which the court ruled that liability for negligence depends not upon the details of the defendant's state of mind, but instead upon the standard of caution that "a man of ordinary prudence would observe." In 1856, the English courts again reaffirmed that "negligence is the omission to do something which a reasonable man, guided upon those considerations which ordinarily regulate the conduct of human affairs, would do, or doing something which a prudent and reasonable man would not do" (*Blyth v Company Proprietors of the Birmingham Water Works*). Similarly, in the United States' case of *Brown v. Kendall* (1850), the Court ruled that a defendant should be liable for negligence only if he failed to act with "ordinary care and prudence," a phrase that legal scholars now recognize as an early use of the reasonable person standard. Whether a person is reasonable depends not in the first place on what she wants, but upon whether her way of thinking and acting conform to a certain socially recognized standard, one that does not always concern the person's perhaps idiosyncratic motives.

Other legal systems, of course, have similar standards. It is often claimed that the reasonable person standard in Anglo-American law is related to the ancient Roman standard for legal care, the standard of the *paterfamilias*. Both mandated that (certain) citizens live up to societal expectations. But the specific duties and expectations associated with each of these differ: the Roman standard granted the *pater* much wider latitude within his own family to act as he deemed fit, and imposed upon him much narrower duties of care to noncitizens. Though both standards impose duties upon citizens, the duties thus imposed are not identical in the two cases.

The parochiality of the concept of reasonable becomes even more evident if we look at other modern legal systems. French and German lawyers, despite having ready-made words to translate the concept of the reasonable, rarely craft laws using such terms. Unlike the rest of Canada, Quebec imposes a duty on everyone to help those in peril. Everyone is to act as a *bon père de famille*—a good head of household—a standard obviously historically related to the Roman *paterfamilias*, but whose specific duties are more wide-reaching than those of both its conceptual ancestor and of the Anglo-American reasonable person standard.

The Israeli example is even more instructive:

When the concept of 'reason' is not in common usage, it is difficult to find a cognate for *reasonable*. In modern Hebrew, for example, the lawyers had considerable difficulty translating phrases employing reasonableness that appeared in the English statutes that they adopted as their own, in particular, James Fitzjames Stephen's draft criminal code, which became standard in many of the former English colonies. Finally, sometime after the founding of the state of Israel, a group of experts convened at the Department of Justice in Jerusalem and decided to introduce the word *savir* as the designated equivalent of *reasonableness*.[4]

Israeli lawyers had to consciously and deliberately import the notion of the reasonable into their nascent legal system, a move that would have been completely unnecessary were the notion universal and timeless. Seeing this helps confirm the hypothesis that the concept of the reasonable is culturally specific in just the way that thick concepts typically are.

Now for all I have said, it remains possible that the culturally specific concept of reasonable is world-guided in a way compatible with Williams' internalism. Just as the correct application of the concept HARMONIOUS, for instance, depends only upon the relations among the internal parts of the object in question, so too the correct application of the concept REASONABLE might depend only upon whether a person's actions and motives align in some favored way. Internalism might be true even if, as I've been arguing, REASONABLE is a thick concept.

But I now want to argue that this is not how our concept of REASONABLE actually works. I think we can best understand the descriptive content of REASONABLE by considering how it may be correctly used by those who do *not* wholeheartedly identify with its directive. Then, the descriptive content of the concept—to borrow an idea of Kant's—shines like a jewel. Like CHASTE, REASONABLE may be used by someone who understands and perhaps even acknowledges the evaluative point of the concept, without fully endorsing that point. Here are a few examples of odd though recognizable uses of the idea of a reasonable person:

Reasonable people adapt themselves to the world. Unreasonable people attempt to adapt the world to themselves. All progress, therefore, depends on unreasonable people.

George Bernard Shaw

A woman in love can't be reasonable—or she probably wouldn't be in love.

Mae West

I tried being reasonable, I didn't like it.

Dirty Harry

Taken together, these examples point to the idea that a good explication of the concept REASONABLE would show that reasonable people display a certain kind of balance. First off, reasonable people tend to be fair-minded; Dirty Harry's point reflects this. A reasonable person doesn't overindulge his or her own idiosyncrasies too much, but makes some effort to fit in with others.

---

[4] Fletcher and Sheppard (2005), 67.

Second, West's quip suggests that reasonable people tend not to be the grip of powerful emotions, and are not excessively single-minded. A reasonable person exercises a modicum of self-control and discipline. It would be hard to imagine describing a wildly imprudent person as reasonable. Reasonable people don't lose sight of their other commitments and values as they pursue any particular one of them.

Third, reasonable people are, for better or worse, somewhat practically conservative and "realistic." If the success of certain projects requires one to ignore or sharply discount foreseeable risks, then only unreasonable people will ever see such projects through—this, I take it, is Shaw's point. Reasonable people pay attention to considerations favoring either stasis or gradual change. Unreasonable people are much more likely to upset the apple cart.

So it would seem that reasonable people take account of interests both short-term and long-term, both their own and those of others. A person may do exactly the only thing she wants to do, and yet fail to be reasonable on this score. So being reasonable isn't simply about doing what you want to do. It's also about weighing multiple considerations—including but not limited to the interests of others—in some fair-minded way. I don't mean to *equate* reasonableness with fairness or justice or prudence. I just think that a reasonable person pays *some* mind to such considerations. They are not in the grip of some one thing.

Let's now re-examine one of Williams's most well-known examples intended to illustrate his internalism about reasons. Suppose I think that some man ought to be nicer to his wife, that he shouldn't abuse her. One might think that he has a reason to be nicer to her. But Williams argued that if there is nothing in this man's motivational set that being nicer to her would serve, then the man in fact does not have reason to be nicer to her. To be sure, Williams emphasizes that this heartless husband is "ungrateful, inconsiderate, hard, sexist, nasty, selfish, brutal, and many other disadvantageous things."[5] But he doesn't have a *reason* to be nicer to her, at least not if acting more nicely serves none of his actual motives. Williams bit the bullet here.

But it seems to me even more unappealing to bite the bullet when it comes to the husband's being *reasonable*. The man who treats his wife so poorly is—unless the circumstances are *very* strange—thereby unreasonable. And the fact that he is unreasonable has little to do with what the man wants. It is no objection to the claim that he is being unreasonable to point out that he isn't motivated to be nicer to her. Indeed, this is just *more* evidence of his unreasonableness. So I really don't see how one would find internalism appealing if one thinks that the concept REASONABLE is thick in the way that I've described.

The more general point is confirmed when we look at how the reasonable person standard in the law is in fact applied. One never can successfully argue that one acted as a reasonable person would have acted merely by noting that one lacked any subjective motivations that would have led to more cautious behavior. Saying truthfully, "But I

---

[5] Williams (1995), 39.

wanted only to act selfishly!" does not suffice to show that one complied with the reasonable person standard. While it might not be true that reasonable people always behave ethically, it is clear that effective pursuit of one's self-absorbed goals does not inoculate against the charge of unreasonableness. Some of the constraints on a reasonable person's behavior are social rather than individual.

So much for the concept of REASONABLE. We still need to understand what bearing it has upon the concept of a REASON. It seems that there is much more to acting reasonably than merely just acting upon a reason. No doubt most of those who act unreasonably still do so for some reason or other. Thus, acting on a reason does not suffice for meeting the reasonable person standard.

But the other direction appears to be much more promising. If a reasonable person in your circumstances would V, then it would seem that you too have a reason to V. It would sound extremely odd to say that it would be reasonable for you to V, but you nevertheless have no reason to V. Instead, the fact that a reasonable person would do something pretty much guarantees that there is some reason to do it. Perhaps this argument doesn't settle the issue. But the burden of proof is clearly upon the person who wants to insist that it can be reasonable for you to do something that you have no reason to do.

Let's take stock. I have argued that the concept of REASONABLE is a fairly thick concept, that a reasonable person is not entirely unmoved by the interests of others, and that reasonable people do things that they have a reason to do. This supports the thought that reasons aren't always internal. I have also tried to draw attention to a tension in Williams's work, in that in some places he emphasized the ubiquity and the importance of thick concepts, while in other places he argued for a very thin understanding of a reason for action.

Looking beyond Williams, if REASONABLE is a fairly thick ethical concept, and if there is a close connection between the REASONABLE and a REASON FOR ACTION, and if OUGHT is a thin concept, then it's very likely that many philosophical projects (for example John Broome's) that try to reduce REASONS to OUGHTS, or OUGHTS to REASONS, will fail. For OUGHTS are usually considered to be neither descriptive nor world-guided nor in the first place culturally dependent. OUGHT is instead a textbook example of a thin concept. And what's REASONABLE is descriptive, world-guided, and culturally dependent. So, they seem very different to me. We are no more likely to reduce what's reasonable to what one ought to do than we are to reduce what's generous or what's kind or what's charitable to what one ought to do. The concept of REASONABLE and its battery of cognates are thicker than either the concept of OUGHT or GOOD.

References

Anscombe, G. E. M. (1957) *Intention* (Oxford: Blackwell).

Fletcher, George and Steve Sheppard (2005) *American Law in a Global Context: The Basics* (Oxford: Oxford University Press).

Williams, Bernard (1981) 'Internal and External Reasons', in his *Moral Luck* (Cambridge: Cambridge University Press, 1981), 101–13. First published in Ross Harrison (ed.) *Rational Action: Studies in Philosophy and Social Science* (Cambridge: Cambridge University Press, 1979), 17–28. [Page references to 1981 version.]

—— (1985) *Ethics and the Limits of Philosophy* (London: Fontana).

—— (1995) 'Internal Reasons and the Obscurity of Blame', in his *Making Sense of Humanity* (Cambridge: Cambridge University Press, 1995), 35–45. First published in William J. Prior *(ed.) Reason and Moral Judgment, Logos,* 10 (1989). [Page references to 1995 version.]

13

Well-being, Wisdom, and Thick Theorizing: on the Division of Labor between Moral Philosophy and Positive Psychology

Valerie Tiberius

13.1 Introduction

We wouldn't attribute well-being to someone who is seriously physically ill and we wouldn't attribute practical wisdom to someone who has poor skills of instrumental reasoning. But when we attribute well-being or wisdom to someone we also mean to say that they have something worth having, something good for them, perhaps even something admirable. Well-being and wisdom are thick concepts: they are tied to the world and they express evaluations at the same time. This fact causes puzzles in metaethics about how to account for concepts that seem to have two directions of fit. I will not be concerned with those puzzles here. Instead, I want to focus on the special promise these concepts might have for moral theory. This promise is suggested by Bernard Williams in his *Ethics and the Limits of Philosophy* who thought that moral knowledge was sustained by thick concepts and undermined as shared thick concepts were lost. But the role of thick concepts in first-order moral theory has not been discussed in much detail.

Interestingly, psychologists have taken a recent interest in thick concepts that used to be the domain of philosophers.[1] Psychologists have proposed theories of well-being and wisdom and have done all sorts of studies to determine the causes and correlates of their theoretical constructs. One might think that this research is irrelevant to philosophical theories because one assumes the following picture: philosophers articulate and defend abstract, formal theories that provide the necessary and sufficient conditions for well-being or wisdom. Psychologists can use these theories to inform their operationalized definitions of the constructs they want to investigate. Then psychologists run their studies and discover the facts about what causes well-being or wisdom so defined, or what kind of people tend to have it.

[1] Of course they're not interested in the concepts, per se; they're interested in the stuff to which the concepts refer. But this is also true of moral philosophers who study virtue and well-being.

For example, philosophers could defend an informed preference theory of well-being and psychologists could tell us what things people prefer when informed, or what kinds of people are more likely to get their informed preferences satisfied. We start with philosophical analysis of the thick concept and then we can turn things over to the scientists.

I will argue in this paper that this is the wrong picture and that things are more complicated than this—at least as far as well-being and wisdom are concerned. In section 13.2 I will explain the wrong picture in more detail and give some needed background. Once we see *how* things are more complicated we can also see that thick concepts do hold out a special promise for making progress in moral theory. Or so I shall argue. I will start in section 13.3 by distinguishing two ways in which normative ideals can be thick, using well-being and wisdom as my examples. I then discuss the alternative picture of how empirical and philosophical research can be brought together in an inquiry about normative ideals in section 13.4. Finally, in section 13.5, I discuss some of the pros and cons of what we might call "thick theorizing" for making progress in moral theory. I use well-being and wisdom as my examples throughout the paper because these are topics I have studied enough to know how the big methodological picture might look. Because the main question of the paper is about methodology, the paper will be somewhat programmatic. I suspect that the conclusions I argue for generalize to other thick concepts, but I also think that well-being and wisdom are important enough topics that these conclusions are of some interest even if they don't generalize.

13.2 Lists and unifying explanations

Psychologists like to make lists. Philosophers like to identify necessary and sufficient conditions for list membership. The most prominent theories in the well-being literature in psychology are lists. For example:

- Ed Diener's theory of subjective well-being (SWB) according to which SWB consists in global life satisfaction, domain satisfaction, positive affect, and low negative affect.[2]
- Martin Seligman's theory of flourishing as positive emotion, engagement, relationships, meaning, and achievement.[3]
- Carol Ryff and Burton Singer's theory that defines psychological well-being in terms of autonomy, personal growth, self-acceptance, life purpose, mastery, and positive relatedness.[4]

It makes sense that psychologists would be drawn to lists of states or conditions that can be measured.[5] But philosophers are going to want to know what unifies the list. What is the nature of well-being such that it includes these items and not others?

---

[2] Kesebir and Diener (2008).   [3] Seligman (2011).   [4] Ryff and Singer (1998).

[5] It's not that psychologists *never* try to justify or explain what's on their list. Ryff and Singer, for instance, do talk about human needs as a unifying concept. But the theoretical justification of the constructs is not their primary concern.

The most prominent philosophical theories of well-being are preference theories, life satisfaction theory, and eudaimonism.[6] Perhaps the most popular of the preference theories is the full information theory, which makes the satisfaction of preferences under idealized conditions (conditions of full information) the key to well-being.[7] Life satisfaction theory, as articulated by L.W. Sumner, holds that authentic satisfaction with your life overall constitutes well-being; authenticity, on his view, requires both information and autonomy.[8] Eudaimonism ties well-being to fulfillment of your nature, in some way, whether that is your nature as a human being or your individual nature.[9] There is (obviously!) much more to say about these theories. The important point for our purposes is that any of these theories could serve to explain how certain items on the above lists get on those lists. For instance, perhaps autonomy, personal growth, self-acceptance, and so on are things that we prefer, when informed, for their own sakes. Perhaps positive emotion, engagement, and meaning speak to deep human needs, the fulfillment of which constitutes our well-being. Or, perhaps life satisfaction, domain satisfaction, and positive affect cause authentic life satisfaction.

When we turn to the wisdom literature, we still see theories and lists, though the disciplinary lines are less clear. The two main psychological theories of wisdom are Paul Baltes's "Berlin Paradigm" and Robert Sternberg's "Balance Theory." The Berlin Paradigm defines wisdom as "expertise in the conduct and meaning of life"[10] and proposes a list of criteria for wisdom:

- rich factual knowledge
- rich procedural knowledge
- lifespan contextualism
- relativism of values and life priorities
- recognition and management of uncertainty.

According to Sternberg:

Wisdom is defined as the application of tacit knowledge as mediated by values toward the goal of achieving a common good (a) through a balance among multiple intrapersonal, interpersonal, and extrapersonal interests and (b) in order to achieve a balance among responses to environmental contexts: adaptation to existing environmental contexts, shaping of existing environmental contexts, and selection of new environmental contexts.[11]

This definition is more like a theory, and Sternberg's argument for it draws on some of the same sources that a philosopher would draw on in defending her theory (thoughts about the nature of a good life and facts about human nature). On the basis of this

---

[6] Parfit's (1984) well known taxonomy of theories of well-being (hedonism, desire-based theories, and objective list theories) is no longer quite representative of the favored theories in philosophy. See Haybron (2008), 34.

[7] See Griffin (1986) and Railton (1986).

[8] Sumner (1996).

[9] For the former, see Nussbaum (2001); for the latter, see Haybron (2008).

[10] Baltes and Staudinger (2000), 124.   [11] Sternberg (1998), 353.

definition, he defines lists of mental processes that are involved in wisdom and the variables that make a difference to how much wisdom people have.

In philosophy there is not a set of venerable theories of wisdom to choose from as there is for well-being. The best developed theories of wisdom are Aristotelian, some of which are more interpretive than others.[12] John McDowell's perceptual model of practical wisdom, which identifies it with a capacity for discernment of the salient features of a situation that is both cognitive and conative, is perhaps the best known. In her critique of McDowell, Rosalind Hursthouse lists a number of capacities that are important to wisdom that are missing from the perceptual model.[13] So, in the wisdom literature we sometimes find philosophers making lists and psychologists defending theories. The important point for our purposes is that there are two kinds of questions about wisdom: one is about the list of capacities and skills that constitute wisdom, the other is about what wisdom is such that these things are on the list but not others.

The distinction between these two different questions and the disciplinary pattern (particularly in the well-being literature) suggests the following division of labor and methodology for proceeding. Philosophers should construct and defend theories, then turn things over to the psychologists. Notice that constructing and defending a theory requires more than providing necessary and sufficient conditions for what items get on the list. Theories must be justified and the tools for this kind of justification are the tools of philosophy: wide reflective equilibrium, conceptual or reconstructive analysis, thought experiments, counter-exampling and other methods are designed to defend philosophical theories of normative concepts.[14] These methods are not empirical, so the job of articulating and defending a theory is a philosophical job for which we don't require the tools of empirical science. Further, since philosophers have no particular expertise in measurement or in constructing operationalizations of concepts to be measured, once the formal analysis is done—once the necessary and sufficient conditions for list membership are set out and defended—our work is done. This is the picture I aim to reject in the rest of this paper.

13.3 Two kinds of thickness

The usual kind of thickness that is attributed to normative concepts is demonstrated by people's use of these concepts. Courage has descriptive and prescriptive content because we do not attribute it unless the person about whom we are speaking is in some way good at facing danger, nor do we attribute it without expressing some admiration or

---

[12] For an excellent example of the interpretive end of the spectrum, see Broadie (1991).

[13] Hursthouse (2006).

[14] Traditional conceptual analysis is under a bit of a cloud among philosophers who are interested in empirically informed ethics. Haybron (2008), 44, suggests "reconstructive analysis" as a better approach; Sumner (1996), 6, advocates philosophical analysis that occupies "a middle ground between the merely conceptual and the fully empirical."

approval. "Well-being" and "wisdom" have this kind of thickness. But there is another kind of thickness we can see if we go back to Aristotle. For Aristotle, there isn't a neat division between the conceptual analysis and the list of causes or constituents of well-being or of wisdom. Aristotle does have a definition of *eudaimonia* as rational activity in accordance with virtue, but his *theory* of eudaimonia is clearly meant to include much more than this. For Aristotle, much of what might now be in the domain of psychology was fair game: the causes and correlates of happiness are as important to his overall theory as the encapsulated definition.

Now I'm not suggesting that the very concept of well-being includes all the virtues Aristotle discussed, but this observation about Aristotle does indicate a way in which *theories* of well-being (or wisdom) may be thick. Theories such as Aristotle's spell out the details of what is unified by the definition: they specify the causes, consequences, and mechanisms of well-being or provide specific descriptions of the skills or capacities required for wisdom.

Theories of the good or the right (thin normative concepts) are not like this. While philosophers do *apply* theories of the right to get conclusions about particular actions, these conclusions are not part of the theory of right; they are not part of what it is for an action to be right. For Aristotle, on the other hand, being temperate, just, and wise in the way that he described, is part of what it is to live a flourishing life. The reason for this difference, it seems to me, is that the two kinds of thickness are related. The reason that specifications of the causes and mechanisms of well-being are part of the theory of well-being is that our concept includes some descriptive content that constrains its application.

The literatures on well-being and wisdom provide examples of both kinds of thickness. We have already seen how certain theories of well-being and wisdom specify the components of these states. There is also evidence that these concepts (or related concepts) have both prescriptive and descriptive content. For example, Jonathan Philips, Sven Nyholm, and Shen-yi Laio have argued that the folk concept of happiness (a concept related to well-being, but usually taken to be more purely psychological) is moralized because people are more likely to judge that someone is happy if he is living a morally good life than if he is living a morally bad life.[15] Similarly, Jonathan Phillips, Luke Misenheimer, and Joshua Knobe show that evaluative judgments play a role in the application of the concept of "happiness," though not for the concept of "unhappiness."[16] This works reveals "happiness" to be closer to "well-being," because it has prescriptive content.

When it comes to wisdom, there are a large number of studies of people's "implicit theories" of wisdom, that is, the notion of wisdom that ordinary people have. The folk notion of wisdom is thick; according to one meta-analysis it includes cognitive or logical ability, insight, deep understanding of others' perspectives, reflectiveness or the

---

[15] Philips, Nyholm, and Laio (forthcoming).   [16] Phillips, Misenheimer, and Knobe (2011).

motivation to think deeply about things, concern for others, and real world skills that allow the wise person to apply her understanding to solve actual problems.[17] Experimental studies can also reveal interesting things about our use of the concept. Few experimental studies have been done in this field, so the results to date are not well substantiated, but there is some evidence that people are more likely to attribute wisdom to older people than to younger people when assessing vignettes, even when the behavior of the people in the vignettes is the same.[18] If these findings are correct, our concept of "wisdom" may have descriptive content that we do not necessarily endorse.

13.4 An alternative model: sharing labor

In this section of the paper, I argue that there are reasons not to accept the neat division of labor I outlined at the end of section 13.2 for theories of thick normative notions like well-being and wisdom.[19] There are two reasons for this. First, insofar as the unifying definition of the concept is tied to people's actual usage of it, empirical research is relevant to the project of articulating a definition. Of course, philosophers, not trained in psychology, do conduct a kind of empirical research: they pay attention to how concepts are used by their friends, families, students, the news media, and so on. But these observations are not systematic and may be biased toward the way concepts are used by people philosophers happen to hear.[20] Second, questions about the causes, mechanisms, and skills involved in well-being and wisdom are not always straightforwardly empirical questions.

The claim that how people actually use their normative concepts is an empirical question should not be controversial. What is controversial is that the empirical facts about our concept use are relevant to philosophical theorizing about these concepts. When it comes to well-being and wisdom (and perhaps similar concepts), there is a reason to think these empirical facts are relevant. This reason has to do with the fact that theories of well-being and wisdom aim to describe states that are normative *for people*. Theories of well-being aim to describe "the goal of life" in a way that this description may ultimately resonate with people who will then be able to make their own lives better or improve the lives of others. This idea that our use of normative concepts is relevant to our philosophical theories of them is behind Julia Annas's insistence that we translate "*eudaimonia*" as happiness (rather than, say, the more esoteric "flourishing"). Annas argues that what the ancients were trying to do is just what modern theorists are trying

---

[17] Bluck and Glück (2005).   [18] Staudinger and Glück (forthcoming).

[19] For an interesting argument for rejecting this division of labor in the field of moral cognition, see Lapsley, Daniel, and Hill (2008).

[20] The method of relying on intuitions has been the subject of much recent controversy. (See DePaul and Ramsey (1998) for a balanced set of papers.) My point here is that even if philosophers recognize the importance of going beyond their own intuitions, they may not have the right tools. The methods of experimental psychology may be better suited for getting an accurate picture of how concepts like well-being and wisdom are used in general.

to do: to describe a "conventionally successful life which the agent finds satisfactory."[21] Annas sees "happiness" as a concept that plays a particular role in ordinary life: it describes the kind of life we want to have, for its own sake. The fact that we use the concept this way (when we wish someone a happy life, when we talk about the pursuit of happiness, and so on), according to Annas, is what makes it the case that the ancients and the moderns are theorizing about the same thing. This fact is, therefore, important to what theories we consider as contenders for theories of happiness.

The relevance of the empirical facts about how we use these concepts also appears in Sumner's discussion of the criteria of adequacy for a theory of well-being. According to Sumner, "descriptive adequacy" is the main criterion against which theories of well-being should be judged: they must make sense of the ordinary judgments we make that use the concept. It is hard to see how empirical research (particularly, research that aims to discover what these ordinary judgments are) would not be relevant to investigating descriptive adequacy.[22]

When it comes to normative concepts, at least, it is important to clarify that our *use* of concepts such as "well-being" or "wisdom" is, in the main, indirectly relevant to the project of constructing a normative specification of these concepts. What is directly relevant to establishing that some end or character trait is normative for a person is a connection to the person's reasons for action. I will assume that in the case of well-being and virtues that contribute to individual flourishing, these reasons should be construed as internal.[23] That is, to show that a person has a reason to pursue well-being or to develop wisdom, one must show that these goals are appropriately related to something the person wants or cares about (or would want or care about under appropriate conditions). How we use concepts such as "well-being" or "wisdom," then, is relevant insofar as it reveals the cares and commitments that give rise to our practical reasons. It seems to me that how we use these concepts often does reveal our commitments in just this way. For example, if people are inclined to call someone happy only if he is living a morally decent life, this suggests that people care about living morally good lives and are motivated (to some extent) to choose morally good lives for themselves. It's not how we use words, per se, that matters to normative theorizing, but what our use of words shows about our understanding of the world and our commitments to action. In Williams's words "critical reflection should seek for as much shared understanding as it can find on any issue, and use any ethical material that, in the context of the reflective discussion, makes some sense and commands some loyalty."[24]

The case I've just made for paying attention to empirical work on how we use our normative concepts needs to be qualified in two further ways. First, it is certainly not the case that every study shows what it purports to show. It may be difficult to get subjects to

---

[21] Annas (1993), 453.   [22] Sumner (1996).
[23] Reasons internalism is controversial, of course, but I think it should be less controversial when it comes to prudential reasons like the reasons to pursue well-being or practical wisdom.
[24] Williams (1985), 116–17.

distinguish different concepts in response to artificial scenarios and some concepts may not be common enough to have a fixed meaning. "Well-being" may very well be such a concept. While we do talk about how well someone is doing ("She's doing well!"), we do not use the word "well-being" very often. If a concept is not in common usage, studies that aim to show how it is used or what commitments its use reveals are problematic.

Second, the facts about how we use a concept do not determine what the best philosophical theory is. To say that this information is relevant is not to say that it will always carry the day. Focusing on the example discussed above, let's grant for the sake of argument, that our concept of "happiness" is moralized such that we do not attribute happiness to people who have morally bad lives and that this is evidence that we have some practical-reason supporting commitment to living well in a way that meets moral standards. Is this relevant to what philosophical theory of happiness is the best one? Yes. Does it rule out a purely hedonistic theory of happiness? No. There may be good reason to defend a hedonistic theory of happiness. For example, if people use the word "happiness" to mean two different things and we need some way to draw the distinction, we might decide to call the hedonistic notion "happiness" and reserve "well-being" for the moralized notion.

Again, similar points can be made for theories of wisdom. Above I discussed research on people's implicit theories of wisdom. And I have argued in this section that the fact that a theory of wisdom is meant to describe an action-guiding ideal gives us some reason to pay attention to the ideal people actually have. But this prima facie reason to pay attention to how people use the concept and what this says about the ideals they accept is not overriding, and the facts about the folk theory of wisdom does not determine what wisdom is. After all, some elements of the folk theory might be incompatible with others. For example, the fact that people seem more likely to attribute wisdom to older people, other things being equal, does not fit with thinking about wisdom as deep understanding and reflective skill. If deep understanding and reflection are what defines wisdom, then attributions of wisdom should vary with changes in these variables, not with changes in age that do not result in other relevant changes.

I now want to turn to the second point against the neat division of labor. One might think that even if empirical evidence bears on philosophical analysis, once we've settled on the right analysis the remaining work is empirical. This would be true if our analysis makes well-being, for example, something purely empirical. For example, if we settle on hedonism as our theory of well-being, it will indeed be the case that questions about the causes of well-being are empirical questions. Once we know that the target is pleasure, psychologists can investigate the causes of it without the help of philosophers. But hedonism is not the most popular theory of well-being.[25] Much more popular in philosophy are idealized subjective theories: theories that take well-being to be identified with a subjective state under certain ideal conditions. The two most prominent views

---

[25] Even hedonists about well-being have some reason to think that theoretical guidance with respect to measurement is useful and important (Feldman makes this case in Part III of Feldman (2010)).

here are the informed desire theory and the authentic happiness theory, which I discussed briefly at the beginning of section 13.2. Taking these two theories as my examples, I'll now argue that determining causes is not always a simple empirical project.

According to Sumner's authentic happiness theory, happiness constitutes well-being when it is informed and autonomous.[26] Autonomy turns out to be tricky to define and Sumner gives us some guidance but no obviously operationalizable criterion. Sumner introduces two ways of thinking about autonomy. We can think of autonomous happiness as happiness with a certain causal history, that is, happiness that is not caused by manipulation, coercion, or political oppression. We can also think of autonomous happiness as having to do with a person's deepest self or the values with which she identifies most. It should be clear that either way of thinking about autonomy makes autonomous happiness something difficult to measure empirically. To decide whether someone's happiness is non-autonomous, we have to decide whether the causal history of that person being made happy by *that* is a history that involves injustice, or whether the person's identity is represented by that happiness. These are difficult questions, but more importantly, they are normative questions. This means that something will be lost in translating "autonomy" into something that can be identified empirically without employing norms. So, if this is your theory of well-being, there will be philosophical work to do in inferring claims about (normative) well-being from claims about (empirical) happiness.

It might seem that this line of thought makes the role for empirical studies too insignificant, because now it sounds like empirical studies on the causes of well-being *never* tell us anything about well-being except indirectly. Psychology looks like the handmaiden to philosophy, which does all the heavy lifting. I do not intend the point to be quite so flattering to philosophy. First, though philosophers specialize in making normative arguments, we do not have a monopoly on this enterprise. Second, there are many cases in which the inferences from empirical facts to normative claims about well-being are uncontroversial. For example, there seems no reason to worry about autonomy in the discovery that relationships are a key cause of happiness.[27] Finally, even in cases in which there is a worry about autonomy, the empirical facts about causes of (unideal) happiness are at least some important evidence for the causes of well-being.

Turning to informed desire theory, we see a similar problem. What a person would desire if she were fully informed about her options is not directly empirically discoverable. This is because people are not vividly aware of all the relevant facts when they form their preferences and this is the sense of "full information" that these theories demand. This means that the empirical facts about what people prefer (even facts about what people prefer when moderately well informed) are merely evidence for what people want when fully informed and, hence, merely evidence about well-being. To get to definite conclusions about well-being, we need to make inferences about what people would want under ideal conditions. Again, the empirical facts about what we desire may

---

[26] Sumner (1996).   [27] Diener and Seligman (2002).

often be extremely good evidence, in cases where there isn't much controversy or cause to doubt what would happen in the ideal.

Whether or not eudaimonist theories, which take well-being to consist in fulfilling your nature, will simplify the measurement of well-being depends on the details of the theory. Any theory that includes virtues on its list of well-being ingredients will make it difficult to measure well-being directly without making any value judgments, since attributions of virtues are evaluative. Indeed, any pluralist theory of well-being has the problem of putting together assessments of how a person is doing on multiple indexes into one overall assessment of well-being. How to weight the different components of well-being (such as friendship, accomplishment, and virtue) does not seem like something that can be settled purely empirically.

This complexity might tempt some to favor a "value-free" theory of well-being (that is, a theory that licenses assessments of well-being that require no evaluative judgments). Psychologists are certainly inclined to go this way. By defining well-being as something purely psychological such as positive affect plus life satisfaction, questions about how people *would* respond under ideal conditions can be avoided.[28] Defining well-being so that it is a purely empirical notion is a less attractive option for philosophers, since the role that well-being plays in welfarist moral theories assumes that well-being is something we have reason to pursue.[29] Of course, there could be a philosophical defense of an account of well-being (hedonism, for example) that makes it the kind of thing that can be measured empirically without any complications. But such an account has to answer the difficult question of why the non-normative facts about certain psychological states (such as pleasures) imply moral imperatives. This may be done, but the mere fact that pleasure is easier to measure empirically is not a sufficient answer.

There are similar reasons for rejecting the neat division of labor between philosophy and psychology when it comes to wisdom. Indeed, the point may be easier to see here since wisdom is a virtue and, therefore, even more obviously a normative concept than "well-being." Consider the question of whether traumatic experiences help wisdom develop. To investigate this question, psychologists might use some measurable criteria of wisdom and investigate whether traumatic experiences cause people to score higher on these criteria than the average population. They might also listen to what people say about their traumatic experiences and gauge from these narratives whether trauma has had an effect on wisdom.[30] In either case, it is necessary to know exactly what counts as an increase in wisdom and if what counts as wisdom cannot be reduced to purely empirical terms, then the neat division of labor is in trouble.

To see the point more clearly, let's take an example of a criterion of wisdom that is constitutive of wisdom according to the Berlin Paradigm, discussed above in section

---

[28] Ed Diener, a key figure in happiness research in psychology, defines what he calls "subjective well-being" as including life satisfaction, domain satisfaction, high positive affect, and low negative affect. See Diener, Scollon, and Lucas (2003), 189.

[29] See Sumner (1996) for a discussion of welfarism.   [30] Ardelt (2005).

13.2. One of the criteria of wisdom according to this theory is "value relativism and tolerance," which is sometimes defined as "an acknowledgment of individual, social, and cultural differences in values and life priorities."[31] Of course, as the psychologists doing this research acknowledge, a thoroughgoing "anything goes" sort of relativism isn't wise; tolerance of *everything* would not be compatible with the other dimensions of wisdom in the Berlin Paradigm. So, value relativism gets refined so that "it means to acknowledge and tolerate interindividual differences in values, while at the same time being geared toward optimizing and balancing the individual and the common good."[32] Constraining tolerance in this way is necessary, but it also makes "value relativism" into a normative criterion. If *wise* value relativism is attuned to optimizing the good, then we can't determine who has it without ourselves making normative judgments. However psychologists operationalize the "value relativism" variable, there will be an ineliminable normative element that invites philosophical reflection on the kind of tolerance that is appropriate.

I have argued in this section that psychological research can tell us something interesting about our normative concepts and philosophical thinking can tell us something important about the causes and correlates of our normative ideals. If this is so, then the neat division of labor according to which philosophers define concepts and psychologists operationalize those concepts to discover correlates and causes is probably not the best arrangement. This does not mean that psychologists need to become philosophers, or vice versa, but it does mean that there is reason to be aware of the work that goes on in each other's fields so that this work can be taken account of when it is relevant. Certain research questions might warrant collaboration, but there are other, low-cost ways of sharing labor: philosophers and psychologists can acknowledge when they are relying on assumptions that go beyond their own expertise and they can make an effort to support these assumptions by reading each other's work. Moreover, there are often other ways of supporting these assumptions that can be conducted by the researcher herself: after all, it is certainly not the case that philosophers are incapable of taking account of the empirical world and psychologists are inept at making normative judgments.

13.5 The pros and cons of thick theorizing

In *Ethics and the Limits of Philosophy* Williams suggests that the turn in our moral discourse from thick concepts such as "wisdom" and the other virtues to thin concepts like "good" and "right" has decreased our ethical knowledge.

Earlier I said that reflection might destroy knowledge, because thick ethical concepts that were used in a less reflective state might be driven from use by reflection, while the more abstract and general ethical thoughts that would probably take their place would not satisfy the conditions of propositional knowledge. To say that knowledge is destroyed in such a case is not to say that

---

[31] Kunzmann and Baltes (2005), 117.   [32] Staudinger and Glück (forthcoming), 14.

particular beliefs that once were true now cease to be true. Nor is it to say that people turn out never to have known the things they thought they knew. What it means is that these people once had beliefs of a certain kind, which were in many cases pieces of knowledge; but now, because after reflection they can no longer use concepts essential to those beliefs, they can no longer form beliefs of that kind.[33]

Reflection impedes our ability to use thick concepts because it puts us in mind of other, potentially better ways that we might "go on." This shakes our confidence in the way we had previously carved up the world, by undermining our sense that our way was the right way.

Williams observes that we can't go back to an unreflective time, but that the kind of knowledge that is associated with lack of reflection isn't necessarily the most important thing. We do, though, need ethical *conviction*, which he understands in terms of confidence in our ethical judgments and ideals: "One question we have to answer is how people, or enough people, can come to possess a practical confidence that, particularly granted both the need for reflection and its pervasive presence in our world, will come from strength and not from the weakness of self-deception and dogmatism."[34] Conviction, according to Williams, will be strengthened by training our critical reflection on finding shared understanding that commands loyalty.

One benefit that the kind of theorizing I have been discussing in this paper might have is to shore up our confidence in thick concepts such as "wisdom" and "well-being" without self-deception and dogmatism. What I have been suggesting is that the construction of a theory of wisdom or well-being involves taking account of people's pre-existing commitments, and refining the ideals by paying attention both to norms for rational improvement (norms that are employed in philosophical reflection) and to empirical data. Through this process, the theorist takes what people care about and what is known about human psychology and articulates a fitting ideal that is credibly normative or reason-giving. Of course the proof is in the pudding and this paper has only discussed recipes for pudding, it hasn't actually made any.[35] But the *promise* is that the method of theorizing articulated here will vindicate thick concepts in our modern world, "marked by a peculiar level of reflectiveness."[36] In this way, rather than reflection destroying knowledge, reflection—at least reflection of a certain kind—can increase our confidence in concepts like well-being and wisdom.

One might wonder what contribution is made by the *thickness* of these concepts. If the point is justification by tracing back to shared values and commitments, what does it matter if we focus on thick or thin concepts? It is certainly not impossible for the method I have outlined to start with thin normative concepts.[37] Thick concepts such as well-

---

[33] Williams (1985), 167.   [34] Williams (1985), 171.

[35] For my own attempts to make the pudding, see Tiberius and Plakias (2010) and Tiberius and Swartwood (2011).

[36] Williams (1985), 163.

[37] Cf. Scanlon (2003) in which he argues that the kind of value-laden justification Williams favors could also be at work in ethical theory that employs thin concepts such as the concept of the right, on this view.

being and wisdom have some advantages, though, because our ideals of wisdom and of a good life are so complex. This complexity gives the theorist a lot of substance to work with and a variety of related commitments to which to appeal.

The promise to restore a kind of confidence in thick concepts such as well-being and wisdom depends on three things: first, the attention to what people actually think about these concepts; second, the fact that people have confidence in what science tells us about human psychology; and third, the power of the argument that the results of this method will be reason-giving. Noticing these conditions can give us hope, because these are at least things over which we have some control. But it should also give us pause. In a way, the biggest advantage of thick theorizing is also its biggest disadvantage. When we construct theories that speak to people's actual commitments, ideals, and values in fundamental ways, we are more likely to construct theories that are action-guiding, reason-giving, and persuasive, theories that can underwrite the sort of confidence Williams thinks is missing in our reflective age. But when we draw on people's actual commitments, ideals, and values to construct theories, we also open ourselves to the charge that our theories will only apply to those who actually share these commitments. The disadvantage of thick theorizing has to do with scope.

We can distinguish two different but related problems of scope. One problem is that there will be people to whom our theory doesn't apply. The other is that this first problem with scope will undermine confidence in the theory for those to whom it *does* apply. Let's consider what it means to say that a theory of well-being has limited scope or that it doesn't apply to everyone. First, a comprehensive theory of well-being will have different layers: at least it will contain a very abstract definition of what counts as well-being (e.g., well-being is informed preference satisfaction) and a substantive theory about what tends to produce informed preference satisfaction in well-being subjects given what we know about human psychology.[38] The substantive part of the theory relies on generalizations about human beings and can admit of exceptions without failing as a theory. So, our question is about people who do not sign on to the abstract definition of well-being that the theorist has defended, because they have very different intuitions about well-being at the outset.

Certainly, if well-being is a policy goal, this fact may cause *political* problems. If I am the prime minister of the UK and I want to start measuring well-being so that I can make it a policy goal, and I think that well-being is physical pleasure, I may have some difficulty in convincing the relevant parties that this is a good idea. But this political problem isn't a problem for thick theorizing per se. It's a problem with implementing theories in the public sphere that could befall any theory and any method of theory construction. Indeed, one might think that thick theorizing would have an advantage against this criticism, if the case can be made that the resulting theory of well-being is implied by what people already thought.

---

[38] See Tiberius (2007).

The mere fact of limited scope might cause political problems, but it does not undermine the theory itself. There is a real problem, though, if the limited scope undermines our warrant in believing the theory. Why would it? If it is assumed that for a theory to be correct it must apply to everyone, then the fact that our theory of wisdom does not would count against it. But why should we assume that a theory of wisdom must apply to everyone for it to be a good theory, worthy of our acceptance? Why should it trouble us if there are people with whom we share so little in terms of what practical problems we have and the kinds of approaches to these problems we find admirable that what counts as wisdom for them is different from what counts as wisdom for us? If we do indeed have the practical problems we have, and we do indeed admire a certain way of solving these problems, why should it matter if some people have a different view? When it comes to well-being and wisdom—things that are good for us, after all—the fact that some people see them differently matters only if the way they see things is better.

So, the real worry about limited scope is that the people to whom the theory doesn't apply represent a way of "going on" that seems better than the one recommended by the theory. This could certainly be the case, but if it were, then we would be in the position of wanting to revise our own theory or reject it in favor of a better one. Consider a toy example in which our community has settled on a theory of well-being that highlights pleasure as the criterion for anything to count on our list of well-being components. Only the things that cause pleasure count as contributing to well-being according to our theory. Then we run across a group of people who don't accept our theory and who have a theory that countenances several experiences, not all of them identical with pleasure, as well-being criteria. These people think that something contributes to your well-being if it produces pleasure, flow, or feelings of personal growth. Further, they have empirical evidence that these three feelings are not identical.[39] We might look at them and think that their lives, insofar as they are living up to their theory, seem richer than ours, or that they have something we want. If so, it seems that we have a reason to change our theory of well-being to reflect this new information (e.g., that pleasure isn't the only thing we want for its own sake). On the other hand, we may look at these people and think they're confused or that they just want different things from us, in which case their being different from us won't give us a reason to change our theory, but it also won't give us a reason to stop thinking the theory we have is the right one for us.

The above example is vastly oversimplified. We don't typically confront communities of people who have a different theory of well-being (or of wisdom). And the above example assumes a single criterion for evaluating theories: what is wanted for its own sake is taken to be the ultimate criterion for the list of well-being ingredients. But the point of the example was not to show how it really works when we confront the limited scope of a favored theory, rather, the point was just to show that when we confront people who don't share our favored theory because they have something *better*, this gives us

---

[39] See Waterman (2008) for a discussion of the position in psychology that eudaimonic experiences are distinct from hedonic experiences such as pleasure.

reasons to change or modify the theory that we have. So, it's true that when there are people who seem to represent a way of going on that is better than the one we have, this does undermine the warrant for our theory, but this is just as it should be. When it comes to theories of well-being and wisdom that are supposed to characterize ways of being in the world that are good ways to be, when we find other people with different ideas who seem to be flourishing more than we are, this should be taken as evidence that there's something wrong with our ideas.

13.6 Conclusion

I have argued that there is a way of constructing theories about thick concepts such as well-being and wisdom that combines empirical and philosophical methods. Thick theorizing results in theories that straddle different layers of abstraction. Such theories include formal definitions and substantive accounts that draw out the real world implications of those definitions. Empirical evidence about our concepts is relevant to formal definitions insofar as we want these definitions to capture ideals that people already have. Philosophical argument is relevant to the task of spelling out the substantive account insofar as the definitions we're employing involve idealization and cannot be straightforwardly operationalized.

The promise for the kind of theorizing I have sketched is that the resulting theories will have two desirable features of any normative theory. They will be reason-giving, because they will draw on recognizable values and ideals in ways that people can see what's good about them. They will also be practically applicable, because they will have enough substantive detail that they will have real implications for what we should do. Williams points to a third advantage. According to Williams, one thing that will make a difference to the possibility of making progress in ethical thought:

Is the extent to which ethical life can still rely on what I have called thick ethical concepts. They are indeed open to being unseated by reflection, but to the extent that they survive it, a practice that uses them is more stable in face of the general, structural reflections about the truth of ethical judgments than a practice that does not use them.[40]

The kind of thick theorizing I've described might lead to the confirmation of our thick concepts, rather than to their destruction and, if Williams is right, this kind of confirmation might provide a stable basis for ethical practice.

References

Annas, Julia (1993) *The Morality of Happiness*. (New York: Oxford University Press).
Ardelt, Monika (2005) 'How Wise People Cope with Crises and Obstacles in Life', *ReVision: A Journal of Consciousness and Transformation* 28: 7–19.

---

[40] Williams (1985), 200.

Baltes, Paul and Ursula Staudinger (2000) 'Wisdom: A Metaheuristic to Orchestrate Mind and Virtue Towards Excellence', *American Psychologist* 55: 122–36.

Bluck, Susan and Judith Glück (2005) 'From the Inside Out', in Robert Sternberg and Jennifer Jordan (eds.) *A Handbook of Wisdom: Psychological Perspectives* (New York: Cambridge University Press), 84–109.

Broadie, Sarah (1991) *Ethics With Aristotle* (New York: Oxford University Press).

DePaul, Michael and William Ramsey, eds. (1998) *Rethinking Intuition: the Psychology of Intuition and its Role in Philosophical Inquiry* (Lanham, MD: Rowman & Littlefield).

Diener, Ed, Christine Scollon, and Richard Lucas (2003) 'The Evolving Concept of Subjective Well-Being: the Multifaceted Nature of Happiness', *Advances in Cell Aging and Gerontology* 15: 187–219.

—— and Martin Seligman, (2002) 'Very Happy People', *Psychological Science* 13: 81–4.

Feldman, Fred (2010) *What Is This Thing Called Happiness?* (Oxford: Oxford University Press).

Griffin, James (1986) *Well-Being: Its Meaning, Measurement, and Moral Importance* (Oxford: Oxford University Press).

Haybron, Daniel (2008) *The Pursuit of Unhappiness* (Oxford: Oxford University Press).

Hursthouse, Rosalind (2006) 'Practical Wisdom: A Mundane Account', *Proceedings of the Aristotelian Society* 106: 283–307.

Kesebir, Pelin and Ed Diener (2008) 'In Pursuit of Happiness: Empirical Answers to Philosophical Questions', *Perspectives in Psychological Science* 3: 117–25.

Kunzmann, Ute and Paul Baltes (2005) 'The Psychology of Wisdom: Theoretical and Empirical Challenges', in Robert Sternberg and Jennifer Jordan (eds.) *A Handbook of Wisdom: Psychological Perspectives* (New York: Cambridge University Press), 110–38.

Lapsley, Daniel and Patrick Hill (2008) 'On Dual Processing and Heuristic Approaches to Moral Cognition', *Journal of Moral Education* 37: 313–32.

Nussbaum, Martha (2001) *Women and Human Development: The Capabilities Approach.* (Cambridge: Cambridge University Press).

Parfit, Derek (1984) *Reasons and Persons* (Oxford: Oxford University Press).

Phillips, Jonathan, Luke Misenheimer, and Joshua Knobe (2011) 'The Ordinary Concept of Happiness (and Others Like It)', *Emotion Review* 71: 929–37.

Phillips, Jonathan, Sven Nyholm, and Shen-yi Liao (forthcoming) 'The Good in Happiness', *Oxford Studies in Experimental Philosophy*.

Railton, Peter (1986) 'Moral Realism', *Philosophical Review* 95: 163–207.

Ryff, Carol and Burton Singer (1998) 'The Contours of Positive Human Health', *Psychological Inquiry* 9: 1–28.

Scanlon, T. M. (2003) 'Thickness and Theory', *Journal of Philosophy* 100: 275–87.

Seligman, Martha (2011) *Flourish: A Visionary New Understanding of Happiness and Well-being* (New York: Free Press).

Staudinger, Ursula and Judith Glück (forthcoming) 'Psychological Wisdom Research: Commonalities and Differences in a Growing Field', *Annual Review of Psychology*.

Sternberg, Robert (1998) 'A Balance Theory of Wisdom', *Review of General Psychology* 2: 347–65.

Sumner, L. W. (1996) *Welfare, Happiness, and Ethics* (New York: Oxford University Press).

Tiberius, Valerie (2007) 'Substance and Procedure in Theories of Prudential Value', *Australasian Journal of Philosophy* 85: 373–91.

—— and Alexandra Plakias (2010) 'Well-Being', in John Doris and the Moral Psychology Research Group (eds.) *The Moral Psychology Handbook* (Oxford: Oxford University Press), 401–31.

—— and Jason Swartwood (2011) 'Wisdom Revisited: A Case Study in Normative Theorizing', *Philosophical Explorations* 14: 277–95.

Waterman, Alan (2008) 'Reconsidering Happiness: a Eudaimonist's Perspective', *The Journal of Positive Psychology* 3: 234–52.

Williams, Bernard (1985) *Ethics and the Limits of Philosophy* (London: Fontana).

General Index

Index of Notable Examples